MOOCs and Their Afterlives

MOOCs and Their Afterlives

Experiments in Scale and Access in Higher Education

EDITED BY ELIZABETH LOSH

The University of Chicago Press
Chicago and London

The University of Chicago Press, Chicago 60637
The University of Chicago Press, Ltd., London
© 2017 by The University of Chicago
Chapter 12 © 2017 by Jessie Daniels, Polly Thistlethwaite, and Shawn(ta) Smith-Cruz
Published 2017
Printed in the United States of America

26 25 24 23 22 21 20 19 18 17   1 2 3 4 5

ISBN-13: 978-0-226-46931-7 (cloth)
ISBN-13: 978-0-226-46945-4 (paper)
ISBN-13: 978-0-226-46959-1 (e-book)
DOI: 10.7208/chicago/9780226469591.001.0001

Library of Congress Cataloging-in-Publication Data

Names: Losh, Elizabeth M. (Elizabeth Mathews), editor.
Title: MOOCs and their afterlives : experiments in scale and access in higher
    education / edited by Elizabeth Losh.
Description: Chicago ; London : The University of Chicago Press, 2017. | Includes
    bibliographical references and index.
Identifiers: LCCN 2017005394 | ISBN 9780226469317 (cloth : alk. paper) | ISBN
    9780226469454 (pbk. : alk. paper) | ISBN 9780226469591 (e-book)
Subjects: LCSH: MOOCs (Web-based instruction)
Classification: LCC LB2395.7.M6556 2017 | DDC 371.33/44678—dc23 LC record
    available at https://lccn.loc.gov/2017005394

♾ This paper meets the requirements of ANSI/NISO Z39.48-1992 (Permanence of
Paper).

To my mother, Llewellyn, who has always been a lifelong learner.

Contents

Acknowledgments

Like teaching, writing can be an intensely collaborative activity. In an edited collection like this one, it is obvious from counting the number of contributors in the table of contents that they merit many thanks for their generosity in giving so much time to conceptualizing, writing, revising, critiquing, and promoting this volume.

I am also extremely grateful for some of my academic collaborators who facilitated interesting scholarly conversations about MOOC problems and possibilities, especially David Theo Goldberg of the University of California Humanities Research Institute; Trebor Scholz, who organized the seminal Mobility Shifts: International Futures of Learning Summit, where I first met many of the authors whom I sought to include; Mimi Ito, who oversaw research activities at the Digital Media and Learning Hub; and Christian Hoeckley of the Gaede Institute for gathering scholars together in 2014 to discuss MOOCs and the liberal arts.

When I began aggregating essays, I was serving as one of three co-facilitators of FemTechNet, which served as an important network for freely discussing the potential shortcomings and blind spots of uncritical MOOC boosterism at a time when many universities were eager to jump on the MOOC bandwagon. I am especially grateful to co-facilitators Sharon Irish and Lisa Nakamura, who organized a number of important dialogues and conferences about digital pedagogy and continued the work of FemTechNet founders Anne Balsamo and Alexandra Juhasz.

Funding to support faculty research from the University of California, Irvine, the University of California, San Diego, and from William & Mary was critical for development of this project and its timely completion, and I am especially thankful to Dean Kate Conley and Vice Provost Dennis Manos of

William & Mary for making the work of digital pedagogy so much easier with their support.

The team at the University of Chicago Press was fantastic from start to finish, especially the enthusiastic David Morrow, the scrupulous Susan Zakin, and Jenni Fry and Elissa Park who managed the logistics of copyediting.

As always, an acknowledgments section would not be complete without thanking my husband, Mel Horan, for the two years of proofreading, listening, and material support that he provided for this endeavor.

Introduction

ELIZABETH LOSH

The *New York Times* dramatically declared 2012 to be "the year of the MOOC."
Attention to so-called massive open online courses (MOOCs) offered to users
for free by companies—such as Coursera, edX, Udacity, and Google Course
Builder—spurred a national conversation about the size and shape of higher
education.

From the perspective of only a few years later, it appears obvious that
MOOCs could never be a panacea for all the issues around scale and access
in higher education. As a Pew Report on "Tracking Online Education in the
United States" indicated in 2014, administrators of elite institutions were often
less likely to trumpet the promise of extremely large "mega-classes" with enrollments in the tens of thousands than they had been in the previous year.
In 2017 it might seem that what some have called "the MOOC Moment" has
largely passed.[1]

Many of these essays argue that what may have been most significant
about the advent of MOOCs was not the courses themselves, which tended to
be remarkably uniform as vehicles for content delivery that used digital learning management systems, but the diversity of pedagogical reactions among
administrators, faculty, students, and members of the general public to this
particular format for free large-scale distance learning. These many different
"afterlives" of MOOCs on campuses around the world could be called the
central concern of this book, which assesses how continuing efforts to adopt
new approaches to both quantity and quality in higher education could be

1. See *The MOOC Moment*, a selection of *Inside Higher Ed* articles and essays on massive
open online courses, which was published as an online pamphlet in 2013 and is available at
https://www.insidehighered.com/content/mooc-moment.

more successful and better reflect the values of experiential and lifelong learning. As attempts to innovate in response to MOOCs have multiplied, acronyms describing these experiments have proliferated: cMOOCs, CLMOOCs, SPOCs, BOOCs, POOCs, DOCCs, and meta-MOOCs, which are all represented in this collection. This volume gathers a wealth of work from a number of contributors with significant firsthand experiences teaching courses that refine, adapt, reconfigure, challenge, or appropriate the MOOC model. It also includes students who participated in these courses, as well as leading public intellectuals who refused to participate in distance-learning experiments that they considered dangerous or unethical.

Rather than emphasize stories of meltdowns, defections, protests, lawsuits, and scandals, which could seem to be as hyperbolically negative as the press releases of 2012 had been hyperbolically positive, this book suggests some ways to negotiate conflict around these technologies that are both new and old. Of course, with retention rates hovering at below 5 percent, few universities are maintaining the revolutionary fervor that characterized the optimistic press releases and photo ops of previous years. Even one-time MOOC guru Sebastian Thrun dramatically took off his rose-colored Google glasses in 2014 and admitted that his company, Udacity, was guilty of churning out a "lousy product" that didn't merit its exalted spot on the "front pages of newspapers and magazines." It might seem easy to dismiss "MOOC madness" or "MOOC mania" as a flash-in-the-pan phenomenon, but the voices that arose in reaction to MOOCs are still reverberating in the academy and urging new policies about distance learning, new types of innovative digital courses, and new approaches to online access and virtual learning communities.

This volume includes essays by faculty who have taught conventional MOOCs with companies like Coursera and edX and continue to serve as advocates, although they have also publicly discussed the limitations of current learning management systems, the challenges of student retention, and the difficulties of scaling up. At the same time, *MOOCs and Their Afterlives* showcases contributions from prominent MOOC critics who are nonetheless articulate advocates for online access and the reform of higher education in the digital age. Moreover, this kind of public debate and discussion about MOOCs has spurred a variety of innovative pedagogical experiments in higher education that appropriate the name recognition associated with the MOOC model: SPOCs (small private online courses), DOCCs (distributed open collaborative courses), POOCs (participatory open online courses), BOOCs (big open online courses), and many other new forms of online teaching. This unique collection of essays recognizes that peer-learning experiments destabilize the traditional student-teacher relationship, and it includes works

by those experimenting with new systems of peer evaluation and with new
ways to study and promote informal learning online so that more challenging material can be learned, retained, applied, and disseminated by a greater
diversity of students in a wider range of knowledge-making communities.

This book is intended to appeal to those concerned about higher education and policies about access to knowledge, lifelong learning, and instructional technology outside the context of a traditional classroom. In framing
the debate, it is important to point out that open education has a long history in the American experience that has shaped our political rhetoric and
public culture for a long time. Any narrative about calls for open access to
higher education should be situated in our nation's conversation around what
public culture means, which has been going on for well over a century, a history that includes the Tuskegee Movable Schools of Booker T. Washington
and George Washington Carver, which began on horse-drawn wagons; the
Chautauqua adult education movement and its tent revival culture; World's
Fairism, in which temporary exhibits educated a newly mobile public; correspondence courses for rural and working-class learners; the adult schools
of the settlement house movement; the University of Chicago's post–World
War II Great Books courses intended to propagate the liberal arts among
those in the workplace; a range of radio and television courses throughout
the twentieth century devoted to civic and practical education; the Freedom
Schools of the civil rights movement; and community consciousness-raising
efforts orchestrated by feminists and activists for immigrants' rights.[2] In other
words, it is difficult to untangle the history of open education from the history of struggles for social justice, and neither history is linear, progressive, or
closed to multiple interpretations.

In *The War on Learning: Gaining Ground in the Digital University* (2014), I
argued that attention to the long history of instructional technology is needed
to balance tendencies in popular culture to romanticize novelty. When lessons from earlier iterations are forgotten, it's difficult for increasingly digital
campuses to genuinely innovate. Many of the supposedly newest edtech innovations had been around for at least a decade or two, including open online courses, educational video games, and large-scale distributions of mobile
computing devices. I argued that the need for highly formalized paradigms
of digital learning, such as MOOCs, was spurred by a desire for command
and control in response to an often chaotic, transitional environment of to-

2. One could even argue that the demonstrations and lectures in the "penny universities"
of early American coffeehouses indicate that the open education movement predated political
independence in the United States.

day's campuses, in which students can use mobile technologies to capture and subvert the traditional college pedagogical performance. After having written that book, I realized the need to have a richer range of stories that included not only instructional technology but also adult education more generally, which I hope will encourage many more future projects on this topic for both established and emerging scholars.

Technology has been an important part of open education for much of this history. Even some of the most antipopulist of intellectuals have been interested in using new media to reach broader audiences and to engage the public. As Florian Cramer (2011) has pointed out, the model of free universities founded by artists and activists in the 1970s, 80s, and 90s using DIY resources has now transitioned to web-based forms of dissemination. Before this wave of avant-garde thinkers, European critics from the Frankfurt School who fled the Nazi racial state joined a "new school" in New York City, which questioned much of the received wisdom about what higher education should be. Although some consider its current curriculum and institutional structure as representative of the worst tendencies of neoliberalism, the New School attempted to honor its legacy of internationalization and experimentation by hosting the week-long Mobility Shifts conference in 2011. This eight-day conference organized by digital labor scholar Trebor Scholz proved to be one of the most important summits on technology and open learning at the cusp of the MOOC moment, an event at which many of the authors of essays in this book had the opportunity to network for the first time.

In the past, rethinking access by approaching challenges to learning from the perspective of universal design often involved aiming to address much younger students than those of college age. Walter Benjamin—who was trapped behind in the genocidal Europe of World War II and never made it to the New School—created educational radio programs for children. Similarly, E. M. Gombrich wrote *A Little History of the World* (*Eine Kurze Weltgeschichte für junge Leser*; 1936) to teach equally little learners. In contrast, the audiences for most of the educational experiments in scale and access in this book are presumed to be much older, well beyond an imagined latency period. By assuming that it is never too late to learn, these experiments are challenging the path dependencies built into our current educational system. They are also confronting the power dynamics of existing learning institutions, because sometimes the students are imagined as potential peers of the instructor, and colearning and the coconstruction of knowledge is one of the book's important themes.

 The book begins with the "M" in MOOC, by examining how massive courses potentially are able to operationalize data in new ways. Daniel Hickey and Suraj Uttamchandani sketch out the history of MOOCs as educational technologies and describe the division between cMOOCs that emphasize qualitative principles of connected learning and xMOOCs that emphasize the quantitative (in focusing on the volume of enrollment, learner analytics, and other numerical indices), which they characterize as the "constructivist" and "instructionist" paradigms, respectively. By assuming that empirical research witll be most persuasive to those likely to dismiss the "hype and hyperbole" surrounding MOOCs, Hickey and Uttamchandani suggest some ways to get the best of both cMOOC and xMOOC worlds by using their own BOOC, or "big open online course," as an examplar, which also incorporates "situative" and "participatory" theories of learning that stress the importance of understanding the social dynamics of learning and the ability of learners to contribute to a class. (Their BOOC focuses on assessment as its subject matter.) Hickey and Uttamchandani's essay is followed by Armando Fox's contribution, which interrogates the biases of MOOC detractors by anticipating their objections. Fox is a computer scientist who—with Professor David Patterson—launched Berkeley's first MOOC on Coursera. Currently the course uses the edX platform and is accompanied by their e-textbook *Engineering Software as a Service* (Fox and Patterson 2014). Fox is known for arguing that introducing computer technologies in learning allows for greater personalization, customization, and individualization and thus courses can be "private" rather than "massive." In this essay, he suggests ways that MOOCs might be useful in traditional instruction beyond their utility for pedagogical research purposes, and he questions why autograders have been demonized. This section of the book closes with journalist Owen Youngman's critical reflection about his experiences teaching a Coursera MOOC that focused on "understanding media by understanding google." Youngman cautions that too much of public opinion has become focused on utopian and dystopian poles of the debates around teaching with technology and not enough attention has been paid to the middle ground of how low retention rates can actually mean that a strong and dedicated cohort finishes a course by learning to adopt sustaining peer learning practices and how empathy can be nurtured in this new learning context. Despite their differences disciplinarily and philosophically, all three of the essays in this section rethink the emphasis on massive enrollments and connect MOOC methods to the values of traditional classroom education that might be occurring simultaneously or in parallel.

If the first group of essays covers the positive possibilities of xMOOCs in varying degrees, the second group of essays emphasizes the promising potentials of the contrasting cMOOC approach, specifically by exploring the theme of so-called connected learning and developing peer learning as a mode of interaction. It opens with Cathy N. Davidson's essay about what she learned by teaching a "meta-MOOC" titled The History and Future of (Mostly) Higher Education using Coursera. Along with David Theo Goldberg, Davidson has codirected the $2 million annual HASTAC/John D. and Catherine T. MacArthur Foundation Digital Media and Learning Competitions. The Digital Media + Learning (DML) organization has been active in recent calls to "reclaim open learning" and embrace connected learning initiatives. One of the DML's core constituents, Howard Rheingold of Smart Mobs fame, follows Davidson's contribution with his essay on "Peerogy." A veteran of many open-learning experiments with his Social Media Classroom and Collaboratory, Rheingold organized the fall 2014 iteration of Connected Courses with co-facilitators Alan Levine and Jim Groom, which included twenty-five instructors overall. In his "Peerogy" essay, Rheingold argues for the value of sometimes-messy processes of colearning and coteaching and against existing regimes of testing and examination. DML participant Jonathan Worth comes next in the collection, with his essay about his open courses on photography that have drawn thousands of participants. Worth claims that the current debate about the crisis of higher education in the Internet age cannot be decoupled from equally contentious issues about copyright and privacy and that, just as the expertise of the photographer has been undermined by digital practices that open new professional possibilities, educators need to be similarly responsive and innovative to keep up with new economic models. Although perhaps less well known nationally than Davidson, Rheingold, and Worth, Mia Zamora has also been a regular contributor to the DML community. Her essay about the CLMOOC (Connected Learning Massive Open Online Collaboration), which uses best practices of connected learning to recast work being done by the National Writing Project, brings the context of literacy education to this collection to ask how "open" might mean open to new modes of connection and composition. In her essay Zamora redirects attention from concept of a "course" as the main unit of acquiring knowledge to the "make."

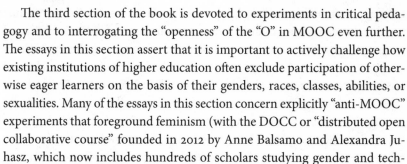

The third section of the book is devoted to experiments in critical pedagogy and to interrogating the "openness" of the "O" in MOOC even further. The essays in this section assert that it is important to actively challenge how existing institutions of higher education often exclude participation of otherwise eager learners on the basis of their genders, races, classes, abilities, or sexualities. Many of the essays in this section concern explicitly "anti-MOOC" experiments that foreground feminism (with the DOCC or "distributed open collaborative course" founded in 2012 by Anne Balsamo and Alexandra Juhasz, which now includes hundreds of scholars studying gender and technology), challenge elitism (along with "town and gown" divisions between universities and their surrounding communities and the perceived "placelessness" of the MOOC format) with the POOC, or "participatory open online course," run in Harlem by the City University of New York, or take Davidson's meta-MOOC experiment to its furthest possible conclusion with what could be considered a meta-meta-MOOC experience on Twitter "MOOC MOOC." In the spirit of collective organizing, almost all the works in this section are written by multiple authors, including contributions by Radhika Gajjala, Erika M. Behrmann, Anca Birzescu, Andrew Corbett, Kayleigh Frances Bondor, Jasmine Rault, T. L. Cowan, Sean Michael Morris, Jesse Stommel, Jessie Daniels, Polly Thistlethwaite, and Shawn(ta) Smith-Cruz. The final essay in this section about the Harlem POOC by Daniels, Thistlethwaite, and Smith-Cruz also suggests that claims of openness are superficial if lacking deeper support for offering all course materials—including books and films—unencumbered by intellectual property restrictions on replication and dissemination. (The vexing role of copyright law in open education will also be featured in the closing essay of the volume.)

The fourth section of the book includes three essays by professors who explore the paradoxes at the heart of the MOOC moment and the pathos of engagement with the implied promises of the MOOC, either as an administrator or as a student. All three essays are produced by rhetoricians and emphasize the emotional turbulence associated with the MOOC zeitgeist. My own essay in this section focuses on how MOOC affects function in the oratory of company founders who preach digital universalism in TED Talks and the disappointment that engenders shame and contempt for participants. Alex Reid uses the posthumanism of Bruno Latour as a way to understand the "EdTech Gold Rush" of the present moment, which represents to participants both rhetorical kairos (opportunity) and metanoia (regret over past choices). As Reid points out, Latour himself stars in a MOOC titled Scientific Humanities, now available on Coursera, although initially designed for a more innovative France Université Numérique (FUN) platform. Reid also suggests that we might look to another online platform for learning, the popular online game about managing resources *Minecraft*, to understand the logics of "digital prospecting." Steven Krause, who in 2014 edited one of the first collections about MOOCs, *Invasion of the MOOCs*, describes a range of experiences that he had as a student in different MOOC courses and how he negotiated intense feelings of isolation and alienation created by connections that only made learners feel more alone.

The book closes with a collection of essays by prominent MOOC critics who object to the MOOC format, its organizational and economic power structures, the deceptiveness of its claims for reforms, and the potential harm caused by either the revolutionary destruction or ineffectual deferral that MOOCs represent. The authors of "An Open Letter to Professor Michael Sandel from the Philosophy Department at San José State University," which appeared in the *Chronicle of Higher Education* in 2013, revise and expand their extensive critique of MOOCs as enforcing an intellectual monoculture for this volume. According to the authors, when MOOCs become required content in classrooms that are "flipped" to avoid conventional live lectures, the variety and range of strains of humanistic inquiry becomes sterile. Their essay is followed by the scathing attack on the sanctimonious appeals of MOOCs by Ian Bogost, who offers his analysis of the "secret lives" of MOOCs and their function in the "contemporary educational, economic, and media ecosystem." The authors at San José State who argue that elite institutions don't necessarily offer the best teaching for diverse student populations is echoed in the contribution of Siva Vaidhyanathan, who compares his own teaching to the labor and care for students expended by his sister, a math teacher in a community college. Like the authors in the San José State Philosophy Department, Vaidhyanathan recounts how bruising battles over MOOCs can exacerbate conflicts between faculty and administration, in telling the story of the attempted ouster of University of Virginia President Teresa Sullivan by the campus's governing board. He also argues that MOOC promoters are poorly positioned to understand the needs and concerns of the developing world, an argument that resonates in the final essay in this volume, in which Nishant Shah asks how a crisis in education could be manufactured and interrogates the many "C" terms of MOOC structures.

Although this collection is organized to articulate separate and distinct themes, there are often overlaps and resonances across these subheadings. For example, assessment is a theme not only in the Hickey essay but also in the essays from Zamora; Morris and Stommel; and Daniels, Thistlethwaite, and Smith-Cruz. Affect is highlighted in the essays from Reid, Krause, and myself, but emotional response to online learning experiences is also emphasized in Zamora's work on "guilt" in distance education, Youngman's work on "empathy" in peer learning, and Rault and Cowan's work on classroom killjoys.

Unfortunately, not every interesting and important experiment of recent years could be documented here, given the constraints of space and the lead times needed in academic publishing. For example, a number of faculty members in the Selfies Research Network collaborated to produce an open online course about selfies and explored how this new genre of photographic self-representation could promote effective teaching about surveillance and microcelebrity, as well as the many ways subaltern experience could be documented. Although the Selfie Course is briefly mentioned as noteworthy in the Gajjala essay, other participants have written about it at greater length elsewhere. Moreover, in response to a year of high-profile shootings of black men by police and widespread hashtag activism deployed in protest, dozens of faculty members collaborated to produce the #Ferguson and #Charleston syllabi. The discussion of hashtag pedagogy in the Rault and Cowan essay, which is also alluded to in several of the other essays in the critical pedagogy section on openness, does not compensate for the relative absence of more work in the collection on digital pedagogies of street action. And in the wake of public attention to online misogyny and headlines about GamerGate and the harassment of feminist game critics, designers, scholars, and fans, online educational resources are being compiled to promote rapid response assistance to those subject to online violence, while also educating potential perpetrators. These emergent large-scale open courses that respond to the latest trends in digital culture may truly be the next wave in distance education. Contemporary innovations in online learning are reflected in a remarkably rich and heterogeneous field to which this volume can only serve as an introduction.

References

Cramer, Florian. 2011. "Is There Hope?" Presented at Mobility Shifts: International Futures of Learning Summit, New York, October 15.

Fox, Armando, and David Patterson. 2014. Engineering Software as a Service: An Agile Approach Using Cloud Computing + $10 AWS Credit. San Francisco: Strawberry Canyon LLC.

Losh, Elizabeth. *The War on Learning: Gaining Ground in the Digital University*. Cambridge: Cambridge: MIT Press, 2014.

PART ONE

Data-Driven Education

1

Beyond Hype, Hyperbole, Myths, and Paradoxes: Scaling Up Participatory Learning and Assessment in a Big Open Online Course

DANIEL T. HICKEY AND
SURAJ L. UTTAMCHANDANI

Most readers of this volume are likely familiar with the distinctive history of massive open online courses (MOOCs). Their rapid expansion contrasts with the more steady expansion of higher-education technologies in prior decades, punctuated by small bursts around the advent of computers, personal computers, multimedia computers, and the Internet. The pace of change quickened around the turn of the century with the open education movement that laid some groundwork for the modern MOOC. The acronym itself was coined in 2008 for an open course on "connectivist" learning offered by George Siemens and Stephen Downes. MOOCs exploded in 2011–12 with Udacity, Coursera, edX, and others, suddenly enrolling tens of thousands of students around the world in free courses designed around the instruction of prominent academics. This outpouring of attention, investment, and learners was unprecedented in higher education.

Even as the *New York Times* dubbed 2012 "The Year of the MOOC" (Pappano 2012), the backlash against MOOCs was already underway. Many observed that the streaming videos and quizzes that dominated the newer MOOCs represented relatively shallow ways of interacting with content (e.g., Kays 2012; Marks 2012; Pope 2012). The acronym "xMOOC" (variously for eXtended or eXtension) was introduced to distinguish these newer offerings from the earlier networked and interactive courses advanced by Siemens and Downes, which quickly came to be called "cMOOCs" in response. Some observers had already commented on the difficulty of connecting with other learners in the cMOOCs (Mackness, Mack, and Williams 2010). It turned out that supporting social interaction in the xMOOCs was proving *much* harder. An effort to include more interaction and group projects in a Coursera course on online learning was widely cited for going "laughably awry"

(Oremus 2013, 1). A study found that engagement in Coursera discussion forums declined significantly over time among completers, and that instructor involvement actually worsened participation (Brinton et al. 2014). While the "hype and hyperbole" over MOOCs continued to pour forth (Billsberry 2013, 739), John Daniel, an influential leader in the open-learning movement, captured the widespread concerns by summarizing the "myths and paradoxes" of xMOOCs (Daniel 2012). These included *number* of students taught (but single-digit completion rates), *value* (dubious certificates of completion), *purpose* (disregard for outcomes and focus on posturing and profits rather than spreading learning), *pedagogy* (essentially behaviorism), *access* (mostly serving elites), and *risks* (MOOCs as degree mills).

Yet the rapid expansion of MOOCs also prompted significant scholarly consideration of "learning at scale." In 2013, the National Science Foundation organized workshops on the topic (Fisher and Fox 2013), while the Bill and Melinda Gates Foundation established the MOOC Research Initiative that supported in-depth investigations for over twenty courses (Gasevic et al. 2014). In 2014, the Association for Computing Machinery initiated the annual Learning@Scale conference, and the number of empirical studies of MOOCs grew rapidly (e.g., Ebben and Murphy 2014; Papamitsiou and Economides 2014). As nicely detailed in the other eighteen chapters in this volume, innovators began pushing the boundaries of the xMOOC platforms and created new cMOOC formats, resulting in many promising formats to support more ambitious forms of learning at scale.

This chapter summarizes one ongoing effort that is intended to inform the entire range of efforts to scale open learning. Like others in this volume, we aimed to move beyond the current rhetoric of MOOCs. More specifically, this effort is part of a broader program of research that is attempting to transcend a forty-year-old debate over instructionist versus constructivist approaches to instruction. Instructionist approaches are rooted in a more "associationist" perspective on learning (e.g., Anderson 1990; Gagné 1985) which assumes that higher order knowledge can and should be broken down into smaller elements that can be individually learned, mastered, and assessed.[1] This perspective is explicitly manifested in artificially intelligent tutors, like those associated with Carnegie Mellon University (Koedinger and Corbett 2006) and competency-based education (Bramante and Colby 2012) and

---

1. Many scholars distinguish between older behaviorist variants and newer cognitivist variants. The former assumes knowledge is represented by behavioral stimulus-response associations, whereas the latter assumes knowledge consists of cognitive associations; both share this same reductionist assumption that makes them largely antithetical to constructivism.

more implicitly manifested in the xMOOCs. The obvious advantage of associationist approaches is that they make little or no demand on instructors, and scale readily. In contrast, constructivist approaches are rooted in more "rationalist" views of learning (e.g., Glaser 1984) that emphasize the construction of higher-level conceptual schema that learners create to make sense of the world (rather than by assembling numerous smaller associations). While there are many variants, constructivist approaches are more open-ended and inquiry-oriented than instructionist approaches. This means that these approaches can support plenty of engagement around more fundamental disciplinary concepts and meaningful social engagement around those concepts. But doing so requires patient instructors with sufficient understanding of both the particular discipline and how knowledge develops in the discipline—the so-called PCK, or pedagogical content knowledge, popularized by Lee Shulman in the 1980s (Shulman 1986).

Constructivist approaches such as problem-based learning have been explored extensively in conventional online contexts (e.g., Kanuka and Anderson 2007). However, as exemplified by the case of the Coursera meltdown mentioned above, constructivist approaches can be very difficult to scale. This is because both the people who design a course and then the instructors and facilitators who teach that course need a lot of TPCK (technological pedagogical content knowledge; Koehler and Mishra 2008) concerning the way that disciplinary knowledge can optimally unfold *within the particular technology*. In many settings this knowledge will be in very short supply, very expensive, or both. The challenge of scaling constructivist learning becomes particularly apparent when it comes to assessing student learning; even knowledgeable instructors are hard pressed to evaluate learner-generated artifacts or student performance efficiently and reliably, and most constructivist assessment practices are exceedingly difficult to automate with computers. Furthermore, assessing constructivist learning with the multiple-choice and short-answer formats associated with instructionist approaches are likely to miss the most important outcomes. For these reasons, the tensions that follow from antithetical assumptions behind constructivist and instructionist approaches are certainly exacerbated in most efforts to scale learning.

The new course described in this chapter attempted to transcend these tensions and produce new practices for scaling learning by drawing on two related sets of contemporary insights. The first are newer "participatory" approaches that can harness the advantages and minimize the disadvantages of both instructionist and constructivist approaches. The new course described in this chapter emerged from prior efforts to create this kind of synthesis in conventional online courses focusing on conventional course content.

The second set of insights comes from learning theorists including Siemens, who set out to exploit the unique nature of digital knowledge networks and interest-driven social networking.

Participatory Learning and Assessment (PLA)

The design of this new course was rooted in an extended program of design-based research of educational multimedia (e.g., Hickey, Taasoobshirazi, and Cross 2012; Hickey and Zuiker 2012), educational video games (e.g., Barab et. al. 2007; Hickey, Ingram-Goble, and Jameson 2009), and secondary language arts instruction (Hickey, McWilliams, and Honeyford 2011). These studies used newer "situative" theories of knowing and learning (Brown, Collins, and Duguid 1989; Lave and Wenger 1991) to uncover new solutions to enduring challenges concerning assessment, feedback, grading, and accountability in technology-rich learning environments. What distinguishes situative theories from the prior theories is that they assume that knowledge primarily resides in the social and cultural practices of knowledgeable humans. This means that learning occurs when humans participate meaningfully in those practices (hence the label "participatory"). Contrary to some characterizations (e.g., Anderson, Reder, and Simon 1996), situative theories do not deny individual knowledge or ignore individual learning. Rather, situative theories assume that individual knowing and learning are "special cases" (i.e., secondary representations) of, primarily, social learning, and that the social, cultural, and technological contexts where knowledge is learned and used is a fundamental aspect of the individual knowledge (Greeno 1998). These assumptions lead to a much broader view of "learning" than the individually oriented instructionist or constructivist perspectives. In addition to the more familiar acquisition of knowledge and skills by individuals, situative theories see learning in moment-to-moment interactions (between learners, materials, and other learners), evolving practices within a cohort of learners (such as a new pattern of interaction in a particular discussion forum), and even broader long-term cultural shifts (such as the way that universities are learning to accommodate MOOCs).

Rather than attempting to prove or demonstrate the situated nature of learning, the prior design studies insistently searched for new approaches to assessing learning given these core situative assumptions about learning. For example, these studies embraced a much broader view of "assessment" that saw assessment taking place wherever learning (broadly construed) was occurring. This in turn pushed aside the conventional distinction between formative assessment (in support of new learning) and summative assessment (of prior learning), leading to focus on the actual functions of assessment (intended *and* unintended) rather than just the intended summative or formative purposes. The assessment framework that emerged from these studies was used to "align" learning across (a) informal socially interactive activities, (b) semiformal classroom assessments, and (c) formal achievement tests. As illustrated below, this alignment is accomplished by "balancing" the formative and summative functions of assessment within each of these "levels." These several multiyear design studies resulted in a number of instruction-assessment "ecosystems" that supported remarkable levels of individual and social engagement with course knowledge. Most importantly, the inclusion of high-quality classroom assessments and rigorous achievement tests showed that such engagement could consistently influence the knowledge of individuals and the achievement of groups without ever "teaching to the test."

The prior program of research referenced above expanded into conventional online courses taught by the first author and others around 2010. The need to organize the findings from the prior research to accomplish this expansion resulted in a general set of design principles. Reflecting a continued focus on participation in sociocultural practices, the larger framework that these principles formed was deemed Participatory Learning and Assessment (PLA). Course features for enacting these principles in the Sakai learning management system were refined in two online graduate-level education courses over several years (Hickey and Rehak 2013). The strategies for organizing the way that students interacted with course content, one another, and the instructor drew significant inspiration from three strands of research that extended situative theories of learning into the era of digital knowledge networks. Two of these were Henry Jenkins's (2009) notion of online "participatory culture" and studies by Ito et al. (2009) of the way young people "geek out" in interest-driven social networks. While both courses involved conventional textbooks, external open educational resources were gradually incorporated over time. Drawing from the notions of connectivist learning advanced by Siemens (2005) and by Downes (2006), the strategies that emerged for supporting disciplinary interactions with those resources emphasized acknowledging a diversity of opinions, making connections within and between disciplines and networks, and identifying current learning resources.

What distinguishes the PLA framework that emerged from these two courses were online strategies for delivering useful evidence that could be used to enhance participation, individual knowledge, and group achievement, without undermining any of them, and without compromising that evidence for making claims about the resulting knowledge or achievement. The next section describes how this framework was used to scale up one of these two courses, Assessment in Schools. The approach to this scaling reflected the concern that the rapid scaling of the xMOOCs had "locked in" the narrow instructional approach with which they started. Hence the new course was capped at five hundred learners to allow the gradual development of more interactive features. This big (rather than massive) course was deemed a "BOOC" and the course was called the Assessment BOOC.

Research and Development Context

After developing the Course Builder platform for a course titled Power Searching with Google, Google released an open-source version and began promoting it for wide usage. The course and consequently the platform featured streaming videos and quizzes, much like the xMOOCs. In contrast to more comprehensive learning management systems, Course Builder was designed to support individual courses and to be easily modifiable.[2] Presumably reflecting concerns about limited interactivity in most MOOCs, Google offered grants to faculty for developing MOOCs that were "more interactive than typical MOOCs." The first author was awarded one of these grants. With university consent, a small team was assembled to develop and promote the Assessment BOOC.

This new course was first delivered as a twelve-week open course offered to the first cohort of students in fall 2013. It was promoted widely using Google and Facebook and 460 people eventually registered. The first assignment was completed by 160 participants, and 60 ultimately completed the course, including 8 students enrolled in a three-credit, graduate-level section. The Assessment BOOC was taught a second time in summer 2014, when some of the new features were automated, and streaming videos and open-ended self-assessments were added. Because most of the energy in 2014 was committed to recording videos and automating features, the course was not as widely promoted, and the instructor and teaching assistant had very limited interaction with individual students. Of the 187 registrants, 76 completed the first assignment and 22 completed the course, including 12 credential students. The course was then refined to allow a self-paced version to be offered in 2015, with little or no direct instructor involvement for the open students.

The following discussion of the BOOC course features is organized around the five PLA design principles. The extensive evidence of student engagement

---

2. Whereas the Open edX platform consists of approximately five hundred thousand lines of code, Course Builder consists of just five thousand lines; the effort described here ultimately added about three thousand additional lines, mostly in the form of course content.

and learning left behind in both courses is currently being analyzed. Some of this evidence of engagement and learning in both courses, as well as details of how each feature was scaled, has already emerged from the peer review process (Hickey, Quick, and Shen 2015). This chapter focuses on how these features embodied the five PLA principles and introduces new theoretical refinements regarding the different kinds of interaction associated with each.

PLA Design Principles, Course Design, and Course Features

The five PLA design principles coordinate activity across different kinds of interactions that support different kinds of learning. Drawing on Hall and Rubin's (1989) study of situated learning in mathematics classrooms, the principles distinguish between interactions that are *public* (presented to every member of the class and potentially beyond), *local* (in public but between specific peers and/or the instructor), or *private* (between individuals). A fourth kind of interaction, *discreet* (i.e., unobtrusive), was added to highlight the core PLA assumption that conventional achievement tests should be used judiciously and inconspicuously.

The PLA principles and features draw inspiration from Engle and Conant's (2002) notions of *productive disciplinary engagement* (PDE). Engle and Conant pointed out that engagement that is *disciplinary* involves both the declarative knowledge of the discipline as well as the social and cultural practices in which disciplinary experts engage. They further argued that disciplinary engagement that is *productive* generates numerous connections between that declarative knowledge and the learner's experiences engaging in disciplinary practices.

As elaborated in Hickey (2015) and summarized below, the PLA framework essentially embeds Engle and Conant's design principles for fostering PDE within the "multilevel" assessment model that emerged in the earlier design research. Because the course features used to enact the five PLA principles are organized around these principles, some features are not introduced in the order that learners encounter them.

1. USE PUBLIC CONTEXTS TO GIVE MEANING TO KNOWLEDGE TOOLS

The first PLA principle embodies the core situative assumption that the context in which disciplinary knowledge is learned and used is a fundamental part of that knowledge. Students' own prior experience, current interests, and future aspirations are used to publically "problematize" the disciplinary knowledge of the course. This is consistent with Engle and Conant's first design principle: *problematize subject matter from the perspective of the learner*. This leads to course features that are different from the more common inquiry-oriented and problem-based approaches (even when such approaches allow students to choose or generate their own problems).

1.1 Personalized learning contexts. In the Assessment BOOC, registrants were directed through a process that asked them questions about their actual or aspirational role in the education system and helped them draft a curricular aim that embodied their practices in that role to personalize their learning in the course. In this way the registration process highlighted the personalized approach that the course would take. This presumably discouraged registrants who were not serious about taking the course and/or who did not find the approach appealing. The information that a registrant entered was then automatically inserted into his or her wikifolio for the first assignment, in which students would further refine that aim. Each subsequent assignment asked learners to restate and reframe their curricular aim as their understanding of that aim grew alongside their knowledge of assessment.

1.2 Networking groups. Registration information regarding primary academic domain and role was used to organize students into networking groups (manually in 2013 and automatically in 2014). Doing so structured local interactions with both similar and different peers and revealed how course content interacted with domains and roles. For example, when learning about portfolio assessment, math teachers find it difficult to even imagine how they would use portfolio assessment, while many composition teachers realize that they are already doing a version of it. Likewise when learning about the validity of evidence for supporting claims about learning, educators are usually most concerned with the content-related evidence relationship (and the relationship between the content of their curriculum and their content of the assessments). Conversely, administrators are usually more concerned with criterion-related evidence (concerning the score needed on a particular assessment to support a particular decision or conclusion), while researchers and doctoral students are often more concerned with construct-related evidence (concerning psychological constructs like motivation). Discussing these differences turns out to be an efficient way to comprehend nuances that would otherwise be impossibly abstract for many learners.

Most existing MOOCs that assign learners to groups employ a relatively rigid structure to allow for manageable assignments in discussion forums.

The fact that discussion forums were not used for group interaction in the Assessment BOOC allowed for a more fluid approach to group membership. This feature was intended to encourage the formation of *affinity spaces* around common interests. Highlighting their central role in participatory culture, Gee (2004, 67) describes the affinity space as "a place or a set of places where people affiliate with others based primarily on shared activities, interests, and goals, not shared race, class culture, ethnicity, or gender." Rather than asking to be assigned to a different group, learners simply chose with whom they wish to engage. Like most interest-driven social networks, this allowed leaders to emerge and "lurkers" to observe, resulting in new affinity spaces within and across the primary networking groups. This participatory goal was explicitly supported with a simple feature added to the third assignment in the Assessment BOOC in 2014: students were invited to extend their usernames to project additional memberships (e.g., "librarian" or "unemployed math teacher") to make it easy to find peers with common interests.

1.3 Public course artifacts. Most MOOC platforms are organized around videos and private engagement with prompts for declarative "known-answer" questions. In contrast, all the BOOC assignments consisted of public (to the class) wikifolios that focused primarily on disciplinary practices. While the wikifolio assignments do involve declarative course knowledge (both directly and indirectly), this knowledge was always presented in the context of disciplinary practices and was never presented in the context of known-answer questions.

The open-field wikis that were refined in the prior online courses (in Sakai) were streamlined in the BOOC. Clicking on each section header reveals or hides the detailed instruction for that section. An edit button reveals a WYSIWYG text-editing window below the instructions. For example, the Performance/Portfolio Assessment assignment includes detailed instructions for specific parts of the assignment. This fairly intensive programming effort simplified the assignments and resulted in a complete artifact, meaningful as a stand-alone page that included both prompts and responses. This feature embodies the assumption that learner-generated artifacts occupy a central role in participatory approaches to learning. In contrast to worksheets and highly structured assignments that students often find arbitrary, abstract, and impersonal, "artifacts" are imbued with personalized meaning and identity. Artifacts that are both public and persistent play a crucial role in the interest-driven social networks that provide much of the inspiration for this instructional approach.

1.4 Relevance ranking. A simple strategy for fostering PDE that had emerged in the prior online courses proved to be remarkably scalable in the BOOC. This strategy has students rank the relevance of elements of disciplinary knowledge or disciplinary resources to their aim and/or role, and then justify that ranking. This serves to problematize the disciplinary knowledge *from the learner's perspective.* In the BOOC, this was initially enacted as an open-field activity, as in the prior course. While the course was underway, the feature was redesigned so that learners simply dragged text boxes to indicate their ordering of personalized relevance. In addition to being much simpler for the students, this allowed output of a spreadsheet that showed the relative ranking for each student, which streamlined the development of the public feedback described below.

Thus, for example, in the Performance/Portfolio Assessment assignment, learners first restate their personalized curricular aim, using their growing understanding of their aim alongside their growing understanding of assessment. They then consider the advantages and disadvantages of the two formats and rank them in order of relevance for their aim and justify that selection. After creating a task for the most relevant format and a scoring rubric, learners engage with the seven criteria for evaluating those tasks by ranking them and providing a rationale for (at minimum) the most relevant and least relevant.

This simple activity is probably the single most important feature of the course for fostering PDE, and one that appears to be infinitely scalable. This is because learners understand the activity immediately and because it can be used to support many types of engagement. A particularly important insight is that even when students lack the experience or understanding to rank something, they must engage with the knowledge to reach that conclusion. This in turn prepares them to quite readily appreciate the rankings and rationales of peers with similar aims.

1.5 Personalized open educational resources (OERs). Several of the BOOC assignments had students rank the relevance of carefully curated OERs and/or search for and share new ones. Connectivist views of learning (Siemens 2005) and the realities of twenty-first-century knowledge networks strongly favor helping students learn to use, locate, annotate, and share OERs. In the BOOC, students posted OER URLs in their wikifolios; the annotated URLs were then automatically placed all together on a separate page, where students could easily review them.

1.6 Streaming instructor videos. The prior course and the 2013 BOOC included two introductory videos. In 2014, the instructional team debated adding videos for each weekly wikifolio. On the one hand, students like online videos and many expect them. Videos can be viewed while commuting or exercising and provide a more personal connection to the instructor. On the other hand, videos might lead some students not to purchase the text or to engage less with the text and their peers. Videos are time consuming to create, and our participatory perspective raises the additional concern that "lecture" videos decontextualize course knowledge while emphasizing "known-answer" declarative knowledge, subsequently discouraging students from explicitly personalizing their wikifolios.

The team ultimately concluded that streaming videos would allow the instructor to model this personalized engagement expected in each weekly assignment relative to the design of the BOOC and the other courses he taught. The new videos also feature the instructor taking positions that diverged from those in the textbook or providing nuanced insights that reflected his own personalized instruction context of teaching this and other courses for many years. Importantly, the videos thus modeled the *practices* associated with disciplinary engagement rather than reiterating declarative knowledge explicated elsewhere.

2. RECOGNIZE AND REWARD PRODUCTIVE DISCIPLINARY ENGAGEMENT (PDE)

This second principle assumes that productive forms of disciplinary engagement should be highlighted and recognized. This is consistent with Engle and Conant's second and third PDE design principles: *give students authority over their disciplinary engagement* and *hold students accountable for their disciplinary engagement*. Put differently, the BOOC *provides resources to support PDE* (their fourth principle), and these features support student authority and accountability over that engagement. The following features were designed to motivate PDE in both public and local interactions. While we argue that PDE should be recognized and rewarded, we further argue that the process should be transparent and occur outside any formal evaluation or accountability practices (i.e., grades).

2.1 Peer commenting and discussion. Each BOOC assignment instructed students to post at least one question to their peers and to review and discuss the work of their peers by commenting on one another's wikifolios. Participants' different rankings and questions are intended to prompt productive local interactions in threaded comments directly at the bottom of each wikifolio. This feature reflects our assumption that commenting directly on artifacts is more likely to foster disciplinary discussion than conventional discussion forums. Further, this feature allowed the instructor to introduce more advanced and nuanced concepts in the comments, rather than in the body of the assignment, where it might confuse or overwhelm less-experienced students.

2.2 *Public feedback.* Within MOOCs and beyond, a great deal of attention is being devoted to "private" learning analytics that give learners individualized guidance and feedback, predict which students are going to succeed, and so on. One of the innovations that was explored extensively in the BOOC was public feedback that highlighted exemplary work and showed aggregated ranking for the class as a whole and for each networking group. Before each weekly deadline, the instructor provided relatively extensive comments to students who posted early (generally the more ambitious and experienced students). These comments would typically address an important issue in the assignment that the other students were likely to encounter as well. But these issues are so nuanced and contextual that including them in the assignment itself would overwhelm the less-experienced learners. A course announcement was posted mentioning the issues and directing others to consult those examples and comments once they started on their own wikifolio. The situative insight here is that the other students would have completed enough of the assignment to have enough context to engage meaningfully with such issues.

After each weekly deadline, the instructor publically summarized how the various networking groups ranked the resources or concepts differently. The later public feedback not only articulated these patterns, but also encouraged learners to engage with students outside of their networking groups to reexamine particular concepts and (ideally) revisit and even revise their own rankings. The feedback also pointed students to wikifolios that explored a concept well, revealed interesting nuances, or asked productive questions. This feedback was expected to both motivate students to be recognized and help students reengage efficiently if they performed poorly on the self-assessment described below.

Postcourse student commentaries confirmed that these features together motivated students to post high-quality work early, and that students found the feedback quite useful. Reflecting our argument about gradual scaling, the ranking information was manually gathered by the instructor in the prior classes and initially by a project intern in the BOOC. The automated ranking feature described above was designed in such a way that the ranking information was exported to a spreadsheet from which graphs could be quickly generated. A central goal for further streamlining this course is automating

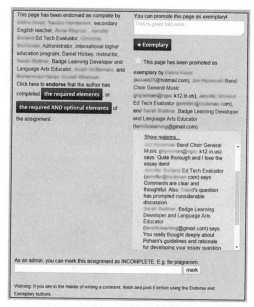

FIGURE 1.1. Completed peer endorsement and peer promotion page
in the 2014 Assessment BOOC (big open online course).

the manner in which this information is consolidated and displayed, as it is
currently one of the most laborious aspects of the course.

2.3 Peer promotion. Peer promotions are central to the functioning of
friendship-driven networks (e.g., "likes" in Facebook), and peer-established
reputations (e.g., badges in the Stack Overflow Q&A sites) are crucial in
interest-driven networks. In the prior online course (Hickey and Rehak 2013),
students were instructed (but not required) to promote particularly productive
examples or exchanges by posting a comment that started with a distinctive
string ("&&&") and providing a warrant. As shown in figure 1.1, this feature
was automated in the BOOC. Each week, students were instructed (but not
required) to promote one peer wikifolio for being "exemplary" and provide a
justification for the selection. The public feedback would indicate which member of each networking group received the most promotions and link to the
promoted wikifolio. The peer promotions were issued alongside the peer endorsements (described below) and were fully automated so that a warrant was
required and each student could only issue one peer promotion each week.

2.4 Evidence-rich digital badges. Digital badges are "web-enabled micro-
credentials" that contain specific claims and detailed evidence supporting

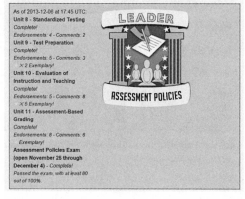

Assessment Policies Leader

Marina Michael, Elementary School Teacher earned this badge by participating in the Educational Assessment BOOC. The earner of this badge has gained and demonstrated expertise by completing four weekly wikifolio assignment concerning policies in educational assessment. These include standardized testing, appropriate test preparation, evaluation of instruction and teaching, and assessment-based grading. Their work has also been recognized as particularly strong by their peers.

Criteria for issuance

In order to earn this Leadership Badge, the awardee had to first:

- Complete four Wikifolio assignments (linked below)
- Engage with peers in discussion (not linked below, for peer privacy)
- Endorse and promote peers' Wikifolios

While engaging in this activity, the wikifolios created by the awardee were marked as "exemplary" more often than any other individual in their peer professional networking group.

Evidence

As of 2013-12-06 at 17:45 UTC:
Unit 8 - Standardized Testing
Complete!
Endorsements: 4 - Comments: 2
Unit 9 - Test Preparation
Complete!
Endorsements: 5 - Comments: 3
✕ 2 Exemplary!
Unit 10 - Evaluation of Instruction and Teaching
Complete!
Endorsements: 5 - Comments: 8
✕ 5 Exemplary!
Unit 11 - Assessment-Based Grading
Complete!
Endorsements: 8 - Comments: 6
Exemplary!
Assessment Policies Exam (open November 25 through December 4) - *Complete!*
Passed the exam, with at least 80 out of 100%.

FIGURE 1.2. Evidence contained in the 2014 Assessment BOOC (big open online course) course completion badge and one module.

those claims. As shown in figure 1.2, BOOC students who completed the wikifolios and the exam for each of the three course modules could earn a corresponding digital badge. The badges were automatically issued to students inside of the course and displayed on their profile pages. When students elected to push a badge out of the course, they could choose to include detailed evidence of their engagement and learning. This included links to their completed wikifolios, number of comments (but not the comments themselves because they could contain student names), number of promotions, rationale for the promotions, and an indication of their performance. Earning all three badges and completing the final exam resulted in an *Assessment Expert* badge that contained the other three badges.

The member of each networking group who earned the most promotions earned a version of each badge that stated *Leader* and clearly indicated that their peers found their work exemplary (see fig. 1.2). In 2014, students who transformed the contents of their wikifolios into a comprehensive term paper that the instructor deemed worthy of sharing with peers earned a customizable badge that linked back to the paper itself and the instructor's comments.

The optional term paper generated extra credit for the credential students and was required to earn a grade of A+ in the course. While six students submitted a paper in 2014, only three were deemed sufficient to earn the badge and/or extra credit.

It is worth noting that this project was well aware of the overly simplistic characterizations of evidence-rich digital badges as "extrinsic incentives." While space does not permit a detailed elaboration, the project acknowledged that badges could be used (and indeed are being used) as arbitrary rewards for activities that students already find intrinsically motivating. Surely such uses of badges will provide yet another example of this "overjustification effect" that has been shown in hundreds of empirical studies (Deci, Koestner, and Ryan 1999). But doing so overlooks the possibility that (1) the specific claims and detailed evidence in *digital* badges makes them intrinsically meaningful; (2) the circulation of claims and evidence in digital networks makes *open* badges particularly meaningful; and (3) that open digital badges have broader sociocultural consequences for learners and ecosystems (Casilli and Hickey 2016).

3. EVALUATE/GRADE ARTIFACTS THROUGH LOCAL ENDORSEMENTS AND REFLECTIONS

In practice, the first two principles result in extensive written student work. Although desired, this creates a new challenge of evaluating and grading all of these artifacts and interactions. The third PLA principle eschews any formal summative evaluation of the content of public artifacts and local interactions. This principle thus builds on existing assessment research that suggests "no marks" (i.e., ungraded) feedback (Harlen 2007) and cautions against overly detailed scoring rubrics in portfolio and performance assessment (Popham 1999). These prior suggestions were reframed using sociocultural approaches to portfolio assessment (Habib and Wittek 2007) and the notion of "portfolio culture" (Gitomer and Duschl 1995). Rather than laboriously evaluating the artifacts for dubious evidence of enduring knowledge and undermining engagement, two features support local interaction that informally assess completion and engagement.

3.1 Instructor and peer endorsement. Students were instructed (but not required) to endorse the wikifolios of at least three peers for being "complete." As shown in figure 1.1, wikifolios could be endorsed as complete for just the required parts or including the optional parts as well, and wikifolios showed the names of all the endorsers. The instructions indicated that students who failed to secure an endorsement could email the teaching assistant, but this almost never happened; while the instructor or a teaching assistant personally reviewed and endorsed the wikifolios of all the credential students, nearly every completed wikifolio earned multiple endorsements. In both BOOCs, students averaged around seven endorsements per week. A systematic review in the over eight hundred wikifolios in the 2013 course confirmed that every peer-endorsed wikifolio was completed.[3] This suggested that the public nature of the wikifolios and endorsements helped eliminate the threat of collusion. One serious instance of plagiarism was quickly identified when a noncredential student recognized that her response to the optional activity of summarizing the "big ideas" in the chapter had been cut and pasted by another noncredential student. An automated comparison algorithm subsequently confirmed that this was indeed an isolated incident and that very little content was duplicated content across wikifolios.

3.2 *Engagement reflections.* One of the optional elements on the wikifolios was writing a reflection that students posted after they had interacted with their peers. This practice and the content of the prompts had been extensively refined in the prior courses. Building on notion of *consequential* engagement introduced by Gresalfi et al. (2009), students were instructed to reflect on their *contextual engagement* ("How suitable was your context for learning this knowledge?"), *collaborative engagement* ("Who else's work and whose comments helped you learn this new knowledge?"), and *consequential engagement* ("What will you do differently in your context and beyond as a consequence of learning this knowledge?").

The assumption here is that students who had not engaged productively with the disciplinary knowledge of the course would have a difficult time drafting a coherent and convincing reflection. Analyses of log files in the prior course confirmed that some students returned to their wikifolios and engaged more *after* starting their reflections. In this way the reflections accomplished a situative assessment goal of summatively assessing one kind of learning (prior engagement) while formatively assessing another kind of learning (understanding the relationship between new disciplinary knowledge and one's disciplinary practices). The ultimate intention of these reflections is rooted in the anthropological notion of prolepsis (the way anticipated future events shape present activity). It is expected (but not yet proven) that the anticipation of

---

3. The only exception was the initial question posted to peers, which was not included in roughly a third of the wikifolios.

having to reflect on these three aspects of engagement will proleptically shape learners' prior engagement accordingly.

In addition to formatively supporting the sort of critical engagement that is largely absent in most MOOCs, these reflections also provide informal summative evidence of that engagement. It turns out that it is very difficult for students to generate coherent responses to these reflection prompts without having engaged accordingly. Students in the prior course and the credential students in the BOOC were awarded full points for posting wikifolio drafts by the deadline and later adding a reasonably coherent reflection. Each wikifolio was worth five points out of a hundred, and students were penalized one point a day for each day they were late to ensure a critical mass of interaction around the weekly deadlines. This grading practice quickly revealed that the rare incoherent reflections were typically associated with incomplete assignments. This made it possible to penalize marginal participation without engaging in the tedious and dubious grading of the content of individual artifacts. In the long term, this seems like a feature that would lend itself well to automation, using a relatively basic automated text analysis routine.

4. ASSESS INDIVIDUAL KNOWLEDGE PRIVATELY

This principle reflects the situative assumption that assessments that efficiently generate valid evidence of enduring knowledge must frame that knowledge in ways that limit the assessment's value for directly supporting *new* learning (as elaborated in Hickey 2015). This further suggests that public and local interactions should not be organized around the static representations of knowledge on formal assessments, and that any formal assessment of knowledge should be carried out privately. But we also assume well-designed "curriculum-oriented" assessments are uniquely suited for evaluating the way course activities were designed and the way individual students enacted those activities. This is because they are "proximal" assessments of the disciplinary knowledge emphasized in the course activities (rather than the more general content of textbook or targeted standards).

4.1 Ungraded open-ended quizzes. In 2014, ungraded quizzes featuring six to eight open-ended assessment items were added to each wikifolio. Students had to enter a response to each item to see the scoring key for the item. These formative assessments were entirely voluntary and students were encouraged to attempt the items from memory. While the system retained student responses, these were not formally evaluated by anyone else. The instructions recommended that students who were unable to answer more than one item from memory should reengage with their classmates (starting with the public feedback) and the text before taking the module exam.

This is a relatively new feature and it is currently being intensively studied. The relationship between the practice items and exam items, the text of the recommendations, and the content of the public feedback seem particularly important here. It is unclear whether the items should be constructed-response or selected-response (or both), or whether the items should focus on disciplinary practices or declarative knowledge (or both). Another question is whether low-performers are recommended to go back and engage more with their peers or go back and review the text. These features are expected to be particularly important in the self-paced BOOC, where credential seekers may be inclined to hastily post their wikifolios in an effort to race through the course with minimal engagement with the disciplinary practices. The situative assumption here is that a formal assessment (even an ungraded one) cannot really capture the extent to which the declarative knowledge sampled by the assessment became contextualized within each learners' personalized disciplinary practices. A related assumption is that the self-assessment represents a small sample of the declarative knowledge that engaged learners should take away from each assignment.[4]

5. MEASURE AGGREGATED ACHIEVEMENT DISCREETLY

The last PLA principle encourages using externally developed multiple-choice achievement test items for very specific purposes. Such "distal" items are "standards oriented." As long as the items are not "cherry picked" to tap into topics of the specific curriculum, they can be used to create an achievement test that is largely independent of the way a particular course was designed. As such they are useful (and indeed necessary) for measuring learning within courses, comparing learning across different versions of the same course, and accurately documenting course improvement over time.

By "discreet" this principle means unobtrusive and ephemeral; course assignments should never be directly aligned to achievement tests. In most cases students should only see their overall score. Most importantly, little if

---

4. This gets at a central concern with prevailing approaches to competency-based education and most MOOCs. Specifically, while on-demand assessments can readily capture declarative knowledge, they can't readily capture (a) knowledge of disciplinary practices, (b) the extent to which declarative knowledge has been connected to disciplinary practices (and therefore, will be subsequently usable), or (c) the entire range of disciplinary knowledge associated with particular competencies. As such, these assessments should be used to sample the declarative knowledge left behind from PDE.

any course time should be devoted to instructing students on how to answer multiple-choice items. This is because doing so yields knowledge that is otherwise useless and compromises the validity of any exam that includes those items or similar items.

5.1 *Time-limited multiple-choice exams.* The exams in the BOOC were timed multiple-choice exams with items selected from the textbook item bank. Items were selected without regard to whether they had been covered in the course, but rather for being difficult or impossible to look up with the limited time available. Test takers only saw their score, and not the correct answer for each item. We experimented with the badge-related evidence associated with the exams and eventually allowed the students to choose to include (a) their actual score, (b) whether they met criteria, or (c) nothing about the exam in their digital badges. For the students who took the course for credit, exam scores were factored into the final course grade.

Findings, Next Steps, and Conclusions

Perhaps the most important finding across the two Assessment BOOCs is that raw engagement for both the credential students and the noncredit students who completed the course increased substantially. The average number of words per wikifolio increased from 1,398/1,207 for the credential/completers in 2013 to 2,820/1,377 in 2014. This suggests that the substantial decline in the amount of local interactions that individual students had with the instructor and teaching assistants did not undermine motivation to work on their wikifolios. One other difference is that the proportion of comments that reference a specific context of practice dropped from around 50 percent in 2013 to about 25 percent in 2014. This appears to have been caused by a 2014 modification that forced students to post a question to their peers before they could share their wikifolios. Most of the other indicators for the two groups were similar across 2013 and 2014, including average comments per wikifolio (4.2/3.4 versus 5.6/3.0), percentage of comments that were deemed disciplinary (for directly referencing the topic of the assignment, both around 95 percent), and exam scores (all around 80 percent).

We are unaware of any other effort to scale up open learning that resulted in these levels of disciplinary engagement, knowledge, and achievement. As such we concluded that this effort to scale up participatory learning was a success. This scaling effort continued in subsequent efforts to create a self-paced version of the Assessment BOOC for summer 2015 with most of these same features. New features are being developed to fully automate registration, testing, and badge issuance, help learners find active peers working on particular assignments, and let learners archive completed wikifolios in a manner that tells subsequent students whether they are willing to reengage with them. To the extent that the course can attract a sufficient number of participants, it should be possible to attain a level of individual and social PDE that is unprecedented for a self-paced course.

The apparent success of this effort brings us to several conclusions about scaling learning that we believe generalize to other efforts. The first conclusion is that *scaling should be done gradually*. To quickly scale up to massive numbers of users, most MOOCs and MOOC platforms were forced to sacrifice interaction and personalization; because the code behind them is already so complex, those platforms are now finding it quite challenging to incorporate new features. Our second conclusion is that *scaling should be done iteratively*. Our efforts were directly shaped by newer design-based research methods that emphasize the development of "local" theories in the context of reform efforts (Cobb et al. 2003). Furthermore, we conclude that such iterative refinements should be done within a coherent theoretical framework. Because the core multilevel assessment model behind this work was rooted in situative theories of learning, we were able to draw additional research and theory carried on in that tradition to generate useful theoretical insights and practical solutions. In particular we found the notion of PDE especially helpful, because we were able to evaluate all our design decisions in terms of their presumed or actual impact on the disciplinarity and productivity of learner interactions.

Finally, we conclude that the PLA framework seems generally useful for guiding efforts to scale learning. A key feature of this framework is that disciplinary knowledge is represented in somewhat different ways across each level. This increases the trustworthiness of the evidence at one level for assessing the impact of refinements at the previous level. For example, the engagement reflections provide useful evidence of the extent to which students were connecting disciplinary knowledge and disciplinary practices in their wikifolios. This evidence was clearly used by students to refine their subsequent engagement (and sometimes their prior wikifolio); this evidence was also used by the instructor and designers to fine-tune assignments and features within and across courses. Similarly, given that the private self-assessment was ungraded and most students who posted a wikifolio completed them, we presume that students used this evidence to determine whether they were ready to take the exam.

In summary, we believe the synchronization of the PLA framework with iterative design-based refinement is a promising way of scaling interactive learning. An ongoing collaboration with a fully online university-run high school is bolstering our confidence that this framework can also "scale out" to large numbers of teachers in conventional online classes. In 2013–14, four English teachers successfully used this approach to create entirely new courses for grades 9–12 using OERs and the newer Canvas learning management system. The new courses were developed as alternatives to individualized "distance education" courses that were being delivered using an antiquated system. When the school was reaccredited in 2014, the evaluators were particularly complimentary toward the new courses and encouraged expanded collaboration. The English courses were offered again in 2014–15, and new teachers developed new courses in history and biology. We are particularly encouraged that some of the extensions to the Canvas learning management systems developed for this work (such as wikifolio commenting) are now being incorporated into the larger learning management system for the hosting university. Certainly much work remains to be done, but quite a bit of progress has been made in this initial effort to scale participatory learning.

References

Anderson, John R. 1990. *Cognitive Psychology and Its Implications*. San Francisco: WH Freeman.

Anderson, John R., Lynne M. Reder, and Herbert A. Simon. 1996. "Situated Learning and Education." *Educational Researcher* 25 (4): 5–11.

Barab, Sasha, Steve Zuiker, Scott Warren, Dan Hickey, Adam Ingram-Goble, Eun-Ju Kwon, Inna Kouper, and Susan C. Herring. 2007. "Situationally Embodied Curriculum: Relating Formalisms and Contexts." *Science Education* 91 (5): 750–82.

Billsberry, Jon. 2013. "MOOCs: Fad or Revolution." *Journal of Management Education* 37 (6): 739–46.

Bramante, Fred, and Rose Colby. 2012. *Off the Clock: Moving Education from Time to Competency*. Thousand Oaks: Corwin Press.

Brinton, Christopher G., Mung Chiang, Sonal Jain, H. K. Lam, Zhenming Liu, and Felix Ming Fai Wong. 2014. "Learning about Social Learning in MOOCs: From Statistical Analysis to Generative Model." *Learning Technologies, IEEE Transactions on Learning Technologies* 7 (4): 346–59.

Brown, John Seely, Allan Collins, and Paul Duguid. 1989. "Situated Cognition and the Culture of Learning." *Educational Researcher* 18 (1): 32–42.

Casilli, Carla, and Daniel Hickey. 2016. "Transcending Conventional Credentialing and Assessment Paradigms with Information-Rich Digital Badges." *Information Society* 32 (2): 117–29.

Cobb, Paul, Jere Confrey, Andrea diSessa, Richard Lehrer, and Leona Schauble. 2003. "Design Experiments in Educational Research." *Educational Researcher* 32 (1): 9–13.

Daniel, John. 2012. "Making sense of MOOCs: Musings in a Maze of Myth, Paradox and Possibility." *Journal of Interactive Media in Education* 3. http://www-jime.open.ac.uk/article/2012-18/html.

Deci, Edward L., Richard Koestner, and Richard M. Ryan. 1999. "A Meta-Analytic Review of

Experiments Examining the Effects of Extrinsic Rewards on Intrinsic Motivation." *Psychological Bulletin* 125 (6): 627.

Downes, Stephen. 2006. "Learning Networks and Connective Knowledge." *Collective Intelligence and eLearning* 20:1–26.

Ebben, Maureen, and Julien S. Murphy. 2014. "Unpacking MOOC Scholarly Discourse: A Review of Nascent MOOC Scholarship." *Learning, Media and Technology* 39 (3): 328–45.

Engle, Randi, and Faith Conant. 2002. "Guiding Principles for Fostering Productive Disciplinary Engagement: Explaining an Emergent Argument in a Community of Learners Classroom." *Cognition and Instruction* 20 (4): 399–483.

Fisher, Douglas H., and Armando Fox. 2013. "Report on the CCC-CRA Workshop on Multidisciplinary Research for Online Education." Alexandria: National Science Foundation. http://archive2.cra.org/ccc/files/docs/meetings/OnlineEducation/CCC-MROE-Report.pdf.

Gagné, Robert Mills. 1985. *The Conditions of Learning and Theory of Instruction.* New York: Holt, Rinehart and Winston.

Gasevic, Dragan, Vitomir Kovanovic, Srecko Joksimovic, and George Siemens. 2014. "Where Is Research on Massive Open Online Courses Headed? A Data Analysis of the MOOC Research Initiative." *International Review of Research in Open and Distributed Learning* 15 (5): 134–76.

Gee, James. 2004. *Situated Language and Learning: A Critique of Traditional Schooling.* New York: Routledge.

Gitomer, Drew, and Richard Duschl. 1995. "Moving toward a Portfolio Culture in Science Education." In *Learning Science in the Schools: Research Reforming Practice,* edited by Sean Glynn and Reinders Duit, 299–326. Mahwah: Lawrence Erlbaum.

Glaser, Robert. 1984. "Education and Thinking: The Role of Knowledge." *American Psychologist* 39 (2): 93–104.

Greeno, James G. 1998. "The Situativity of Knowing, Learning, and Research." *American Psychologist* 53 (1): 5–26.

Gresalfi, Melissa, Sasha Barab, Sinem Siyahhan, and Tyler Christensen. 2009. "Virtual Worlds, Conceptual Understanding, and Me: Designing for Consequential Engagement." *On the Horizon* 17 (1): 21–34.

Habib, Laurence, and Line Wittek. 2007. "The Portfolio as Artifact and Actor." *Mind, Culture, and Activity* 14 (4): 266–82.

Hall, Rogers, and Andee Rubin. 1989. "There's Five Little Notches in Here: Dilemmas in Teaching and Learning the Conventional Structure of Rate." In *Thinking Practices in Mathematics and Science Learning,* edited by James Greeno and Shelly Goldman, 189–235. Mahwah: Lawrence Erlbaum.

Harlen, Wynne. 2007. "Criteria for Evaluating Systems for Student Assessment." *Studies in Educational Evaluation* 33 (1): 15–28.

Hickey, Daniel T. 2015. "A Situative Response to the Conundrum of Formative Assessment." *Assessment in Education: Principles, Policy and Practice* 22 (2): 202–23.

Hickey, Daniel, Adam Ingram-Goble, and Ellen Jameson. 2009. "Designing Assessments and Assessing Designs in Virtual Educational Environments." *Journal of Science Education and Technology* 18 (2): 187–208.

Hickey, Daniel, Jenna McWilliams, and Michelle Honeyford. 2011. "Reading Moby-Dick in a Participatory Culture: Organizing Assessment for Engagement in a New Media Era." *Journal of Educational Computing Research* 45 (2): 247–63.

Hickey, Daniel, and Andrea Rehak. 2013. "Wikifolios and Participatory Assessment for Engagement, Understanding, and Achievement in Online Courses." *Journal of Educational Multimedia and Hypermedia* 22 (4): 407–41.

Hickey, Daniel, Gita Taasoobshirazi, and Dionne Cross. 2012. "Assessment as Learning: Enhancing Discourse, Understanding, and Achievement in Innovative Science Curricula." *Journal of Research in Science Teaching* 49 (10): 1240–70.

Hickey, Daniel, Joshua Quick, and Xinyi Shen. 2015. "Formative and Summative Analyses of Disciplinary Engagement and Learning in a Big Open Online Course." In *Proceedings of the Fifth International Conference on Learning Analytics and Knowledge*. New York: Association for Computing Machinery. http://dx.doi.org/10.1145/2723576.2723639.

Hickey, Daniel, and Steven J. Zuiker. 2012. "Multilevel Assessment for Discourse, Understanding, and Achievement." *Journal of the Learning Sciences* 21 (4): 522–82.

Ito, Mizuko, Sonja Baumer, Matteo Bittanti, danah boyd, Rachel Cody, Becky Herr, Heather A. Horst, et al. 2009. *Hanging Out, Messing Around, Geeking Out: Living and Learning with New Media*. Cambridge: MIT Press.

Jenkins, Henry. 2009. *Confronting the Challenges of Participatory Culture: Media Education for the 21st Century*. Cambridge: MIT Press.

Kanuka, Heather, and Terry Anderson. 2007. "Ethical Issues in Qualitative E-Learning Research." *International Journal of Qualitative Methods* 6 (2): 20–39.

Kays, Trent. 2012. "MOOCs will never Replace Traditional Higher Ed." *Minnesota Daily*, October 22. http://www.mndaily.com/2012/10/22/moocs-will-never-replace-traditional -higher-ed.

Koedinger, Kenneth R., and Albert Corbett. 2006. "Cognitive Tutors: Technology Bringing Learning Sciences to the Classroom." In *The Cambridge Handbook of the Learning Sciences*, edited by Keith Sawyer, 61–78. New York: Cambridge University Press.

Koehler, Matthew J., and Punya Mishra. 2008. "Introducing TPCK." In *Handbook of Technological Pedagogical Content Knowledge (TPCK) for Educators*, edited by the AACTE Committee on Innovation and Technology, 3–29. New York: Routledge.

Lave, Jean, and Etienne Wenger. 1991. *Situated Learning: Legitimate Peripheral Participation*. New York: Cambridge University Press.

Mackness, Jenny, Sui Mak, and Roy Williams. 2010. "The Ideals and Reality of Participating in a MOOC." In *Proceedings of the 7th International Conference on Networked Learning 2010*, edited by Lone Dircknick-Holmfeld, Vivien Hodgson, Chris Jones, Maarten de Laat, David McConnell, and Thomas Ryberg, 266–75. Lancaster: Lancaster University.

Marks, Jonathan. 2012. "Who's Afraid of the Big Bad Disruption?" *Inside Higher Ed*, October 5. http://www.insidehighered.com/views/2012/10/05/why-moocs-wont replace-traditional -instruction-essay.

Oremus, Will. 2013. "Online Class on How to Teach Online Goes Laughably Awry." *Slate*, February 5. http://www.slate.com/blogs/future_tense/2013/02/05/mooc_meltdown_coursera _course_on_fundamentals_of_online_education_ends_in.html.

Papamitsiou, Zacharoula, and Anastasios A. Economides. 2014. "Learning Analytics and Educational Data Mining in Practice: A Systematic Literature Review of Empirical Evidence." *Journal of Educational Technology and Society* 17 (4): 49–64.

Pappano, Laura. 2012. "The Year of the MOOC." *New York Times*, November 2. http://www .nytimes.com/2012/11/04/education/edlife/massive-open-online-courses-are-multiplying -at-a-rapid-pace.html.

Pope, Justin. 2012. "Uncertainty Abounds as MOOCs Move Toward Credit." *Diverse: Issues in Higher Education*, November 19. http://diverseeducation.com/article/49594/.

Popham, W. James. 1997. "What's Wrong—And What's Right—with Rubrics." *Educational Leadership* 55:72–75.

Shulman, Lee S. 1986. "Those Who Understand: Knowledge Growth in Teaching." *Educational Researcher* 15 (2): 4–14.

Siemens, George. 2005. "Connectivism: A Learning Theory for the Digital Age." *International Journal of Instructional Technology and Distance Learning* 2 (1): 3–10.

2

Can MOOCs and SPOCs Help Scale Residential Education While Maintaining High Quality?

ARMANDO FOX

Now that the media honeymoon with massive open online courses (MOOCs) is apparently over, MOOCs have variously been denounced for dumbing down college courses, homogenizing the presentation of a course based on a single professor's topic, and relegating professors who use the materials to the status of high-level teaching assistants. Universities and MOOC providers have variously been accused of using MOOCs as an instrument to strip faculty of intellectual property rights, to privatize education or otherwise outsource it to commercial providers, to justify laying off faculty or "adjunct-ifying" their teaching budgets, to unfairly monetize faculty efforts to create courses, or to cram more students into least-common-denominator course formats while sacrificing education quality. I propose an alternate perspective: MOOCs have triggered new considerations around scalable course technology, course formats, and the potential for better insight into student learning, and these benefits are "scaling down" from MOOCs to small private online courses (SPOCs) that can be offered by offering highly customizable copies of MOOC materials to classroom students.

As MOOCs and SPOCs are still in their early stages, much of what I report in this essay must be taken as a personal view: while it is all supported by the direct experience of my colleagues and me, it is not rigorous and I don't present it as such. It will also appear to focus disproportionately on our experience with a particular course; this is because I prefer to provide concrete examples to support each of my positions, and space constraints make it impossible to do so for a range of courses.

That said, I believe the material here represents the collective viewpoint of a contingent of academics who have been quietly taking advantage of some of the overlooked benefits of SPOCs, and I hope it spurs others to consider doing the same.

From First MOOC to Institutional Goals:
How Berkeley's First MOOC Happened Almost by Accident

In 2009, my colleague David Patterson and I took over Berkeley's undergraduate course in software engineering with the intent of retooling it to better match modern software practice (Fox and Patterson 2012). Because of the course's surging popularity (see fig. 2.1), we had begun investigating the possibility of constructing automatic graders—not just for multiple-choice "scantron" quizzes, but for providing detailed feedback on complete programming assignments, by repurposing the tools that professional programmers use to test and evaluate their own programs. Two faculty team-teach the course, with one twenty-hour-a-week teaching assistant (TA) per thirty-five students. The in-progress spring 2015 course has 237 enrollees. SPOC technology has been used since spring 2012. The upper line indicates the student's rating of instructor effectiveness (7 is best) for each offering.

Coincidentally, at around this time (fall 2011), our Stanford colleagues Daphne Koller and Andrew Ng invited us to try adapting part of our course as a MOOC, Stanford having no comparable course at the time. (Coursera had not yet been incorporated, so the opportunity was presented to us as an experiment in pedagogy.) We agreed, believing that our commitment would force us to follow through on the autograder challenge: Stanford's MOOCs were enrolling tens of thousands of students, and only fully automated grading would be feasible at that scale. Shortly thereafter, Coursera was incorporated, and our MOOC became the second course offered on that platform and the first from UC Berkeley. Significantly, we asked Coursera to create a separate copy of the MOOC accessible only to Berkeley students enrolled in our campus course, in part because we needed to release materials to Berkeley students earlier, both to meet campus deadlines and to "shake down" the materials before releasing them to MOOC students. In retrospect, this was the first SPOC.

The intensive press around MOOCs soon got the university's attention, and a steering committee was convened by then-chancellor Robert Birgeneau, led by vice chancellors, and staffed by deans and chairs of various departments. Its charter was to unify and rationalize institutional MOOC strategy and resourcing with that of existing online programs. Significantly, and in contrast to the tone of many popular press articles about universities and MOOCs at the time, the steering committee came to the early conclusion that

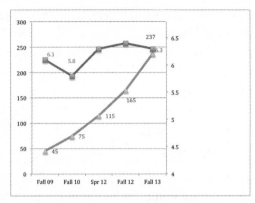

FIGURE 2.1. Enrollment in the revised version of UC Berkeley's undergraduate software engineering course. The lower line with green triangles indicates enrollment. The upper line with squares indicates student's rating of instructor effectiveness (7 is best) for each course offering.

MOOCs were unlikely to become major revenue generators. Therefore, the strategic priorities for MOOCs would align with Berkeley's existing mission of "access and excellence" as follows:

*Support and improve on-campus teaching and pedagogy research by tak-*ing advantage of the large enrollments of MOOCs, which offer new analytics opportunities that don't work at smaller scales (Lord 1980) and the ability to test pedagogical interventions using between-subjects experiments ("A/B testing"). Indeed, as individual instructors start to pay attention to this data to improve their materials, student expectations will rise to the point that instructors *not* taking advantage of the data will become the exception.

Investigate alternative and hybrid on-campus course formats that leverage MOOC technology, both to enrich course experiences and improve access to high-demand courses.

Expose current faculty and graduate students (future faculty) to these new teaching tools and modalities and train them in the use of the new tools, since future generations of students will surely expect their instructors to be facile with online learning.

Burnish the university's brand and public service mission by featuring our best courses and teachers in free offerings, thereby demonstrating the diversity and excellence of Berkeley's people and intellectual pursuits.

Based on the above goals, the committee ultimate chose to align Berkeley with edX for several reasons, including edX's nonprofit status (given the determination that significant revenue was unlikely) and the open nature of the edX platform (since a customizable and modifiable platform was considered a necessary component of the test bed for doing pedagogy research to improve on-campus teaching). The four existing Berkeley MOOCs were migrated to edX and have remained there since.

The rest of this essay describes the effect of the decision to make MOOCs first and foremost a vehicle for enriching the teaching and learning experience for our own faculty and students.

From MOOCs to SPOCs: Our SPOC Experience, and Dispelling Some SPOC Misconceptions

The constraint of scale had led us to explore parts of the design space for MOOC courseware that we would not have considered but for the need to scale. We were stupidly surprised to realize that the technology we had built to deploy the MOOC "in the large" was exceptionally useful "in the small," that is, in our own classrooms: having a single shared artifact (the Open edX courseware delivery system) to "bridge" the two paradigms is what helped us identify these benefits and gave us the idea to offer them to our colleagues at other universities. We did end up building four different autograders for different types of software engineering assignments; these represent close to a thousand engineer-hours of work by our teaching assistants (TAs) and us, and work by Coursera (and later edX) to provide us with a way to integrate them into the Open edX courseware system. But the effort amortizes well: they have graded hundreds of thousands of programming assignments so far. In addition, because of these autograders, our classroom students get finer-grained feedback than they'd get from human TAs, who can spend at most a few minutes per assignment. In addition, we could now give our classroom students the opportunity to resubmit homework to improve on their previous score and increase mastery, something previous cohorts of campus students had requested but which we had been unable to grant because of the increased course staff it would have required (Fox 2014).

Given the success of our MOOC and campus course, we wondered if our materials could help other instructors teach software engineering in the way we developed. We were inspired by a recent experiment at San José State University in California, in which students in an analog circuits course used MIT-authored MOOC lectures and homework assignments created by Professor Anant Agarwal (Lewin and Markoff 2013). The students' in-classroom time was spent working on lab and design problems with local faculty and TAs. These students scored 5 percentage points higher on the first exam and 10 points on the second exam than the previous cohort that had used the traditional material only. Even more strikingly, the proportion of students receiving credit for the course ("C" or better grade) increased from 59 percent to 91 percent. So educational quality arguably increased, costs were lowered by helping students graduate more quickly, and faculty time was shifted from what the faculty perceived as a lower-value activity—creating and delivering lectures on content that hasn't changed recently—to the higher-value activity of working directly with students on the material. This model seemed to us to take advantage of important MOOC features, including access to high-quality materials and rapid feedback to students via autograding, to maximize the leverage of the scarce resource—instructor time.

Inspired by that example, in spring 2013 we reached out to the approximately 10 percent of enrollees in the initial MOOC who had self-identified as computer science instructors potentially interested in using our MOOC materials in their classrooms. Our colleagues at edX were interested in trying a new model for using MOOC materials, so they arranged for each of five instructors (four at US four-year universities and one at Tsinghua University in China) to receive a complete and customizable deployment of the course with access limited to their classroom students and instructional staff. Since these courses were neither large nor open, we coined the term SPOC for *small private online course* to describe this deployment scenario. As we have reported elsewhere (Fox et al. 2014), far from delivering "clones" of "our" course to their students, the SPOC instructors used our materials in a variety of ways. All watched our lectures to prepare for the course; some assigned a subset of our videos for their students to watch, while others watched our videos to help prepare their own live lectures. Three of the four made some use of our exams. Two contributed new homework assignments created for their own students that take advantage of our autograding technology; we provide these assignments to our UC Berkeley students as well. One contributed scaffolded "walk-throughs" for one of the more complex homework assignments, based on observing specific trouble spots experienced by students in her course. All but one use our autograders to some degree. Our discussions with the instructors revealed a particular area of difficulty their students were having on one of the assignments, and when we surveyed our UC Berkeley students, we were surprised that they had the same complaint but had not voiced it; as a result we worked with the SPOC instructors to create a new homework assignment to provide more depth on that topic, which is being "field tested" in the Berkeley course in spring 2015 and will be made available in the MOOC and all SPOCs by summer 2015.

In short, the experience with the SPOC instructor community (which has since grown to encompass several dozen other instructors in the United States and abroad) showed that, while computer science instructors as a group have always been eager to share curriculum and materials, sharing materials *around a common artifact*, namely a SPOC on the Open edX platform, means that the materials so created are not one-way but two-way: not just an assignment, but an autograder to grade it with built-in knowledge of the instructors' grading rubrics; not just a brief quiz, but an online offering of that quiz that students can take in class or at home; and so on. And since the platform and the course format documentation are open and available at the website code .edx.org, there is no risk that the materials created become beholden to a particular vendor's proprietary format.

Indeed, the standard packaging has also made it easier for us to continually refine our course: we now have three complete captures of the live lectures from which we are assembling a "definitive" version containing the best treatments (in our opinion) of each topic, while still making the other source materials available. In between offerings, we have enriched the material with additional resources not available to us in the initial offering, such as live informal interviews with famous software engineers and materials created by our "SPOC'ers" in connection with the course.

This core group of SPOC'ers still have a biweekly conference call and website where they share best practices, discuss difficulties they are having, and so on, and some even helped organize a panel on SPOCs at the major computer science education conference (Roth et al. 2015). This admittedly anecdotal experience suggests to us that some objections to SPOCs that have been voiced by our colleagues may turn out to be misconceptions. We address a few in the rest of this section.

Objection: SPOCs are a potential manifestation of a "winner-take-all" paradigm in which one dominant version of a course squelches other instructors' editorial voices and pedagogical choices, relegating the other instructors to high-level TAs (Lucas 2014).

Both a textbook and a course plan represent a set of editorial choices, among other things. Most of us have used others' textbooks to teach courses without feeling that we were thereby handing editorial control of the course over to the textbook authors. We may excerpt from those books or skip around; we may augment what's in the book with our own materials; or we may comment on the current state of research or industry practice, adding currency and perspective to those materials. In other words, beyond creating *content* for students, we create *context* for them (Dillenbourg et al. 2014).

As demonstrated by our initial group of SPOC'ers, a SPOC affords the same level of customization, but comes with a set of field-tested materials that work well together and are packaged for distribution using a standard software framework, in our case the open-source Open edX framework. The pattern of activity we've experienced is hardly consistent with the "winner-take-all" scenario—each instructor has both customized the material to their students' needs and contributed ideas and materials back to the common artifact. Yet, at the same time, instructors interested in using our materials "out of the box" could easily start from our ready-to-use lecture materials and cloud-based autograders, freeing them and their TAs from the burden (and few of our computer science colleagues would characterize it otherwise) of grading simple programming assignments when they could instead be working with individual students on more sophisticated design projects that put the basic concepts into practice. After all, there is no a priori reason to expect that someone who is good at creating content is good at delivering lectures, scaffolding assignments, creating exercises, and so on, even though most faculty are expected to perform all these functions competently as part of their teaching role.

Objection: We've long been able to distribute PDFs of our own notes and even videos of our own lectures, so SPOCs don't offer fundamentally new opportunities to share courseware.

While true, this argument falls short because PDF and video distribution are *one-way* channels. We receive no information about how those assets are being used, which might give us clues as to whether learners find them useful. Which sections of the material do students review repeatedly? At what point do they indicate a loss of interest in our presentation of a topic, for example, by clicking the stop button on a video? Previously, most systems that could provide such information were not readily available to individual instructors in smaller schools. While the tooling of current MOOC/SPOC environments is still evolving rapidly, tools such as VisMOOC (Shi et al. 2015), built as part of a research project on visualizing large-scale MOOC data, make such information available to instructors in near real time in a friendly visual format. That is, while the early emphasis on MOOCs appears to have focused on video lectures, the instant feedback provided by interactive components such as autograded assignments is the true differentiating advantage of MOOCs.

Indeed, because MOOC + SPOC platforms such as Open edX are implemented as software-as-a-service (e.g., hosted in the cloud, accessed via a browser, no installation required for students or instructors), getting new technologies into instructors' hands is quicker and easier than if software or other artifacts had to be distributed. For example, Gulwani (2014) has built technology that can generate questions and step-by-step solutions for reasoning tasks such as geometry proofs, logic problems, algebra-equation solving, and other fields, some of which has begun to be integrated into MOOC platforms. While the scale of MOOCs motivates the application of this technology to education, I predict that such technologies will find rapid uptake in SPOCs as well, and students will come to expect it in their courses.

Objection: SPOCs and MOOCs are a ploy by vendors and/or universities to privatize education or arrogate the intellectual property rights of the faculty who create the courses.

While I was preparing this essay, a colleague brought to my attention that some have taken the "P" in "SPOC" to stand for *privatization* (the usurpation of education by commercial entities) rather than the intended *private* (designating an online course in which enrollment is limited to a specific group, e.g., the students also enrolled in a corresponding residential course). But even without this confusion, it should be clear that an *open* courseware platform effectively empowers individual faculty to publish their courseware, just as e-books and print on demand have facilitated book publishing for individual authors who might never get the attention of a publisher (or who might be dissatisfied with the publishers' intellectual property terms). That is, what is new is the availability to anyone of a channel for distributing one's work widely. While the courses on the edX.org website are all offered by edX-affiliate universities, any instructor at any non-edX university (or, for that matter, anyone wishing to deliver an online or hybrid course) can download and deploy the Open edX courseware delivery system royalty-free to distribute one's own courses on it, whether to a classroom of twenty or as an open MOOC that could serve twenty thousand. Of course, operating a system that can serve thousands rather than tens requires technical expertise and expense, but universities already support similar facilities such as email and student information systems, either in-house or through contracts with private vendors.

A related concern is whether faculty who provide courseware for MOOCs or SPOCs are giving up (potentially valuable) intellectual property rights. This is a valid concern, although many of those same faculty routinely sign away copyright on their original research papers when submitting to a journal or conference. In any case, it is certainly helpful to understand one's employer's intellectual property policies for courseware. At UC Berkeley, the long-established shared-governance model has led to an intellectual property policy that is very faculty-centric, wherein faculty own all the intellectual property they create for their courses and the university must obtain faculty permission to republish or redistribute it. That policy has not been modified for MOOCs: faculty who create them retain 100 percent of the intellectual property rights in their content, and indeed UC Berkeley and edX cannot offer a faculty member's MOOC without an explicit grant of permission (i.e., a license) from the author.

Objection: MOOCs "dumb down" campus courses by forcing all course elements to fit existing MOOC technology affordances.

Many aspects of traditional classes, such as small-group discussions and face-to-face time with instructors, do not work in the MOOC format. This assertion is true, but it implicitly and incorrectly assumes that replicating the classroom experience is the proper goal for an online course. In the SPOC format, a simple response to this objection is "if it hurts, don't do it."

For example, our campus course, like those of most of our SPOC'ers, includes an open-ended design project that both the instructors and the students consider integral to the course. By its nature it is instructor interaction intensive, since each team's project is different and the students encounter design issues they have not faced in the scaffolded homework assignments. The project is entirely absent from the MOOC, since mentoring design projects scales poorly. Yet the automation of the autograders for the "skill-building" components of the course has resulted in *better projects*. The students start the project with better preparation since they have received instant feedback on their homework assignments and been able to resubmit them multiple times to improve mastery. The TAs and professors can spend more time during office hours working with students on the design project, since they are freed from the drudgery of grading. Our ratio of TAs to students has not changed, but the TAs are spending nearly 100 percent of their time on the high-touch activity of answering individual student questions, and essentially none on grading skill-building assignments.

SPOC Influence on Campus Teaching

In fall 2013, enrollment in UC Berkeley's introductory computer science course exceeded 1,000 for the first time, and as of this writing stands at about 1,300, reflecting exploding demand for computing education (Patterson and Lazowska 2013). And unlike MOOCs, whose completion rates range from 2 percent to 10 percent (as listed on http://www.katyjordan.com /MOOCproject.html as of June 12, 2015) for a 1,300-student campus course the norm is that most students will complete the course (in the sense of sticking it out to the end, if not necessarily receiving a passing grade). At this scale, campus courses start to exhibit MOOC-scale challenges: variation in student ability is wider, and different subcohorts of students have difficulty with different concepts, making a "synchronous" course increasingly challenging to run. While "flipping the classroom" using MOOC materials has been widely publicized as one way to use MOOC technology on campus (Brame 2013), with some instructors now exploring "flipping" using contents drawn from several MOOCs (Bruff et al. 2013), instructors should not overlook the op-portunity to improve productivity within their existing teaching formats by allowing faculty time to be focused on higher-leverage activities.

We believe our SPOC experience can inform efforts to meet the demands of scale while maintaining high course quality. In particular, since careful use of SPOCs allow certain aspects of the course to be handled by teaching staff other than the professor, we can improve faculty productivity *if* we are able to make some structural changes in how courses are staffed, resourced, and administered.

One key innovation is new teaching staff roles: in addition to TAs, our large courses employ lab assistants and tutors who may contribute only a few hours a week but have mastered the material. How can such assistants, who have minimal if any teaching training, be trained to be effective in such roles? Interestingly, we and other MOOC instructors had encountered a similar problem in the MOOC: given the MOOC's worldwide reach, there's always some student somewhere awake and working on the course, so we rely heav-ily on volunteers recruited from previous MOOC offerings to serve as "com-munity TAs" in the MOOC (this is now common practice in many MOOCs). Most of these volunteers had mastered the course material, but had little or no prior experience in an instructor role. One of these volunteers who *did* have teaching experience, Professor Samuel Joseph of Hawai'i Pacific University (an alumnus of our first MOOC offering and now the lead facilitator for our MOOC), created an entirely new and separate SPOC, hosted on edX, as an introduction/orientation to serving in the community TA role. Enrollment is limited to and required for those who have been selected as volunteer com-munity TAs; enrollees learn about the role and importance of community TAs in the MOOC, receive hints for moderating forums and facilitating remote pair-programming (an exercise in which remote students work collaboratively on a programming problem with community TAs "dropping in" virtually to coach them), and get advice on helping students having difficulty on specific assignments without providing answers outright. In essence, this effort uses the MOOC format as a distribution mechanism for instructor-facing guid-ance on how to effectively mediate the course. At UC Berkeley, we now ask our TAs for the campus version of this course to enroll in that SPOC, and we are planning to enhance the SPOC to make it available as supporting material for professors and TAs at other institutions interested in using our materials.

The idea of using MOOCs and SPOCs to help teach the teachers is not our innovation; "teacher-training SPOCs" are being produced by the non-profit Code.org and by the National Science Foundation's CS10K project (cs10kcommunity.org), both of which aim to train high school teachers to deliver computer science courses. These teacher-training SPOCs will be combined with live workshops and remote interaction (Google Hangouts) to train instructors on the use of materials. In other words, the MOOC format can potentially be used to scale up the teaching not only of students but also of teachers.

We have also identified ways that campus SPOC'ers can benefit from the scale of MOOCs. For example, we are building an autograder that gives students feedback on code style—a somewhat subjective but important attribute of program code—by comparing a student's solution to those of her peers and providing feedback based on the differences (Moghadam et al. 2015). Our approach relies on automatically analyzing enough submissions so that one can always be found that is "just a little better" than the one being evaluated; we have found this to be the case when we look at thousands of submissions to a homework assignment, but less often true when considering only the two hundred or so submissions of that assignment from our own campus students. If we pool our students' submissions with those of MOOC students, our technique works.

Challenges for Instructors and Administrators

These new approaches entail structural challenges, since so many elements of the calculus of faculty compensation are tied to traditional course formats.

For example, creating materials to orient and scaffold other instructors may not only help scale a local course, therefore increasing local faculty productivity, but also can encourage colleagues at other universities to adopt the materials, which would presumably reflect well on the course author and institution. Creating such materials is at least as difficult and time consuming as creating student-facing materials, if not more so. Yet most universities do not explicitly reward time spent creating materials other than those that are student facing, so this task may represent an unacceptable opportunity cost for a busy instructor. And if such materials are created and successfully used to train new teaching roles such as informal tutors, adjustments to existing campus policies, budgets, and personnel allocations may be required to recognize and compensate those roles.

Many faculty workload calculations are based on student contact hours. Committee approvals may be required to change course delivery formats—for example, to allow a flipped-classroom course in which lectures are watched online—to recognize the difference between a "contact hour" spent meeting with a small group of students and a "contact hour" spent delivering a lecture to a room of hundreds.

We have been navigating these challenges at UC Berkeley in the quest to scale up our already highly demanded computing courses, and our experience so far is that the gain in scalability justifies these nontrivial structural changes.

Finally, too often lost in MOOC and SPOC discussions is the students' perspective. Our surveys of our campus students consistently show that students like having lectures available online, both for review and because there is no stigma associated with pressing "Rewind" when a concept goes by just a bit too quickly. At office hours, I no longer get questions of the form "Can you review what you said about X in lecture yesterday" because the students can review it themselves, online. Students still attend lecture, but they value it all the more since lecture time is increasingly spent on going into more depth on a topic or working a real-world example based on the topic. Students rarely visit TAs asking if their homework approach is correct, because they can get feedback from autograders instantly. Students like this format and are doing better in courses that take advantage of it (as evidenced, e.g., by the higher quality of the course projects), and we are able to serve more of them. Indeed, our sense at UC Berkeley is that MOOCs and SPOCs are raising the bar for course evaluations in the departments that are embracing them.

Conclusions and Looking Ahead

It should surprise no one that much of what I have described was envisioned long ago: in *Education Automation* (Fuller 1964), inventor and futurist R. Buckminster Fuller presented a vision of remote education remarkably prescient of both MOOCs and SPOCs, albeit couched in the technological milieu of his time. Far from eviscerating the university, he argued, the ability to capture, incrementally refine, and share "self-service" educational materials would be a boon to both faculty and students. Faculty would spend more time on research and on meaningful interactions with students rather than rote repetition and grading, and students would benefit from not just a *particular* presentation of a lecture or topic by their instructor but also *the best* presentation of that lecture or topic, perhaps refined incrementally over a long period.

I have presented our anecdotal but provocative evidence that the scale of MOOCs can be exploited in novel ways to provide pedagogically innovative help for classroom students: MOOCs can thus help education be rich because of scale. MOOC materials can be used in a blended setting called a SPOC to supplement the classroom experience: SPOCs therefore hold out the possibility that MOOC scale can work to the benefit of small (classroom-sized) groups of students. Our experience has been that instructors using SPOCs are not parroting the content created by the authors but rather infusing it with their own voices and making contributions back to the material in ways that would be difficult or impossible with traditional teaching media such as textbooks and lecture slides alone.

To serve more students in the classroom, we can separate the scalable from the nonscalable parts of a course. Making the scalable parts rich despite scale requires two things: first, investing in MOOC technology to scale up the teaching of teachers as well as the teaching of students, by creating instructor-facing material that improve scale-up leverage; and second, rethinking teaching compensation in light of this change, by rewarding time spent to create such materials and recognizing new and possibly informal teaching roles that take advantage of them.

Properly combined, MOOCs and SPOCs together can help deliver the best of both worlds—rich because of scale as well as rich despite scale.

References

Bruff, Derek O., Douglas H. Fisher, Kathryn E. McEwen, and Blaine E. Smith. 2013. "Wrapping a MOOC: Student Perceptions of an Experiment in Blended Learning." *Journal of Online Learning and Teaching* 9 (2). http://jolt.merlot.org/vol9no2/bruff_0613.htm.

Dillenbourg, Pierre, Armando Fox, Claude Kirchner, John Mitchell, and Martin Wirsing. 2014. "Massive Open Online Courses: Current State and Perspectives." *Dagstuhl Manifestos* 4 (1). Proceedings of Dagstuhl Perspectives Workshop 14112. http://drops.dagstuhl.de/opus/voll texte/2014/4786/.

Fox, Armando. 2014. "Curricular Technology Transfer for the 21st Century: MOOCs and Technology to Advance Learning and Learning Research (Ubiquity Symposium)." *Ubiquity*, Article 3, June. doi:10.1145/2618397.

Fox, Armando, and David Patterson. 2012. "Crossing the Software Education Chasm." *Communications of the ACM* 55 (5): 44–49.

Fox, Armando, David Patterson, Richard Ilson, Samuel Joseph, Kristen Walcott-Justice, and Rose Williams. 2014. *Software Engineering Curriculum Technology Transfer: Lessons Learned from MOOCs and SPOCs.* Technical report no. UCB/EECS-2014-17. Berkeley: Department of Electrical Engineering and Computer Sciences, University of California, Berkeley.

Fuller, R. Buckminster. 1964. *Education Automation: Freeing the Scholar to Return to His Studies.* Carbondale: Southern Illinois University Press.

Gulwani, Sumit. 2014. "Example-Based Learning in Computer-Aided STEM Education." *Communications of the ACM* 57 (8): 70–80. doi:10.1145/2634273.

Lucas, Henry. 2014. "Disrupting and Transforming the University." *Communications of the ACM* 57 (10): 32–35. doi:10.1145/2661055.

Lewin, Tamar, and John Markoff. 2013. "California to Give Web Courses a Big Trial." *New York Times*, January 15.

Lord, F. M. 1980. *Applications of Item Response Theory to Practical Testing Problems*. Mahwah: Lawrence Erlbaum.

Moghadam, Joseph, Rohan Roy Choudhury, He Zheng Yin, and Armando Fox. 2015. "AutoStyle: Toward Coding Style Feedback at Scale." Second ACM Symposium on Learning At Scale, Vancouver, March.

Patterson, David, and Ed Lazowska. 2013. "Why Are English Majors Studying Computer Science?" *Berkeley Blog: Campus Scholars' Perspectives on Topical Issues*, November 26. http://blogs.berkeley.edu/2013/11/26/why-are-english-majors-studying-computer-science.

Roth, Gerald, Armando Fox, Janet Burge, Dan Grossman, and Joe Warren. 2015. "SPOCs: What, Why, and How." Panel presented at 46th ACM Technical Symposium on Computer Science Education (SIGCSE 2015), Kansas City, March.

Shi, Conglei, Siwei Fu, Qing Chen, and Huamin Qu. 2015. "VisMOOC: Visualizing Video Clickstream Data from Massive Open Online Courses." IEEE Pacific Visualization Symposium, Hangzhou, April.

3

Measuring the Impact of a MOOC Experience

OWEN R. YOUNGMAN

Since I began working on one of Northwestern University's first massive open online course (MOOC) in 2013 (Understanding Media by Understanding Google, offered through Coursera), reporters, colleagues, students, and friends have asked me many questions—and, indeed, many of the same questions—about online education in general and "massively open" online education in particular. Some have been asked so often that my first public presentation on the topic took the most common one as its title, "Who's Going to Grade All Those Papers?" (Youngman 2013f).

I came to Northwestern's Medill School of Journalism, Media, Integrated Marketing Communications, after thirty-seven years in the news industry, where at the *Chicago Tribune* I oversaw the creation and launch of its first Internet sites (Ziv 2003). I therefore do not find it surprising that these questions generally arise from views at two ends of a spectrum that can be characterized variously as running from rejection to acceptance, from excitement to fear, from skepticism to unquestioning acceptance, or even from the utopian to the dystopian.

This was very much the way that similar people reacted to the rapid spread of the commercial Internet following the 1993 release of the Mozilla browser by the University of Illinois at Urbana–Champaign. Thus, in the early days of MOOCs, the answers to many of these questions have been as open to dispute and interpretation as were those about the World Wide Web in the late 1990s; in fact, one of the common questions is identical in form: "Why would [name of newspaper or university] ever give away [its expensive news or education] for free?"

Since a *New York Times* article proclaimed 2012 to have been the "Year of the MOOC" (Pappano 2012), hardly a week has gone by without the publication of reporting, observation, or scholarship representing each extreme. (Wondering what the "Year of the Internet" might have been? According to James Gleick [2001], author among other things of *The Information: A History, a Theory, A Flood*, it was 1994.)

This wide variety of only partially answerable questions particularly are found in the discussions over just what sort of education takes place when tens of thousands of students pursue learning largely on their own, without in-person contact with their peers or their instructors—even after acknowledging that many of the enrollees are already highly educated adults with advanced degrees. Some days I read anecdotes about apparently unalloyed success (Kolowich 2014), but more often I read about high-profile failures (Lewin 2013), especially in the context of efforts to use them within a more traditional framework. From the start, my colleagues' and my goal at Northwestern was to pursue student learning by making the rigor of the MOOC that I would create at least similar to that of our on-campus offerings.

Nuanced, though pointed, discussions among academics have proliferated. I was present when, at its February 2014 "Conversation on the Liberal Arts," the Gaede Institute at Westmont College invited a number of scholars to provoke reflection among attendees on whether "the relational nature of liberal arts education can be captured—perhaps even enhanced—in a virtual environment" (Gaede Institute 2014).

For example, Dr. Peter J. Hadreas, chair of the Philosophy Department at San José State University, asked in part whether we could hold education in MOOCs to standards drawn from Plato, among which he listed three: "to honor and respect knowledge; to have good will for the student; and . . . bold speech, in which one speaks one's mind" (Hadreas 2014, citing Plato's *Gorgias*).

Dr. Alexander W. Astin, emeritus professor of higher education at the University of California, Los Angeles, placed the desired outcomes of a liberal education in direct contrast with those of a "course content" approach; he cited "leadership, citizenship and social responsibility, self-understanding, critical thinking, empathy and concern for others, and [intellectual] honesty" near the end of his presentation as hallmarks of an approach that depends on the engagement of faculty and student alike (Astin 2014).

My own interest tends in this particular direction. While I can and do observe how participants in my MOOC treat the ideas, context, and content that I am presenting, even before I heard Dr. Astin speak I sought to ascertain whether they were deriving benefits from their MOOC exposure that went beyond learning the material. This includes, of course, observing student progress through the course, but, as I wrote after the course's first session (Youngman 2013e), I believe it also requires surveying the students, which I have done with a twenty-minute postcourse survey instrument.

My MOOC is based on a Medill course that I began teaching at Northwestern in the winter term of the 2011–12 academic year, American Media through the Lens of Google. That class has enrolled up to forty undergraduates each time it has been offered, with one-third of the seats set aside for students from other parts of the university than the journalism school; one objective is "to use scholarship, reporting, and reflection about one of the key business success stories of the Internet era—Google—to understand today's American media landscape, and how Google's success and ideas have caused dramatic changes not only in journalism, but also in American business and culture" (Youngman 2012). It thus is a class about media, not about a class about Google, partially in the spirit of Siva Vaidhyanathan's 2011 book, *The Googlization of Everything*. His is one of the books I assign, and I include interviews with him in both the Medill course and the MOOC.

The on-campus offering comprises twenty sessions over ten weeks and covers nearly that many individual topics, from research to news to video to social media to privacy and its implications. The Coursera version focuses on just eight topics within six weeks and, given the international nature of the course, reduces the focus on some US-centric topics.

Both syllabi are built around core ideas from recent books by Ken Auletta (2009), John Battelle (2005), Jeff Jarvis (2009), Steven Levy (2011), Eli Pariser (2011), and Siva Vaidhyanathan (2011), which are supplemented and brought up to the present moment with newspaper and magazine articles, blog posts, videos, and other online material (in the case of the online class, around eighty of the latter resources are included in the syllabus to accompany the prerecorded video lectures). Both classes include interviews with and appearances by some of the books' authors—on campus or via videoconference in the case of the undergraduate course; in prerecorded conversations or live online "hangouts" for the MOOC, in some of which a selection of students can participate.

The inclusion of material from books that they are encouraged to buy or borrow has been an obstacle for some people, though the syllabus includes alternate materials for those who cannot, or choose not to, obtain them. The amount of additional reading material has been an obstacle for others, many of whom, in the course's discussion forums, have indicated a preference for MOOCs where all the "requirements" are contained in the video lectures that typically are the most prominent feature of these classes.

As noted earlier, at Northwestern, those involved agreed early on that we wanted enrollees who fulfilled this MOOC's requirements to achieve many of the same objectives we have for on-campus students: that they "learn to think analytically about news events related to the media and journalism businesses, become comfortable in interpreting both the news and the newsmakers, and learn when the implications of an event or an idea may necessitate a change in their own opinions, activities, and practices" (Youngman 2012).

One consequence of this decision, then, is that the lengthy postcourse surveys necessarily required a particular subset of learners: those who agreed to these conditions and then pursued them with achievement in mind. As I wrote in the *Atlantic*'s affiliated site *Quartz* (Youngman 2013a), in the first instance of my MOOC fully two-thirds of those who signed up never watched a single lecture, many without even having viewed the syllabus. That amounted to roughly thirty-six thousand of the fifty-five thousand who clicked the inviting "Join for Free" button on Coursera. (This may be true in part because, as Alan Finder (2013) wrote, "Signing up takes less time than creating an iTunes account," and there are no consequences for "defection.") Of the remainder in that session, another seventeen thousand decided along the way to "audit"— that is, not to submit any of the required homework that might lead to what Coursera calls a "Statement of Accomplishment."

Of those who signed up, only two thousand tried to "pass" the course by submitting the required quizzes and written homework. When I asked all the students, in an open-ended question during session one, what denominator I should use in thinking about completion percentages, one of the most-discussed numbers that was bandied about in discussing MOOCs, discernible effort is what the 302 respondents overwhelmingly preferred.

Some, who agreed to be quoted in an article such as this, set the bar high:

> Completing a MOOC should not be compared against traditional course completion/retention rates. The best metrics to compare it against are conversion rates, and particularly those of online ads. Signing up for Coursera is as easy as Googling or clicking an ad. This is not "enrollment" in the traditional sense. It's creating an account online and nothing more. Those of us who do the work are "conversions." I would even say that it's the students who've done the work for at least ½ of the course who should be considered as "enrolled," because anyone can spend a few minutes a week posting or taking a quiz. Those of us who are invested enough to do ½ the work have "bought" the product after being exposed to it online. (response to Coursera discussion thread, October 10, 2013, 3:59 p.m.)

> My idea of completing a course is doing the assigned readings, watching the lectures, and turning in the assignments. Auditing is different. . . . I would not, as an auditor of a course, expect to be factored into the number of people who

take the course as you would a paid class at a university (response to Coursera discussion thread, October 9, 2013, 4:09 p.m.).

While there undoubtedly is some sample bias reflected in these responses, a fair number of others pushed back by saying that since all they wanted to do was watch the lectures and do the accompanying readings, they'd also think of themselves as having completed the work. Still, after considering all arguments, I went on record in *Quartz* as preferring the middle ground that these 302 respondents settled on.

So what does that look like in hard numbers? At the time of this writing in October 2014, two sessions of the course had been completed. In those first two six-week sessions, 99,407 registered, and 37,949 students watched a single lecture. Of 4,381 students who pursued some sort of credential, 1,939 were successful in earning one, by scoring seventy of one hundred possible points in the grading scheme I created within the Coursera platform.

Those 1,939 were the targets of the main quantitative postcourse research I conducted in 2013 and 2014 (although I sent a shorter survey to 911 others who had scored at least twenty of one hundred possible points before discontinuing active participation). Of the students who completed the course, at least partial responses to the twenty-eight-question survey were received from 1,329, or 68.5 percent. Earlier in each session, I had surveyed students while the classes were running and received 2,829 responses to a different set of twenty-five questions.

As constructed (before I heard either Dr. Astin or Dr. Hadreas speak), this survey instrument cannot address a student's acquisition of "leadership, citizenship and social responsibility," though certainly I saw some students succeed in assuming leadership roles among their peers, as indicated through their online conversations. (As Dr. Astin [2014] did note, "It may be that students teach each other more stuff than we teach them.") I fear intellectual honesty seems beyond my ability to measure in any but a subjective way. But both the survey and the forty thousand forum discussion posts, all of which were read by at least one of my student teaching assistants or me, may give evidence of "empathy and concern for others," self-understanding, and critical thinking.

First, empathy. One question in particular on a midcourse survey attempted to understand how the enrollees were interacting with one another: "On a scale of 1 (disagree completely) to 5 (agree completely), rate your degree of agreement with each of the following statements about the discussion forums." This question placed emphasis on the forums specifically because

TABLE 3.1. Perceptions of individual and shared value derived discussion forums

Prompt (n = 1,814 across two sessions)	Rating "4" or "5" on 5-point scale, %	Average rating on 5-point scale
I want the other class members who participate in the forums to succeed in this course	81.8	4.27
I enjoy reading other students' perspectives and comments	74.4	3.90
I am learning new ideas from the forums	71.3	3.84
I enjoy sharing my perspectives and comments with other students	56.0	3.56
I think the other class members who participate in the forums have similar goals to mine	50.6	3.48
I enjoy helping other students by answering their questions in the forums	43.2	3.39
I am benefiting from having other students answer my questions in the forums	44.7	3.38
I often tell a friend, family member, or coworker about an idea I encountered in the forums	45.6	3.21
I feel connected to the other class members who participate in the forums	37.9	3.16

Note: Data from Youngman (2014a, 2014b).

it was the most visible and routine place where interaction takes place (the other being the peer-assessment process, which provides the answer to the most common question I'm asked: they grade each other, typically five at a time, though there is no upper limit and some graded dozens per week). Across the two sessions, responses to this question on the forums were received from 1,814 of those surveyed, and table 3.1 summarizes the aggregate results, sorted by sentiment on a five-point scale.

As I wrote on my own website (Youngman 2013c), one of my Medill colleagues, Dr. Stephanie Edgerly, remarked on seeing the numbers that "those are high mean scores (and the percentages of 4 or 5s back that up). Especially the high scores on reading others' perspectives, learning from others, and wanting others to succeed. People in your class are not on a digital island by themselves."

This is not to say that the majority of enrollees used or even enjoyed the forums, satisfaction with which was the lowest of any course element I asked them to rate (3.82 on a similar five-point scale, whereas satisfaction with the video lectures came in at 4.5, written homework assignments at 4.37, and the assigned readings at 4.24). Still, her observation was helpful in the immediate aftermath of my having published some early thoughts on the *Guardian*'s website (Youngman 2013b), where the strongly held views of commenters about this very topic were plentiful: for example, "I can imagine nothing more demotivating than never being in the same room with fellow students (anonymous comment, October 18, 2013, 5:43 a.m.)."

Anecdotal evidence within the course also tends to support the view that this empathy is real. As in most MOOCs (Christensen et al. 2013), the majority of enrolled students come from outside the United States (73 percent in the first session and 77 percent in the second, according to Coursera data), and a significant number are native speakers of languages other than English (58 percent and 52 percent, respectively, in the first and second session, according to my own survey).

Language is not much of a barrier for anyone in the casual environment of forum commenting. For instance, in my own surveys, less than 10 percent of the nonnative speakers of English said doing so was "fairly difficult" or "very difficult." The peer-assessment process was sometimes another matter: these same people often worried "out loud" in the forums that their lack of facility may lead their peers to assign them lower grades, clear or no clear rubric.

That's not how I saw it play out, however. The comments from the people who were grading them tended toward empathy:

> Particularly from the assignments I'm grading that were written by non-English-speaking students, I'm learning how to read for **intended** meaning [emphasis in original]. This has always been particularly difficult for me and because of that I think it's a seriously useful skill to have. If there's an odd syntax, muddled idiom, or missing verb, I can still get the main drift of the writer's intent and grade accordingly (response to Coursera discussion thread, October 30, 2013, 5:03 a.m.).

> It's been a bit challenging sometimes reading people's papers when their English skills aren't great, but I think of what it must be to try and write complex ideas in another language. . . . I have felt deeply appreciative of the students who have so generously shared their world view through their homework assignments (response to Coursera discussion thread, October 31, 2013, 12:11 a.m.).

> I enjoy the peer grading since I was able to learn so much from the other students here, even when English was not their first language. I felt a lot of the students are making a difference and taking risks in expressing their views associated with their culture in English (response to Coursera discussion thread, July 24, 2014, 4:12 p.m.).

As it happens, when students have flagged their homework grades as unfair and requested staff review, we have found that the culprit is not poor

English; more often, the petitioner has made a required point so carefully and subtly that someone grading hurriedly seems to have just plain missed it. This is perhaps a byproduct of the educational background of the "student body," to which I have alluded. According to Coursera data, the percentage of students in the first two sessions of my MOOC who held no less than a bachelor's degree were 79 percent and 75 percent, respectively. According to my postcourse surveys, those percentages were higher, 90 percent and 82 percent. Thus the widespread observation that MOOCs are best serving people who "already know how to learn" (Signorelli and Hovious 2014) is not without merit.

A further inference about the forums seems worth reporting here. An exchange I had with one of my Northwestern students who was serving as a "community teaching assistant"—largely by monitoring the discussion forums for trends and student questions, so that I could appear or intervene as needed—unknowingly advanced Dr. Edgerly's point further one afternoon. "I have a confession to make," he said upon dropping by my office after a class. "Well, two confessions." I indicated I was interested. "First, being a TA is making me a better student," he continued. "When I see how all these people from around the world, with jobs and busy lives, are fitting in all those readings and the homework and the lectures, it makes me think about how I can be as focused."

"Great," I said. "What's the second confession?" "You won't like this one as much," he said. "They have a closer, more supportive community than anything I am in at Northwestern, and I'm a senior."

That, I suppose, is a point that also is made by the first row of data in table 3.1: "I want the other class members who participate in the forums to succeed in this course." Around 82 percent of each cohort (the percentage varied by less than 1 percent across the two surveys) felt invested in the success of thousands of people they had not met in person. Why might that be?

On the Coursera side, I infer that they saw they were getting value from their classmates' posts (rows 2 and 3 of table 3.1). On the Northwestern side? I asked some of the other teaching assistants. The most interesting answer came from a Medill senior. "It's different in Coursera than it is here, I think," she said. "These people are not in competition with each other. Here if someone fails, it might wind up being good for us." Whether there can be circumstances where empathy for, and competition with, the same people can comfortably coexist is not something on which I have either sufficient data or a treasure trove of anecdotes.

Still, "empathy and concern for others" does not and should not take place in a vacuum. Dr. Astin (2014) stated them in the context of an expectation

TABLE 3.2. Perceptions of individual learning outcomes

Prompt (n = 1,329 across two sessions)	Rating "4" or "5" on 5-point scale, %	Average rating on 5-point scale
I learned things in this course that I shared with friends, family, or coworkers	86.8	4.37
I learned what I was hoping to learn in this course	85.6	4.27
I learned things in this course that I did not expect to learn	84.9	4.32
I learned things in this course that changed some of my opinions, habits, or ideas	84.6	4.27

Note: Data from Youngman (2014a, 2014b).

of faculty and student engagement, of course, as well as alongside more inwardly directed outcomes as the second outcome I'm examining here, "self-understanding." Again, I tried to get at this idea by examining both student comments in discussion forums and through online surveys. Here are the aggregate results from a question on the postcourse surveys, which again sought agreement on a five-point scale (table 3.2).

Among this sample of extremely qualified, extremely committed, and extremely engaged students who completed the course's requirements, the average ratings unsurprisingly were higher than those in the broader midcourse sample. One purpose of this set of questions was in fact to get at the results of student engagement, a topic that Medill professors have been studying for some time in the context of media (Peck and Malthouse 2011). For example, both survey questions include statements about sharing new ideas with others. Well before the use of social media had gained its current level of importance for media entities, this sort of consumer behavior had been demonstrated to work to their benefit: "When people believe that a media brand satisfies their appetite for things to talk about, they will want to use it," Medill professor Steven S. Duke has pointed out, citing prior work at the Readership Institute by Northwestern's Limor Peer, Bobby Calder, and Mary Nesbitt (Duke 2011, 178 and notes).

Further, the opportunity for ideas contained in Northwestern courses to spread in such fashion was part of the university's motivation for experimenting with MOOCs, according to Provost Daniel S. Linzer: "to reach a new and broader audience and to have an impact that extends beyond the campus" (quoted in Rowley 2013). Others were to experiment with new teaching tools, evaluate outcomes from new modes of education, and explore new pedagogical methods (Rowley 2013). And as indicated in the earlier excerpt from my syllabus, one of my goals in creating this course was to see whether students could learn when they need to make "a change in their own opinions, activities, and practices." Another was to test the reach of my interpretations beyond the undergraduate audience—and, based on my experience in the news business at a time of disruptive change, evaluate the potential for disruption that, as already has been noted, are widely and regularly attributed to MOOCs.

Examples of students reporting that they were making changes in their habits or ideas were easy enough to come by.

> Actually the situation appears to be even worse than I thought. We are the product and I would rather be free than use free products. I have changed my strategy plan. . . . I am definitely going to start spend money on buying services rather than trading my data and therefore my power for services (response to Coursera discussion thread, October 14, 2013, 10:19 p.m.).

> The course made me more conscious about some of my online behaviour. The CHANGE I have suffered is regarding mobile phones: I am completely traumatized with the side effect that mobile technology is having on us! I am trying to forget my phone more often, and also trying to spend some hours a week without using the cellphone AT ALL (response to Coursera discussion thread, October 29, 2013, 11:00 a.m.) [emphases in original]

> Week 5 has provided a catalyst for re-examining my multi-tasking and compulsive mobile device behavior. And I don't like what I see. I am the constant multi-tasker, frequently with up to five devices engaged. . . . I was a believer that this level of multi-tasking is smart and efficient. Now, I have my doubts. I recognize that at times it is down right rude. I see this in others. Now I am seeing it more and more in myself. I had not expected to get this level of personal insight from this course. For this I am grateful and committed to making appropriate changes (response to Coursera discussion thread, June 28, 2014, 3:51 p.m.).

> Before, I was happily surfing the Internet but now I'll never be the same again and I'll never view the internet/data collection the same again either. Information really is power (response to Coursera discussion thread, October 28, 2013, 4:36 p.m.).

It is perhaps self-evident that self-understanding is not altogether different from the fact that critical thinking also takes place—though, in both my on-campus course and in the MOOC, it tends to emerge over time as students encounter vastly different points of view on the main topic of the course, Google's impact on media (and, to a lesser extent, culture). For example, some assigned readings either embrace or reject the idea that Google is crippling our intelligence (e.g., Carr 2008 and, conversely, Cascio 2009). Others hold that the effects of Google on how the news is delivered and consumed are either beneficial or the farthest thing from it. These brief examples aim to demonstrate the point.

> I don't see that Google can make you stupid or intelligent. . . . Perhaps it makes us all a little lazy, and erodes our self-reliance and ability to adapt? I think this view is supported by the earlier thread that asked what would life be like without Google, or what if Google crashed. The answers in many cases can be summed up by two themes, "I couldn't survive" and "life would be impossible." Neither is true. There was life before Google, and there will be life long after Google has disappeared (response to Coursera discussion thread, October 10, 2013, 10:01 a.m.).

> I disagree with [Carr's] conclusion that relying on computers to mediate our understanding of the world flattens our intelligence into artificial intelligence. Simply put, these devices enhance my intelligence. . . . [I]n the future, continuing to experience newness, staying engaged, and staying connected to everyone will be just as desirable for one's well-being as it is desirable for a cell in one's body to remain connected to that body (response to Coursera discussion thread, October 18, 2013, 9:47 a.m.).

> Look at the information that Google gives you but then ask for more from a different perspective. Go to the library and learn about your subject, without the help of Google. Talk with experts. Develop your intuition—does this information "smell" right? Is your gut feeling asking you to dig deeper? (response to Coursera discussion thread, September 19, 2013, 7:51 a.m.).

If these data and comments are markers of desirable outcomes, they also are markers of the type of deep engagement that Medill's scholarship has argued should make these effects longer lasting. In my chapter in *Medill on Media Engagement* (Youngman 2011), I provide, in many ways, an explicit link to education, in that its focus is the media experience called "make me smarter," the elements of which include the following:

- It addresses issues or topics of special concern to me.
- It updates me on things I try to keep up with.
- It's important I remember later what I have read/looked at.
- Even if I disagree, I feel I have learned something valuable.
- I look at it as educational. I am gaining knowledge.

Most of the ideas I raised for agreement or disavowal in my postcourse surveys on the perceived value of completing the MOOC were utilitarian

TABLE 3.3. Perception of self-improvement

Prompt (n = 1,006 across two sessions)	Scale					Average
	1	2	3	4	5	
Taking this course has made me feel smarter, better educated, and/or better informed	9	13	103	465	516	4.37

Note: Data from Youngman (2014a, 2014b).

(see Youngman 2013e). But one question was explicitly focused on students' subjective experiences, and it was the one that elicited the highest degree of agreement among respondents (see table 3.3).

No matter whether the respondents said they expected to do better at work or in school thanks to the course (average score 3.78), and no matter whether they said they intended to use their certificate to try to get a new job or promotion (3.87), this not only resonated strongly but also most closely matched a goal listed in the online syllabus, that students come "to understand the tactics that modern media companies, journalists, marketers, politicians, technologists, and social networks are using to reach you and affect your behavior . . . [and to] learn how to anticipate the future impact of [Google] and its competitors on information consumption, creation, and distribution" (Youngman 2013d). And so I intend that my further exploration of this and other data will help show my colleagues and me "how to anticipate the future impact" of the broadly visible, but far from fully developed, teaching tool that is the MOOC.

References

Astin, Alexander W. 2014. "To MOOC or Not to MOOC the Liberal Arts." Presented at the 13th Annual Conversation on the Liberal Arts of the Gaede Institute at Westmont College, Montecito, February 15. YouTube video, 27:09. Posted May 6. https://www.youtube.com/watch?v=J_ALK2gMaFE&t=18m51s.

Auletta, Ken. 2009. *Googled: The End of the World As We Know It*. New York: Penguin Press.

Battelle, John. 2005. *The Search: How Google and Its Rivals Rewrote the Business and Transformed Our Culture*. New York: Portfolio.

Carr, Nicholas. 2008. "Is Google Making Us Stupid?" *Atlantic*, July/August. http://www.theatlantic.com/magazine/archive/2008/07/is-google-making-us-stupid/306868/.

Cascio, Jamais. 2009. "Get Smarter." *Atlantic*, July/August. http://www.theatlantic.com/magazine/archive/2009/07/get-smarter/307548/.

Christensen, Gayle, Andrew Steinmetz, Brandon Alcorn, Amy Bennett, Deirdre Woods, and Ezekial J. Emanuel. 2013. "The MOOC Phenomenon: Who Takes Massive Open Online Courses and Why?" November 6. Social Science Research Network. http://dx.doi.org/10.2139/ssrn.2350964.

Duke, Steven S. 2011. "The Talk About and Share Experience." In Peck and Malthouse, *Medill on Media Engagement*, 178 and notes.

Finder, Alan. 2013. "A Surge in Growth for a New Kind of Online Course." *New York Times*, September 26, B10.

Gaede Institute for the Liberal Arts. 2014. Agenda for "MOOCing the Liberal Arts? Technology and Relationship in Liberal Arts," Montecito, February 14–15. http://www.westmont.edu /institute/conversations/2014_program/ConvOverview.html.

Gleick, James. 2001. "Inescapably Connected: Life in the Wireless Age." *New York Times*, April 22. http://www.nytimes.com/2001/04/22/magazine/22CONNECTIVITY.html.

Hadreas, Peter J. 2014. "The Open Letter to Michael Sandel and Thoughts About Online Teaching." Presented at the 13th Annual Conversation on the Liberal Arts of the Gaede Institute at Westmont College, Montecito, February 14. YouTube video, 38:44. Posted May 5. http:// www.youtube.com/watch?v=6OhkZ2LxxE8&t=19m28s.

Jarvis, Jeff. 2009. *What Would Google Do?* New York: Collins Business.

Kolowich, Steve. 2014. "The MOOC Where Everybody Learned." *Chronicle of Higher Education*, September 16. http://chronicle.com/blogs/wiredcampus/the-mooc-where-everybody -learned/54571.

Levy, Steven. 2011. *In the Plex: How Google Thinks, Works, and Shapes Our Lives.* New York: Simon & Schuster.

Lewin, Tamar. 2013. "After Setbacks, Online Courses Are Rethought." *New York Times*, December 10. http://www.nytimes.com/2013/12/11/us/after-setbacks-online-courses-are-rethought .html.

Pappano, Laura. 2012. "The Year of the MOOC." *New York Times*, November 2. http://www .nytimes.com/2012/11/04/education/edlife/massive-open-online-courses-are-multiplying -at-a-rapid-pace.html.

Pariser, Eli. 2011. *The Filter Bubble: What the Internet is Hiding from You.* New York: Penguin Press.

Peck, Abe, and Edward C. Malthouse, eds. 2011. *Medill on Media Engagement*. Cresskill: Hampton Press.

Rowley, Storer. 2013. "Northwestern Partners with Coursera on MOOCs: Northwestern University News." *Northwestern*, January 21. http://www.northwestern.edu/newscenter/stories/2013 /02/northwestern-partners-with-coursera-on-moocs.html.

Signorelli, Paul and Amanda Hovious. 2014. "Two Takes on How Massive Open Online Courses May Affect Librarians and Library Services." *American Libraries*, May 27. https:// americanlibrariesmagazine.org/2014/05/27/moocs/.

Vaidhyanathan, Siva. 2011. *The Googlization of Everything (and Why We Should Worry)*. Berkeley: University of California Press.

Youngman, Owen. 2011. "The Makes Me Smarter Experience." In Peck and Malthouse, *Medill on Media Engagement*, 33–46.

———. 2012. Syllabi for American Media through the Lens of Google (JOUR 390 and 343). Northwestern University's Medill School, Winter 2012.

———. 2013a. "How Two-Thirds of My Students Never Showed Up, But Half of Them Passed." *Quartz*, November 21. http://qz.com/149406/how-two-thirds-of-my-students-never-showed -up-but-half-of-them-passed/.

———. 2013b. "Massive Open Online Courses: A First Report Card." *Guardian*, October 17. http://www.theguardian.com/commentisfree/2013/oct/17/massive-open-online-courses -report-card.

———. 2013c. "So Is It Lonely in MOOClandia?" *The next miracle (v11.1)*, October 21. http://owenyoungman.com/2013/10/21/mooclandia/.

———. 2013d. Syllabus for Understanding Media by Understanding Google. Coursera, September. https://www.coursera.org/course/googlemedia.

———. 2013e. "To Measure a MOOC's Value, Just Ask Students." *Chronicle of Higher Education*, December 13. http://www.chronicle.com/article/To-Measure-a-MOOCs-Value/143495.

———. 2013f. "Who's Going to Grade All Those Papers?: Assessing Student Achievement at Scale." Presented at the 2013 Learning, Teaching and Assessment Forum of Northwestern University's Searle Center, Evanston, October 18.

———. 2014a. Data from midcourse research conducted October 7–13, 2013, and June 16–22, 2014, via SurveyMonkey.com.

———. 2014b. Data from postcourse research conducted November 11–17, 2013, and July 17–28, 2014, via SurveyMonkey.com.

Ziv, Niva. 2003. "The Chicagotribune.com." In *Strategic Management: Concepts and Cases*, edited by Arthur A. Thompson and A. J. Strickland, 13th edition, C339–C355. New York: McGraw Hill/Irvin.

PART TWO

Connected Learning

4

Connecting Learning:
What I Learned from Teaching a Meta-MOOC

CATHY N. DAVIDSON

In May 2013 I began work on an intellectual and pedagogical extravaganza that I came to refer to as "Meta-MOOC." Although the basic platform and structure I used was a standard-issue massive open online course (MOOC) offered through Duke University via Coursera, everything else about this on-line course was planned to interrogate the very nature, substance, and effi-cacy of MOOCs as a phenomenon, genre, business model, and pedagogy. For six weeks, beginning January 27, 2014, I taught a MOOC along with several others, including fourteen undergraduate, master's, MFA, and doctoral students from Duke, University of North Carolina, and North Carolina State University. The course was called The History and Future of (Mostly) Higher Education: Or, How We Can Unlearn Our Old Patterns and Relearn for a Happier, More Productive, Ethical, and Socially Engaged Future.

That whimsical subtitle was designed to signal the "meta" ambitions for engaged, connected learning built into the collaborative enterprise, extending far beyond a content-delivery model of the hierarchical, "doc on the laptop," passive model of learning associated with MOOCs. Our meta-MOOC was also a different model than the traditional university lecture hall. In addition to the Coursera MOOC, the Humanities, Arts, Science, and Technology Al-liance and Collaboratory (hastac.org), an open-access online network of over

Adapted from the *Chronicle of Higher Education*, January 23, 2014, and March 14, 2014, FutureEd blog (http://www.chronicle.com/blogs/future/2014/01/23/when-meta-mooc-meets -wiki-transforming-higher-education/ and http://www.chronicle.com/blogs/future/2014/03/14 /changing-higher-education-to-change-the-world/, respectively).

Special thanks to Futures Initiative Research Fellow and City University of New York Gradu-ate Center English doctoral student Danica Savonick for her assistance in the final draft of this paper.

thirteen thousand members dedicated to "Changing the Way We Teach and Learn," launched a partner project called FutureEd. HASTAC is an exceptionally active and interactive network that has inspired many learning innovations in collaborative methods, peer teaching, peer learning, and blended learning. FutureEd was designed to spark an international conversation on the need for public investment in educational innovation as a public good. As noted on the HASTAC website, "the #FutureEd Initiative is led by those with the most at stake in transforming higher education: students and faculty. Open, worldwide, HASTAC-led and user-inspired, 'The History and Future of Higher Education' assesses the educational legacies we've inherited in order to design new ways of learning for present needs and future aspirations" (http://www.hastac.org/future-higher-ed).

Implicitly and explicitly, the meta-MOOC and the FutureEd Initiative were launched to investigate the true potentials of connected, online, collaborative, cross-institutional, and cross-disciplinary learning apart from the profit motive. In the conversation that swarmed around the general public in 2013, MOOCs were being presented as if they were revolutionary as pedagogy, sound as a business model, and brilliant as technology. In fact, the pedagogy in and of itself was the lecture—an outmoded instructional arrangement if ever there were one. The technology was quite clunky (but also quite stable)—that is, basically a video platform attached to social networking, chiefly dialoguing, tools. Finally, the business model has yet to turn a profit or to save any university money in addressing the needs of its own target audience of students. In fact, by February 2013, the argument was flipped to suggest that, although MOOCs were not making or saving much money, their "educational impact is invaluable" (Tharpe 2014). As of this writing in September 2014, neither the business nor pedagogical model of the MOOC has proven to be either valuable as commodity or invaluable as learning.

The implicit and explicit premise of the meta-MOOC and FutureEd was that the claims for innovation advanced by the commercial, for-profit companies such as Coursera that were launching MOOCs were drowning out the efforts of many other educators who were dedicated to finding better learning models that might actually save student tuition dollars (not make profits for venture capitalists). So far, MOOCs have stolen the show, as if they are the only innovation in town and as if for-profit companies are the only place to go for educational innovation. That is flatly untrue. The "meta-MOOC" was partly designed to showcase successful innovations in order that others may be inspired to change, too. The meta-MOOC was designed to extend the HASTAC campaign on behalf of true learning innovation to thousands of participants worldwide.

The rhetoric about the conservatism of higher education is simply not true. However, it is true that those making change often feel solitary within their departments, disciplines, or institutions. The FutureEd Initiative was partly designed to make alliances across disciplines and institutions. Approximately thirty courses offered by diverse institutions of higher learning, from community colleges to Ivy League universities, championed educational innovation and using tools, email lists, and other ways to connect students and faculty members across institutions.

HASTAC also hosted three wikis to which anyone could contribute their ideas. One was a bibliography of resources (e.g., books, articles, videos, and websites) on educational innovation. The second was a wiki devoted to pedagogical and classroom innovations. Finally, there was a collaboratively created, crowdsourced wiki dedicated to institution building, in which participants were encouraged to share narratives of successful change that had spearheaded at their own institution. No legislators or venture capitalists rushed forth to fund these ideas, but we heard from students, parents, and the general public who were hungry for meaningful transformation of education, from kindergarten through lifelong learning. MOOCs are one response to this need for educational transformation. Meta-MOOC shows how many other ways of meeting exist. It offered pathways to leadership for those who want them.

Our methods included learning by doing, learning by connecting, and learning by experiencing, teaching, and sharing. In medical school, the classic formulation for this method is "See one. Do one. Teach one." We extended that triptych to a fourth principle: "Share one." The idea is that if the Internet extends our human reach and our need for human judgment in ways both heady and precarious, then our current educational system is doing it all exactly wrong. Learning content and being tested in standardized exams on the best answer from four or five items is exactly wrong in a world where content is massively available, easily remixed, potentially unreliable, and always changing. Learning how to learn, learning how to judge wisely, learning how to connect, and learning how to translate what one learns to situations that can improve lives (whether from the lessons of history or mastery of C++) are the real metrics of success in our world.

To that end, in addition to the MOOC and FutureEd in spring 2014 I also taught a face-to-face graduate class titled (you guessed it) The History and Future of Higher Education. The course was sponsored by our interdisciplinary program in Information Science + Information Studies. My students read extensively in the history of higher education, in what I call an "activist, purposive history," one designed to help us see how the status quo came to be this way to help us to see a way to changing it. They worked in teams of two or three and each took charge of one week of the MOOC and worked to make that experience as interactive, participatory, and two-directional as possible. They kept office hours, posing challenges on the forums, interacting with participants, and learning from this vast international community.

Under the model of "see one, do one, teach one, share one," the students communicated what they learned on the various social media tools we had set up for the course. They also interacted with face-to-face students being taught at the same time in similar classes. Christopher Newfield, a professor of English at the University of California at Santa Barbara, was teaching English Majoring After College (Histories and Futures of Higher Education). David Palumbo-Liu, professor of comparative literature at Stanford, taught Histories and Futures of Humanistic Education: Culture and Crisis, Books and MOOCs. Books and articles by each of the three instructors were included in the course, and we used Google Hangouts so the students at each university could ask questions of the other professors. These Hangouts were also open to a larger public. During these Hangouts, students and the public were informed of and invited to participate in various online and face-to-face projects of relevance to the future of higher education. My students also published their insights in biweekly posts on the FutureEd blog established for our course by the *Chronicle of Higher Education.*

The finale of all this meta-MOOCing was the collaborative design of three models of what we are calling "Designing Higher Education From Scratch," where the students, again working in teams, developed and blogged about three radically different models of what higher learning might look like. Our College was designed as a "small, low-cost junior/community college aimed at equipping promising students with the skills they need to succeed in a rigorous higher education environment." Hand, Head, Heart University was dedicated to "learning yourself to engage the world, engaging the world to learn yourself." It was basically a humane, socially engaged version of an elite private university. The third university, Libertates University, was dedicated to "an education system that is personalized—not standardized, comprehensive but not a check-list, and exploratory not mandatory" (Holman 2014).

The students involved, including those participating in the MOOC, collected some two hundred questions about the meaning and structures of higher education, asking, "What is it for, who is it for, in what way does it serve society, and what are the best ways to deliver on our mission?" Rarely do students have the opportunity to reconceive everything, on the deepest level and on the most practical, of what education should be. They named their new universities, made online models, provided as much detail as possible of everything from learning models to the physical plant, right down to designing the T-shirts. And then they posted their universities for the more than eighteen thousand Coursera students to comment on and share.

That's a long way from the top-down, broadcast delivery model of education that seems to be preserved in conventional MOOCs or in the conventional lecture hall or in our outmoded ways of testing, accrediting, credentialing, grading, or keeping up our "standards." If the standards themselves are outmoded, at what are we excelling? If the model of learning was designed for building Model Ts and not the next Twitter, who cares if you are top of your class? If as a teacher, you are still doing in the classroom what your teachers did in your classrooms, even as you see your own students or your children learning by themselves in astonishingly creative, inventive new ways, something is drastically wrong. It's not easy to change. This is why the FutureEd Initiative offered a massive open invitation to learn, to participate, and to find partners: See, do, teach, and share. It works for educators as well as for those we educate.

But a question persists: What remains from a MOOC after the final video has ended and the last paper has been peer assessed? To my mind, the most exciting part of our meta-MOOC was the spirited exchanges among the course participants. So that is the question. How can a MOOC be more than a "one off"? What remains for the participants after the MOOC is over? What infrastructure is required beyond the MOOC platform to turn a massive learning experience into a movement in the real world? And what real problem do MOOCs solve—or not solve?

The research is by no means definitive on these issues but one thing is clear: as presently conceived, the Coursera-style, top-down MOOCs are not a "solution" to the problem of rising costs at American universities today. The Coursera data indicate the primary audience of MOOCs isn't the traditional college-bound student. The typical MOOC participant is a thirty-year-old with a college or even a postbaccalaureate degree. Two-thirds live outside the United States (see fig. 4.1).

MOOCs don't do much of anything to make higher education less expensive but, given the outrage academics expressed toward them when they first burst on the scene, it is also important to underscore that MOOCs are also not the cause of all problems facing American universities today. MOOCs did not create our adjunct crisis, our overstuffed lecture halls, or our crushing faculty workloads. The distress in higher education is a product of fifty years of neoliberalism, including the actual defunding of public higher education by state legislatures. In California, for example, Aaron Brady and economist Mike Konczal note that, "For every $1,000 of personal income in California,

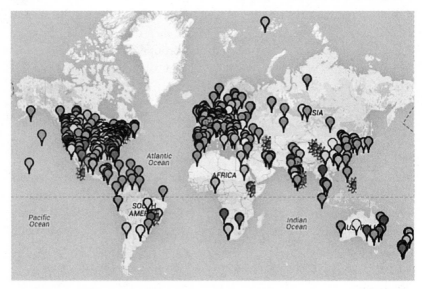

FIGURE 4.1. Class map of meta-MOOC (massive open online course) The History and Future of (Mostly) Higher Education. Students added markers for their own location. Built with ZeeMaps.

the state invested only $7.71 for higher education in 2008, about 40 percent below the $12.86 invested as late as 1980" (Brady and Konczal 2012). One reason academics are so suspicious of MOOCs is that corporate investors and corporatized administrators often promulgate (or buy into) the specious "magical thinking" that CEOs can run universities more cost-effectively than faculty members. They don't. The major push to "corporatize" higher education has coincided with a rise, not a decrease, in costs. The greedy, corporate brutality of far too many contemporary universities—where salary distribution mirrors that for the 1 percent in corporations—is reminiscent of the power exerted in the Middle Ages by the great monasteries that both captured land and ruled over the populace. Some universities are clearly being powered these days as much by real estate barons as intellectuals. Let's call it "turf and serf": real estate land grabs, exploitation of faculty labor, and burdening of students with crushing debt. MOOCs may be a manifestation of the economic problems besetting higher education, but they are hardly its cause.

Yet sympathy for the stressed academic who has had to face decades of diminishing resources does not mean one can let academics off the hook for unwillingness to reconsider the structures (intellectual and otherwise) of the contemporary university. Another reason I ran my MOOC was that we wanted to see if the more than eighteen thousand participants who ended up registering for the course could help galvanize a movement on behalf of educational changes that any professor, department, or school could begin to

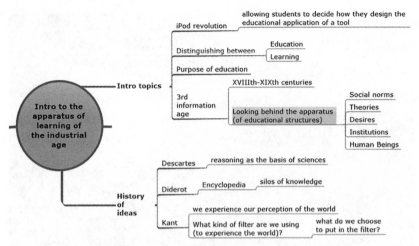

FIGURE 4.2. Summary of videos from week 2 of meta-MOOC (massive open online course)
The History and Future of (Mostly) Higher Education in a mindmap (close-up).
Courtesy of MOOC participant Vahid Masrour

carry out today. The short answer (surprise, surprise!) is that it takes infra-structure, planning, and human labor to make real change. I believe parts of this could be replicated by anyone wishing to create a real-world movement from a MOOC.

First was laying the conceptual groundwork. I made it clear that there was an activist purpose behind my retelling the story of the nineteenth-century transformation of the liberal arts college into the modern research university to train people for the standardized, Taylorized, specialized, hierarchical Industrial Age that reflected ideologies of scientific management for factory efficiency. I urged participants to be part of a public movement to recreate the Industrial Age university we had inherited for the world we all live in now. The "future" portion of my MOOC posed conceptual and practical ways of rethinking curriculum, pedagogy, assessment, and institutional structures for an interactive, DIY, information-heavy world and invited MOOC participants to contribute their own ideas.

Not everyone in this MOOC ended up liking the activist dimension of the course, but, for those who did, it provided a place for deep dialogue. Individual participants often took the lead with astonishing generosity. For example, a learning designer from Ecuador, Vahid Masrour, created beautiful, inspiring mind maps summarizing the ideas and connections across my four or five videos each week and put them up on Google+ for others who were not in the MOOC to share (see, e.g., fig. 4.2). More collectively, over seventy courses, reading groups, workshops, or conferences were organized directly

Robin Heyden @rheyden · 1h
First meeting of the Second Life study group for #FutureEd. Great
fun! pic.twitter.com/8wvNqq7iO3
↩ Reply ↻ Retweet ★ Favorite   Flag media

FIGURE 4.3. Photograph of *Second Life* virtual FutureEd Initiative study group.
Courtesy of Robin Heyden (Twitter).

or loosely as spinoffs, some organized before the MOOC began and some
during the course of the MOOC.

Here's where the HASTAC FutureEd Initiative provided supplementary
infrastructure that contributed to the real-world impact. We built a platform
where anyone could list their contribution and sent out a newsletter twice a
month highlighting models of successful change. Among the many notable
examples are the twenty to twenty-five people who met weekly at Fordham to
discuss the MOOC and who are now working toward a future digital-literacy
program. There was a Friday lunch group at the City University of New York
Graduate Center sponsored by JustPublics; Provost Terry Brown's faculty
working group at the State University of New York at Fredonia looked toward
curricular change; and the Ocelot Scholars at Schoolcraft, a community college in Livonia, Michigan, led by Professor Steven Berg, ran a digital-literacy
project with competitions, classes, blogging events, and conferences alongside
the MOOC. At least two participants, Professor Katie King (University of
Maryland) and the educational consultant Robin Heyden, ran topical discussions in *Second Life* (see fig. 4.3). Jesse Stommel, CEO, and Sean Michael
Morris, managing editor, of the digital journal of learning, teaching, and technology *Hybrid Pedagogy* ran an irreverent weekly Twitter "MOOC MOOC"
to stir the pot. The 240 graduate students in the HASTAC Scholars program

are blogging daily as part of the Pedagogy Project. Finally, three wikis on hastac.org continue to collect community-sourced bibliography, classroom innovations, and models of successful institutional change.

That's a significant impetus to change in many directions at once. And it was not easy. The costs were larger in terms of human labor, time, and actual costs. Because it was a learning experiment for me and an add-on to my regular Duke duties, I put the $10,000 I was paid to create the MOOC into an account that funded FutureEd—teaching assistants, meals for our classes about the MOOC, travel to conferences for the students, research agendas, equipment, and so forth. We ended up with a MOOC team of nearly twenty people working on this effort—students, colleagues, and HASTAC administrative staff members. All held office hours, participated in MOOC discussions, answered questions, and communicated ideas beyond the MOOC both through twice-weekly blog posts to this publication and on hastac.org.

Will the stirring, rich debates in The History and Future of (Mostly) Higher Education continue? If the participants in the MOOC have their say, the answer is yes. They may live in different countries, thousands of miles apart, but they share a zeal that could become a movement. As one participant noted, "The learners who signed up for this course obviously have a passion for learning and changing education. I only hope that each of us will try to do something to change our learning culture; perhaps as a movement or perhaps as an individual. The rewards would be worth it." Or, in the inspiring words of another: "If every student in this class did only one thing to change the tide of education, we'd have a tidal wave!"

References

Brady, Aaron, and Mike Konczal. 2012. "From Master Plan to No Plan: The Slow Death of Public Higher Education," *Dissent*, Fall. https://www.dissentmagazine.org/article/from-master-plan -to-no-plan-the-slow-death-of-public-higher-education.

Holman, Kaysi. 2014. "Designing Higher Education from Scratch." *HASTAC*, February 17. http:// www.hastac.org/blogs/kaysi-holman/2014/02/17/designing-higher-education-scratch.

Tharpe, Coleman. 2014. "MOOCs May Not Make Much Money, But Their Educational Impact Is Invaluable." *Daily Texan*, February 17. http://www.dailytexanonline.com/opinion/2014/02/17 /moocs-may-not-make-much-money-but-their-educational-impact-is-invaluable.

5

Toward Peerogy

HOWARD RHEINGOLD

The more I give my teacher power to students and encourage them to take more responsibility for their own learning, the more they show me how to redesign my ways of teaching.

At the end of the first course I taught solo, I asked students for their frank opinions of what was working and what could work better. I didn't want to wait for anonymous evaluations, which don't afford dialogue or collaboration. The first pushback was a strong request for more project-based collaboration, shared earlier in the semester. From the beginning, I had asked students to use the tools we were studying and using—social bookmarking, forum discussions, blog posts and comment threads, and collaboratively edited wiki documents—to organize team projects of four to six students. The first year I tried this, we discovered that four students work better than six for a semester-long project—division of labor, intragroup communication, assessment, and the nature of the final presentation rapidly grow more complex with more than four collaborators. When teams presented their projects at the end of the term, we were all so astounded that one student astutely asked (to general acclamation): "Why can't we show each other this kind of collaboration earlier than the last class meeting?" We had learned that *learning to collaborate ought to be collaborative*—the teams should interact with the other students in the class as co-responsible learners during the collaboration process, not just as an audience for the final product.

The next year, I asked several students to take responsibility each week for conveying the main points of the texts and helping me to engage others

Adapted from Howard Rheingold, "Toward Peeragogy," *DML Central: Digital Media and Learning*, January 23, 2012, http://dmlcentral.net/blog/howard-rheingold/toward-peeragogy.

in classroom discussions about the readings. The experiment was well received, but we all agreed by the end of the semester that student presentations sometimes devolved into book reports with a few questions tacked on, lacking sufficient interconnection between that week's different presentations. So the year after that, I started asking students to form "coteaching" teams who would work with me to focus on key points from the readings and to organize activities that would engage students in directing their own inquiry into our topic of virtual community and social media. When coteaching teams started using PowerPoint to present their key points, one student asked: "If we are going to study social media, don't presentation media qualify?" That question led me to develop a list of more than one hundred not-PowerPoint presentation media for project presentations, which emphasize how collaborative multimedia presentations enable small groups like teaching teams to work together. Such tools include mind maps, screencasts, social-bookmarking programs, and curatorial storyboards for postings from social media, such as Storify. These tools allow peer learners to present knowledge in different and compelling ways, as well as to engage active participation by the entire class instead of broadcasting to a passive audience.

Community of Committed Colearners

Between the coteaching teams, the collaborative projects, and our inquiries into the nature of community—online and face-to-face—the powerful idea of making our class into a community of colearners who cooperated to help each other learn began to take over. The goal of using our physical class time and online interactions to grow into a learning community is now baked into the syllabus—I ask prospective students to read and commit to fulfilling their role in the community's colearning before they are admitted to the class.

I confronted the laptop-in-classroom issue by initiating "attention probes," such as showing the class a video of themselves and "what it looked like from where I stood" (Rheingold 2009) or asking them to close the lids of their laptops when they weren't actively using them. Now (again at students' suggestion) I open a forum discussion thread at the beginning of the term, soliciting the students' suggestions about potential attention probes to try in class. I am no longer surprised when student variations on my bright ideas turn out better than my original version. I know now that the syllabus and lesson plans will always change from year to year—as long as I pay attention to my colearners.

"Colearners" came into my vocabulary and practice when I started experimenting with my own purely online courses. I had grown accustomed to addressing my weekly emails to "esteemed students" in my university teaching. The first time I started composing a message to my online class, I called them "colearners" instead of "students," and the simple change in nomenclature—together with my by-now ingrained habit of codesigning my teaching with my students—led to immediate and remarkable enthusiasm. The difference might just be semantic, but it proved to be a surprisingly powerful demonstration of word magic. In my next university class, I plan to start using the term with my university students. We won't be able to eliminate the institutional fact of life that my grading matters more to their careers than their evaluations matter to mine. But I know they will perceive my sincerity when I tell them I'm attuned to learning from them while they are learning from me. I have not abdicated my role as "expert learner," but opening up to colearning has produced nothing but positive results so far.

I've run four cohorts of the course Introduction to Mind Amplifiers (Rheingold 2015c) and one cohort of Toward a Literacy of Cooperation (Rheingold 2015b). I limit each cohort to thirty. Each time, a few colearners told me they were overwhelmed—"informational waterboarding" and "hot-dog eating contest" were two particularly pungent evaluations. Not every colearner felt that way, however—each time a cohort completed a five-week course, a few of them had digested all the info we threw at each other and were hungry for more. When I become a better teacher, I'll find better solutions for those who are overwhelmed. My immediate instinct has been to respond to those who asked for more. At the request of these colearners, I created an online forum where alumni could convene. Each time a course finishes, two or three hungry self-learners join the alumni community.

A couple dozen alumni now organize their own live sessions with guest lecturers. One colearner showed us what he learned to do with Yahoo Pipes after my course introduced him to the tool. Another gave a presentation about her use of graphic facilitation techniques to provide the visual notes she had shared with us during the course. Guest authors were invited. I realized that some colearners become adept quickly at self-organized learning—and will continue to learn cooperatively whether I continue to facilitate them.

R.I.P. Lecture-Discussion-Test

In retrospect, I can see the coevolution of my learning journey. My first step was to shift from conventional lecture-discussion-test classroom techniques to lessons that incorporated social media. My second step gave students co-teaching power and responsibility. And my third step was to elevate students to the status of colearner. It began to dawn on me that the next step was to explore ways of instigating completely self-organized, peer-to-peer (p2p) online learning.

The ultimate test of peer learning is to organize a course without the direction of an instructor. Although subject-matter experts and skilled learning facilitators are always a bonus, it is becoming clear that with today's tools and some understanding of how to go about it, groups of self-directed learners can organize their own courses online. P2PU and other examples are harbingers. In *Deschooling Society*, Ivan Illich (1971) predicted that learners of the future would find each other and use information technologies to form "learning webs" and "networks"—prescient terms, considering that the ARPANET was only two years old at the time. It didn't take long for my initial explorations to uncover dozens of nascent p2p learning platforms, new learning forms such as massive open online courses (MOOCs), and emerging theories of "paragogy."

P2P Learning Explosion

A rich and growing proliferation—a Cambrian explosion of p2p learning platforms—seems to be in progress. I have collected hundreds of links to materials on p2p learning platforms, which I have shared with thousands of my fellow colearners (Rheingold 2015a). P2PU is one of the leaders in the field. I'm particularly interested in Anya Kamenetz's P2PU course titled Getting Started with Self-Learning. There are, I have found, many others: Stack Exchange ("a network of question and answer sites on diverse topics"), Open Study ("make the world your study group"), Quora ("a continually improving collection of questions and answers created, edited, and organized by everyone who uses it"), BetterAt ("learning from other people and teaching others is the best way to learn"), World University ("which anyone can add to or edit"), Skillshare ("classes to learn anything from anyone"), and School of Everything ("Nobody likes to be told what to do. School of Everything is here to organize your education however you please")—the list grows every day.

I also discovered, through a colearner in a Rheingold U class, about "paragogy"—the nascent theory of peer-to-peer pedagogy. The colearner, Charles Danoff, wrote a paper about it with Joseph Corneli (2008): "Paragogy: Synthesizing Individual and Organizational Learning." Searching for "paragogy" reveals more resources—but not so many that they can't be surveyed quickly. The field is just beginning to grow.

I intend to expand the paragogy universe by instigating a peer-created guide to pure p2p learning. I'm calling it "peeragogy." While paragogy" is more etymologically correct, peeragogy is self-explanatory. Can we self-organize our research, discover, summarize, and prioritize what is known through theory and practice, then propose, argue, and share a tentative resource guide for peeragogical groups? In theory, those who use our guide to pursue their own explorations can edit the guide to reflect new learning.

It's not exactly a matter of making my own role of teacher obsolete. If we do this right, I'll learn more about facilitating others to self-organize learning.

References

BetterAt. 2015. http://better.at/. Accessed May 20.

Classes—Skillshare. 2015. http://www.skillshare.com/classes. Accessed May 20.

Cornell, Joseph, and Charles Jeffrey Danoff. 2008. "Paragogy: Synthesizing Individual and Organizational Learning." http://metameso.org/~joe/docs/paragogy-final.pdf.

———. 2012. "Paragogy.net." http://paragogy.net/Main_Page.

Corneli, Joseph, and Alexander Mikroyannidis. 2012. "Crowdsourcing Education on the Web: A Role-Based Analysis of Online Learning Communities." In *Collaborative Learning 2.0: Open Educational Resources*. InfoSci-Books.

Hot Questions—Stack Exchange. 2015. http://stackexchange.com/. Accessed May 20.

Illich, Ivan. 1971. *Deschooling Society.* New York: Harper & Row.

OpenStudy: Study Together. 2015. http://openstudy.com/. Accessed May 20.

P2PU | DIY U: Getting Started With Self Learning. 2015. https://p2pu.org/en/groups/diy-u -getting-started-with-self-learning/. Accessed May 20.

Peer 2 Peer University. 2015. https://p2pu.org/en/. Accessed May 20.

Pipes: Rewire the Web. 2015. http://pipes.yahoo.com/pipes/. Accessed May 20.

Quora—The Best Answer to Any Question. 2015. https://www.quora.com/. Accessed May 20.

Illich, Ivan. 1971. *Deschooling Society.* New York: Harper and Row.

Rheingold, Howard. 2009. "Watch Attention in the Classroom | HowardRheingold Episodes | Learning Videos | Blip." http://blip.tv/howardrheingold/attention-in-the-classroom-4073 002. Accessed June 13, 2015.

———. 2015a. "@hrheingold—Delicious." https://delicious.com/hrheingold/p2pu.

———. 2015b. "Introduction to Cooperation Theory." http://socialmediaclassroom.com/host /cooperation/lockedwiki/main-page. Accessed June 13, 2015.

———. 2015c. "Introduction to Mind Amplifiers." http://socialmediaclassroom.com/host /mindamplifier4/lockedwiki/main-page.

———. 2015d. "Rheingold U." http://www.rheingold.com/university/.

———. 2015e. "Wiki: Interactive Media Resources | Social Media CoLab." http://socialmedia classroom.com/host/vircom/wiki/interactive-media-resources.

———. 2015f. "Wiki: Welcome from the Instructor | Social Media CoLab." http://socialmedia classroom.com/host/vircom/lockedwiki/welcome-instructor.

School of Everything | Learn More. 2015. http://schoolofeverything.com/. Accessed May 20.

World University. 2015. http://worlduniversity.wikia.com/wiki/World_University. Accessed May 20.

6

The Learning Cliff: Peer Learning
in a Time of Rapid Change

JONATHAN WORTH

Introduction

What follows is a particular teaching moment that's located on a learning
curve so steep as to appear to be overhanging. On reflection it was an innovative moment for me, but needs to be understood within a much broader and
holistic set of attempts, some successful, some not successful, to solve a whole
raft of problems: problems that were both disciplinary—and approached from
a practitioner perspective—and personal—and approached from the perspective of someone having to learn how to teach quickly and in a live environment. This is a narrative about synthesizing approaches to openness, and it
begins in the 2008 academic year, around the same time as Dave Cormier
coined the term massive open online course, or MOOC.

Context

In his book *What Would Google Do?*, Jeff Jarvis (2009) describes a failing
Harvard student who has been spending his term on a web project unrelated
to his course. At the last moment he throws up a website and spreads the
word among his fellow students that the site is a collaborative study aid and
everyone should add in the missing information about the various topics, à la
Tom Sawyer's fence painting. His Harvard peers diligently do as directed and
the boy aces his exam. The boy was Mark Zuckerberg, and the web project
he'd been noodling around with turned into Facebook, but the really interesting thing about this story for me was that his professor said that this collaborative cohort was the highest passing class he'd ever taught.
 While Mark Zuckerberg was getting other people to do his homework
for him, I was (and media producers like me were) living through seismic
changes in the media economy. As an editorial photographer in New York I

had a business model in which my product (photographs) was a scarce commodity, relying on legacy media gatekeepers (newspapers and magazines) to control its supply to maintain its price. The final consumer, the reader, never actually paid me directly for my photographs. Instead they would pay for the newspapers and magazines that my pictures came wrapped in (the mode of distribution). However, the Internet was redefining this business model as well as the whole media landscape in which it existed. My photographs were becoming images, and the magazines and newspapers were becoming websites.

The Internet cookie was about to show advertisers that they didn't have to pay a premium for carpet bomb advertising in a national newspaper; instead they could pay for individually targeted ads that followed their customers from one site to another and would be available to the highest bidder. My scarce analog photographic product had turned into a nondiminishing digital one whose unit costs were zero, and transmissions were instantaneous and free.

For many of us at the time our only means to wrest back control of the supply was to use copyright. I would dedicate time every week at first and then later, every day, to trawling the Internet looking for copyright abuses (usually by Google searching my name as this was before the days of image search) and firing off takedown notices, until eventually a clearly terrified and very young person responded. She promised to remove the offending Heath Ledger pictures, and then, concerned about the legal consequences of her piratical actions, she begged me not to tell her parents.

This was a defining moment for me. I'd never set out to be this person. Here I was, an adult, shouting and threatening (albeit digitally) a child, who'd done nothing more than I'd done as a young person, as had generations of young people before us. Humans have historically surrounded themselves with images of their heroes, be they in churches as paintings, murals, and tapestries, or as idols. They were the cultural signifiers declaring to which group we belonged.

I wondered who alive today hadn't pulled pictures of their heroes from magazines and stuck them to their teenage bedroom wall or used them to cover their schoolbooks? This was no different. It was just that the walls of their generation aren't in bedrooms; they're social. They're on Facebook, Tumbler, and Pinterest, and their schoolbooks are more likely to be blogs. Sure the digital has moved us from the tangible to the intangible, but it is still underpinned by the same impulse of association, both in private homage and public association.

If anything I wanted to be telling this young fan's story, and quite quickly (mostly to appease my own guilt) I sent her previously unseen outtakes from the shoot. These are the images of most value to the geek (the unpublished backstory to the shoot), and access to this content is highly prized. They're similarly prized by paying publications and had previously formed an essential part of my editorial business model, but I had now given it all away for free, to an anonymous fourteen-year-old blogger, because I was ashamed. And I thought the story would end there, but it turned out that she wasn't just any old blogger. It turned out (and probably the reason why she'd turned up so highly in the Google-ranked search), that she was the "go-to" girl for Heath Ledger. She was a trusted and credible source, and her blog was a hub for other Heath Ledger fans from which I began to see a steady flow of traffic to my site. This was a flow of people not satisfied with the free low-resolution screen images, but instead people who wanted to buy original photographic prints and any other ephemera from the day. Everything was a potential collector's item, and the more the digital made us all archivists of the intangible, so it reminded us of the physical events and tangible artifacts that had born firsthand witness to those events. The photograph was not evidence enough.

This phenomenon of people (fans or geeks as I'm referring to them) wanting to pay for something that was apparently freely available was in direct contradiction to what my economics 1.0 understanding told me were the factors that should affect price. Not in the sense of the artifact that had borne witness to the event, like the mug Heath had drunk from in one picture or the book he had left behind—those things were loaded with meaning, but the images didn't come into that bracket. There was an infinitely free supply of them, yet a demand to pay remained. What these fourteen-year-old bloggers were showing me was that pixels weren't paper and that photographs were very different from images, and that these had their own inherent value structures, which was something that I investigated further by offering to work for editorial clients for links rather than fees—and then, in a widely publicized experiment with the science fiction author Cory Doctorow (2009), let consumers choose their own price points.

I was navigating photography's paradigm shift with the only reference points I had, like describing images as photographs. As Marshall McLuhan (McLuhan, Fiore, and Agel 1967) puts it, describing new media in terms of old, where the term "photograph" is used as a metaphor for the image, is a way of leveraging something familiar to describe something new and unfamiliar. Thematic references built from what technology looks like traditionally can used be at the expense of what that technology might come to mean, and history has taught us this. For example, the first car was described as a horseless carriage, rather than a climate changer, or obesity wagon.

The darkened rooms of the Italian Renaissance, onto whose walls were projected images from outside, were called camera obscuras, from which we get the name camera. Those rooms were effective for safely viewing solar eclipses, and later their portable boxlike variants were useful for artists to trace accurate illustrations. They have little in common, however, with the mobile supercomputers from which we habitually capture and share both our own data and the data of others, including but not limited to the things we see. Calling them phones or cameras reference previous technologies that they resemble physically but not what, in the age of data, they are coming to mean.

These paradigm shifts aren't limited to cars or photography, but instead are an expected aspect of technological change punctuated by moments of *retrospective* significance. We are as McLuhan (McLuhan, Fiore, and Agel 1967) said, the people of the rear view mirror, always walking backward into a future seen in the reflection of old technologies.

But as a new teacher I wasn't familiar with or wedded to the traditional modes of university teaching—which was scary, but I now appreciate how it freed me to consider these questions from new perspectives; I also didn't know how to teach these ideas of constant redefinition and paradigm shift speculation. As David Campbell puts it, "as they stormed the Bastille, no one turned to anyone else and said *hey, this is the first day of the French revolution.* It was only with the benefit of an historical perspective that this and other pieces of information can be stitched together to form a narrative" (Campbell 2014). We (me and my students) would have to learn the subject together.

By professional necessity I was already reaching out to other people making sense of this changing media landscape. Cory Doctorow was one of them, a science fiction writer who made e-versions of his books openly available for downloading with a Creative Commons license. These licenses are as Joi Ito (2008) describes: a user interface that sits on top of the traditional All Rights Reserved Copyright. It enables the creator to explicitly allow certain kinds of usage and reuse of their works without the user having to seek permission, and these licenses sit along a scale of openness. The most restrictive disallows remixing or commercial usage, whereas the least restrictive allows both but only stipulates that the original work must be attributed to the author. Usage of these licenses at the same time as publishing hard copies was making good economic sense for Cory, as he says himself, "my problem isn't piracy, it's obscurity" (Rich 2009).

Other people within the photographic industry were also experimenting with creative new approaches to the business of photography like Stephen Mayes, then director of VII photographic agency, and John Levy, publisher of the photojournalism magazine FOTO8 and director of HOST gallery. Professor David Campbell of the Durham Centre for Advanced Photographic Studies had stopped writing for closed academic publications and instead was publishing his thoughts and reflections on a blog (https://www.david -campbell.org/); eventually he left his institution to become a freelance academic. Fred Ritchin had predicted this paradigm shift at the birth of Photoshop in 1988; Ritchin (2000) developed these ideas with his seminal text *After Photography*. Ritchin (2013) then went on to map out the work of a series of practitioners who have since developed and are developing exciting approaches that are redefining what the twenty-first century photographer and their business models might become. And Tim Hetherington[1] was out in the field redefining what photojournalism and lens-based story telling might be.

But none of us really knew how this future of photography might unfold, so it made sense to make that the starting point of the class. I did this both with the students in the room and those people who were not but still might be interested in the conversations that Stephen, David, John, Fred, and I were having, so it seemed appropriate to run the class on a blog.

#PicBod and the Doctorow Experiment

The first course I designed and delivered for the Coventry University BA Photography degree was titled Picturing the Body (#PicBod), a class about representations of the body in art. I was never going to be an expert in this field, but I did have something to say about the artifact, the crafted, the artisanal, the rare, and the valuable physical thing forever locked in time and space. I thought of this both in terms of the photographic fine print, framed and on a wall, but also by analogy, as the face-to-face teaching and learning moment, "the class." Both of these were, as Kevin Kelly (2008) describes, "generative" physical experiences that could not be digitized, only simulated. Chris Anderson (2009) speaks to this as well when he says that with every abundance we also find scarcity, and although in that case he's talking of the abundance of material accessible via the Internet versus the time it would take to consume

---

1. Tim Hetherington produced books, films, and other work that "ranged from multi-screen installations, to fly-poster exhibitions, to handheld device downloads"; he was killed by a mortar in 2011 while working as a photojournalist in Libya. "Tim Hetherington," *Wikipedia*. https://en .wikipedia.org/wiki/Tim_Hetherington#cite_note-guardobit-5. Accessed June 14, 2016.

it all. If the digital were being leveraged as a nondiminishing simulacrum, then the more people who saw it, and the wider it reached outward through time and space across the Internet, then access to the artifact of which it was a trace/representation would become relatively scarcer.

In a prominent experiment, Cory Doctorow and I had placed this phenomenon in a market context. After shooting a portrait of Doctorow,[2] I made, numbered, and signed special archival chrome-ink prints that were bundled along with pages from a photocopied version of Cory's latest manuscript, each page of which Cory had signed. Everything went on sale using a variable pricing system that relied on participatory price setting of the kind described by Yochai Benkler (2011), but, crucially, our "free" version was also available alongside. This high-resolution file of the image was (and is) available for download and can be printed at high definition up to a meter square. It also means you can zoom in and read the titles of the books lining the shelves, which Cory then augmented further by annotating the image to describe what the ephemera within it was. Finally, we limited the length of time that they would be on sale at this price and warned potential buyers that any remaining images would go on sale at ten times the price a month later and then that any remaining would be destroyed.

Since Cory Doctorow has a cult following, it turned out that one of the things we had in fact done was to provide a public forum for Doctorow fans to make statements to their peers (and Cory) about how much they valued his work (evident in the good natured in-fighting via social media to find out who had secured the number one and most expensive print).

There were a number of precedents for this variable pricing most notably in the music industry, such as Radiohead's pay-what-you-like album launch of *In Rainbows*, or where artists such as Madonna were switching to live performances for their main revenue streams and thus leveraging bits to sell generative atomic experiences.

---

2. We began with a portrait of the author at work in his office, which we decided was something that had a universal currency with avid readers. Reading is after all a very intimate experience but largely one-sided. We might spend hours or days with the voice of the author in our heads, following us around whatever spaces we choose to read, but that intimacy is asynchronous and unreciprocated. We never get to share in the moment of creation. We can only imagine what the author saw as they conjured up the next story twist, or what it feels like to sit in the writer's chair, look out from the desk or down at the blank page as the words march across it. The image shows Cory seated at his desk surrounded by books and all manner of personal ephemera. He is small in the frame, only head and shoulders visible above a monitor, which sits in the lower right corner and from which blasts the scene's only source of light. (Cory actually had to sit staring into a high-powered flash head for about ten minutes.)

This was what and how I was learning, and it seemed and seems an appropriate and holistic way to teach, being both in and of the digital at the same time.

Innovation Moment: Role of the Teacher

Throughout that first year my thinking, and so the class's, was dominated by Chris Anderson's (2009) *Free*, Clay Shirky's (2010) *Cognitive Surplus*, Laurence Lessig's (2008) *Remix Culture*, William Poundstone's (2010) *Priceless*, and Jeff Jarvis's (2009) *What Would Google Do?* Jarvis (2009) tells us to think of our sites (for which I heard "classes") as being *means* rather than *destinations* and as aggregating hubs rather than broadcast units, as well as platforms on which collaborators can build and add their value. Shirky (2010) makes us thinks of collaborative beta processes to join, with their associated compound benefits of support and engagement, rather than finished products to be sold and consumed. Lessig (2008) reminds us that learning with the digital is both atomized and quantum, existing as it does in multiple environments and experiences simultaneously. He also made me rethink how the learning materials should be licensed if my intention was for them to benefit from remix and adaptation, à la Jarvis and Shirky. Anderson (2009) was pushing us to think about new economies and to identify and unpick mirror metaphors, whereas Poundstone (2010) introduced us to the world of behavioral theory via the pricing structures of restaurant menus. All these things fed into both the design and delivery of what became better known as Phonar (Photography and Narrative; http://www.phonar.org).

The class was and has remained "in beta." Every class has led with a statement about schedule subject to change according to the dynamics of the class and also inviting visitors (via a site button) to point out any inaccuracies and suggest improvements. A separate section (http://phonar.org/staffroom) also details opportunities for collaboration or adaptation of the course. And at the beginning of each iteration, we've made it explicitly clear that we don't have definitive answers to the key questions we pose; instead the participant is invited to reflect on a series of interviews and creatively respond to a series of rapid-fire tasks, which will form a portfolio submission. There is no pressure to develop fully resolved solutions, but emphasis is instead placed on the iterative processes, so the inevitable "failures" are seen as an opportunity to dramatically steepen our learning curves. Marks are awarded for the reflections on these "failures," rather than deducted for the failures themselves.

This iterative *thinking through doing* is both a way of chipping away at a big complex problem with a number of smaller simpler ones, forcing us to apply and test the knowledge we're developing. It is also a fertile environment for innovation as, in comparison to the student's learning experiences so far, this represents an adverse set of circumstances. There are no exams to be taken or algorithmic solutions to be drilled. One cannot excel by being the strongest photographic-craftsperson in the group alone. There are no defined solutions to these problems. Instead one must find new solutions that speak to the student's own interpretation of the problem and are appropriate for the student's particular audience.

Model Assignment: A Post-Photographic Portrait

The culmination of this module will be the production of a "post-photographic portrait" of Jill Jarman's Piece for Cello performed by Laura Ritchie. Your decisions throughout this process should build upon and further develop the work we've begun in creative workshop and throughout the lecture series. This process should be evidenced explicitly and succinctly on your blog as well (a 500 word reflective summary would do the trick).

Then when an online participant probed for more direction via Twitter I answered:

Here's a slightly longer answer than the 140 characters Twitter allows: Perhaps see the task as a license (should one be needed) to "break out of the frame." To break out of stills, to use sound, explore multi-point perspective, and grapple with non-linear narratives. It's the chance to make a bigger and more ambitious project than the weekly tasks, and now that you've established a weekly turnaround of work, you should find it easier to build something substantial. Revisit the lectures and interviews, look over your task outputs, and then think of something you feel passionate about (love or hate) and craft us a narrative. (https://phonar.org/?s=post-photographic)

What is not said here in this example—but is explicit throughout the course—is the critical need to identify, speak clearly to, and move to action the communities of interest who surround your work.

The Phonar classes do not train you to be a twentieth-century algorithmic supplier of photographs. Rather, they seek to develop heuristic problem solvers who are visually literate and digitally fluent, people who can speak clearly with images and move people to action. It is photography and education as agents for change.

We don't begin from the position voiced by traditional legacy media that "we are constantly bombarded with too much information" (Cunningham 2015) and in need of more professional journalists to make authoritative sense of it all for us passive and docile consumers. Instead we need to challenge those traditional arbiters of meaning, and all need to be active interrogators of the media we consume; "in the digital age, participation is a part of genuine literacy" (Gillmor 2010, 60). Our [photographer's] journalistic "product" no longer speaks for other people but instead enables them to speak authoritatively for themselves, for their voices to be heard and crucially for their stories to move people to action. If there is one image that sums this moment, it is the World Press Award winning photograph of 2014. It is an image titled "Signal" by John Stanmeyer and shows migrants at night, on the shores of Djibouti holding their mobile devices high into the air. They are trying to capture a free telephone signal to connect with friends and relatives left at home or to a home to which they're trying to journey. It is tragic that so many of these people continue to die in boats unfit for the passage, and even though many are holding smart devices and connecting successfully to the network, it *still* takes a photojournalist from New York to bring us their story.

The subjects have the means to tell their own stories, but not the social capital to be heard. The postdigital reality is that with so many people speaking this language of images at once, we have moved to a point where seeing is no longer naturally synonymous with believing.

The past hundred years of photography's evidential currency have ended. The image has inherited its cultural legacy but not its evidential currency. The pixel-based image is not trace representation; it is an algorithm, a string of editable code rather than a fixed compound of silver halides—so regularly bearing false witness as to no be longer credible.

The image is now, as Stephen Mayes assert, experiential (Brook 2012). Its end users share them as easily as texts, a form of language in their own right. Snapchat is a great example, where images are shared among friends and then self-destruct, something that would be anathema to the photographer who's grown up carefully archiving every photographically witnessed moment.

Therefore the big underlying question that the class tries to address is: *What is a twenty-first century photographer when everyone is a photographer?* In many ways, the twenty-first century photographer is analogous to the twentieth-century teacher since, before *the digital*, they were both arbiters of meaning. The photographer's job was to provide a definitive representation of events informed by a rigorous application of journalistic values and integrity. Their currency and status—part learned (skills) and part earned (social capital)—legitimized them as both a credible witness and a trusted source and, without that reputation, they were worse than valueless. Teachers have historically played a similar conduit for the one-to-many mode of information broadcast, relying on their collateral wealth of knowledge to define them as the most valuable and reliable source of information in the room.

The technologically connected room, however, is smarter than the teacher. It has access to more information than any human can possibly draw on, and the technologically connected crowd of eyewitnesses can offer more (literal) points of view than can the one professional photographer, no matter how fleet of foot or well positioned, or the one instructor. So it was appropriate to question what both of their new roles might be in a technologically connected society, by opening a digital version of the class online and making it free to join.

This approach drew mixed reactions from professional photographers, teachers, and managers. The *British Journal of Photography* questioned whether I was a "Freetard or Visionary" (the comments were very firmly in favor of the former), and the senior manager at my institution who'd been tasked by our vice chancellor with helping me, helped by sharing that *he'd given lots of things away for free in his time, and all it'd ever taught him was that it made people not want to pay for anything.* On the other hand, I was made a Fellow of the Royal Society of Arts and Commerce for my research developing sustainable business models and chosen by MIT Media Lab Director Joi Ito to feature as the lead case study in The Power Of Open publication, but nevertheless . . .

I reflected on how my thinking had changed from the way I'd previously seen the economic drivers at work with my old business model, which helped me to understand that in most of these cases the people just didn't realize their postdigital value asset. And it was as scary for them as it had been for me, but I was not the cause of their folding business models. At best, I was a symptom.

As a photographer I used to think my value asset was photographs, and when the business model for the mode of distribution of my photography failed, so did my business. But when I stopped fixating on the mode of delivery and instead focused on what the technologist Richard Stacy calls "the mode of information" (Stacy 2009) (which was photography or, more broadly, visual storytelling), my model began to thrive. He speaks of an imagined village where two lamplighters live, one who considers himself a lighter of lamps and the other a maker of light. No prizes are awarded for whose philosophical outlook enabled them to thrive after the invention of the gas lamp.

The general opinion that open meant free reflected a point of view that considered the value asset of a teacher to be information, and so understandably it led to administrators and instructors thinking that by freeing up the mode of delivery (the class), they'd have nothing to charge for. It's a similar way of thinking that would see the value asset in a library be the books (the sources of information). But without the librarian to take the learner by the hand and guide the individual through a coherent learning journey, the library is just a room of books, with unrealized and potential knowledge. And if one seriously considers information to be the value asset of the teacher in the technologically connected classroom, then that puts them in the no-win situation of having to go head-to-head with the biggest information library in the world—the Internet itself.[3]

The Phonar structure doesn't posit the teacher as being the most knowledgeable person in the connected classroom. Instead they are curator and contextualizer: someone with an overview of the landscape and an idea of the destination but in need of the connected class of colearners to chart their best routes through.

The iterative *thinking through doing* speaks to the maker philosophy of hands-on independent crafting and tinkering and of failing fast and often, both in the products that the students are making (photographs, for instance) and their learning experience, which is, in turn, my version of the analogous maker product. But it is one that we are *all* involved in. The students come to a class that I coordinate and produce learning artifacts, the success of which they reflect on and then iterate. I reflect on the success of class in terms of their experience, which I gauge in terms of their outputs and feedback, before likewise iterating on that, and so on.

Open Class: Weeks Two to Nine

As such, class sessions vary as they respond to the dynamics of the particular cohort, but the success and impact of the weekly interviews with tweeted notes has dominated the evolution of the class. At the start of term I have a number of new contributors, plus the bank of previous ones, but then the group is invited to identify, reach out to, and organize additional interviewees. This is posed as something of a challenge, but identifying, reaching out to, and engaging audiences is a key learning objective, so by introducing this problem early and implicitly, we chip away at it as a group from the safe mentored class space. It means we can together address questions of how one should identify and approach a prospective subject/collaborator/employer via digital means.

As the sessions progress, we listen to these interviews (recorded from Skype) sharing both our reactions (via Twitter) and later our longer form

---

3. Five years later the course became the *Guardian*'s UK Number 1 and one of the most oversubscribed at the university even with charging the highest fees allowed.

reflections (on blogs). This moment of open and reactive tweeted note sharing has become a cornerstone of the open classes, which comes directly from Jarvis's reference to Zuckerberg's collaborative Harvard class.

Students electing to take the Phonar class openly are not allowed to use pens and paper for notes. All notes must be collaborative and tweeted using the hashtag #Phonar. So a typical class session might be that I've interviewed a particular photographer or academic in advance, either recording a Skype conversation using something like Call Recorder or doing a Google Hangout On Air, and then posted the video on YouTube. I then use the class blog/site to announce that *at x o'clock GMT on Wednesday we'll be listening to (for example) Fred Ritchin from New York and Lars Cuzner from Norway in discussion with Jonathan Worth. It'll be freely accessible, so please tweet your notes using the #Phonar hashtag, and if you do a search on the same you'll be able to see everyone else's notes in turn.*

This hashtag moment of live sharing their notes and finding those of others is central to the Phonar digital moment. Participants new to Twitter will usually arrive with their experience of Twitter being the unadulterated torrent of tweeted meal images and personal updates. Those who have gone through the Twitter sign-up process have possibly also had a bunch of suggested celebrities pushed at them to follow, which to the skeptical user can make a bad situation worse.

A more fruitful way for the Phonar participant to approach social media participation is to consider that if Facebook is all the people they went to school with, then Twitter should be all the people they wish they'd gone to school with. On this basis, we begin this process of tuning Twitter, by looking for those people whom the user feels are expert in their field. If they're not contemporaries or peers, they seek contemporary credible authorities and, once found, we encourage them to follow them—but crucially we look to see whom they follow, in just the same way that one might go to the sources of an article.

By visualizing the voices that are informing our expert, we begin to deconstruct the expert's view of the world and so contextualize the expert's comments. In a similar way we can map relations between Twitterers and data mine individual tweets, which is a particularly effective tool when researching communities of context surrounding particular threads or conversations to draw those individuals into further conversations and/or move them to action.

I'm calling this tuning of clearer signals from the digital noise "digital fluency," since this approach is more than just reading and writing, which literacy might imply. To be fluent is also to be able to speak clearly and be understood, and thus one also has to be sensitive to the audience and their context, especially if the intention is to move an audience to positive action. In digital spaces this becomes even harder when interactions can be dislocated from real-time experience. A face-to-face conversation in a shared physical environment has all the benefits of shared ambience and potential for interpersonal empathy. If the room is hot and noisy, or my interlocutor arrives with puffy, wet eyes appearing distressed, I can be sympathetic in both what I say and how I say it, whereas in an email I can't. In other words, I need to be sensitive to whom I'm talking.

Meanwhile, the class is listening (each from their own device and with earphones) at their own pace,[4] free to stop, rewind, replay, or pause to tweet a note or read someone else's, and I am streaming a column of the hashtag and projecting it at the front of the class. I use a platform like Storify to aggregate the tweets, as well as YouTube or Archive.org to host the interview, as well as add my own thoughts and augment this metaclass set of notes with other linked material. It is admittedly, an intense experience, and its open nature quickly establishes a normative behavior for the group with regard to their note sharing, in terms of both quality and quantity. The fact that there is a unique norm for this "group" demarcating them from other years is also a powerful dynamic and a motivating factor that we build into the classes.

As a reinforcement (pedagogical tactic) of this norm, I make it explicit that each year builds on the last with new themes, new contributors, and new responses from the students to both the questions and tasks, but also in that the new cohort can remix the work of the previous year, but only because the previous year enabled them to do so by agreeing at this point to license their work with Creative Commons licenses and so pay the benefits forward. Again the explicit question is: how much further will they be able to see by standing on the shoulders of their alumni peers? And again, are they going to reciprocate in this sharing economy of creative innovation by paying their work forward, too? If so, they will be known and associated among the members of this community, by virtue of their year of participation, the work they produce, and whatever Phonar artwork, logo, or hashtag they design, which they are free to exploit financially. #Phonar12 was best exemplified by and lives on in #Photosense and #Photography Magazine; #Phonar13's impact was around issues of privacy; and #Phonar14 was "Photography for Your Ears" and ended with a flash mob cello concert performed by the entire class, led by concert cellist Laura Ritchie and introduced from Hawaii by musician Duane Padilla.

The rapid-fire nature of the tweeted note sharing does mean that it is more

4. A twenty-minute interview typically takes forty minutes for everyone to complete.

of a reactive exercise, but this has proven to provide a rich foundation of material for discussion during class and for longer form reflective blog posts afterward. And, of course, as the week progresses and more people from the distributed class listen to the videos and add their comments, the global set of notes get better and better. Because the class materials and the site they gathered on remain open year-round and available for any teacher to teach, should we choose to revisit an interview in another iteration then we can draw on the accumulated long-tail benefit of all the previous and intervening contributions as our starting point.

This opening up of the conversation asynchronously through the use of Twitter and blogs also has had other positive results in terms of employability as well as internationalization. The mechanics of Twitter mean that whenever one's Twitter ID is used the user is alerted, so I direct students to include the Twitter IDs of the people they're citing, quoting, or discussing.

This means that in any one class the contributor (usually high profile in their field) receives repeated alerts that they're being talked about and invariably they will come along and look in, often to actually join the conversation. This is a magical moment for any class, when the person they're listening to and commenting on begins to talk back. Students have responded that this both outward-facing and industry-centered experience changes the classroom dynamic. It forces them to focus on their note taking, which is happening publicly among their peers, and to be sensitive to the fact that every lesson is a potential industry contact/networking opportunity, and potentially even a job interview—a pertinent frame for the class, as the digital footprints and learning data of each new student is more likely to be harvested by future employers anyway.

The Storify platform also affords the teacher a means to be sensitive to how the metaclass set of notes evolves. A student lacking the confidence to fully and openly engage in class discussion might feel more comfortable otherwise engaging via Twitter, where they don't have to raise their hand. Since the tutor sees that this student has tweeted comments, the tutor can reassure the student by dragging and dropping a proportionately higher number of the student's tweets into the timeline with other similar notes or perhaps situate them visually next to a popular/successful/high-profile student.

This pedagogical approach leverages the core properties of a connected learning experience, both sharing a purpose and being openly connected.

Open Class: Week One (Privacy and Trust)

The public nature of learning digitally has also become a space for reflective engagement. In 2013 Nishant Shah asked at the Digital Media and Learning awards what his rights might be (as an imaginary sixteen-year-old in the world of Phonar digital learning) to be forgotten, and I had no answer. I was colearning the digital while teaching with and in the digital.

Unlike my postdigital students, my school reports were buried somewhere in someone else's attic. I was no longer held accountable for the questionable views I'd had in 1988 or my embarrassing actions. RFID chips had not recorded the times I'd gone to my high school library, and universities hadn't analyzed that data to assess my likelihood of completing their degree courses. My information searches were my own business, which were made in the confidence that, regardless of how trivial or earnest they were, no one would ever know. I could browse and search my library for the innocent and private joy of browsing and searching without consequence. No one was storing my private correspondences or algorithmically analyzing their contents. Back then I'd written private letters that were sealed and public postcards that said nothing. I didn't have a mobile phone to triangulate my locations, movements, or modes of travel; to record my conversations; or map my relationships. Insurance companies weren't analyzing my buying habits, and no prospective employer would ever be able to drill into the soap opera of my social profile for the backstory on my resume. My formative years were what would now be described as "off-grid."

In technologically connected societies we habitually share this seemingly inconsequential data by default. We share our own and that of others by association, and others share ours. Mobile devices, pacemakers, hearing aids, library books, store cards, Twitter lists, Facebook friends, and photographs all store and hemorrhage data that can be harvested, algorithmically collated, cross referenced, and interpreted. Data that is of us and by us, but usually not for us, which is bought and sold by data brokers, the consequences of which are fed back to us via an obfuscated feedback loop.

At the start of each year's open class I now go through some of the ways in which we as participants are already leaking data and ask that we model out some of the threats and risks that we might possibly be vulnerable to, but this is an incredibly hard task since we consistently underestimate the risks associated with some things and overestimate the risks associated with others. Like the smoker who's afraid of flying (even though they're statistically much more likely to die of lung cancer than in a plane crash), we are as Dan Ariely (2008) describes *predictably irrational.*

Once we have identified the things we feel are most at risk, we consider
who or what might represent a potential threat and then how we might miti-
gate against any consequences. Unfortunately, even if we do assess rationally,
it would be impossible to account conclusively for every digital byproduct
and eventuality. As a teacher, and open agitator, it is those unforeseen digital
externalities that worry me the most.

Externalities are an economics term used to describe the positive or negative side effects of a process. Imagine a chocolate factory that produces not
only delicious aromas as part of the cooking process (a positive externality)
but also a toxic effluent from part of the cocoa bean washing process (a negative externality).

Companies concerned with maximizing profits will tend to try and ex-
ternalize (pass on) rather than internalize (pay for themselves) the costs of
dealing with negative externalities, even though the cost to society is much
higher as a result. Imagine the river on which our imagined chocolate factory
sits. Once polluted, the entire river now has to be filtered at a much greater
expense than would have been the case had the pollutants been filtered at the
source. Economists refer to this as *true costs*.

The negative externalities of learning/living with the digital are for the
majority of us still passing around an obfuscated feedback loop. The consequences of the data trail that we as academics and, even more acutely in ethical terms, the trails of our students as we teach and learn within the digital
are extremely hard to quantify, assay, or evaluate. It's a machine loop, not a
human one wherein otherwise unrelated information is associatively and algorithmically mapped by third parties to create otherwise unimaginable connections and conclusions. Imagine a single forty-year-old woman who stops
buying birth control from her supermarket and whose sister has a history of
preeclampsia. Would she draw a direct connection between her store card,
Facebook friends/relations, and the subsequent denial of her mortgage application because of an algorithmically calculated potential of a fall in income?
And by the time she does make those connections between what amounts to
being constantly surveilled and the inequitable outcome, she is unlikely to
find herself in an informed position to challenge it, since this surveillance isn't
mutual or transparent. There is no effective transparency of accountability in
a seventy-two-page document listing the terms and conditions written in le-
galese (https://www.apple.com/legal/internet-services/itunes/us/terms.html).
Imagine what exposures we will be opened to as LinkedIn, Lynda.com, Slide-
Share, and Pulse (now all part of the same group) start to coalesce our learning data with say Pearson, who are collaborating with Knewton's Adaptive

Learning Platform and Arizona State University to offer level one of many of their degrees (Kolowich 2013).

In class we begin by examining our "frequently visited locations" (see fig. 6.1) on an iPhone by navigating to:

>Settings
>Privacy
>Location Services
>System Services
>Frequent Locations

We do this to recognize "anchor points," or places most visited, and then the times that they're visited. We can use this information to predict where people work (do they spend daylight hours there?) and where they might live (do they spend evening hours there?), and most likely we also have indicators as to how they travel between those two locations. Analyzing these behavior patterns can reveal a great deal about us, and abnormalities in those patterns can say even more (i.e., where you are says more about you than any other point of data).

We run thought experiments on who might possibly find it useful right now: (1) where we live; (2) where we work; (3) our route between both; (4) probable mode of transport; (5) and with whom we associate; and (6) then who might find an archive of this data useful in the future. What would five years spent driving to work versus walking or cycling say about me to a company selling healthcare or life insurance? Combine with that my store card, my credit card–buying histories, my social media posts, and their associated metadata (data about the data), my Internet browsing history, my location data, and, if one is wearing smart technology, my biometric data, and it becomes hard to imagine knowing more about oneself than the person or entity who owns the sum total of this aggregated data.

We also consider what our associations can say about us: not our best friend or flatmate, but the people with whom we share a bus ride, a coffee shop, or a building. For instance, if I spent three years studying in a class or in the classroom next door to someone who was later convicted of terrorism charges, or if I bought coffee at a coffee shop at the same time a drug deal was transpiring nearby, or if I shared the same holiday destination and hotel Wi-Fi as a child pornographer, what does our "relationship," however tacit or selective, say about me? The reality is that in the world of big data, these associations can indicate anything that the entity in control of the data set wants them to mean.

FIGURE 6.1. Screenshots of Apple
iPhone display showing location services
and frequent locations.

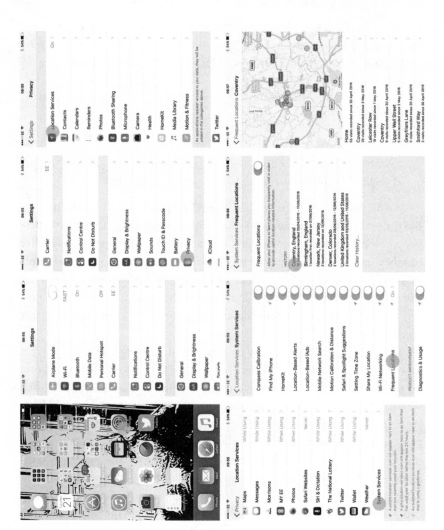

#Phonar is a class on narrative and we think of narrative as the thread that stitches together what might otherwise be unrelated information. As photographers we are the entity in control of that narrative, but as students and inhabitants of the digital we are not.

In the class, I assign each of the twenty-one chapters of Doctorow's (2008) *Little Brother* to be read by different people over one week. When we come back together, each person summarizes his or her chapter for the rest of the group. The book is a young adult science fiction novel set in a dystopian future world where high school kids find themselves on the frontline of the fight to reclaim their data. Our conversation in the classroom expands to wonder what the technologies we're using might come to mean. Take, for example, the main character Marcus Yallow's description of the dangers of the false positive (which I've been driving toward in the previous passages):

> This is the paradox of the false positive and here's how it applies to terrorism:
> Terrorists are really rare. In a city of twenty million like New York, there might be one or two terrorists. Maybe ten of them at the outside. $10/20{,}000{,}000 = 0.00005$ percent. One twenty-thousandth of a percent.
> That's pretty rare alright. Now say, you've got some software that can sift through all the bank records, or toll pass records, or public transport records, or phone records in the city and can catch terrorists 99 percent of the time.
> In a pool of twenty million people, a 99 percent accurate test will identify two hundred thousand people as being terrorists. But only ten are terrorists. To catch ten bad guys you have to haul in and investigate two hundred thousand innocent people.
> Guess what? Terrorism tests aren't anywhere close to 99 percent accurate. More like 60 percent accurate. Even 40 percent accurate, sometimes. (Doctorow 2008, 129)

All this is considered *before* we begin to work in our open class. This issue about false positives extends beyond our mobile smart devices to the software we use on them. I also ask students to investigate a website called Take This Lollipop (www.takethislollipop.com), wherein the data from their Facebook accounts is harvested and incorporated into a short horror movie that depicts the viewer as a stalker's target and includes their currently shared Facebook information and associated information, after which tweeting our notes in class suddenly seems incredibly tame compared with the data we habitually share.

I encourage participants to take both a metacognitive view of their current behavior and then a third-person perspective on their historical profiles by asking what they think their data says about them, and then what might a prospective employer infer from the same information. For some, this "light-bulb" moment can be disconcerting, like going into a mirrored changing room and seeing one's profile for the first time. For others this can be much more sobering, both figuratively and literally, and for those people I recommend Julia Angwin's (2014) *Dragnet Nation: A Quest for Privacy, Security, and Freedom in a World of Relentless Surveillance* with its wealth of information on how to reign in data sharing from browsers, websites, and devices.

As learners we are trying to move ourselves from positions of default, or worse, statutory consent, to positions of *informed consent*, a place where we can learn of the digital from within. As photographers we have to consider the gravity and responsibilities of the postdigital storyteller and what sort of consent our work will ultimately ask of our subjects. Because in both cases the readers of our learning and photographic data are both human and algorithmic and not either/or. And one can just as easily substitute any other form of digital communication, a Facebook update, a tweet, a text, and even a sign-in to a Wi-Fi hotspot. In fact this practice paid us to stop thinking of our images as photographs and to start thinking of them more as data visualizations.

Conclusion

I've tried to describe a particular teaching and learning moment that, on reflection and after five years of development, seems like a positive innovation and outcome from the open classes, but one that is also set within a much bigger contextual caveat. Note sharing among peer learners both home and abroad, with the use of hashtags in public social-media platforms, has been both positively received by the students and brought numerous indirect associated benefits.

The profile of the course and afforded learner opportunities for collaboration and networking, both with those in the industry and peers, on an otherwise unimaginably global scale have all been very positive externalities, though the long-term externalities of learning and living in the digital are less clear, and I don't feel able to approach that as anything other than transparently as a colearner.

In 2015 the BA Honors Photography course at Coventry University in the United Kingdom will be running a newly written degree course to be delivered by a new team of staff. #PicBod and #Phonar, or 251MC and 351MC, respectively, may appear in some guise, but their design and delivery will rightly reflect the interests and passions of the new members of staff assigned to teach them. It would be entirely inappropriate for someone new to feel as though they had to answer the same questions that my colleague Matt Johnston and I had wrestled with, to arrive at the same answers, and to teach in the same way, because the questions we've asked ourselves were moving targets, which is one of the most valuable takeaways from the last five years of open teaching.

What it means to be a photographer today and what constitute sustainable practices are evolving problems, which requires the class to be responsive to be an appropriate solution. Those moving targets are key principals of what I'm coming to think of as a holistic open pedagogy, one that shares many of the drivers and design principals of connected learning.

For my next class I'm trying to come up with a set of questions to challenge myself and although not definitive or exclusive I currently have four:

- Have I enabled my class to give their informed consent to *learn with the digital*?
- Is there an equitable share of the power within and without the class, and if not, is that dynamic transparent?
- Do any of my teaching decisions constitute barriers to entry/engagement, such as geographical, cultural, technological, linguistic or academic?
- Who owns our data?

References

Anderson, Chris. 2009. *Free: The Future of a Radical Price*. New York: Hyperion.

Angwin, Julia. 2014. *Dragnet Nation: A Quest for Privacy, Security, and Freedom in a World of Relentless Surveillance*. New York: Times Books, Henry Holt and Company.

Apple. "Apple Media Services Terms and Conditions." https://www.apple.com/legal/internet -services/itunes/us/terms.html. Accessed June 14, 2016.

Ariely, Dan. 2008. *Predictably Irrational: The Hidden Forces That Shape Our Decisions*. New York: Harper.

———. 2010. *The Upside of Irrationality: The Unexpected Benefits of Defying Logic at Work and at Home*. New York: Harper.

Arthur, Charles. 2009. "Want to Live Like Commons People?" *Guardian*, September 23, sec. Technology. https://www.theguardian.com/technology/2009/sep/23/joi-ito-creative -commons-twitter.

Benkler, Yochai. 2011. *The Penguin and the Leviathan: The Triumph of Cooperation Over Self-Interest*. New York: Crown Business.

Bill Penuel, Jean Rhodes, Julian Sefton-Green, Juliet Schor, Katie Salen, Kris Gutiérrez, Mizuko Ito, Sonia Livingstone, and S. Craig Watkins. 2013. *Connected Learning: An Agenda for Research and Design*. Digital Media and Learning Research Hub.

Brook, Pete. 2012. "Photographs Are No Longer Things, They're Experiences." *WIRED*, November 15. http://www.wired.com/2012/11/stephen-mayes-vii-photography/.

Campbell, David. 2014. *Professor David Campbell on Narrative, Power and Responsibility*. October 22. https://phonar.org/2014/10/professor-david-campbell-on-narrative-power-and -responsibilty/.

Creative Commons. 2011. *Power of Open*. San Francisco: Creative Commons Corporation.

Cunningham, Francine. 2015. Panel I: How the Digital World Redefines Our Lives. "Disrupt Europe! How to Turn the Challenges of the Digital World into Opportunities," EU Parliament, Brussels, July 1. ALDE Group. Livecasts. https://alde.livecasts.eu/disrupt-europe.

Dietl, Andreas. 2010. "Andreas Dietl: Reporter: Copyright Fight." *Andreas Dietl* (blog), July 13. http://brusselsguy.blogspot.co.uk/2010/07/reporter-copyright-fight.html.

Doctorow, Cory. 2008. *Little Brother*. New York: Tom Doherty Associates.

———. 2009. "Jonathan Worth's Copy-Friendly Photography Business Experiment." Craphound .com. October 20. http://craphound.com/news/2009/10/20/jonathan-worths-copy-friend -photography-business-experiment/.

———. 2015. "Why Give Away Your Work for Free?—Medium Writing Prompts." *Medium*. https://medium.com/medium-writing-prompts/why-give-away-your-work-for-free -5ed4513d5fa8.

FOTO8. 2010. "Beyond Perceivable Benefits: Jonathan Worth's Experiment." January 28. http:// www.foto8.com/live/beyond-perceivable-benefits-jonathan-worths-creative-commons -license-experiment/.

Gillmor, Dan. 2010. *Mediactive*. [United States]: Dan Gillmor.

Guardian. 2014. "University Guide 2015: League Table for Film Production and Photography," June 3. https://www.theguardian.com/education/ng-interactive/2014/jun/03/university -guide-2015-league-table-for-film-production-and-photography.

Ito, Joi. 2008. "Creative Commons & The Sharing Economy." *Japan Society*. November 20. http:// www.japansociety.org/page/multimedia/articles/creative_commons_the_sharing_economy.

Ito, Mizuko, Kris Gutiérrez, Sonia Livingstone, Bill Penuel, Jean Rhodes, Katie Salen, Juliet Schor, Julian Sefton-Green, and S. Craig Watkins. 2013. *Connected Learning: An Agenda for Research and Design*. Irvine: Digital Media and Learning Research Hub.

Jarvis, Jeff. 2009. *What Would Google Do?* New York: Collins Business.

Kelly, Kevin. 2008. "The Technium: Better Than Free." *Kevin Kelly*, January 31. http://kk.org /thetechnium/better-than-fre/.

Kolowich, Steve. 2013. "The New Intelligence." *Inside Higher Ed*, January 25. https://www .insidehighered.com/news/2013/01/25/arizona-st-and-knewtons-grand-experiment -adaptive-learning

Lessig, Lawrence. 2008. *Remix: Making Art and Commerce Thrive in the Hybrid Economy*. New York: Penguin Press.

McLuhan, Marshall, Quentin Fiore, and Jerome Agel. 1967. *The Medium Is the Message*. New York: Bantam Books.

Poundstone, William. 2010. *Priceless: The Myth of Fair Value (and How to Take Advantage of It)*. New York: Hill and Wang.

Rich, Motoko. 2009. "With E-Readers Comes Wider Piracy of Books." *The New York Times*. May 11. http://www.nytimes.com/2009/05/12/technology/internet/12digital.html.

Ritchin, Fred. 2000. *After Photography*. New York: W.W. Norton, 2009.

———. 2013. *Bending the Frame: Photojournalism, Documentary, and the Citizen*. New York. Aperture Foundation.

Shirky, Clay. 2008. *Here Comes Everybody: The Power of Organizing Without Organizations*. New York: Penguin Press.

———. 2010. *Cognitive Surplus: Creativity and Generosity in a Connected Age*. New York: Penguin Press

Smyth, Diane. 2011. "Freetard or Visionary?" *British Journal of Photography*. September. http://www.bjp-online.com/british-journal-of-photography/profile/2108237/freetard-visionary.

Staas, David. 2012. "Using Location Patterns to Power Big Data on Mobile." Signal Conference, Chicago, September 11. Cited in Angwin, *Dragnet Nation*, 149–50.

Stacy, Richard. 2009. "Free Content Is Not the Issue—Its Free Distribution Richard Stacy." *Richard Stacy*, May 11. http://richardstacy.com/2009/05/11/free-content-is-not-the-issue-its-free-distribution/.

Stanmeyer, John. 2014. "Signal." World Press Photo Foundation. 2014 World Press Photo of the Year. http://www.worldpressphoto.org/collection/photo/2014/contemporary-issues/john-stanmeyer.

"The Today Show Adobe Photoshop Debut." n.d. YouTube video, 6:28. Posted February 19, 2015. https://www.youtube.com/watch?v=OHbM4QJYVYM.

7

Reimagining Learning in CLMOOC

MIA ZAMORA

Introduction: The CLMOOC

This book firmly establishes that not all massive open online courses (MOOCs) are created equally. The diversity of MOOC adaptation is in and of itself an important aspect of the new affordances of open online distance-learning paradigms. As we consider the question *What does "open" mean?*, this chapter will hold up a particular adaptation of the massive open online phenomenon that ultimately reinvigorates the potential of "open." The term "open" has set to course many interpretations, many of which seem to be the source of anxiety for those who seek to protect their own market share in the business of higher education. Traditional brick-and-mortar institutions of education are threatened by the suggestion of "open." Why should we give the milk away for free? In comes marching a world in which traditional lectures are rigged to reach "the many" and upheld as a disruptive moment in the educational landscape. The hype has set the stage for technologically pow-ered content delivery paradigms masquerading as innovation. Yes, a flood of MOOCs most certainly presents new methods for content delivery. And content designed to reach the masses most certainly presents a challenge to those who uphold a traditional business model for education. These MOOCs are often offered by universities on platforms such as Coursera and edX, and involve lectures via original videos (Kolowich 2013), automated quizzes, and peer-reviewed assignments (Guzdial 2013). "Massive" refers to the number of enrolled students. However, that is, according to Morris and Stommel (2013), "a fundamental misperception of how teaching works" since these MOOCs privilege teacher-centered pedagogy, and meaningful learning is unlikely to result from this kind of prepackaged instruction. This formulation is a myopic lens for what "open" might confer to higher education, blindsiding any poten-tial for real innovation in the realm of learning. The question of what "open" means is crucial, and a fearful or limited notion of "open" will prevent us from developing institutional change that matters. The thwarted interpretation of the language of openness might keep at bay the truly transformative power of "open." The crucial question now should be: With the new affordances of networked learning in an open environment, how can we reimagine *what learning is* in the twenty-first century? And how might the phenomenon of MOOCs in higher education affect learning across the entire educational landscape? In what ways have MOOCs affected K–12 learning? Some answers to these questions lie in a particular case study. This chapter highlights how the phenomenon of open networked learning has been appropriated by the National Writing Project (NWP; http://www.nwp.org). Founded in 1974, the NWP is the only federally funded program that focuses on the teaching of writing. The NWP is a network of teacher professional development sites anchored at colleges and universities and serving teachers across disciplines and at all levels, from early childhood through university. Codirected by faculty from local universities and from K–12 schools, nearly two hundred local sites serve all fifty states, the District of Columbia, Puerto Rico, and the US Virgin Islands. Sites work in partnership with area school districts to offer high-quality professional development programs for educators. This established community of teachers has leveraged their established network as they have apprehended the potential of truly open learning. They have launched their own version of a MOOC entitled Making Learning Connected—also known as #CLMOOC (#CLMOOC Blog 2014). When considering the case of CLMOOC, perhaps a more productive entry point to an understanding of "open" is to ask: What is open for? (Campbell 2014). And who is open for?

These questions have indeed been answered in powerful ways. The "alternative" or connectivist MOOCs (cMOOCs), which are often highlighted within this book, have probed what is possible as they have brought to light powerful new ways to learn. cMOOCs provide minimally structured timeframes, topics, resources, and an initial digital platform or collective starting point. Participants are expected to connect, interact, and collaborate openly with each other to develop, extend, and amplify the content of the course (Bali et al. 2015). A cMOOC is "based on connection rather than content, which looks more like an online community than a course, . . . [it] doesn't have a defined curriculum or formal assignments" (Downes 2012); and "cMOOCs are based on a connectivist pedagogical model that views knowledge as a networked state and learning as the process of generating those networks and adding and pruning connections" (Siemens 2013).

The organizers of cMOOCs operate as well-informed process hosts rather than as authoritative content experts. Instead of using a learning management system (LMS) to deliver information and assignments, they provide a reposi-tory for participant work (Bali et al. 2015)

CLMOOC (#CLMOOC Blog 2014) is a connectivist case study highlight-ing these particular affordances of a networked online learning environment. Designed for educators, CLMOOC has focused on creating things and the DIY ethos of the recent maker movement. Emphasizing learning-through-doing in a social environment, maker culture has emphasized informal, net-worked, peer led, and shared learning motivated by hands-on production and fun. The CLMOOC adoption of maker culture is a key insight into what "open" can mean for education as a whole. CLMOOC has ultimately redi-rected the concept of open to mean connected. The CLMOOC experiment in massive open online learning has highlighted that open can indeed en-gender empowerment for educators and learners. The upshot of CLMOOC is most certainly not institutional vulnerability born of "free learning." Rather, CLMOOC foregrounds that learning can be a *freeing experience* rooted in the connections we make (Campbell 2014). This central paradigm shift paves the way for new pathways to learning. And as education continues to adjust to the new affordances of a networked society, educators must gain and pass on the digital literacies that serve as the foundation for navigating this new reality.

CLMOOC stands for "Connected Learning Massive Open Online *Col-laboration.*" The word "course" in the MOOC acronym is purposely shunned. The "C" has been rewritten to emphasize certain inherent values. As a col-laboration (rather than a course), CLMOOC's participatory design and con-nectivist underpinnings distinguish it from the many MOOCs that value ef-ficiency, reproduction, and knowledge transfer. The notion of collaboration has been an important emphasis from CLMOOC's onset. There have been three iterations of the CLMOOC event—the first in summer 2013, the sec-ond in summer 2014, and the third in summer 2015. The third iteration was offered during *The Summer to Make, Play & Connect* (Make Summer 2016) by Educator Innovator, which is both a blog and a growing community of educators, supporters, and partners, including the National Writing Project, and powered by educators from the NWP.

Participants in CLMOOC play with new tools and processes for mak-ing projects, share their results and their learning, and explore the educa-tional model known as "connected learning." Designed to help educators reimagine learning, CLMOOC is a collaborative, knowledge-building and knowledge-sharing experience open to anyone who's interested in making and creating. In CLMOOC, participants are invited to design and then engage in "makes"—creative and productive projects—that tap into their personal (and professional) interests. A make is any project or work where a CLMOOC participant creates something. Drawn heavily from the principles of connected learning that emphasize creating and production-centered learning, CLMOOC makes include a vast array of creations. For example, makes might be written (e.g., a story, poem, or play), drawn (e.g., a painting, comic, or animation), or designed (e.g., a web page, game, meme, or map). A make might be something you bake, compose, code, solder or stitch. A make might be a social network or connection you form. CLMOOC makes are inspired by weekly prompts that invite vast forms of interpretation. CLMOOC suggestions for makes are merely that—suggestions. Makes are posted and shared, as well as commented and reflected on, within the networked community.

The CLMOOC experience is primarily directed toward K–12 teachers, university professors, writers, youth workers, mentors, librarians, and museum educators, and is offered for six weeks during the summer. By working to adopt a collaborative approach and a reflective stance toward the processes of making and learning, the CLMOOC also provides an opportunity for participants to plan for an enactment of these experiences in their own teaching and learning contexts and settings. In other words, participants are invited to bring their own creative learning "home." The principles of connected learning are ultimately the language and tools to support teacher and learner agency.

What Is Connected Learning?

Having a real, personal connection is so valuable and so important. It's at the heart of learning and teaching. We need to be acknowledged and seen and often in the hyper-connected world we're shocked when someone pauses and really engages.
    —CHRIS CAMPBELL, CLMOOC participant (#CLMOOC Quotes 2014)

The hallmark of CLMOOC is the use of the connected learning principles as a design "spine." Connected learning is an approach that sees learning as interest driven and peer supported and oriented toward powerful outcomes. Emerging from the MacArthur Foundation's Digital Media and Learning Initiative, these principles have now been more fully described in a report entitled *Connected Learning: An Agenda for Research and Design* (Ito et al. 2012). In the report the authors describe how the principles knit together three crucial contexts for learning:

1. *Peer supported*: In their everyday exchanges with peers and friends, young people are contributing, sharing, and giving feedback in inclusive social experiences that are fluid and highly engaging.

2. *Interest powered*: When a subject is personally interesting and relevant, learners achieve much higher-order learning outcomes.
3. *Academically oriented*: Learners flourish and realize their potential when they can connect their interests and social engagement to academic studies, civic engagement, and career opportunity.

They also describe the design principles of connected learning experiences:

4. *Production centered*: Digital tools provide opportunities for producing and creating a wide variety of media, knowledge, and cultural content in experimental and active ways.
5. *Shared purpose*: Social media and web-based communities provide unprecedented opportunities for cross-generational and cross-cultural learning and connection to unfold and thrive around common goals and interests.
6. *Openly networked*: Online platforms and digital tools can make learning resources abundant, accessible, and visible across all learner settings.

Additionally, connected learning environments embody values of equity, social belonging, and participation. The CLMOOC is a meta-MOOC in the sense that it uses praxis as the gateway for acquisition of the learning theory. If you are a part of CLMOOC, you make and create first and analyze later (in other words, your own learning becomes the basis for a critical lens into learning).

For forty years, the practice of placing educators in the position of learners has been a hallmark methodology of the NWP. Dedicated to the effective teaching of writing in its many forms, the NWP envisions a future where every person is an accomplished writer, engaged learner, and active participant in a digital, interconnected world (Connected Learning 2015). NWP began in 1974 in the Graduate School of Education at the UC Berkeley, where James Gray and his colleagues established a university-based program for K–16 teachers called the Bay Area Writing Project (BAWP). Gray, a teacher-educator and former high school English teacher, was motivated to create a different form of professional development for teachers ("History of NWP"; http://www.nwp.org/cs/public/print/doc/about/history.csp). He sought to develop a professional development (PD) model that made central the knowledge, leadership, and best practices of effective teachers, and that promoted the sharing of that knowledge with other teachers. The foundation of the NWP philosophy is rooted in a vision of peer-supported learning. Forty years later, the NWP's teachers-teaching-teachers model of professional development is reinvigorated. The recent development of Educator Innovator (http://

educatorinnovator.org) furthers this vision of the early model. Educator Innovator is a consortium of networks that gather together like-minded colleagues and organizations that value open learning for educators and whose
interests and values exemplify connected learning. In short, the potential of
open raises the bar for the most successful teacher professional development
network in America. The NWP has always harnessed both the power of peer
learning and the power of a scalable network. In many ways, connectedness
is not new for the NWP. But what is new with CLMOOC and the linking of
this broader network is that the NWP has leveraged its well-founded wisdom
in an open twenty-first-century digital environment. In the best sense, the
marriage of the NWP's wisdom with the tools of the twenty-first century have
laid the groundwork for education's exponential gain.

Designing for Open: Conceiving of CLMOOC

What comes first is inspiration.
—MARK SCHROEDER, CLMOOC participant (#CLMOOC Quotes 2015)

The CLMOOC facilitation team—Christina Cantrill, Joe Dillon, Elyse
Eidman-Aadahl, Terry Elliot, Karen Fasimpaur, Kevin Hodgson, Jordan
Lusink, Paul Oh, Chad Sansing, Anna Smith, and Stephanie West-Puckett—
spent a great deal of time planning for the first iteration in 2013. The challenge for the team was to conceive of a professional development experience
that used connected learning principles to showcase the power of connected
learning experiences. An important early team decision was to place the
CLMOOC learner/participant at the center. With the participants themselves
at the heart of the enterprise, it followed suit that the relationships among
learners also took center stage. The result was to spotlight how connections
(both intellectual and personal) are essential to authentic learning. CLMOOC
inherently linked the definition of open to the creation of personal learning
networks that break outside the typical walled gardens of a traditional course.
    Although the connected learning tenets outlined above were used as a
set of design principles for inspiration and grounding, ultimately much of
the true design tension for CLMOOC resided in how to go about *building*
CLMOOC. The key to CLMOOC's vision is bound to a simple question:
What should come first: the theory of connected learning or "the making"
(production-centered activities)? After much discussion, the early facilitation
team took a great leap of faith. The role of production-centered learning (i.e.,
"the make") was chosen as the lead out for all CLMOOC activity. This pur-

poseful move away from *consumption* (acquisition of content) to *production* (creation through multimodal writing with new digital tools) became the central reorientation. The unforeseen artifacts generated within CLMOOC have consisted of diverse forms, multimedia mash-ups, and playful remix. With this shift away from prescribed content, the early design team purposely chose to forgo the prescriptive assertion of particular learning outcomes. Facilitators did not outline a particular place of "arrival." CLMOOC has thus been characterized by "bursts" and "drifts" of both production and collaboration too complex and dynamic to capture in a linear narrative (Smith et al. 2016).

There were no instructions offered to participants. Rather, playful prompts were designed to invite folks to jump in to activity. Weekly "Make Cycles" replaced the more traditional lesson structure of curricular units. The CLMOOC design team relinquished any role of authority as they consciously chose to assume the position of colearners. By embracing a notion of colearning, the design team forfeited any expert impulse and allowed the community to take shape, take charge, and emerge in dynamic and unpredictable ways. From this stance, the team witnessed the organic growth of the community and let the collective wisdom of the many lead the way. In short, they trusted the community connections. And in turn, the community brought forth meaningful learning as individuals identified their own goals for the experience. Furthermore, the community took the instinctive step to move from making to reflecting on process. The design team's early design strategy to trust in community emergence and to shun an authoritative stance was a foundational building block to the authentic openness of CLMOOC.

Establishing Openness: The Ethos of CLMOOC

And maybe that is what I find appealing—the opportunity to play and explore without the stress of having to be perfect.
—JANET CHOW, CLMOOC participant (#CLMOOC Quotes 2015)

There is often significant fear and caution regarding the openness of the Internet in the context of education. Moreover, there is much less about the positive potential of the Internet as a gateway for learning. At the heart of this resistance lies a trust issue. Portals to the open Internet are often framed in educational culture as toys, tools, or even add-ons that might invite chaos or anarchy in learning contexts (Losh and Jenkins 2012). This perception needs to be reconsidered. Perhaps a better way to think of the open net is to consider it as a set of decisions about how we choose to communicate. A trusted learning environment is a space where people can take risks in the open and actually trust each other. But how do we ensure such a space? For CLMOOC, the trust in community emergence might not have worked without a complementary notion of collaborative culture or a strategically honed ethos. How is open effectively facilitated? How is the colearning model sustained throughout the event? How did CLMOOC ensure the growth and expansion of this democratic learning space?

The issue of trust was confronted head on in the design of CLMOOC. A culture of affirmation was planned quite purposely. From the onset, a commitment to a supportive inclusive message helped expand the CLMOOC community. The goal was to create a MOOC that did not only cater to technophile or veteran MOOCers. CLMOOC is about bringing curious learners on board. But exactly how did the team help newcomers orient themselves to online learning? How did they engage so many newcomers, while keeping at bay that often experienced sensation of being overwhelmed? (The accounts of these disheartening experiences leave predictable traces in cMOOCs. Newcomers often tweet about feeling deluged by information overload. They blog to apologize for not blogging. They post that they are lost.) There was considerable concern about "drop out." "The struggling participant" was a hypothetical challenge before CLMOOC even got started.

In response to this justified concern, the facilitation team arrived upon the notion of affirmation. The culture included an "always open" invitation to join (no matter how far into the six-week period) and a philosophy of acceptance (any amount of engagement was welcome). The team determined a set of culture-building principles (an on-point message if you will) that became a continued insistence throughout:

- To accept and honor lurkers[1]
- To communicate to participants that they can come and go without fear of violating norms or falling behind
- To welcome and encourage both collaborative efforts and individual work
- To affirm all participants—to let them know they are OK, since people creating and sharing in online spaces can be unsure (Dillon 2013)

Joe Dillon, an early CLMOOC team facilitator and key architect of the "ethos of CLMOOC," drafted an open newsletter message of encouragement that set the tone:

1. For those who might not be familiar with the term within the context of online behavior, to "lurk" means to click here and there (and check out what content and commentary is being generated by a community) while remaining an observer more than a contributor to the unfolding conversation

This is just a note to say that your participation so far has been perfect!

If you've lurked, that's perfect! You are learning while you lurk, waiting to jump in.

If you've been posting like mad, you've been leading and making our community more inviting! If you've been hot and cold in #clmooc, posting in fits of productivity and disappearing for a while, that's great. You have kids to feed, dogs to walk, and laundry that doesn't fold itself, after all. We get it. Even when you're catching up on your beauty sleep, you help make #clmooc massive!

Regardless of how you've participated, consider yourself caught up and ready for your next (or first) creative act in #clmooc. You're ripe for your next (or first) connection. (Dillon 2013)

This explicit CLMOOC ethos has been sustained to the present, playing just as much a role in summer 2014 and summer 2015 iterations as it did in the first iteration. The overall network upheld this approach of generosity and people felt comfortable coming and going and sharing their learning at will. The Google+ community grew to approximately 2,217 in CLMOOC 2014,[2] resulting in approximately 1,600 publically shared and distributed artifacts ("makes") about writing-as-making. The successful growth of CLMOOC is in part because of this established sense of security, equity, and trust as a foundation for true openness.

As the world has changed because of affordances of the open net, our educational system has resisted this paradigm shift. Earlier laws designed to protect our students might ultimately prevent them from learning in a connected environment. Obviously, school policy needs to be reconsidered. But the larger question remains: How might we open doors for students while keeping them safe? Part of the answer lies in a need to establish new social norms. Educators can play a significant role in establishing an ethics of connected learning. In many ways, CLMOOC has modeled a powerful community-building strategy of openness that is first and foremost predicated on trust.

CLMOOC Entry: Getting Past Guilt

Between our first year of CLMOOC and the second, . . . we heard later stories of folks who lurked, brought ideas to the classroom or professional spaces, and then came back strong in the second year as active participants, grateful for the ongoing message of valuing those who lurk to learn.

—KEVIN HODGSON, CLMOOC facilitator (#CLMOOC Quotes 2015)

2. Of the participants, 2217 educators opted in, composing and distributing compositions using Twitter (n = 18,656 tweets), a Google+ community (n = 1,658 members), a Facebook community (n = 55), and personal websites (n = 133 blogs).

In summer 2013, I was one of the more than one thousand CLMOOC participants. As the director of the Kean University Writing Project (KUWP), I knew the NWP network well and was excited to see how the NWP would adapt to the open online learning context. I had previously participated in a few cMOOCs (i.e., I registered for #MOOCMOOC and #ETMOOC). I was interested in #MOOCMOOC in particular since it came at a key moment in the MOOC hype and offered a timely crowdsourced query of the emergent MOOC phenomenon. But as much as I wanted to think critically about the emergence of MOOCs, I had yet to understand or experience the nature of truly open learning. I opted to remain a lurker as I still did not feel prepared to become a regular contributor. I chose to observe as I acclimated to networked forms of online learning. In hindsight, I recognize that I learned a great deal while simply lurking in those earlier networked learning contexts. I became familiar for the first time with the colocated infrastructure that cMOOC participants inhabit. But at that early point in my online learning experiences, I also felt that I was not really a valid participant because I was not yet actively posting contributions to ongoing discussions. I disliked the feeling of not being able to complete something that I had made a formal commitment to (via registration). I recognize now that I had yet to grasp a true understanding of openness. I remember my reluctance to sign-up for further online learning opportunities since I was concerned with the time commitment involved. I had my doubts if I would be able to keep up with the pace of CLMOOC, but since it was my own community taking the plunge, I signed up anyway. I worried that I would experience guilt more than anything (for not being the robust participant I wanted to be). Guilt is indeed a backlash emotion for many who give the online learning model a try. This aftereffect of the MOOC phenomenon should not be underestimated. Many learners are prone to that familiar fear of losing momentum, or (heaven forbid)—the dreaded sense of failure that can so easily seep into the (academically wired) mindscape. There is work to be done in unlearning the message from the hidden curriculum of lifelong schooling. The unwritten and unintended values passed down in a formal educational context rigs learners to certain expectations (e.g., the teacher is the authority and therefore knows best, and there are only right and wrong answers). Educators and learners have been pummeled for years by evaluations, deadlines, tests, and authorized outcomes. One consequence of these hidden values is the guilt stemming from fear of not meeting prescribed expectations. But people need time to process before entering into the fray of an open online discussion. Those who lurk also learn. The trick to emboldening an open-learning community is to build a culture of guilt-free participation. People should know that is okay to dip in and out of the open online networked experience because it is a dynamic, ever unfolding phenomenon, and each perspective brings new energy. The culture of affirmation developed from the onset within CLMOOC pushed me forth, alleviating this unnecessary but deeply instinctive guilt.

CLMOOC Emergence: The Dandelion as Connected Learning Metaphor

> Nobody loves the head of a dandelion, maybe because they are so many, strong and soon.
>
> —TONI MORRISON, *The Bluest Eye*

I had shared with colleagues that I felt a bit like a dandelion seed on the wind when I first participated in CLMOOC. For many educators who participated in this grand experiment, the experience was transformative. CLMOOC changed the way we approach our classrooms, and for many, I know it has changed the way we understand the experience of learning. Unfortunately, in so many classrooms, the proposition of learning has been bound to fixed outcomes and content. But in this day and age—with the dynamism of open online technologies—learning can be driven by self-interest, research can be conducted with powerful global collaboration and crowdsourcing, and teachers and students can discover alongside each other as they break down old hierarchies that have limited the production of new knowledge. This is the heart of the connected learning experience. Like so many NWP educators, I embraced this experience more fully when I took the plunge with CLMOOC last summer. I let go of my expert impulse, embraced my inner imposter-syndrome self, and started to make, create, and reflect. Like a dandelion seed caught in a wind gust floating over a fertile field of wild flowers, I was taken here and there, and I wasn't quite sure where I would land. My learning in CLMOOC (as I hacked toys, created avatars, made maps, and met a lot of great new colleagues) was never about fixed learning outcomes, but rather it was an unfolding process that was partially intuitive, partially serendipitous.

But such a vision of learning threatens institutionalized notions of what learning should look like. A dandelion seed that takes root disrupts the aspirational uniformity of the pristine green lawn. Nonetheless, children cannot see the dandelion as a weed with its yellow face greeting them as the world warms again. Children play away the hours, learning so very much, asking themselves powerful fundamental questions as the afternoon rolls on. But as we come to be socialized and adulterated, we accept those dandelions as weeds, as undesirable. So, too, we learn to hem our curiosity and we rifle for the "correct" answers, making it harder to just play.

Nevertheless, real (transformative) learning is just that. It is play and discovery. It is asking powerful fundamental questions while embarking on a quest for new answers in earnest. How can we harness the wisdom of child's play back into the life of our twenty-first-century classrooms? Higher education could take a cue from educators in the K–12 arena who have understood that play constitutes serious learning. *Hybrid Pedagogy* editors Sean Michael Morris, Pete Rorabaugh, and Jesse Stommel (2011) assert that play constitutes a new form of critical inquiry. We must find a way to incorporate play into education, making school something that students enjoy as they discover that learning can be fun and freeing. I am quite sure that like a gust of spring wind, open technologies and connected learning principles can set us on a new course, breathing new life into our collective classroom inquiries. Despite the current educational landscape (of relentless assessment and institutionalized testing), we can craft learning potential like an open field, punctuated by all kinds of wild flowers, even the dandelions.

As I reflect on my own learning in CLMOOC 2013, it strikes me that the dandelion might serve as the perfect metaphor, since it points to an ecology of openness. Still, where is the hub or center of CLMOOC knowledge production? This dandelion metaphor seems to suggest a scattered drifting paradigm for learning. But there is a powerful (and counterintuitive) aspect of groundedness in this. The essential openness of that field of learning allows for you (the participant seed) to be the true center of the CLMOOC experience. Learning becomes deeply personalized and inherently meaningful when you take the generative center. And the *playful* aspect (that the open field affords) creates a reason for people to want to engage. In truly transformative open online learning, the learners themselves are the heart of the enterprise and as they drift and play, they connect to something larger. The seed is where the knowledge germinates, and the fertile soil of the open landscape ensures that growth. Learners carve out identities and then reach out to other communities and networks, expanding knowledge and connections (Koh 2014).

After being a CLMOOC participant in 2013, I became a CLMOOC facilitator in 2014. The ease in which my role evolved reflects the opportunity that the CLMOOC version of open affords. I took the helm for the fourth Make Cycle in CLMOOC 2014 as I prompted everyone to "Hack Your Writing" (#CLMOOC 2014). Encouraging participants to consider a broader use of the term "hack," I asked the community to consider hacking as playful exploration. According to Suiter (2103), to hack is to make innovative customizations (perhaps exploiting the "weakness" in something). Hacking involves the use of playful creation to enrich knowledge of complex systems. This useful term has been applied to the academy itself. The academy is approaching a new integration with revolutionary technologies. We have quickly gone from computers in the classroom to classrooms in the computer (Suiter 2013). A playful hacker ethos (at this critical juncture for higher education) is key to reinvention and change that will matter.

I pointed out in my "Hack Your Writing" newsletter prompt (CLMOOC—Making Learning Connected 2014) that hackers often undermine authoritative systems. Hackers crack systems for fun, pursuing civic or collective action. The creative response to this call was nothing short of phenomenal. The diversity and depth of the makes that week highlighted how much the affordances of new digital tools and technologies have opened up our understanding of what it means to write. After a fun week of invoking a culture of remix and exploration, writing did in fact emerge as making with a multitude of innovative approaches (Zamora 2014).

Facilitating Open

It is what we filter out that speaks.
—SUSAN ANGEL, CLMOOC participant (#CLMOOC Quotes 2015)

The move from CLMOOC participant to facilitator posed new challenges. Because of my on-the-ground role as director of the KUWP, I was simultaneously at the helm of shaping two distinct networks (both the local face-to-face network of the KUWP Summer Institute,[3] as well the open online CLMOOC network; http://www.nwp.org/cs/public/print/doc/nwpsites /summer_institute.csp). I learned quickly that the two networks were not necessarily interchangeable, but still, they were not disparate. In anticipation of these two leadership roles converging in one summer, I led my KUWP team to consider how to incorporate the connected learning principles into our professional development summer institute offerings for local teachers. I knew that what I experienced as a participant in CLMOOC 2013 needed to be at the center of what I was doing locally to help transform teachers into teacher-leaders. Teachers come to the NWP summer institutes to be reinvigorated. Many of today's teachers are overwhelmed by the prospect of using new technologies and digital tools. Technological savvy has been framed as

---

3. Each of the nearly two hundred NWP sites holds an invitational summer institute every summer. Several thousand teachers participate each year in these summer institutes, and every year new groups of summer fellows at local sites describe their experience as "a space for critical reflection so essential to good practice," "causing a noticeable and great shift in all of my teaching," or "the best professional development I have had in all my years of teaching."

a particular skill set, which is often inaccurately ascribed to the young (Selwyn 2009). This unfounded impression further exacerbates a growing digital divide between educators and students. It has been a great disservice to education overall to formulate technology as an intrinsic classroom skill. And often the result is the problematic understanding that the acquisition of digital skills (in and of themselves) will ensure a teacher's ability to teach effectively. In the most obvious sense, a great teacher is so much more than a person who can navigate apps with ease. Yet I have found that by demystifying the tools and trade of openness and helping teachers get "connected," they rediscover their passion for learning. In turn, they are repositioned to infuse their own classrooms with that passion. As someone in the position to support the revitalization of teacher practice, I recognized the need for a paradigm shift in perception around educational technology. What better way to empower our local teacher-consultants than to share with them the connected learning principles in an open network?

Connecting Online and Offline Participants

"What can you do?" has been replaced with "What can you and your network connections do?" Knowledge itself is moving from the individual to the individual and his contacts.
—HOWARD RHEINGOLD, *Net Smart*

If teachers enter into professional development from the gateway of connected learning, they should no longer see technology as a skill set that is added on. In the past at KUWP we used to have a choice of tracks that a teacher could choose from when joining our summer institute. One of those tracks was the "tech track." In other words, gaining more facility with technology and digital tools was an option. Gaining more digital confidence was essentially an elective aspect of their summer professional development plan. But I knew after CLMOOC 2013 that this administrative frame for gaining digital confidence would no longer serve learning in a twenty-first-century context. We decided to take a new approach. "Tech" would no longer exist as a "track" to be selected, but instead the introduction of connected learning principles via participation in CLMOOC would be a foundational design for our 2014 Summer Institute. The CLMOOC was not originally conceived to be implemented as a built-in experience for local teachers joining the NWP through our local summer institutes. But at the KUWP, the CLMOOC has become a foundation for the transformative process that has always been key to the NWP philosophy.

As an NWP leader in both the local and online context, I have recognized the need for an essential identity shift for teachers. Who is open for? In the case of CLMOOC, open is for teachers who are more importantly colearners. Teachers are the crucial bridge connecting K–12 learning to the expectations that lie ahead in higher education. Everyday teachers model how to learn. CLMOOC has given many educators an opportunity to experience learning anew—as a collaborative, playful, and connected experience. The educators of CLMOOC have taken that profound CLMOOC lesson home to their own classrooms. Teachers today should also know themselves as designers. By embracing connected learning through the CLMOOC, our local teachers not only built a new professional learning community but also learned the power of navigating open. They were able to experience the kind of networked creativity that will be so essential to leading students to learn in this century. This is not an intuitive or easy step for teachers to take. But with the blending of both the local and online networks to support this vision, our teachers were able to step into new territory and grow in a multitude of ways.

Learning Pathways and Drift

> How do you move . . . be in the flow . . . pick things up . . . feel it in your body . . . be in
> it, not just above it? . . . How do we create an arc of life-learning?
> —CLMOOC participant (#CLMOOC Quotes 2015)

Perhaps one of the most powerful legacies of CLMOOC is the way in which it has laid bare multiple learning pathways. Pathways not as established trails to set out on, but rather trailblazing as a journey not yet made. With CLMOOC, learning is in part about movement. Making room for the emergent to be possible, the CLMOOC experience rises to the paradoxical challenge of determining a purposeful space for learning while allowing for freedom in learning. The kind of learning that has occurred in CLMOOC foregrounds the reality that school may only be one node in a learner's network. The makes (and the resulting community conversations) highlight the myriad ways people come to learn something. This special MOOC experiment ultimately reminds us that we must all widen our lens regarding the where and when as we are considering how learning takes place. As CLMOOC illustrates, transformative learning is rhizomatic rather than linear. One significant upshot of the CLMOOC's particular establishment of "open" is to make us ask more directly: How does learning take shape as we move through different contexts? This is an important question for educators to consider. At this moment in education, we are hyperfocused on destination markers: our curriculum, our standards, and our assessments. What counts as learning is being confined by such markers. The awareness and acknowledgment of different learning pathways (and the drift that takes place as one moves through different learning contexts) is key to understanding what is possible as we attempt to envision what education should be in this century. Learning should not be a directive, but rather, a holistic experience. *So what is open for?* It is for enhancing and ensuring this aspect of learning rather than relegating learning to the sidelines of programmatic agendas and planned outcomes.

CLMOOC's particular version of "open" models a critical reconsideration of learning in the twenty-first century. CLMOOC has inspired so many educators by situating them as learners, and it has generated new learning experiences that push beyond a traditional top-down hierarchical model for extending knowledge. Institutional change that matters will start with this reckoning. For the classroom is no longer bound by four walls. CLMOOC has already played a critical role in bridging this divide between K–12 learning contexts and higher-education expectation. As higher education continues to tinker and toy with new educational technologies, it is teachers who must lead our collective way by designing connected learning experiences.

References

Bali, Maha, Maureen Crawford, Rhonda Jessen, Paul Signorelli, and Mia Zamora. 2015. "What Makes a CMOOC Community Endure? Multiple Participant Perspectives from Diverse CMOOCs." *Educational Media International* 52 (2): 100–15.

Campbell, Gardner. 2014. "From Open To Connected." *Gardner Writes*, August 9. Accessed August 15, 2014.

#CLMOOC Blog. 2014. "#CLMOOC—Making Learning Connected." http://clmooc.educator innovator.org/2014/.

#CLMOOC. 2014. "Make Cycle #4: Hack Your Writing." July 7. http://clmooc.educatorinnovator .org/2014/2014/07/07/make-cycle-4-hack-your-writing/.

#CLMOOC Quotes. 2014. Google Docs. https://docs.google.com/presentation/d/1is4lKaS -as274myjkTKRR6UZ4fafBzu9aUIAU5ysEnY/preview?slide=id.g390f8eeb7_0202.

———. 2015. Google Docs. https://docs.google.com/presentation/d/1is4lKaS-as274myjkTKR R6UZ4fafBzu9aUIAU5ysEnY/preview?slide=id.g390f8eeb7_0202.

Connected Learning. 2015. "Connected Learning: Reimagining the Experience of Education in the Innovation Age." May 20. http://connectedlearning.tv/connected-learning-principles.

Dillon, Joe. 2013. "Affirmations in Community." *Digital Is*, February 3. http://digitalis.nwp.org /resource/5917.

Downes, Stephen. 2012. *Connectivism and Connective Knowledge: Essays on Meaning and Learning Networks.* 1st ed. Creative Commons. http://www.downes.ca/files/books/Connective _Knowledge-19May2012.pdf.

Guzdial, Mark. 2013. "MOOCs Are a Fundamental Misperception of How Teaching Works." *Computing Education Blog*, January 4. https://computinged.wordpress.com/2013/01/04 /moocs-are-a-fundamental-misperception-of-how-learning-works/.

Ito, Mizuko, Kris Gutiérrez, Sonia Livingstone, Bill Penuel, Jean Rhodes, Katie Selen, Juliet Schor, Julian Sefton-Green, and S. Craig Watkins. 2012. "Connected Learning: An Agenda for Research and Design." DML Research Hub, December 31. http://eprints.lse.ac.uk/48114/.

Koh, Adeline. 2014. "The Political Power of Play." *Hybrid Pedagogy*, April 3. http://www.hybrid pedagogy.com/journal/political-power-of-play/.

Kolowich, Steve. 2013. "The Professors Behind the MOOC Hype." *Chronicle of Higher Education*, March 24. http://www.chronicle.com/article/The-Professors-Behind-the-MOOC/137905.

Losh, Elizabeth, and Henry Jenkins. 2012. "Can Public Education Coexist with Participatory Culture?" *Knowledge Quest* 41 (1 September–October): 16–21.

Make Summer: Make, Play and Connect. 2016. http://www.makesummer.org/?ref=ei.

Morris, Sean Michael, Peter Rorabaugh and Jesse Stommel. 2011. *Hybrid Pedagogy*. http://www .hybridpedagogy.com.

Morris, Sean Michael, and Jesse Stommel. 2013. "MOOCagogy: Assessment, Networked Learning, and the Meta-MOOC." *Hybrid Pedagogy*, July 22.

Selwyn, Neil. 2009. "The Digital Native—Myth And Reality." *Aslib Proceedings* 61 (4): 364–79.

Siemens, George. 2013. "Massive Open Online Courses: Innovation in Education?" In *Open Educational Resources: Innovation, Research and Practice*, edited by Rory McGreal, Wanjira Kinuthia, and Stewart Marshall, 5–14. Vancouver: Commonwealth of Learning and Athabasca University.

Smith, Anna, Stephanie West-Puckett, Christina Cantrill, and Mia Zamora. 2016. "Remix as Professional Learning: Fostering Transformative Teacherly Identities in CLMOOC." *Educational Sciences* 6 (1): 12.

Suiter, Tad. 2013. "Why 'Hacking'?" In *Hacking the Academy: New Approaches to Scholarship and Teaching from Digital Humanities*, edited by Daniel J. Cohen and Tom Scheinfeldt, 6–12. Ann Arbor: University of Michigan Press.

Zamora, Mia. 2014. "Hack Your Writing: Reflections and Connections from #clmooc." *Digital Is*, July 29. http://digitalis.nwp.org/resource/6140.

PART THREE

Openness and Critical Pedagogy

8

Feminist Pedagogy in the Digital Age:
Experimenting between MOOCs and DOCCs

ADELINE KOH

Massive open online courses (MOOCs) burst onto the landscape of US higher education in February 2012 with the launch of the online school Udacity. The promises of MOOCs were utopian: they lent themselves to scale easily for the same cost of production, therefore promising to make education more afford-able and accessible for both people within the United States and the rest of the world. These promises, however, also led to sharp criticisms. Many decried that MOOCs demonstrated bad pedagogy, as they were content based and lecture style rather than student focused. Statistics emerging from the courses also showed that MOOCs had very low retention rates (Parr 2013). Even the idealistic promises of access for marginalized groups were soon questioned, once a study (Christensen and Alcorn 2014) was released showing that the majority of MOOC takers were educated, employed, first world, white men.

Much of the criticism that have been applied to MOOCs, however, has already been raised by many who have developed radical feminist pedagogy, much of which emphasizes community and connectedness over the model of an all-powerful sage on the stage. This traditional model of education, with the instructor at the center and front of the room, is used by MOOCs and functions on what Paolo Freire (1996) called the "banking system of educa-tion," where it is assumed that knowledge is acquired, stored, and given from the lecturer to the lectured. This banking system is part and parcel of what Cathy Davidson (2014) has called the industrial system of education, which focuses on the mass production of students the way products are mass pro-duced in factories. In this regard, the structure of most MOOCs mirror what is increasingly coming under scrutiny in the conventional education system.

In this essay I want to evaluate two digital "feminist pedagogy" experi-ments that use transformative feminist pedagogy to circumvent conventional power structures in online education: in particular, the FemTechNet DOCC (distributed online collaborative course), and an experiment using the Coursera MOOC The History and Future of (Mostly) Higher Education by Cathy Davidson as a DOCC. In the latter, Davidson makes use of the MOOC platform to experiment with a DOCC alternative. I take my definition of feminist pedagogy primarily from the work of bell hooks, Paolo Freire (1996), Audre Lorde (1984) and Carolyn Shrewsbury (1987), all of whom emphasize the importance of building community and allowing for spaces for political, intellectual, and emotional discomfort in the classroom as liberational feminist pedagogy. In short, feminist pedagogy in this essay is defined by approaches that decenter the instructor's authority in the classroom and focus on building strong learning communities. I draw my evaluation of these experiments from my own experience taking part in the FemTechNet DOCC and the Coursera MOOC/DOCC as an instructor in two separate classes that I taught, one in spring 2014 and another in fall 2014 at Richard Stockton College. This chapter evaluates some of the ways in which each example attempts to address fundamental feminist pedagogy issues within the digital environment, some of their limitations, their connectedness with the other experiments, and possible ways forward.

Two major concepts dominate my understanding of transformative feminist pedagogy: (1) student empowerment and restructuring classroom power dynamics, which hinge on decentralizing the power of the teacher as sole authority, and (2) reenvisioning the classroom as a community of learners rather than as a space for a teacher to dole out knowledge to passive recipients. In Teaching to Transgress, bell hooks (1994) defines radical liberation pedagogy as one of student empowerment as well as of community development. For hooks, "making the classroom a democratic setting where everyone feels a responsibility to contribute is a central goal of transformative pedagogy" (39). Similar sentiments are echoed in Carolyn Shrewsbury's "What Is Feminist Pedagogy" (1987), where she insists that a feminist classroom is one with "persons connected in a net of relationship with people who care about each other's learning as well as their own," rather than a "classroom that is comprised of teacher and students" (6).

Emphasis on student empowerment and creating learning communities poses some fundamental challenges to traditional systems of education. hooks writes that the creation of a community is integral to her pedagogy, that "a feeling of community creates a sense that there is one shared commitment and a common good that binds us" (40). To "recognize the value of each individual voice" (40), however, the class as community has to withdraw a noticeable amount of power and influence from the instructor. This move makes many educators uncomfortable since traditional training dictates that the instructor should be the voice of authority as she bears the burden of communicating her knowledge to others. This unease also derives from centering the knowledge and lived experience of others in the room outside of the instructor. This can mean, for example, centering other races and ethnicities in the classroom rather than whiteness as a norm, to place women at the center of the classroom rather than men, or to place LGBT issues rather than women's issues at the forefront of a class about gender.

This shift of power often leads to panic for many instructors, because such a classroom does not morph into the comforting "melting pot" of happy smiling characters of United Colors of Benetton multiculturalism, but rather, one that uncomfortably calls attention to social inequalities within the classroom and outside of it. Such pedagogy draws attention to the practice of social oppression, particularly in relation to gender, sexuality, race, and ability. Thus it may throw the instructor's own biases into sharp relief and make for uncomfortable tensions when students acknowledge the unequal power relations that exist between them. It may call into question the texts that are chosen for the class, the methodologies used in the class to read these texts, and the approaches used for teaching. For these reasons, radical feminist pedagogy is challenging enough to enact in a face-to-face classroom, let alone in a more unfamiliar digital context.

Indeed, online education potentially exacerbates the risky nature of feminist pedagogy because of the different ways the classroom is embodied. Unlike classes and communities that meet in person, where people get to know one another through the presence of their physical bodies, physical movement, and physical space, social interaction in a digital course is reduced to screen names or avatars on online forums or social media spaces or synchronous but isolating video lectures. Without physical embodiment, working through the difficult emotions and situations that may arise can be arduous, especially if the class does not have a face-to-face component. How critical is physical embodiment to community creation and empowerment, and how have recent experiments in online learning navigated these goals? As a means of addressing this important question, the rest of my essay focuses on my experiences with a node of the FemTechNet DOCC and an experiment using a Coursera MOOC as part of a DOCC.

FemTechNet

FemTechNet describes itself as "an activated network of hundreds of scholars, students and artists who work on, with, and at the borders of technology, science and feminism in a variety of fields including Science and Technology Studies (STS), Media and Visual Studies, Art, Women's, Queer and Ethnic Studies" (FemTechNet 2014a). One of FemTechNet's central projects has been the creation of a DOCC as a feminist "anti-MOOC." Unlike a MOOC, which is typically created by one or two instructors and then distributed by an institution (universities or companies), a DOCC emphasizes networked learning and is "built on the understanding that expertise is distributed throughout networks, among participants situated in diverse institutional contexts, within diverse material, geographic and national settings, and who embody and perform diverse identities" (2014c). In other words, in place of a top-down MOOC where the same content is delivered to various computer screens and students more or less left on their own, a DOCC emphasizes building communities of learning over content delivery and establishing connections among these learning communities. Within a DOCC, the communal aspect of learning is the most important part of pedagogy.

In place of a typical MOOC course run by Coursera or Udacity, where content produced by the instructors is made freely available, but participants do not get individualized feedback from instructors or a sense of a classroom community, a DOCC focuses on the network of people within the course rather than the content. FemTechNet (2014c) states that the "key principles of a DOCC" are that it

- recognizes and engages expertise DISTRIBUTED throughout a network;
- affirms that there are many ways and methods of LEARNING;
- embodies COLLABORATIVE peer-to-peer communication modes and learning activities;
- respects DIVERSITY, SPECIFICITY and DIFFERENCES among people and in bandwidth across networks;
- encourages the collaborative creation of a HISTORICAL archive; and
- enacts a collaborative EXPERIMENT in the use of online pedagogies.

FemTechNet ran its first iteration of the DOCC in 2012–13 in a "beta cycle" and then ran its first full cycle in 2013–14, with classes taught across thirteen campuses in the United States and Canada. I participated in the 2014–15 cycle using my Feminist Theory course at Stockton University (then known as Richard Stockton College) in fall 2014. With Brian Jara from West Virginia University and Marla Jaksch from the College of New Jersey, I formed a Feminist Theory DOCC course node that connected three classes on feminist theory in different locations. At Stockton University, Feminist Theory is taught as the capstone course for the Women, Gender and Sexuality Studies minor, and is usually taken by a mixture of more advanced and beginning students.

For the Feminist Theory FemTechNet node, Jara, Jaksch, and I created a Facebook group in which we invited our students to participate for extra credit. We encouraged students to share content with one another, often posting links that resonated with issues that came up in our three separate classes. Jara also led an activity using the social media platform Vine at the beginning of the semester, where he had students at West Virginia University making videos interviewing one another and students outside the class on what feminism means to them.

Our shared activity was a slight remix of the game *Twitter vs. Zombies* (now known as TvsZ), a self-regulated and community-developed game to teach Twitter literacy to participants originally conceived by Jesse Stommel and Pete Rorabaugh. Players begin the game initially starting off as human, and various students were planted in the game as Patient Zero zombies who would "#bite" humans to turn them into zombies. Zombies could only #bite at certain intervals, and humans could defend themselves from these swipes either by using #dodge or asking another human for a #swipe. All these actions could only be used once until the assigned time was over (e.g., a zombie could #bite once every five minutes, and humans could either #dodge to defend themselves or #swipe to protect another human only once every five minutes). The assigned time changed as the game progressed, and we instructors released rule changes at intervals every one or two hours, which changed how people interacted within the game: for example, by shortening or lengthening #bite/#dodge/#swipe intervals, by allowing players additional actions if they fulfilled certain tasks (e.g., zombies got an #extrabite for rhyming in their tweets, humans got to stay in a #safezone or #cure a zombie [turning it back into a human]), and by linking to a post on why feminism is important.

We played the game from 2:00–8:00 p.m. EST on September 25, 2014. This was a much more condensed version of the original game, which can stretch out over the course of an entire week. This also changed the dynamics of the game because urgency became more important. We also invited people from the general FemTechNet group to join in the game, and were happy that a few of the other FemTechNet instructors did join us for a while. While the other iterations of *Twitter vs. Zombies* had emergent rules sourced from its participants, the brevity of the game made making changes based on participant feedback more difficult to incorporate in our iteration.

Outside our Facebook group and *Twitter vs. Zombies*, the Feminist Theories node had little engagement with each other and the FemTechNet community at large. While I incorporated wiki storming, a key FemTechNet learning project (FemTechNet 2014b), into my course syllabus, Jara and Jaksch did not manage to do so. All three of us also did not use the suggested video schedule for FemTechNet for content, as we had too much base content from feminist theory to cover within the course. The instructors did take part in the main FemTechNet Facebook group by contributing content and interacting with others.

How did my participation in FemTechNet help me navigate digital pedagogy in a digital space? To be honest, I think this is a more difficult question for me to answer because my class and our "node" did not engage with the main FemTechNet network that much outside the two activities I outlined here. This limited the ways in which we could have drawn more greatly from the network and community at large, and it is something I would amend if I were to go into this experiment again.

But the two "connected" activities that we did use—the Facebook group for the Feminist Theory node and the *Twitter vs. Zombies* game—did contribute to student empowerment. My students reported that they were excited by posting reflections on feminism in the contemporary world on Facebook and were excited when people from other schools "liked" their material and engaged with them. The *Twitter vs. Zombies* game also allowed them to play with the reversal of traditional power dynamics—I had a student zombie turn me from human to zombie, as well as a human "cure" me back into humanness (against my volition). A great deal of what my students used in the game as reasons why feminism is important was also quite significant and demonstrated that they had been learning quite a bit from the class itself.

In all, I think that the digital component to the classes did help add a space for "safe" play for my students in which they could experiment with forms that centralized their thoughts rather than those of the professors, and to play with traditional power structures. Our Facebook nodal group was especially "safe" since the group was open only to people who were enrolled in the three classes. We also did not encounter much, if any, trolling or hostility while running our iteration of a feminist *Twitter vs. Zombies*.

However, because participation in this digital component was secondary to our face-to-face meetings, we did not sufficiently take part in the "milieu" of the FemTechNet enough to have some of the more uncomfortable social tensions result. The majority of my students in the class were already well versed in intersectional feminism before the class had begun. Additionally, not being present enough in a digital space means that we lack embodiment in that space, which can be the most nerve-wracking but powerful aspect of learning where one stands in the construction of knowledge. By "embodiment" in this sense I am referring to intellectual and social presence and contributions to the digital community. By being absent, my students and I did not take up space or serve as a useful part of the community; indeed, we were not even visible, hence our lack of embodiment. In brief, then, we were not "embodied" enough in the digital network for potential benefits and complications that can result in that space to develop.

The History and Future of (Mostly) Higher Education

I now turn to another example of my experience with digital feminist pedagogy in between MOOCs and DOCCs. In spring 2014 I taught a graduate seminar, Introduction to the Digital Humanities, in Richard Stockton College's Masters of American Studies program that met once a week. For half the class, my students participated in a Coursera MOOC titled The History and Future of (Mostly) Higher Education by Cathy Davidson. In this sense, my graduate course was both an introduction to methods and theories in the digital humanities, as well as an encouraged self-meditation by my students on how they were learning and why they were learning, as well as thinking critically about the educational system that they had grown up in. While I originally conceived of the course as a hybrid graduate seminar that would meet online three times a month and one time a month face-to-face, feedback from my students led me to change this to a face-to-face weekly course.

The History and Future of (Mostly) Higher Education only took up six weeks of the course, after which we turned back to digital humanities material to consider the intersections of our critique of the industrial system of education with the digital humanities. The Coursera class devoted to historicizing the current model of most education systems as a Fordist industrial model, which placed focus on students as "products" all being "mass" educated in the same way. It invited the community that took the class—both on the Coursera network as well as the accompanying Humanities, Arts, Science, and Technology Alliance and Collaboratory (HASTAC) group that was set up for it—to participate in a massive redesign of this industrial model. Key group learning assignments that all course students were asked to take part in involved coming up with their own joint "class manifesto," remixing their syllabus, and deciding on their own "grading contracts." My students also read and watched the core content from the Coursera course, which included assigned readings that were made available freely, as well as instructional videos made by Davidson for distribution through the Coursera website.

My experience with The History and Future of (Mostly) Higher Education was very different from the one I had with the FemTechNet nodal group:

the emphasis on decentering the instructor and creating an active learning community was much more successful in the former than in the latter. A number of reasons accounted for this difference. First, I taught The History and Future of (Mostly) Higher Education as a graduate seminar with a small enrollment of only six students, compared with *Seminar in Feminist Theory*, which enrolled thirty students and was an undergraduate class. The small number worked in favor of the former, allowing them to bond quickly and to come together as a community.

Secondly, the "key learning activities" from Davidson's Coursera course directly invited students to practice the two central elements of transformative feminist pedagogy: (1) to decentralize the teacher's authority and (2) to focus on the classroom community as invested, self-directed learners who would learn from each other and not simply the professor. These "key learning activities" were getting students to form their own (1) class manifesto, (2) syllabus remix, and (3) grading contracts. To encourage my students to take on more autonomy, I left them alone to complete all three activities on different days, only returning to the discussion in the last half hour of class. I also left them with some examples of each exercise that Davidson had shared on HASTAC as a template that they could reuse or model off if they wanted to.

I was amazed by the degree of engagement and motivation these key learning activities generated in my students, and how well they took to them to genuinely take their own leadership in the classroom. Below I list some highlights from their class manifesto and grading contracts that they generated on their own (italics mine):

[From Their Class Manifesto:]

AMST 5011 is an experimental graduate level course committed to identifying, evaluating, creating and rethinking solutions to educational challenges that our changing society faces in the twenty-first century. We aim to seize opportunities to fully realize and harness the possibilities of twenty-first-century literacies, which we define as the mindsets, skills, and collaborative techniques needed to make full use of the Internet as a space of learning. We believe that the Internet and technology are changing how individuals and communities understand themselves and the world around them, and that this connected age offers a tremendous opportunity to make teaching, learning, and knowledge more accessible, more affordable, and more meaningful for everyone involved. *AMST 5011's purpose is to examine the ways in which technology influences educational dynamics and to collaboratively propose and share new possibilities for the Information Age so that we—scholars, teachers, and students—can best respond collectively to the challenges this new paradigm poses for learning.*

AMST 5011 Class Goals and Practices for the Semester (Spring 2014)

- Create an evolving individual online presence aimed at advancing our digital literacy to exemplify the possibilities of technology in higher education.
- Collaborate in a constructive manner as we assign, guide, and assess the work of peers.
- Practice judicious time management in assigning tasks to others and completing our own.
- Arrive to class on time, fully prepared to participate, having completed assignments on time.
- Represent ourselves and the class both online and face-to-face as engaged scholars who are committed to advancing the above principles.

[From Their Grading Contracts:]

Contract Grading + Peer Evaluation: Explanation and Contract

Evaluation Method:
You determine your grade for this course by fulfilling a contract that spells out in advance the requirements as well as the penalties for not fulfilling the terms of your contract.

Learning together giving and receiving feedback is the core concept of our class. Every student will be responsible for submitting to Professor Koh anonymous peer-grading of his classmates twice this semester, a midterm evaluation (due by March 7th) and the final (due by April 23d). A peer grader will evaluate the work of his / her classmates using Satisfactory / Unsatisfactory descriptive evaluation format (up to 300 words). The unsatisfactory midterm peer assessment is intended to provide the opportunity for a student to improve his / her performance by the final evaluation. In case of a student receiving an Unsatisfactory peer evaluation, recommendations for improvements are to be determined by the peers collaboratively. *The goal is for everyone to produce satisfactory work, and the peers will work with each student to achieve that goal.*

The advantage of contract grading is that, the student, decides how much work he/she wishes to do this semester; if the work is completed on time and satisfactorily, the student will receive the grade for which he / she contracted. This means planning ahead, thinking about all of the obligations and responsibilities this semester and also determining desired grade in the course.

More than any course I have ever taught, the students in this class used these key learning activities to take control of their own learning. The levels of engagement that resulted were very impressive, as well as the level of commitment most students showed both to the class itself as well as the learning and welfare of the other students.

Importantly, though, this class worked well in terms of restructuring my class at Stockton University *internally* but not in terms of commitment with the rest of the HASTAC network that the Coursera course had generated. My students did not decenter authority in the HASTAC learning community; simply they applied these key concepts to radically change their experience of a classroom at Stockton.

My Feminist Pedagogy and Its Lack of Digital Embodiment

These two experiments to implement digital feminist pedagogy yielded very different results in my courses. In the Coursera course, class authority structures shifted greatly, and students experienced much higher levels of engagement than in any courses I have taught. This was not the case for the majority of the Feminist Theory course that I taught under the aegis of the FemTech-Net DOCC.

Several factors account for this difference. First, my Coursera course was a lot smaller than the FemTechNet DOCC course and was taught at the graduate level, where I felt free to give my students much more autonomy that I generally do at the undergraduate level. Second, the key learning activities that I employed using the Coursera course actually helped me to achieve the feminist goals of decentering authority and fostering community—while the FemTechNet activities I employed helped boost community, they did not radically change classroom dynamics in relation to transformational feminist pedagogy in quite the same way. My students who took part in the Coursera course also used much more of the core materials for the class from Coursera itself, as opposed to the Feminist Theory class, where I felt compelled to cover the content generally taught in a standard section of such a class. Because of all these divergent factors, my Coursera course managed to more effectively cover feminist pedagogy goals, compared with that of my FemTechNet nodal course.

It is important to note, however, that I concentrated efforts in both my classes on embodiment *in the physical classroom*, and only used the digital network as a supplement for the course. While each course had online components, they were both "hybrid"—meaning that the physical face-to-face component was still essential to decentering authority and building community. Neither course spent enough effort in trying to engaging with the digital space as the default medium of communication; in all honesty because the efforts I was undertaking to change the structure of my face-to-face classroom already seemed too radical to some of my students, and I was afraid of overwhelming them with too much change. Thus, while they both provided, to varying degrees of success, an alternative to Freire's "banking system" and Davidson's "industrial system" of education, I did not have to fully grapple with the tensions (and learning opportunities) that result when education takes place in a fully digital space, without the comfortable medium of the face-to-face setting to fall back to.

From these two experiments, I have learned the following and would recommend this to others wishing to experiment with digital feminist pedagogy. First, make the key learning activities for your classroom central to decentering instructor authority and about building community. The exercises Davidson used in her MOOC/DOCC, specifically the class manifesto and grading contracts, were invaluable to deeply transforming the environment of my classes. Secondly, build in more of the class where students have to directly engage with the larger digital network—be it either through low-stakes assignments or more comprehensive group activities. I regretted not encouraging my students in both instances to take advantage of the vast network and to see themselves as joint learners in a greater community of knowledge.

I also note the following two challenges. First, students who are used to and have benefited from the traditional system of learning may resist this pedagogy as it goes against what they are used to. Second, the two aspects of feminist pedagogy that I consider central take up a great deal of instructional time, as students rearrange class dynamics and learn to listen to one another differently. Instructors who want to cover as much as possible in their classes might find the time this recalibration takes place to be frustrating.

In sum, though, the horizon for digital feminist pedagogy is bright and encouraging, particularly with networks of teacher-scholars such as HAS-TAC and FemTechNet willing to participate and experiment in this method of teaching. I look forward to reading about future experiments and learning from them.

References

Christensen, Gayle and Brandon Alcorn. 2014. "Online University Courses Can't Change the World Alone." *New Scientist*, March 5. https://www.newscientist.com/article/mg22129590-200-online-university-courses-cant-change-the-world-alone/

Davidson, Cathy. "History and Future of (Mostly) Higher Education." 2014. https://online.duke.edu/projects/history-future-mostly-higher-education/.

FemTechNet. 2014a. "About the Network." http://femtechnet.org/about/.

———. 2014b. "Key Learning Projects." http://femtechnet.org/get-involved/self-directed-learners/key-learning-project/.

———. 2014c. "What is a DOCC?" http://femtechnet.org/docc/.

Freire, Paulo. 1996. *Pedagogy of the Oppressed*. London: Penguin.

hooks, bell. 1994. *Teaching to Transgress: Education as the Practice of Freedom*. New York: Routledge.

Parr, Chris. 2013. "Not Staying the Course: New Study Examines the Low Completion Rates of MOOCs." *Inside Higher Education*, May 10. https://www.insidehighered.com/news/2013/05/10/new-study-low-mooc-completion-rates.

Shrewsbury, Carolyn M. 1987. "What Is Feminist Pedagogy?" *Women's Studies Quarterly* 15 (3/4): 6–14.

9

Epistemologies of Doing: Engaging Online Learning through Feminist Pedagogy

RADHIKA GAJJALA, ERIKA M. BEHRMANN,
ANCA BIRZESCU, ANDREW CORBETT,
AND KAYLEIGH FRANCES BONDOR

"Seriously? You're on Yik Yak? That's crazy!," said K, an undergraduate student in my class, when I mentioned the use of Yik Yak as a potential activity for a future class.

As various modes of technology become more pervasive, self-reflexive and ethical communication become a key issue in the classroom. As we write this chapter it is against the backdrop of many scandals involving Yik Yak in which peaceful protestors of Colgate College were defamed with racist commentary (Koenig 2014) and in which three professors at Eastern Michigan University were attacked with sexist and hostile Yik Yak tweets during an honors lecture that included over two hundred students (Schmidt 2015). The negative attention toward Yik Yak has even led some schools to consider banning Yik Yak. Yet, is this the most effective way to educate students?

As a student from the class who is also now one of our coauthors, Kayleigh, notes in response to the work done in this class, such an approach to teaching becomes important and necessary because, "This is the generation that will soon be controlling online spaces without realizing the implications because, as they see it, 'everyone' has a laptop, cell-phone, and other mediated technologies." The class we refer to was a class on intercultural communication that was taught in fall 2014. In this class, students were asked to examine how sociocultural power systems exist within the coding and usage of various technologies. These technologies include Yik Yak, the various forms of selfies, and Wikipedia. Although, the course itself was not a massive open online course (MOOC), we argue that the pedagogical methods used in this course can, and should, be applied to the MOOC moment. Whether it is the MOOC where many students share their acquired knowledge as a whole,

Wikipedia where writers are documenting knowledge, or Yik Yak where students are shaping cultural knowledge, all three share the commonality of crowdsourcing. Furthermore, all three were designed without cognizance of how sociocultural power operates in mediated spaces. This chapter examines feminist pedagogical engagements with online tools in a seated class context where the class assignments were designed specifically to explore power differentials within technological spaces. The first author of this chapter was the instructor, while the second and third authors were observers. These three authors have varied levels of experience teaching in US educational institutions. The fourth author is a master's student who comes to the class with life experience that contributes to his understanding of university pedagogy in a more sophisticated way than is the case for most master's students who come straight from undergraduate education. The last author is the youngest member of the team and an undergraduate student who was a very lively and enthusiastic member of the class.

In the context of what Elizabeth Losh refers to as the "MOOC moment" in organizing this collection and after, our exploration and discussion pushes toward a rethinking of the disembodied learning and teaching practices that seem to have been perpetuated through the standardization of online teaching. We are not critiquing the MOOC model per se. To simplify and flatten the MOOC model as a straw opponent to the points we try to make would be disregarding the amount of hard and sincere work put in by coders, designers, educators, and administrators in experimenting with that model. The crucial work of coders, designers, software developers, and administrators is often not revealed in the way that much online education is discussed. If the work is spoken of it is usually dismissed as background work on the one hand or as controlling, counterproductive work on the other. Dismissing this crucial work of designing, setting up, and maintaining a learning management system not only does injustice to those who are making honest efforts to work with educators to give us what we might need but also dismisses the need for educators to work collaboratively with these behind-the-scenes workers.

But do we think that all MOOCs are wonderful, however? No. But they are an iteration of online teaching and an attempt at spreading knowledge in a particular way, and not all fell into the trap of transmitting knowledge and exploiting crowdsourcing and underpaying teaching assistants. Some did—but not all. Yet it is not only MOOCs that fall into this trap of exploitation of unpaid labor in the name of experimentation—this is built into contemporary forms of online prosumerism and occurs in various well-meaning settings. So there would be no sense in our pointing to only one model of teaching as exploitative of free labor.

The examples we look at in this chapter are a part of the experimentation and exploration that three of the coauthors have participated in at various levels and periods in their teaching and learning career. We draw on these in an effort to engage online activities of learning. Thus in trying to think of what comes after the MOOC moment we return to an emphasis on the embodied aspect of *doing* as integral to the process of learning. The next wave of digitally mediated classroom may take on/continue Wikipedia editing, as well as the use of selfies, Yik Yak and/or Snapchat in different ways, or it may refocus on innovative uses of discussion boards and online chat and video. Whatever the technology, if we focus these explorations through an engagement with epistemologies of doing, class, access, literacy, and multiple cultures of entry, the next moments in learning through digital technologies may allow us to unpack our understandings of and reveal our very own biases in seeing binaries of men's work and women's work in these settings. Not all feminists may agree on process, product, or implementation, but there will be valuable learning and engagement. Feminists teaching in these contexts have differing opinions on safe spaces and maintenance of instructor power in the classroom. For instance, Kishimoto and Mwangi (2009) ask "if it was possible to really create a 'safe' classroom. If it is possible, who creates it? Do faculty have the power and authority to create a 'safe' environment?" (87). Feminist pedagogues also have differing opinions on how the teacher's authority should be used in the feminist classroom. Feminists such as Luke and Gore (2014) claim that avoidance of authority places the teacher in the subject position of nurturer and the student as the object of nurturance, which may or may not be a productive relationship for learning. Yet even given differing opinions on some basic issues such as how to wield authority in the classroom and how to maintain safe spaces—which take on additional nuances in a fully online setting—feminist experimentation in various modes of teaching and learning provides valuable insight into techniques for inclusion and transformation. Complexity and diversity in teaching through such frameworks creates dynamic learning environments. Feminist pedagogy as a whole, therefore, has allowed for complexity in thought and action working against the flattening of, and elision of, issues around race, class, sexuality, and geography through the use digital technologies.

The use of the latest and cutest form of information exchange or gadget/ thing to play with is not what we emphasize, even if our examples take on contemporary technologies. Rather, in our exploration and thinking through of newer interfaces, the basic underlying feminist pedagogy of doing and engaging returns us to the last twenty years of work by feminist scholars, practitioners, and teachers using online technology for empowerment (and who call themselves "cyberfeminists"). These individuals learn from participatory frameworks developed by fan communities and others—crowdsourcing in their organic every day in efforts to negotiate the use of these technologies. This allows us to simultaneously gain a close involved understanding and a critical thoughtful distance in relation to multiple entry points into these environments.

We find, for instance, that many universal forms of technology often fail to receive attention from educators because they are uncertain territory for the educators themselves. In this essay the coauthors occupy multiple identities in a tiered hierarchy of teaching and learning. For instance, Andy was a student in one of the classes we write about along with Kayleigh; yet because the course was an undergraduate-to-masters bridge course, Andy enters our collaboration as a master's student who teaches classes (offered to majors and as general education classes) in American Culture Studies. Ostensibly he ends up with considerable more life experience than Kayleigh who is a sophomore entering college straight after high school. Other coauthors are also both students and instructors, with Anca having recently graduated with a PhD in media and communication, and Erika doing her coursework toward her doctoral degree. Radhika, on the other hand, might claim to be a student of life but it has been over a decade since Radhika was in a formal classroom as student. Yet, because of the tiered nature of this collaboration, the collaboration itself becomes a space of learning and engagement for the five of us.

In the case of those of us who teach in a formal classroom, we are required to hold firm authoritative ground in front of our students, and therefore we often hesitate to enter into spaces where we are not already experts. However, if we do not enter environments in which we ourselves are uncomfortable in or need to learn to maneuver we are at a disadvantage. This is why educators are required to be researchers as well. We must learn about things happening around us in context to teach our students how to face the real world. In the current ethos of online teaching and learning, we are often painted as nonexperts because academics do not inhabit the supposed "real world" of corporate technology use, nor are we part of the generations named as "digital natives." Digital natives, Shah and Abraham (2009) note, are young consumers of digital gadgets. The phrase is based on Mark Prensky's (2001) use of the phrase as a way of identifying a new demography for markets to focus on and "refers to 'populations born after the 1980s'" who "at face value—have contributed to the growing discourse on Digital Natives." Thus, even though there is much debate on whether these generations are actually digitally adept even though they are comfortable in their use of digital technologies as consumers, the fact remains that these young people are growing up in a world where our everyday is enveloped in communicative and interactional logics shaped through digital ontologies. This means that our challenge in teaching this generation is often about methods and process, while making them look at their gadgets in less taken-for-granted ways.

As we bring in these technologies into classroom settings and enter the play spaces of our students and try to repurpose them in pedagogical contexts, we often face contradictions. We enter these spaces ourselves—the teachers—as experimenters and researchers even as we ourselves are immersed in the use of these technologies in our everyday. Because we are learning to use these technologies simultaneously with our students or sometimes after they have encountered them, we risk appearing like amateurs in the use of these technologies. Thus sometimes educators that venture into these spaces also make the mistake of privileging student experience as that of "digital native" expertise rather than use our own theoretical and academic experience and research insights to help the students contextualize and think through their engagement with these new forms. Yet, as danah boyd (2015) notes, "Just because teens are comfortable using social media to hang out does not mean that they're fluent in or with technology. Many teens are not nearly as digitally adept as the often-used assumption that they are 'digital natives' would suggest."

For example, using selfies to examine the process of meaning making and contestation, as well as emerging forms of social exchange, is rarely seen as a valid teaching tool or method. Through the lens of education as transmission of information (which is implicit in the distance-learning model that MOOCs are premised on), selfies are perceived as nonserious. Selfies are acknowledged as tools for networking and marketing within the global entrepreneurial market economy ethos—so they do get used in the classroom and are studied as modes of communication. Even though some MOOCs have used them as objects of study and as a process of interaction, such as University of Maryland's Android Capstone Project that has a unit on selfies, these course modules rarely focus on a critical engagement with selfies as representative of an embodied and as everyday practice that shapes the epistemology of knowledge as well as information transfer and circulation.

Yet scholars such as Theresa Senft and Jill Walker Rettberg (2015) who were part of a team of Internet researchers who set up the selfieresearchers .com site have used this contemporary practice and made it into a mode of teaching and learning about a variety of interrelated subject areas from art to everyday popular culture or the quantification and coding of identity for surveillance and governmentality. They, along with a team of media scholars from across various time zones, developed and taught the Selfie Course modules[1] in fall 2014 to try to dismantle the notion of the information delivery paradigm by putting selfies at the center of research. The course focused on two main questions. First, how do selfies speak as cultural objects? Second, what methods might we develop to better understand what is being said? Both questions circumscribe the primary theme of the course, which is to better understand selfies as a discourse, evidence, affect, ethics, and performance/presentation of one's self. Similar to Yik Yak and MOOCs, selfies also are shaped through sociocultural systems in which structures of power form its usage and dissemination.

As Rettberg (2014) points out in her recent work, selfies serve a wide range of social, historical, and technical purposes and are part of an emerging record of contemporary life. Knowing this and being aware of this, how might we convey an understanding of the sociocultural, political, and historic importance of such contemporary practices? Is it enough to crowdsource in masses the information (however well presented and coded) and prior publications on these subject matters? What affordances exist in the use of the practice itself to think through various theoretical concepts such as representation of self and other, as well as the datafication of everyday activities? Thus the scholars who set up the Selfie Course put out modules online but, in practice, there were multiple possible embodied negotiations and results that emerged from the use of this material in diverse locations where the course was used freely.

In translating the research on self-presentation into the classroom, for instance, using Snapchat and selfies, which are seen as ephemeral technologies, we have found students responses to be overwhelmingly positive—not because it is a format that is "fun" or that they consider themselves as expert users of these modes of digital self-representation, but rather because they were delighted to be making connections with serious academic work and theoretical frameworks from within the course subject matter through platforms that, for at least several of them, were everyday platforms. They faced the challenge of negotiating the formal classroom space through informal social technologies and worked through these concerns in ways that they themselves began to realize would be highly relevant and beneficial to them as they stepped out into the real world of paid work and professionalization. Using these technologies as a site for knowledge is often overlooked by

---

1. The Selfie Course was created by the following individuals: Theresa Senft, Jill Walker Rettberg, Elizabeth Losh, Kath Albury, Radhika Gajjala, Gaby David, Alice Marwick, Crystal Abidin, Magda Olszanowski, Fatima Aziz, Katie Warfield, and Negar Mottahedeh. The course can be accessed at http://www.selfieresearchers.com/the-selfie-course/.

learning management systems of MOOCs since they center their structure on the dissemination of content instead of learning through experience and doing. Thus, for instance, by using Snapchat in the classroom, the pervasive element that transpires is *awareness* (Losh 2014). We must be aware of the space beyond self-preservation. Instead we want students to look for a more community-based responsibility in a global world. Snapchat gives opportunities to draw on individual experiences while adding a community component. Students become aware of lives outside their own experiences that are often masked in a traditional seated classroom and even in an online class set up as just information exchange—be it a MOOC or some other kind of online class.

Similarly, we have found that the best pedagogical practices enter technological spaces and examine identity formation, sociocultural history, and context. In fall 2014 a group of professors from Colgate University decided to respond to harmful posts on Yik Yak, a platform in which students are able to post anonymous comments about their local community. Originally intended as a confessions website, Yik Yak quickly became a space full of racist and sexist posts. These posts catalyzed a hundred-hour sit-in that challenged the university's racist policies and practices (Koenig 2014). It was then that biology professor Jeff Holm decided to "occupy" Yik Yak with twenty other colleagues during finals week. Their bombarding posts focused on positive messages (like wishing students luck on finals) and subverting anonymity by posting their name. Although well intended, we would like to expand on this moment and suggest that "occupying" Yik Yak is not enough. Merely posting positive messages on Yik Yak does not examine the sociocultural structures that shape race and identity in this cyberspace. Moreover, this misses opportunities to give students the space to build their own conclusions about their personal identity, self-presentation, and marginalized voices.

The five coauthors of this chapter hail from four generations of feminist and queering experience with education and technology. The professor teaching in this mode for over eighteen years, the postdoctoral independent researcher who has been working with the professor in her classes over the past five years, the second-year doctoral student working on gender, gaming, and feminist pedagogy issues, the master's student who straddles the identity of student and teacher, and the undergraduate student who was a member of the fall 2014 class referenced above, all offer insight and retrospective reflection into the pedagogical process. We felt it was important to give credit to our student's thoughts and ideas in the writing process. After all, we are feminist teachers, and writing a feminist pedagogy piece without student feedback and coauthoring might seem a bit of a contradiction. In what follows, we first lay the background to this pedagogy of "epistemologies of doing" and "cyberfeminist tactics" using the experience from Radhika's prior teaching and research. We follow this more theoretical section with a second part of the article where we draw from examples in the fall 2014 class on intercultural communication taught by Radhika to tease out some themes.

Since the mid-1990s, we noted a sense of urgency and rush toward moving our millennial students (and the future workforce) toward Internet connectivity so we could help our students understand the use and its implications of various kinds of technologies. Yet now in 2014, in the techno-saturated milieu, students rarely come to office hours and prefer to send text messages to their instructors rather than check their email for an announcement, let alone look for answers in the (often) largely detailed syllabus uploaded as a PDF in their course-management portal. In the present essay, Radhika narrates her journey into the world of computers as a writer and as a teacher with a focus on issues of access. She encountered many issues over the years as a (cyber)-feminist pedagogue while navigating Internet-facilitated teaching and learning. Together, all five of us ask: What do we mean by global access and distribution of knowledge in this paradigm? How is knowledge building and circulation shaped through an informationalized economy where the visual and textual streaming of anything might be mistaken for actual knowledge or dissemination of truth? What are the challenges in such a context for critical and feminist pedagogy? Internet-facilitated information production and distribution is often described through the use of terms such as global access and knowledge flows. We speak of shifting paradigms of teaching and learning. Yet where is this knowledge flowing to and from? Why is it flowing, if indeed it is flowing? What is shifting our teaching? Is it the technological platforms based in situated design or the ideas of inclusion and access coming to us through grassroots movements that challenges power through social media? Is anonymity or pseudoanonymity a boon or a curse? What are we missing when we treat digitally mediated existence and our digital everyday as a "virtuality" outside our "reality" when we teach in class?

In this article, we raise critical concerns about the shifts in the way teachers are encouraged to use digital technologies. These are shifts that lead to the current MOOC paradigm where "massive" dissemination and crowdsourcing is considered/mistaken as "participation" and "inclusion." We also question the hierarchies of collaboration and access and ask whether these modes of teaching inevitably reinscribe colonial frameworks packaged in neoliberal individual empowerment discourse of participation. We leave the readers with questions and problems in the hope that we can together work on finding answers.

Drawing from Experience

RADHIKA

Drawing on my own twenty-five-year history of living on the edge of the computer screen, speaking, writing, and teaching with keyboard-facilitated strokes, I question the encouragement for educators to shift to digital technology. Every academic year, if not every semester, since 1995 when I was first permitted to incorporate web bulletin boards and text-based MOOs (early multiuser domains with object-oriented features) in my teaching as a graduate student at the University of Pittsburgh, I have reworked my course syllabi (whatever the topic of the course may be) to include a current online mode of interaction as a site of study and ethnographic/immersive engagement. Further, as Bryce Peake (2014), a guest presenter in one of these classes and close advisor on the Wikipedia assignment, notes, "Ethnography exceeds the capacities of quantitative—especially 'big data'—methods, providing a snap shot of those 'power plays' and conflict in action." Even in present times when online interaction for teaching and learning is standardized through course-management tools such as Blackboard and Canvas, I make it a point to try and design activities using online, digital, or wireless tools based in mobile gadgets of some sort in a way that students may not all be comfortable with or familiar with as producers. In some cases the tool is something they use every day but have not thought about in ways that my class assignment requires them to, such as when I've asked them to use Snapchat, *Second Life*, or a gaming platform of their choice for a class assignment. In such assignments, it is the way I design the assignment and require them to explore the environment/tool that allows them to rethink and situate that particular tool or gadget in the context of the class content and course goals.

In some cases, and for some students, the very technology or software introduced in class is new. Thus in classes I taught between 1997 and 2004, when I taught using text-based MOOs (using LinguaMOO for the most part), hardly anyone but a very few of the class members had ever heard about the environment. Using these digital tools in a communication disciplinary context is easy because all these tools are about communicating. But most often teaching about this tools is done in a "how to" fashion. Although there are MOOCs that are more focused on applied communication, such as West Chester University's MOOC entitled A World of Difference: Exploring Intercultural Communication (Tomsen 2015), because these tools used from a producer frame are perceived as "doing technology" in an engineering or technical sense, there never ceases to be a question (or many questions) about why we are using these tools in class. It is also likely that the question about the use of these tools in class context arises because of the way in which the assignments frame their use. The tools are not there for skill gathering in a functional way (although that happens anyway and the smartest of the students are quick to realize and appreciate the real-world-skill-acquiring aspect and potential of the assignments). The tools are introduced in class strategically so as to make the students think about issues of access, power relations, hierarchies of literacy, culture and society, and so on.

ERIKA [2]

MOOCs have had a short, but complicated, history. Many view MOOCs as a liberatory form of education for the masses while others are more hesitant. Notably, few critics of MOOCs have acknowledged the deep-seated past of challenging top-down systems of education steered by feminists for almost a century. As a budding feminist teacher, I have learned that *connection* is central to feminist pedagogy (Sandal 1991). By this, I mean that feminist scholarship has advocated that, as humans, we draw from our own experiences and understandings. Eliminating connection (an often criticized element of MOOCs) takes away some of the most rewarding parts of education: to be able to inspire, educate, and learn with our students. Notably there are various forms of MOOCs (including traditional top-down xMOOCs that imitate conventional college courses and the more connective peer-to-peer cMOOCs that use social media practices for informal learning), so it would be problematic to assume that all MOOCs fail to examine connections between student and teacher. Yet, what is central to feminist pedagogy is the constant reflexivity of power and privilege. Although cMOOCs encourage autonomy, diversity, openness, and interactivity (as described by Downes 2012), most do not consider the various sociocultural issues raised in this essay.

Moreover, as Radhika (and several other individuals involved with Fem-TechNet) have shown, students need to be a part of the education process. Adrienne Rich (1977) once said students need to "claim an education" rather than "receive one." Yet, how do feminist educators work with structural systems that draw from a techno-deterministic ideology that presumes MOOCs to be liberating? Feminist pedagogues have argued that students need to help build and create their own learning spaces. This is why Wikipedia editing has

2. Erika has been working with Radhika and independently as a FemTechNet member in implementing some related assignments.

been such a useful assignment. Radhika initially developed a feminist process for her Wikipedia assignments to be used in her classes when she and Alexandra Juhasz (of Pitzer College) taught a beta version of FemTechNet's distributed open collaborative course (DOCC) in tandem with one another's courses. The syllabus for the course Feminist Dialogues in Technology was also codeveloped and expanded by other beta experiments in classes taught by Elizabeth Losh, Lisa Cartwright, Tara McPherson, and others. When Radhika worked on developing the details of this assignment, she received help and advice from other collaborators, such as Nishant Shah who had implemented Wikipedia editing pedagogically in workshop and classroom contexts in Bangalore, India; Adrianne Wadewitz who was working with the FemTechNet team; Sarah Stierch who was working with the Fembot Collective; and Bryce Peake who was the then-webmistress for Fembot and for *ADA: Journal of Gender and New Media*. This syllabus and the assignments developed were meant to be models for what was to be a pilot for a DOCC model of open-access teaching.[3]

The Wikipedia assignment in this particular class was structured around the course's main theme: intercultural communication in global contexts. This meant that students were to edit and observe how participation in wiki editing lead to intercultural encounter (in the talk feature of Wikipedia), as well as build from global knowledge. Students had to think through what this meant. The exercise was a challenge to the expectations in a class of students (even when they were international students) who expected to stay on stable ground observing and learning about intercultural Others and their communication patterns. Andy and Kayleigh who were students in this class have noted the transformative potential of this assignment even though the assignment itself required very basic and routine (weekly) Wikipedia editing from students. The students had to self-learn and thus challenge themselves and their peers because of their own curiosity, interest, and drive. They also began to understand that Wikipedia was not just a given form of knowledge—rather it existed because people like them contributed to it.

By structuring course material around techno-artifacts central to student lives, the everyday, mundane technology becomes the epicenter of learning. To my surprise, when I discuss Wikipedia in my classroom, most of my students know very little. Many don't read Wikipedia because they have been told since high school (or, for some, elementary school) that Wikipedia is

---

3. The leadership of Anne Balsamo, Sharon Irish, Alexandra Juhasz, Elizabeth Losh, Lisa Nakamura, and Carol Stabile have helped spearhead FemTechNet (http://femtechnet.org/) and the Fembot Collective (http://fembotcollective.org).

biased. This is where the conversation stops. I ask them to elaborate on this and very few are able to.

By using Wikipedia as an artifact, we can easily see how digital formations are grounded in social structures. The talk tab on Wikipedia alone offers great insight into how neutrality is illusory. Neutrality would imply that all voices are heard on equal grounds. However, women and individuals of color are often left out of Wikipedia's archives because of a lack of exposure or through categorizing women and individuals of color as Other.

One can draw parallels between how the structure of Wikipedia and MOOCs operate. They both function through forms of crowdsourcing and by requiring self-learning. In a sense they adopt a neoliberal, prosumer model (Bruns 2009) where the contradiction of individual control over learning encounters online surveillance and digital platform design. Algorithm and community bylaws together produce opaque hierarchies and invisible control over the process where the rules of so-called open participation and the level playing field have the potential to exploit and oppress. Yet, whether it is the bylaws for Wikipedia about unbiased editing or the professor's rubric, both online platforms possess a gatekeeper. As Peake (2015) points out, "rules of reason" are often used as a tool for Wikipedians to assert power over knowledge production. In his example on sexual assault, Wikipedia was not concerned with the veracity of the information but rather if Wikipedia should be a site to host that form of knowledge production—one that draws attention to sexual assault on campus. Similarly, MOOCs often disseminate labor among students. Students often are required to comment, edit, and even grade other student's work. Yet, despite its decentralization of labor, its centralization of power still exists as MOOCs render very little opportunity for knowledge production beyond the limits of the MOOC's objective. Furthermore, both promote education through the guise of neutrality. The MOOC professor assumes the position of the omnipotent gatekeeper of knowledge who draws from fact. Similarly, Wikipedia expects its twenty-two million editors to do the same. Therefore, how is it possible to encourage feminist epistemology when the structures of MOOCs minimize the ability for students to alter and shift course content to empower marginalized voices? It is my hope that through feminist rebuilding of the MOOC through carefully planned assignments and the DOCC by FemTechNet, we will move toward a more equitable way of knowing.

ANDREW

The creation of an active learning space is central to feminist pedagogical techniques as Erika pointed out above by invoking feminist scholars and members of FemTechNet. It encourages the learner to be engaged in learning and the production of knowledge from start to finish. It is also, largely, a form of pedagogy with which the average American student is unlikely to be familiar. Educator and scholar John Taylor Gatto (2003), an advocate for homeschooling, unschooling (a learning method that encourages learner chosen activities), and open-source learning states that the American school system has three purposes that are "roughly" the following: to make good people, to make good citizens, and to make each person his or her personal best. While these may seem laudable goals, in practice the American education system, up until postsecondary education by and large is focused on the first two of these goals, while the third falls by the wayside. Gatto invokes H. L. Mencken's writings in *The American Mercury* in 1924 by stating that the true aim of public education is not knowledge creation and awakened intelligence but rather to create an easily controlled and standardized citizenry. Because students are fed information, facts, and scripts for behavior in the classroom that amount to a schema for learning to pay attention, be quiet, and do not question authority, they are filled with trepidation when they are asked to be responsible for their own learning.

Wikipedia editing is a perfect site for students to begin claiming responsibility for their own learning and a place to combat that trepidation. It serves a dual purpose in that it forces the student to actively contribute to the creation of knowledge by requiring edits to get credit for the assignment and that it serves as an introduction to the negotiations that we must go through when producing knowledge. As I worked on my own edits for Radhika's class, in which I was one of several graduate students mixed in with undergraduates, I noticed several trends in the undergraduates' work. In the class discussion boards, several students indicated apprehension about editing actual content, preferring instead to edit grammar. This reluctance to generate knowledge and content seems to point to the idea that education as empowerment is failing in traditional pedagogy, as these students trust neither their own authorship nor their ability to research and provide sources to back up that authorship. They also reported a discomfort with the idea of making mistakes and being chastised by wiki users for their errors. Fortunately though, Wikipedia offers a relatively low-stakes environment for empowerment by allowing for pages and edits to be reverted to previous states. It does not erase the complex epistemic negotiations of the production of knowledge on Wikipedia, but it does somewhat ameliorate them. It offers a low-pressure entry point, despite student claims of anxiety, into the complex world of knowledge production, and how and why that knowledge is produced.

KAYLEIGH[4]

Radhika's course assignments frequently required students to place their physical bodies into online spaces. For students to register a space in online worlds such as Wikipedia, they created "user names" linking their real persons to their respective online accounts. Thus, our first classroom task—the seemingly mundane act of creating a user name—served as a key component to our creation of an online identity. I initially took for granted the fact that many of us borrowed from aspects of our real, physical selves as we began to craft our online identities.

The importance of our real identities in navigating virtual identities quickly emerged. One person placed the word "brown" in her user name to denote her skin color. Others used a combination of letters and sounds from their legal names, paired with clandestine numbers referencing, perhaps, important dates or ages. Already our real intersecting identities of age, name, and race were becoming important in our navigation of online spaces. This navigation was sometimes hindered because of other aspects of our identities, particularly in the arena of technological literacy.

Students completed assignments through their virtual selves with varying degrees of success, which depended greatly on the abilities and agencies of their real selves. The presence of a gendered body, for example, became important. A white male discussed his lack of identification with an assignment involving a Wikipedia movement that sought to create articles about notable global female figures of ethnic minorities. Like many others in the class, the student's various lack of identification with the assignment's target population led to an inability to fully understand that resulted in a lack of interest.

Even when his gendered, raced (male, white) body was not blatantly present online, it was also not absent. Those aspects of him directly affected how he would interact with assignment materials in cyberspace. This trend of indirect identity impacts emerged, too, when students were tasked with editing Wikipedia articles of our choice. In the initial editing process, many of us chose topics with which we were comfortable—movies, movements, subjects, or objects that reflected our interests and external realities on which we

4. Kayleigh was an undergraduate student in the fall 2014 class taught by Radhika.

forged our identities. We thus continued to feed into these comfortable topics, furthering our identification with them and, perhaps most importantly, our un-identification with absent others.

Further, many of us began our editing assignment with minor grammatical edits fueled by a fear of incorrectly attempting to make a well-meaning yet ultimately wrong major edit. Our un-identities as Wikipedia editors reflected both our lack of agency and knowledge in editing, but also ultimately hindered potential growth in learning these skills. As many of us settled with becoming proud at successfully inserting a comma into a Wikipedia article or successfully summarizing our online endeavors in the virtual classroom space, I cannot help but wonder if we stunted our ability to further our knowledge (and subsequent knowledge sharing) by simply ending with the least possible contribution to receive the grade.

The weekly discussion posts began to serve as an outlet for students to contemplate inabilities and successes with the college's classroom operating software, with other online users, with moments of boredom, or with moments of discovery. Students discussed cognitive dissonance stemming from Wikipedia's policy of objectivity in creating a space where raced/gendered/classed bodies were not allowed, even though raced/gendered/classed bodies were always the ones contributing information.

As an entire generation becomes raised on technology, students discovered the illusion that the world rests at everyone's fingertips through the Internet is flawed. Through our online assignments, we discovered that the voices of millions of people who have access to the Internet continue to remain marginalized daily. The lack of a nongendered option in creating a user account, for example, excludes those whose identities do not fall on the gender binary. A website's policies written in highly technical language excludes those seeking valuable information in an accessible format. An Indonesian teenager researching World War II will likely find importance in a different narrative than a German teenager who is Jewish.

The policies seeking to equalize information are merely serving to perpetuate an unequal hierarchy. Millennials and those who follow must understand the complexity of identity within the real world and recognize its importance in the navigation of online spaces. Radhika's assignments, while educational and informational, seem to have served only to raise more questions about the implications of technologically mediated interactions rather than provide solutions.

Epistemologies of Doing and the Production of Selves

In developing these class assignments, our imperative was that students were thrown into some sort of unfamiliar zone as they engaged a particular technological interface. The unfamiliarity could be based in an element of surprise—"Yik Yak in a classroom?!"—which then leads to an unexpected use of traditional classroom assignment formats and textbooks. Thus the technological interface, because of its design, combined with the design of the assignment built around it for specific classroom subject matter, forces students (and instructors alike and in different ways) to negotiate cultural cues that function differently in familiar everyday life and reveals the process of production of our everyday culture.

For instance, as Pauline Hope Cheong and Kishonna Gray (2011) point out, "virtual worlds and their complex affordances for self-representations compel attention to the performances of online identities, which are still often constituted through gender, race, class, and other markers of difference" (266). This is brought into a setting where students are learning gender and communication or intercultural communication, thus allowing students to experience their everydayness in a way that permits them to see ruptures in the fabric of the "normal" around them. The instructor can then clearly use these ruptures as points of evidence to show students how the theories of social construction, or identity production and marginalization of specific groups, occur in day-to-day social interaction. Spaces for discussion and contestation are opened up which sometimes empowers the marginalized student, sometimes angers students from various backgrounds whether marginalized or not, and sometimes delight and make learning fun. When the instructor effectively manages the ensuing chaos and sudden outburst of energy and emotion—the instructor can channel these moments into intense learning moments. For example, Radhika requires contemplation and journal writing, however mundane the writing may seem when it is being done as a strategy for allowing students to settle down and sort through their encounters with these unusual classroom exercises. By the end of the semester, what may have seemed like "busy work" for some students results in learning evidenced through the papers they produce for class.

Epistemologies of doing suggest that the researcher/teacher and researcher/student must engage in the production of culture and subjectivity in the specific context while interacting with others who are doing the same. This enables them to really talk about the meaning making and the contestation of meaning that goes on while making visible at least some of the hierarchies.

ANCA[5]

Immersion in these digitally mediated spaces and collaborative engagement with these digital tools deeply resonates with the *learning-by-doing* desideratum that philosopher and educational reformer John Dewey (1916) advocated almost a century ago, which still remains a goal to be fulfilled despite the lures and promises of the network—horizontal, active, interactive, collaborative, participatory educational patterns assumed by the widely promoted massive online courses. Contrary to these assumptions, concerns are increasingly voiced about, according to Juhasz (2013), "the current MOOC-osphere, where for-profit or other highly-funded models are dominating the landscape and leading to top-down, static, one-way delivery flows that are surprisingly ill-suited for their web 2.0 home." Notably, the FemTechNet Whitepaper Committee (2013) draws attention to the tendency within the MOOCs education paradigm to ignore the value of knowledge as embodied learning and to perpetuate the limits of conventional education. The authors also stress the missed opportunities for transformative education—ideally informed by genuinely dialogic, collaborative interactions among students and teachers—since crowdsourcing and peer evaluation are used instead "as a labor management technique" (5).

Dewey's questions and statements are therefore as relevant for today's educational settings against the backdrop of a technological culture as they were one hundred years ago:

> Why is it that, in spite of the fact that teaching by pouring in, learning by passive absorption, are universally condemned, that they are still so entrenched in practice? That education is not an affair of "telling" and being told, but an active constructive process, is a principle almost as generally violated in practice as conceded in theory. . . . But its enactment in practice requires that the school environment be equipped with agencies for doing. . . . It requires that methods of instruction and administration be modified to allow and to secure continuous occupations with things. . . . These things mean equipment with the instrumentalities of cooperative or joint activity (1916, 46).

When translated to the diverse technological environments that the first author—and other cyberfeminist pedagogues alike—has relentlessly introduced to cohorts of students in her classes, the "continuous occupations with things" and the "instrumentalities of cooperative activity" urged by Dewey reflect very productively in the technospatial praxis in which students are

---

5. Anca has been working with Radhika for over six years both as student and collaborator in teaching innovations.

prompted to be a part of. This, oftentimes challenging, process of studying through "doing" becomes concurrently a fertile ground for subjectivity and meaning production where students are at once agents and subjects. Therefore, *epistemologies of doing*, coined by Gajjala and Altman (2006), were actively present in the classes where the Wikipedia editing assignment was incorporated.

One of the pedagogical projects Radhika invited me to collaborate on represented an action research study. Action research is different from conventional academic research since it is repurposed to yield practical knowledge and outcomes rather than findings only. It is a participatory undertaking that combines action and reflection and theory and practice "in the pursuit of practical solutions to issues of pressing concern to people, and more generally the flourishing of individual persons and their communities" (Reason and Bradbury 2008, 4). In the education setting, action research is usually used for "improving conditions and practice in classrooms" (Craig 2009, 3). Our collaborative inquiry aimed to assess some of the characteristics and outcomes of students' engagement with the Wikipedia editing assignment in one of Radhika's recent Intercultural Communication courses. The semester-long assignment required students to make weekly contributions (at first editing and, at later stages, content addition) to Wikipedia. One of the objectives of the assignment was to have students assess—also through their own content contribution to Wikipedia—the global knowledge production taking place on Wikipedia. The purpose of our action research was to acquire knowledge regarding the ways students perceive the complex process of Wikipedia editing. The thematic analysis of the weekly short journals that students posted on Canvas revealed four main themes that appeared to constitute students' different reactions, attitudes, and opinions in relation to the chronological sequencing of the Wikipedia assignment stages.

The first theme evoked students' surprise and frustration during the incipient stage of the project. Some students, for instance, expressed feelings of nervousness and being overwhelmed once they created their own Wikipedia accounts, given the multitude of options available for editing and the codes that showed up the moment they were typing in their content. Other students experienced frustration when their edits were changed or simply erased by other Wikipedia editors. The second theme reflected students' growing interest with editing during the stages when their edits, though not major, were not rejected by the Wikipedia editing community. The third theme corresponded to students becoming more comfortable and excited after realizing, despite times when their efforts were not productive, that they were more familiar with the rules and expectations for Wikipedia editing and that they had become content generators in an online space that has global visibility.[6] Finally, the fourth theme identified that students increasingly critically examined how knowledge is produced in the seemingly global, democratic space of Wikipedia.[7] Most importantly, these recurrent themes instantiate the reflective learning stages that students undertook whereby they analyzed their own technospatial praxis represented by their engagement with Wikipedia. These themes map the challenging and rewarding learning journey made possible by an *epistemologies of doing* methodology.

Critical Feminist Pedagogy

Critical pedagogy is rooted in Paulo Freire's (1971) canonical work. Freire draws a metaphor for the traditional education system. Like a bank, students sit patiently while teachers "deposit" information into the student's brains. This model is still commonly accepted today as student-to-faculty ratios become larger. Yet, what is most prominent about Freire's work is the concept that education can serve as a liberatory practice. His work argues that, "besides being an act of knowing, education is also a political act. That is why no pedagogy is neutral" (Freire and Shor 1987, 13).

Efforts are being undertaken to apply and adapt Freire's call to transform education arenas into prospective sites of resistance and liberation to today's technology-mediated education. In one instance that is relevant to our discussion, Sean Michael Morris and Jesse Stommel (2014) draw on Freire's principles to advance tentative strategies that can help to reimagine the current logics and goals of MOOCs. One thesis states that a course should be "a

6. Similarly to other classmates' postings, Andrew Corbett mentions about the phenomenon of patrolling: "I was patrolled earlier in the semester. I think it's just literally someone who volunteers to check on the nature of your work and make sure you aren't doing anything you aren't supposed to. Sort of just to let you know someone is watching. . . . I was also patrolled by another user this week, but they didn't leave me a message, nor can I find anything they reverted or changed, so I'm guessing that means I passed the criteria for good edits so far."

7. Andrew Corbett's post on Canvas reflects the fourth theme: "This week, again I was mostly on talk pages, debating in the topics presented about the content of the page. I found it interesting that some of the people who were commenting weren't signing their comments, but still seemed to have an air of authority about them. One of the interesting ones that I came across was the lack of a career infobox on Hillary Clinton's page. The main debate was that it would be too difficult to boil down a rich and varied career into one or two things for an infobox, and as such, the article itself should explain it. I felt that the infobox could contain the term political figure or politician since that has been a major portion of her career, but others were arguing that things like mother should be included in her infobox, or that she wasn't really a politician, but better known as the First Lady, or a lawyer, which I disagreed with."

conversation, not a static reservoir or receptacle for content," which comes as a corrective to several current manifestations of MOOCs where "content replaces the teacher, making the interchangeability of the teacher's and students' roles impossible." Another thesis stresses that "education cannot be compulsory" but that "the work of learning starts with agency." This imperative challenges the current reality where "MOOC designers have removed even further the opportunity for students to take control of their own learning by disconnecting them utterly from the power of the teacher." According to yet another thesis, "outcomes should give way to epiphanies," contrary to current MOOC practices where "outcomes tell learners what is important in advance, making the act of learning neat and tidy, while deterring the unexpected and unruly epiphanies that arise organically from within a learning environment."

Although Freire's work is the genesis of critical pedagogy, bell hooks (1994) challenges Freire's work by stating that as she read Freire his use of sexist language served as a constant reminder of his "phallocentric paradigm of liberation" (49). This becomes an entry point for many feminist teachers—to disrupt the traditional education setting that places privileged epistemologies at its center.

Notably the feminist classroom no longer focuses on gender alone. Instead the critical feminist pedagogue centrally focuses on how power operates through gender, race, class, nation, ability, and sexual orientation. Many feminists of colors have addressed the importance of the intersection of multiple positionalities with gender (Smith 1983; Moraga and Anzaldua 1983; Lorde 1984; Collins 1990). Through an intersectional lens, we are able to influence student learning in novel ways beyond gender. Their scholarship challenges feminist educators to examine knowledge production and its relationship to power. Moreover, their political engagement inspires a "rehacking" of the traditional education system. After all, it was also bell hooks (1991) that noted "no education is politically neutral" (37).

Parallel to hooks's work, both Gayatri Spivak and Chandra Mohanty call for new modes of epistemology in education. Spivak (1993) contends that education needs to disrupt the colonial process of the Western canon. Her work focuses on representation of marginalized people of the world. She calls for a shift in the way we perceive the idea of learning and understanding. Similarly, Mohanty (2003) challenges the Western academy to critically survey knowledge formation by privileging the examination of links between social forms and histories of oppression. Both scholars have been transformative to both feminist politics and academia alike and have laid the groundwork for those studying the manifestation of the social subject in digital spaces.

Notably, the work of these individuals is still timely. As MOOCs become more popular around the words, some scholars are concerned that MOOCs will become an intellectual neocolonization in which the North educates the South (Sharma 2015). South African scholars raised this issue during the 2009 World Conference of Higher Education. As we examine empire and its linkages to power, we must be cognizant of how MOOCs, more often than not, encourage an epistemology rooted in Western European traditions and fail to give credence to the knowledge built in countries from the global South.

Theoretically, critical feminist pedagogy challenges systems of power. Yet, when put into practice feminist pedagogy possess four elements: (1) participatory learning; (2) validation of personal experience; (3) encouragement of social understanding and activism; and (4) development of critical thinking and open-mindedness (Hoffman and Stake 1998). In no way does the feminist classroom claim neutrality as it fosters sensitivity and draws focus toward marginalized experiences. A closer examination of the four aforementioned elements engenders a better understanding of how issues of neutrality are dismantled. Furthermore, education is one among other domains and institutions that constitute, along cyberspace, the vast scope of cyberfeminist interventions that help "shape the layout and experience of cyberspace" (Gajjala and Oh 2012). Cyberfeminism thus calls for the unpacking and examination of the power logics at the level of these institutional structures through "decentered, multiple, and participatory practices" (1).

Participatory learning is invaluable in the feminist classroom. Students are central to the learning process. The top-down model of learning fails to give an open space for dialogue between teacher and student. The climate should give students the feeling that their voices are a valuable part of the learning process. Instead of having the banking model, like Freire mentions, participatory learning engenders students to become agents of their own, and each other's, learning. Through this process, students become teachers and vice versa.

Notably, a participatory learning space can only exist with the validation of the personal experience. Specifically, the personal becomes political and important in drawing connections between the student's heuristic experiences and those of their classmates. The student's experience becomes legitimized as an important source of knowledge in the feminist classroom. Yet, with personal experience comes the expectation of personal change. Rooted in consciousness raising, the change (and learning) is often best achieved through personal experience.

In addition to consciousness raising of the student's experiences, the feminist classroom encourages social understanding and activism. Dewey (1938) once noted that the best learning is through experiential learning. Similarly, students learn best through feminist praxis. Praxis comes in many forms: service learning, volunteering, zine writing, protesting, or, in the case of this essay, Wikipedia editing.

The final objective is to using participatory learning to validate experience and apply it through praxis. By doing this, the feminist classroom develops critical thinking skills and open-mindedness. As Belenky et al. (1986) surmise, the feminist classroom creates connected knowing or "the ability to put the voices of 'experts' in dialogue with one's own and other's voices and experiences" (101). As critical thinkers, students should be able to examine authority and its relationship to power and knowledge. Open-mindfulness, then, becomes the ability to change one's own opinion when given alternative evidence or experiences from their own.

Since the late 1990s, feminists have speculated what a feminist rhetoric of technology might look like. Koerber (2000) notes that an important characteristic of the rhetoric of technology is that it serves as meaning-making tool. Other feminist educators have used this concept to build meaning in their classroom. For example, Le Court (1998) explored how technology might build critical literacy skills. Similarly, others have used technology as a tool to build narratives around women's and girls' experiences (Hass, Tulley, and Blair 2002). Finally, Bomberger (2004) examines the manifestation of race in online spaces.

Often feminist scholars (and nonfeminist scholars) claim that they want to empower students in the classroom through technology. Instead of claiming to empower student's equality with the teaching in the classroom, feminist scholars ground their work in particular values and ideologies while encouraging processes that reframe various manifestations of power. The focal point then becomes not to dispel the student-teacher hierarchy (as this is impossible when one ultimately grades the other) but rather to give marginalized voices a space in the classroom through text and other frames of reference. In an attempt to contribute to the understanding of how critical feminist pedagogy can open different ways for examining issues of race, gender, class and geography in cyberspace, this reframing becomes the impetus for the student assignments in Radhika's classroom.

WHITENESS

I think the presence or absence of a raced/classed/gendered body within an online environment is an interesting concept. We argue intersecting identities matter in negotiating online interactions—but do they really? We argue that they do, because they inherently provide varying levels of agency long before the self can be negotiated within the online space. We argue that they don't, because you can hide a lack of privilege within an online space. But agency as it exists in cyberspace is so exceedingly complex. Agency inherently combines the "real" (can you afford a computer, can you access the internet?) and "virtual" worlds (are you technologically literate, do you speak the language?). Kayleigh Bondor (personal observation 2014)

This comment from Kayleigh's journal resonates with earlier explorations that Radhika has done in this regard preceding developments in web 2.0 when she used text-based MOOs. This point made by Kayleigh about white males in class resonates with what Radhika's student, Ray, wrote in his journal:

> The very idea that a mediated form of communication technology could serve to disguise identity and even prevent those of privilege from asserting their identity (particularly white, European-American males) became a center to my engagement with course materials. . . . Such technology has shown to have the ability to disguise one's true identity. . . . The main issue underlying all of this is that there are certain forms of technology within the realm of communication that in some form or another make it difficult for people to assert their physical identity (Gajjala and Altman 2006, 78).

In this instance, coauthor and graduate student Melissa Altman who was in the same class (thus had the opportunity to more closely watch her fellow classmates engage these forms in simultaneous resistance to the instructor's critical questionings and in awe of new technologies introduced for learning in the classroom) and who later wrote about epistemologies of doing as form of pedagogy with Radhika, observed that there seemed to be an "unsettling of white privilege." While the notion that there is no race or gender in cyberspace has long been contested by critical scholars and inhabitants of online spaces, the use of cyberspatial praxis and the experience of habitus in cyberspace in pedagogic environments allows us to see how specific socioculturally and linguistically situated practices of literacy and interpersonal sharing contribute to the production of hierarchies in contemporary experiences of race are employed in cyberspaces and the real spaces with which they intersect (Nakamura 2002; Nelson, Tu, and Hines 2001). To understand his experience, we have to look at the real-world context in which he engaged the technological interface—as described above, the classroom context was designed specifically to try to counter the insistence that race remains unremarked. First, the visible identity markers of the instructor identified her as a third-world woman. Next, the context of the course readings was heavily influenced by critical theory and postcolonial feminist theory. Third, we had the makeup of the classroom participants to consider. Ray, for example, was one of only two white males in the class. The other class members included three international students (two Chinese and one Indian), one African American, and one "out" lesbian, and several white women, some of whom were fluent and articulate in the theoretical language of postcolonial feminism and critical theory used in class readings.

Conclusion

Although, these five themes parallel the timeline set forth in the assignment, on a macrolevel we can observe the journey students take to gain a greater understanding of their self-presentation and formation of identity in cyberspaces. In the case of Kayleigh's experience we are able to document her understanding of how sociocultural formations shape cybertexts like Wikipedia. Her analysis of her white, male classmate's grappling with the Wikipedia project serves as a marker of her own understanding of how marginalized voices are often forgotten by the mere act of editing wiki pages. Similarly, Kayleigh's awareness of how real, physical identities shape the cyberself demonstrates how assignments that focus on technospace formation is a valuable pedagogical tool.

References

Belenky, Mary Field, Blythe McVicker Clinchy, Nancy Rule Goldberger, and Jill Mattuck Tarule. 1986. *Women's Ways of Knowing: The Development of Self, Voice and Mind.* New York: Basic Books.

Bomberger, Ann M. 2004. "Ranting about Race: Crushed Eggshells in Computer-Mediated Communication." *Computers and Composition* 21:197–216.

boyd, danah. 2015. *It's Complicated: The Social Lives of Networked Teens.* New Haven: Yale University Press.

Bruns, Axel (2009) From Prosumer to Produser: Understanding User-Led Content Creation. In *Transforming Audiences 2009,* 3-4 Sep, 2009, London.

Cheong, Pauline Hope, and Kishonna Gray. 2011. "Mediated Intercultural Dialectics: Identity Perceptions and Performances in Virtual Worlds." *Journal of International and Intercultural Communication* 4:265–71.

Collins, Patricia Hill. 1990. *Black Feminist Thought: Knowledge, Consciousness and the Politics of Empowerment.* Boston: Unwin Hyman.

Craig, Dorothy Valcarcel. 2009. *Action Research Essentials.* San Francisco: Jossey-Bass.

Dewey, John. 1916. *Democracy and Education: An Introduction to the Philosophy of Education.* Macmillan.

———. 1938. *Experience and Education.* New York: Collier Books.

FemTechNet Whitepaper Committee. 2013. "Transforming Higher Education with Distributed

Open Collaborative Courses (DOCCs): Feminist Pedagogies and Networked Learning." September 30. http://femtechnet.newschool.edu/femtechnet-whitepaper/.

Freire, Paulo. 1971. *Pedagogy of the Oppressed*. New York: Herder and Herder.

Freire, Paulo, and Ira Shor. 1987. *A Pedagogy for Liberation*. Basingstoke: Macmillan.

Gajjala, Radhika, and Melissa Altman. 2006. "Producing Cyberselves through Technospatial Praxis: Studying through Doing." In *Health Research in Cyberspace*, edited by Pranee Liamputtong, 67–84. New York: Nova Publishers.

Gajjala, Radhika, and Yeon Ju Oh. 2012. "Cyberfeminism 2.0: Where Have All the Cyberfeminists Gone?" In *Cyberfeminism 2.0*, edited by Radhika Gajjala and Yeon Ju Oh, 1–10. New York: Peter Lang, 2012.

Gajjala, Radihika, Natalia Rybas, and Yuhui Zhang. 2010. "Producing Digitally Mediated Environments as Sites for Critical Feminist Pedagogy," In *The SAGE Handbook of Communication and Instruction*, edited by Deanna Fassett and John Warren, 411–36. New York: Sage Publications.

Gatto, John Taylor. 2003. "AGAINST SCHOOL." *Harper's Magazine* 307 (1840): 33.

Hass, Angela, Christine Tulley, and Kristine Blair. 2002. "Mentors Versus Masters: Women's and Girl's Narratives of (Re)negotiation in Web-Based Writing Spaces." *Computers and Composition* 19:231–49.

Hoffman, Frances, and Jayne Stake. 1998. "Feminist Pedagogy in Theory and Practice: An Empirical Investigation." *NSWA Journal* 10:79–97.

hooks, bell. 1994. *Teaching to Transgress: Education as the Practice of Freedom*. New York: Routledge.

Juhasz, Alexandra. 2013. "Evolution of the MOOCs?" *FemTechNet*, November 26. http://femtechnet.newschool.edu/blog/evolution-of-the-moocs-2/.

Kishimoto, Kyoto, and Mumbi Mwangi. 2009. "Critiquing the Rhetoric of 'Safety' in Feminist Pedagogy: Women of Color Offering an Account of Ourselves." *Feminist Teacher* 19:87

Koenig, Rebecca. 2014. "What You Need to Know about Yik Yak, an App Causing Trouble on Campuses." *Chronicle of Higher Education*, September 26. http://chronicle.com/article/What-You-Need-to-Know-About/149005/.

Koerber, Amy. 2000. "Toward a Feminist Rhetoric of Technology." *Journal of Business and Technical Communication* 14:58–73.

Le Court, Donna. 1998. "Critical Pedagogy in the Computer Classroom: Politicizing the Writing Space." *Computer and Composition* 15:275–95.

Lorde, Audre. 1984. *Sister Outsider: Essays and Speeches*. New York: Crossing Press.

Losh, Elizabeth. 2014. "Selfies, Snapchat and Distance Learning." *Dmlcentral.net*, April 28. http://dmlcentral.net/blog/liz-losh/selfies-snapchat-and-distance-learning.

Luke, Carmen, and Jennifer Gore. 2014. *Feminisms and Critical Pedagogy*. New York: Routledge.

McPherson Tara. 2014. "Designing for Difference: The Gendered and Racial Epistemologies of Electronic Media." Presentation at Bowling Green State University's School of Cultural and Critical Studies, Bowling Green, November 18.

Mohanty, Chandra Talpade. 2003. *Feminism without Borders: Decolonizing Theory, Practicing Solidarity*. Durham: Duke University Press Books.

Moraga, Cherrie, and Gloria Anzaldua. 1983. *This Bridge Called My Back: Writings by Radical Women of Color*. New York: Kitchen Table Women of Color Press.

Morris, Sean Michael, and Jesse Stommel. 2014. "If Freire Made a MOOC: Open Education as Resistance." *Hybrid Pedagogy: A Digital Journal of Learning, Teaching, and Technology*,

November 20. http://www.hybridpedagogy.com/journal/freire-made-mooc-open-education
-resistance/.

Nakamura, Lisa. 2002. *Cybertypes: Race, Ethnicity, and Identity on the Internet*. New York: Routledge.

Nelson, Alondra, Thuy Lihn Tu, and Alicia Headlam Hines. 2001. *Technicolor: Race, Technology,
and Everyday Life*. New York: New York University Press.

Peake, Bryce. 2014. "Editing Wikipedia for Diversity." Guest Lecture, Bowling Green State University's COMM 5080: Intercultural Communication, Bowling Green State University, Fall.

———. 2015. "WP: THREATENING2MEN: Misogynist Infopolitics and the Hegemony of the
Asshole Consensus on English Wikipedia." *ADA: Journal of Gender and New Media 7*. http://
adanewmedia.org/2015/04/issue7-peake/.

Prensky, Mark. 2001. "Digital Natives, Digital Immigrants." *On the Horizon*, 9: 1-6.

Reason, Peter, and Hilary Bradbury. 2008. "Introduction." In *Sage Handbook of Action Research:
Participative Inquiry and Practice*, edited by Peter Reason and Hilary Bradbury, 1–10. Los
Angeles: SAGE.

Rettberg, Jill Walker. 2014. *Seeing Ourselves through Technology: How We Use Selfies, Blogs and
Wearable Devices to See and Shape Ourselves*. New York: Palgrave.

Rich, Adrienne. 1977. "Claiming an Education." Convocation speech at Douglass College.

Sandal, Renee. 1991. "The Liberating Relevance of Feminist Pedagogy." *Studies in Art Education*
32:178–87.

Schmidt, Peter. 2015. "A New Faculty Challenge: Fending Off Abuse on Yik Yack." *Chronicle
of Higher Education*, January 29. http://chronicle.com/article/A-New-Faculty-Challenge
-/151463. Accessed January 29, 2015.

Senft, Theresa, and Jill Walker Rettberg. 2015. "The Selfie Course." http://www.selfieresearchers
.com/the-selfie-course/.

Shah, Nishant, and Sunil Abraham. 2009. *DIGITAL NATIVES WITH A CAUSE? A Knowledge
Survey and Framework*. San Francisco: Hivos Knowledge Program.

Sharma, Ghanashyam. 2013. "A MOOC Delusion: Why Visions to Educate the World Are Ab-
surd." *Chronicle of Higher Education*, July 15. http://chronicle.com/blogs/worldwise/a-mooc
-delusion-why-visions-to-educate-the-world-are-absurd/32599.

Smith, Barbara. 1983. *Home Girls: A Black Feminist Anthology*. New York: Kitchen Table Women
of Color Press.

Spivak, Gayatri Chakravorty. 1993. *Outside in the Teaching Machine*. New York: Routledge.

10

Haven't You Ever Heard of Tumblr? FemTechNet's Distributed Open Collaborative Course (DOCC), Pedagogical Publics, and Classroom Incivility

JASMINE RAULT AND T. L. COWAN

#blacklivesmatter calls us to prepare the kind of space where grief and anger are okay, where rage is not fearful but necessary, where public outcries make sense. (Bynum 2015)

FemTechNet is fueled by our civil rights, anti-racist, queer, decolonizing, trans-feminist pedagogies as we work within the belly of the beast of neoliberal austerity, normalized precarity, neo-colonial techno-missionary evangelism and MOOC fever towards the radical redistribution, reinvention, and repurposing of technological, material, emotional, academic, and monetary resources. ("We Are FemTechNet," FemTechNet)

The future of feminism can not be left to the hands of white women. (Cooper 2014b)

Over the course of 2011–12, a shifting group of feminist scholars mostly working in colleges and universities in the United States and Canada began to meet under the banner of the Feminist Technology Network (FemTechNet) to design what would become the distributed open collaborative course (DOCC) (Juhasz and Balsamo 2012). The DOCC was offered as Dialogues in Feminism and Technology in a beta version of three nodes (January–May 2013) and in a full version in about fifteen nodes (August–December 2013), and as Collaborations in Feminism and Technology across another forty or so nodes, in addition to an online open-source syllabus in 2014, 2015, and 2016. The course includes an ever-expanding catalogue of Video Dialogues—moderated

We would like to thank, first, our students at Eugene Lang College, the New School, and Yale University who have contributed so much to our thinking about classroom affects. Additionally, the research for this chapter has been funded by the Social Sciences and Humanities Research Council of Canada (SSHRC) Insight Development and Standard Research Grant programmes, for which we are grateful. And, finally, to our FemTechNet colleagues and to all the people who populate the pedagogical publics, thanks a million.

discussions among prominent feminist scholars, artists, and activists in the associated fields of feminist science, technology, art, and media studies. It also includes an (also ever-expanding) set of collaboratively developed Key Learning Projects, including feminist wiki storming, keyword videos, feminist mapping, social media, and gaming projects (i.e., blog commenting, Tumblr, Twitter, and Twine assignments); video ReMIX, an object making/exchange; and *signal/noise*, an online publication of student works generated in the DOCC. In addition to building an open-source archive of feminist scholarship, organizing, and cultural production in these fields, the development of FemTechNet's DOCC also, importantly, contributes an online course design and publication model structured by feminist pedagogical praxis, and adds this model to the recent proliferation of open, online teaching and learning experiments that are the topic of this collection. Perhaps this is a fairly obvious observation. What might be less obvious is that FemTechNet's DOCC also entered into another preexisting constellation of experiments in teaching, learning, and sociality: online feminism, especially at a particularly potent moment.

If, in January 2014, you were following the English-language blogosphere, you would have learned that online feminism had "become toxic" (Goldberg 2014). According to an incendiary article in the *Nation*, online feminism has been paralyzed by a Twitter effect—the easy circulation and publication of "attack"-affects against feminists just trying to do good work "for the movement" (Goldberg 2014). Here, we take up attack-*affects*, rather than simply attacks, as it seems to be from the tone and sentiment rather than the content of online feminism that this apparently movement-threatening "toxicity" emerges and spreads. From the *Guardian*, we got a slightly more measured warning that "Feminism is in danger of becoming toxic" because these attack-affects focus on individuals and individualized symptoms of power inequality rather than contribute to the "great social movement" that is feminism from the 1970s–90s (Bindel 2014). If you've been following this "great social movement" for any of the past forty or hundred years, you will be unsurprised to learn that the affects being cast as attacking, toxic, and disabling are those generated by antiracist, decolonizing/anticolonial, class-conscious, and transfeminist activists refusing to allow online feminism to be dominated by white middle- to upper-class, US-centric, Anglo-settler-colonial knowledges and priorities. That discourses of civility are being deployed to discredit and diminish critiques of power and privilege is nothing new, but we are seeing this old trick played out on a more public and visible scale in the interaction between professionalized, authorized, and often paid publications (e.g., *Na-*

tion and *Guardian*) and the unwaged, unprofessional "nattering" (Spender 1995) on social media like Twitter, Facebook, and Tumblr.[1] While the dynamics of white supremacist "respectability politics" and discourses of civility, as well as access to legitimatized, institutionalized, and professionalized publics, are familiar elements of feminist activism, theory, and pedagogy, we are interested in recent online manifestations and circulations of these feminist affective politics as they shape both online pedagogical publics and our hybrid face-to-face (F2F)/online college classrooms.

In this essay, we trace the contours of what might be called online feminist pedagogical publics and how they contribute to experiments in scale and access in higher education. These feminist pedagogical publics are comprised of the paid and unpaid content produced and circulated as black, decolonizing, queer, and transfeminist consciousness-raising, organizing, movement-building, hybrid intellectual (or so-called immaterial), and very on-the-streets material pedagogy.[2] This is related to what has been theorized as "public pedagogy" (Giroux 2000, 2003, 2004), but we want to focus on a few distinguishing characteristics of these feminist pedagogical publics: (1) the pedagogue or teacher is collective, aggregate, unstable, replaceable, and often anonymous; (2) the public is intensely productive, regularly taking on the role of teacher and challenging, redirecting, and reconfiguring the content of the lesson; and (3) the affective pedagogical register of these publics would be banned by most classroom codes of civility. In the context of the United States, investments in online educational software/platforms are increasingly offered as the solution to the "crisis of higher education" (Blumenstyk 2014), characterized by unprecedented and relentless increases in tuition costs and student debt loads, combined with the radical upward distribution of resources away from students and faculty and toward upper-administrative, managerial, and consultant costs. We want to consider what higher education can learn from

1. The case of Steven Salaita is on our minds as we write this essay. Salaita's tenured position as professor of American Indian Studies at the University of Illinois at Urbana–Champaign was revoked because of what Chancellor Phyllis Wise described as his lack of social-media "civility." Salaita had apparently used the wrong affective tone in his tweeted criticisms of the Israeli military attacks on Gaza, in summer 2014. This is a poignant performance of the ways that disciplinary discourses of civility are deployed in the service of settler colonial and imperial power (see Nyong'o 2014).

2. Our thinking has been greatly influenced by Lisa Nakamura's recent analysis of "unwanted labour," which focuses on "how often efforts by feminists and social justice advocates to reduce misogyny and sexism online are unwanted, punished, and viewed as censorship, uncivil behaviour, or themselves forms of sexism" (Nakamura 2015, 111).

the experiments in open education that are already at work in online feminist pedagogical publics—or, what our students refer to as "the *real* open university," the three sisters, Twitter, Facebook, and Tumblr.

The two main questions we explore are as follows. (1) How have online social media influenced our feminist pedagogies and teaching spaces? (2) How might the FemTechNet DOCC participate in these hybrid spaces (online/F2F and paid/unpaid pedagogical labors)? That is, in what ways can and do we contribute to these online pedagogical publics, and how can new teaching platforms accommodate an affective range that accompanies the teaching and learning of difficult knowledges?

Online Feminist Pedagogical Publics

In their introduction to the *Handbook of Public Pedagogy*, Jennifer Sandlin, Brian Schultz, and Jake Burdick (2010, 2) explain, "public pedagogy has come to signify a crucial concept within educational scholarship—that schools are not the sole sites of teaching, learning, or curricula, and that perhaps they are not even the most influential." In the proliferation of feminist blogs, pages, handles, and hashtags, we can see the workings of a distinct pedagogical culture—creating, debating, analyzing, and reorienting the critical frameworks through which to better recognize to denaturalize and challenge the structures of power in which we live. The framework of "public pedagogies" is centrally organized by the understanding of "culture" as an epistemological and ideological contest of influence:

> Culture now plays a central role in producing narratives, metaphors, and images that exercise a powerful pedagogical force over how people think of themselves and their relationship to others. . . . [C]ulture is the primary sphere in which individuals, groups, and institutions engage in the art of translating the diverse and multiple relations that mediate between private life and public concerns. It is also the sphere in which the translating possibilities of culture are under assault, particularly as the forces of neo-liberalism dissolve public issues into utterly privatized and individualistic concerns. (Giroux 2004, 62)

The formulation of public pedagogies relies on paying attention to the teaching that happens in public. What we want to draw attention to in the work of online feminist pedagogical publics are the contested terrains of the publics themselves, as well as the dynamics of distributed, proliferating, dialectical discursive praxes that are shaping contemporary political, social thought, and participation.

The online feminist pedagogical publics that we consider are those social media pages, blogs, hashtags, listicles, and memes oriented around sharing, learning, and teaching antiracist, decolonizing, queer, trans, body-positive, fat, and crip feminist knowledges. Students in our classes have been regular users of blogs such as the following: *Black Girl Dangerous*, started by Mia McKenzie "as a scream of anguish" that has become a site to "amplify the voices, experiences and expressions of queer and trans* people of color"; *Son of Baldwin*, Robert Jones Jr.'s Tumblr and active Twitter account, "[t]he literary, sociopolitical, sexual, pop-cultural blog. Live from Bedford-Stuyvesant"; *Last Real Indians*, which "highlight[s] Indigenous artists, writers, speakers, movers, shakers, content-creators, leaders, successes, struggles, & current events as viewed through Indigenous eyes"; *Stand With Palestine*, a blog of news analysis and resources for justice in Palestine; *Dear Cis People*, "a place for trans people to send an anonymous message to the cis population as a whole"; *Is This Ableism*, "a safe space for open discussion and genuine questions"; and *Queers with Disabilities*, "a way to connect people with disabilities that identify somewhere in the queer spectrum." Each of these blogs are archives-in-action and social scenes of proliferating knowledges, debates, politics, styles, and discourses of social justice content, which sometimes come from and just as often make their way into our classrooms.

One of the most striking effects of our students' involvement with these media has been intensifying the knowledge gap that manifests as a kind of affect clash in the classroom. For example, half the students in our classes are fully enmeshed in these online pedagogical publics—the combined social and pedagogical lives of media like Tumblr, Twitter, and Facebook. Teaching in a university without a women's and/or gender studies department or major, our feminist/queer courses can never assume a shared or even rudimentary introduction to feminist/queer studies, and we tend to find our classrooms rather split between students intensely identified or at least mostly comfortable with concepts and discourses such as "white privilege" and "white supremacy," "intersectionality," "microaggressions," "PGPs," "heteropatriachy" and "heteronormativity," "homonormativity" and "homonationalism," "orientalis," and "exoticization," "appropriation," "POCs," "WOCs," "QPOCs," "TWOCs," "HIV-poz folks," and so on, and students who have never heard of these words and have a very difficult time believing that these things exist or matter.

Indeed, sometimes it feels like our classrooms mirror the kinds of dynamics typical of, for example, the collaboratively moderated Tumblr blog *Intersectional Feminism for Beginners*, "A basic breakdown of third-wave feminism concepts for the genuinely curious and the terribly ignorant." As "an educational blog," the creators (or "Mods") seek questions or "ask" because they would "like the opportunity to teach or discuss issues with our followers, and any other curious people out there!" (January 17, 2015). Questions range from general ones about key concepts, "How does intersectionality affect women?" (February 18, 2015), to those dealing with perceived attack-affects like,

> What do you think of certain SJ [social justice] bloggers who literally want all white people to die? Like I understand white people have done a lot of horrible things but really? Am I supposed to grab my family and have a mass suicide to appease these people? (January 26, 2015)

The response advises the asker to not use the rage as an excuse to disregard "certain SJ bloggers" who focus on social justice issues but to "look at the context, see why this person is angry. Are you participating in the behaviour that prompted the anger? If so, work to change. If not, this situation is not about you and it is best not to be involved" (January 26, 2015). Blogs like these model the scope of affective registers through which social and political thought is developed, taught, and learned.

We find that one challenge we are dealing with in our post-Tumblr classrooms, compared with that in our pre-Tumblr classrooms, is an increased divide between those students who have sought us out as feminist/queer theory professors *because of* their participation in this social justice–oriented sphere of social media and so hope for/expect a tone and content that they have found/made online and, on the other hand, those who are in our classes because of degree requirements, scheduling convenience, or general curiosity. While we will and have always struggled with differences in familiarity and comfort with feminist/queer politics, studies, theories, and discourses in our classes (certainly this predates the Internet), we are still negotiating a somewhat new pedagogical challenge given the relatively easily available social justice content online, the ways in which this online content is both consumed and produced by our students (highly active produsers), and the hybrid pedagogical, social, and erotic (cruising) uses/functions of these spaces—we would wager to guess that we are encountering greater numbers of and rather different expectations from these self-taught students. These students tend to comport themselves in the manner of the "toxic feminists"—indeed, as soon as they find Sara Ahmed, they find themselves in her description of the "feminist killjoy": she who "'spoils' the happiness of others [. . .] because she refuses to convene, to assemble, to meet up over happiness," even feminist happiness (Ahmed 2010, 65–67). That is, these self-taught students—for whom this learning is a survival tactic—respond to the other students' often unintentionally (but not always unintentionally) racist, homophobic, transphobic, fat-phobic, ableist comments and questions, and general unfamil-

iarity with social justice common-sense knowledges and debates, as well as
their rapidly changing vernaculars through attack affects (e.g., shutting down,
calling out, shaming with exasperated sighs, eye-rolling, and other embodied
emoticons)—treating fellow students as "terribly ignorant," a response that
blogs like *Intersectional Feminism for Beginners* might be seen to engender. In
an age where these knowledges seem so readily available online, uninformed
in-class comments indicate a perceived failure to self-educate and a willful
ignorance that reproduces microaggressions. The students who have participated in these wider pedagogical publics and their affective valences before entering the classroom, who are sometimes read by our other students as "social
justice bullies," respond similarly to other students as they do to scholarly
readings or media examples with an exasperated, "Haven't you ever heard of
Tumblr?"

That is, they enact what Eve Kosofsky Sedgwick (2003) would call a pro-
foundly "paranoid reading" that dismisses an object—usually something written before 2012—for not knowing what we know now. Sedgwick uses "paranoid" not as a pathologizing diagnosis but as a way to describe a prevailing
interpretive method that has come "to seem entirely coextensive with critical
theoretical inquiry," particularly inquiry into matters of social justice and systemic oppressions (126). These methods are motivated by a proactive, protective certainty that violence and oppression inform most actions and can be
found in the interstices of every utterance (which is often true, especially for
those living in targeted bodies) and that anticipation and exposure are the
first steps to undoing and surviving them: for Sedgwick, "paranoia requires
that bad news be always already known. . . . *There must be no bad surprises*"
(130). The "unequivocally future-oriented vigilance" of the paranoid method
insists that "no time could be too early for having-already-known, for its
having-already-been-inevitable, that something bad would happen" (131). Although Sedgwick is hyperbolizing and roasting the long histories of paranoid
reading that sustain feminist and queer studies in the service of suggesting an
alternate method of reparative reading, her glee in describing paranoid practices accounts, on a formal level, for the pleasure and bonding that paranoid
readers experience when we share our analyses with those who share our vigilance. We want to consider what it means to teach *within* the affective space of
paranoia, rage, and political depression, rather than to try to overcome, cover
up, or penalize these totally reasonable reactions to unreasonable life situations. Our students' application of what we have started to call the "Tumblr
standard" reflects the new media-inspired but not entirely new paradox of
feminist/gender studies pedagogy: respecting the classroom as a site for new
encounters with feminist knowledges *while also* acknowledging and building

on the generatively paranoid teaching and learning of pedagogical publics well beyond the classroom.

The students on the receiving end of these paranoid readings and attack-affects sometimes respond defensively (or protectively, and just stop talking: "we just can't say *anything*") or, like the interlocutor of *Intersectional Feminism for Beginners*, respond with indignant overstatement—"Am I supposed to grab my family and have a mass suicide to appease these people?" Rather than rushing to ease the tension and discord in the classroom, we might learn from feminist online pedagogical publics to understand the ways that these conflicted affects can also work to call students *in* rather than *out* and thus galvanize and proliferate the killjoys in the room. Prioritizing a productive tension to foreground the risky business of teaching difficult knowledges, these learning spaces move through and by affective difference rather than settle into a static affective register. As Ahmed writes (2010, 143), "[t]he moral task" for those experiencing racism, for example, is "'to get over it,' as if when you are over it, it is gone." We suggest here that feminist teaching/learning spaces—F2F classrooms and online pedagogical environments—can productively work against the grain of this moral task of "getting over it." Thus one challenge of access in and to feminist learning spaces is the challenge to be open enough to allow students to contend with and account for the "it" that shall not be named as a knowledge practice.

So many of us feminist teachers are proud to sing the killjoy anthem, until the joy gets killed in our classrooms. That is, most feminist professors also find ourselves in Ahmed's (2010, 66) feminist killjoy—as "[f]eminist subjects [who] might bring others down not only by talking about unhappy topics such as sexism but by exposing how happiness is sustained by erasing the very signs of not getting along"—but feel compelled to perform, promote, and maintain a happy accord in our classrooms, even if that means "erasing [rather than naming and engaging] the very signs of not getting along." We might teach Audre Lorde's "The Uses of Anger" as a feminist foundation:

> My anger is a response to racist attitudes, to the actions and presumptions that arise out of those attitudes. . . . My anger and your attendant fears, perhaps, are spotlights that can be used for your growth in the same way I have had to use learning to express anger for my growth. (Lorde 1997, 287)

How many of us, though, are ready, willing and/or able to deal with this rage in our classrooms? How do we engage, rather than shut down the rage expressed in online pedagogical publics—that is, the anger that Lorde reminds us is the result of the (political, social, and consciousness) *labors of achieving* this generative affect? This is some of the affective and epistemological hybrid context that has shifted the pedagogical dynamics and possibilities of the (online or F2F) feminist classroom, from which the DOCC emerges and lives.

Goldberg's (2014) "Toxic Twitter Wars" story in the *Nation* with its sanctimonious discourses of disciplinary white liberalism might have been dismissed and forgotten without much comment had it not taken aim at precisely the thriving coalitional feminist intellectual and activist public that the article insists is imperiled. The article set out to show that online feminism is failed and broken: "mean," "bullying," "insular, protective, brittle, depressing," suffocatingly "dogmatic," "chastising," in a state of "perpetual psychodrama," "furious," "angry," "vitriolic," and "misinformed." That is, it repeats the predictable cliché that feminism is always already dead:

> Beginning in the early 1970s, before many media outlets had turned any serious attention to the women's movement, others were declaring it dead, dying, or permanently disabled. . . . The diagnoses vary slightly, but feminists are almost always to blame. (Rhodes 1995, 691)

This declaration of feminism's demise relies on the very robust work of several women of color and transfeminists—Mikki Kendall, Brittney Cooper, Katherine Cross, Kimberlé Crenshaw, Samhita Mukhopadhyay, Anna Holmes, and Jamia Wilson—which, despite the *Nation*'s publishing reach and authority, the article cannot successfully diminish or undermine. Almost as soon as it went online, most of the feminists quoted, and many of those implicated, took to their various publishing outlets (i.e., Twitter, Facebook, blogs, and online journals) to contest, complicate, reframe, and nuance the article that had worked so hard to flatten, decontextualize, and misunderstand their work. Feminista Jones, a blogger, put it succinctly on her Twitter blog: "what you have done is contributed to the silencing of women who have, for centuries, been taught to keep quiet"; "Michelle, don't ever type my name in print again" (@*FeministaJones* Twitter, January 29, 2014; quoted in John and Jones 2014). Cooper refuses to have her analysis—that black feminism risks being "rendered reactionary, emotional, angry and short-sighted" in social media—reduced to the "larger okey-doke" of the article, and explains that

> Goldberg dishonestly characterizes this demand to be heard as both censorial and anti-democratic, even though, truth be told, it is the very expansion of the number of voices that has white liberals so shook. . . . These campaigns force white folks to actually listen to people of color. (Cooper 2014a)

Cross, whose work and words were used extensively throughout the article, explained that they had somehow been evacuated of her analysis:

The discussion that Goldberg dove into was one that had been started chiefly by marginalised people. . . . It was a discussion about how we, as people on the margins, hurt *each other* using activist logics we either did not create, or created under unacknowledged and compromised positions. . . . For many of us, this was a culture we neither created nor asked for, dominated by norms, argot, mores, and rage sired by a predominantly white, cis middle-class core that had always presumed itself implicitly more knowledgeable about "what the real issues are." (Cross 2014)

What the numerous and various replies and corrections to Goldberg's article reveal is that "solidarity clearly exists within the intersectional community" (Khan 2014) and that it flourishes and thrives in these online feminist pedagogical publics. Tweets and hashtag activism work simultaneously to communicate individuals' ideas, synthesize collective analysis, bring people in, call people out, aggregate a movement, and connect people politically and socially, across space and time. Thus the creation, and ongoingness, of hashtags like #BlackLivesMatter, #IdleNoMore, #SolidarityIsForWhite-Women, and #NotYourAsianSidekick are also the creation and sustaining of a public. The hashtags become agential, building and constituting a shared understanding, responding to public events, and often making links among events, historical moments, and individual and shared experiences.

Distributed, Open, and Collaborative:
The Affective Aspirations of FemTechNet

We contend here that FemTechNet's online pedagogical efforts, as well as other "distributed," "open," and "collaborative" teaching and learning experiments, must be understood as part of these broader pedagogical publics. As we seek to encourage widespread access to the resources that FemTechNet has developed, and to continue to archive feminist genealogies in science, technology, arts, and media studies, it is important that these archives be situated within and in conversation with contemporary praxes. Our online locale—built collectively and always under development—is not only a digital-resource storage facility and content delivery system but also, and necessarily, a technique of feminist online inquiry, analysis, debate, critique, and politically engaged knowledge production. Inasmuch as the DOCC offers a series of well-packaged resources, it is also a site of messy experimentation, with many supplementary projects and initiatives in the 2014–15 Collaborations in Feminism and Technology, including Situated Knowledges Map, Open Online Office Hours (OOOHs), Teach-In on Feminist Game Studies, Town Hall

Meetings on Feminist Digital Media Praxis and Online Safety/Risk, and Feminist International Collaboration & Anti-Violence Organizing, FemTechNet's coalitional experiments are affectively volatile and inseparable from the wider field of online feminist pedagogical publics.

These experiments in open learning and distributed expertise are informed by and part of the broader projects of online feminist engagement through social media participation and agitation, as much as they contribute to and hail from a scholarly project of feminist education and theory formation. One of the risks of organizing open-access resources using the language and logics of the bricks-and-mortar university (e.g., a "course," "office hours," etc.), is that we might find ourselves loading on the ideological implications and affective constraints of the closed-access university and its codes of conduct, as well as its disciplinary mechanisms of decorum and civility, which have proven successful at suppressing dissent, or those knowledges that are toxic to a dominant social, political order (what bell hooks (1994) usefully—toxically—calls white supremacist, imperialist, capitalist patriarchy). As Miriame Kaba and Andrea Smith note in their (reluctant but necessary) response to mainstream feminist cries of white woundedness:

> The only way we can avoid toxicity is to actually end white supremacy, settler colonialism, capitalism and patriarchy. Women of color know that when we leave the supposed "toxicity" of Twitter, we are not going to another place that is not toxic. Thus, our goal is not to avoid toxicity, as if that is even possible, but to dismantle the structures that create toxicity. The work of feminism whether online or off must be to create space for a critical and engaged discussion on a global level about how to end oppression. Then we must mobilize to take actions to make it so. (Kaba and Smith 2014)

While FemTechNet's DOCCs to date have focused on genealogies of feminist technology studies, its organizing principles of collective design can be used to develop DOCCs that even more explicitly build literacies for learners who are new to online feminist pedagogical publics and for participants to share expertise and skills toward that "critical and engaged discussion on a global level" called for by Kaba and Smith "to end oppression." These resources already exist online, from the many reading lists posted on Tumblrs and other blog sites, to the #FergusonSyllabus started by *@FeministaJones*; to massively citational articles like Susana Loza's "Hashtag Feminism, #SolidarityIsForWhiteWomen and the Other #FemFuture" (Loza 2014); Jessie Daniels's "The Trouble with White Women and White Feminism" series on *Racism Review* (Daniels 2014); and curatorial projects like Tara Conley's

HashTagFeminism.com. Indeed, a defining feature of a feminist pedagogical public, including FemTechNet's DOCC, Twitter feminism, and the feminist blogosphere, is its commitment to massively citational practices that do the decolonizing work of increasing access while enabling nonappropriative attribution, accountability, distributed, and situated knowledges.

FemTechNet's collaboratively written and aspirationally driven manifesto (see fig. 10.1) identifies us and the structures of political feeling by which we are oriented and the feminist pedagogical publics within which we are enmeshed. In identifying a range of affective structures—accountability, collaboration, collectivity, care, irony, comedy, messiness, and gravitas—as feminist technologies, we hope to articulate the ways that FemTechNet itself is committed to the difficult and often uncomfortable work of working together. The phrase "FemTechNet is an experiment in solidarity" is tweeted at Kendall's #SolidarityIsForWhiteWomen and its viral analyses, thus situating FemTechNet as participating in, not simply observing, feminist online pedagogical publics.

Conclusion: Affective Labor Market

FemTechNet and the DOCC are part of these online pedagogical publics—where participatory media work as both social and pedagogical platforms, where the line between student and teacher is blurred, and where the work of producing and consuming is deliberately inseparable. Moreover, the DOCC is structured as a method for feminist teaching and learning—the many-to-many pedagogy. As a hybrid space, it lives both online and in our F2F classrooms, through our cross-institutional teacher and student collaborations, and between paid and unpaid teaching and learning. These are the digital, material, and affective labor conditions in which we can no longer merely talk about "teaching the public" or study "how the public is taught," but instead need to contend with the ways that the unpaid public is rendered teacherly and that the work of teaching is increasingly unpaid.

Academics have always been prone to this sort of exploitation—resistant as we have traditionally been to seeing ourselves as workers, preferring to imagine ourselves as something like highly trained and relatively well-paid artists or activists "doing what we love" (Gregg 2009; Cowan and Rault 2014; Tokumitsu 2014)—but with decreasing resources being administered concomitantly with increasing expectations for productivity, engagement, presence, and availability, we are dealing with neoliberalized labor conditions that are inseparable from new digital economies, which rely in very old/familiar ways on obscured, invisibilized, and low- or unpaid (gendered and racialized)

We Are FemTechNet

FemTechNet is committed to making the accessible, open, accountable, transformative and transforming educational institutions of our dreams. We are feminist academic hacktivism.

FemTechNet is an international movement of feminist thinkers, researchers, writers, teachers, artists, professors, librarians, mentors, organizers and activists sharing resources and engaging in activities that demonstrate connected feminist thinking about technology and innovation.

FemTechNet understands that technologies are complex systems with divergent values and cultural assumptions. We work to expand critical literacies about the social and political implications of these systems.

FemTechNet is cyberfeminist praxis: we recognize digital and other technologies can both subvert and reinscribe oppressive relations of power and we work to make these complex relations of power transparent.

FemTechNet is hard at work creating better tools.
FemTechNet has no observers, only participants.

Accountability is a feminist technology.
Collaboration is a feminist technology.
Collectivity is a feminist technology.
Care is a feminist technology.
Irony, comedy, making a mess, and gravitas are feminist technologies.

No one holds the trademark on feminist pedagogy—it is collective intellectual property.
FemTechNet is part of and bigger than the contemporary university.

FemTechNet is fueled by our civil rights, anti-racist, queer, decolonizing, trans- feminist pedagogies as we work within the belly of the beast of neoliberal austerity, normalized precarity, neo-colonial techno-missionary evangelism and MOOC fever towards the radical redistribution, reinvention, and repurposing of technological, material, emotional, academic, and monetary resources.

FemTechNet is a power tool.
FemTechNet is distributed expertise.
FemTechNet is an experiment in solidarity.

FemTechNet recognizes the often-prohibitive tuition fees and other costs associated with post-secondary education and so works both within and well beyond university and college classrooms to open learning opportunities for and from a wide range of participants.

FemTechNet knows that the majority of us are not paid a sustainable wage, and works for economic justice as a feminist principle.

FemTechNet knows that ultimately none of us is protected by our institutions, so we need to take care of each other.

FemTechNet works across rank, to record feminist genealogies and technological innovations of the past, present and future.

We are a work group.
We are a social network.
We are many genders.
We are an innovative learning technology.
We are FemTechNet.

FemTechNet.org

For further information (including press inquiries), contact the Communication Committee, femtechnetinquiries@gmail.com

FIGURE 10.1. "We are FemTechNet" (2014). http://femtechnet.org/publications/manifesto/. Courtesy of FemTechNet.

labor. Feminists have always understood our pedagogical praxis as necessarily linked to theory and activism, as community engaged and accountable, thematizing the intra-action between sites of institutionalized and noninstitutionalized knowledge production. The distributed knowledge aspirations of the DOCC not only *mirror* these longstanding feminist goals but also *live* precariously in the tension among self-exploitation, institutional instrumentalization, and good politics.

The always-in-progress FemTechNet commons (FemTechNet.org) offers resources for enrolled students who are paying for the intellectual capital of credit accumulation at one of the college- or university-administered DOCC nodes, as well as self-directed learners and faculty who open their office hours—institutionally paid or unpaid, depending on your appointment—to online drop-ins. However, as we have already indicated, our enrolled students are also self-directed learners. By contributing to the DOCC's online resources, we are producing teaching and learning materials that operate alongside the Tumblr sites, Facebook pages, Twitter feeds, and other online pedagogical public resources, but which also dangerously operate as a supplement to, making up for the absent center of, the corporatized university.

The affective space of DOCC and FemTechNet offers far more collegial supportive, egalitarian, and sustaining camaraderie than the neglect and de-resourcing that so many DOCC faculty contend with in our home institutions. Thus, we need to consider the ways that the DOCC might function to navigate these affect clashes between the "civil" feminist classroom and the "toxic" public of online feminism. Our effort then is to cultivate the DOCC as a method that attends to the ranges of affects and unequally valued labors of feminist organizing, as well as knowledge production and circulation, rather than simply normalizing the affective code of conduct legislated in and regulated by both the conventional university and conventionalizing online discourse.

References

Ahmed, Sara. 2010. *The Promise of Happiness.* Durham: Duke University Press.

Anonymous. 2015. Question on *Intersectional Feminism for Beginners* (blog), January 26. http://intersectionalfeminism101.tumblr.com/post/109220875778/what-do-you-think-of-certain-sj-bloggers-who.

Bindel, Julie. 2014. "Feminism Is in Danger of Becoming Toxic." *Guardian*, November 18. http://www.theguardian.com/commentisfree/2014/nov/18/feminism-rosetta-scientist-shirt-dapper-laughs-julien-blanc-inequality.

Blumenstyk, Goldie. 2014. *American Higher Education in Crisis? What Everyone Needs to Know.* Oxford: Oxford University Press.

Bynum, Tara. 2015. "Of Hashtags and Home." *Avidly*, March 6. http://avidly.lareviewofbooks.org /2015/03/06/of-hashtags-and-home/.

Cooper, Brittney. 2014a. "It's Not about You, White Liberals: Why Attacks on Radical People of Color Are So Misguided." *Salon*, April 8. http://www.salon.com/2014/04/08/its_not_about _you_white_liberals_why_attacks_on_radical_people_of_color_are_so_misguided/.

———. 2014b. "Feminism's Ugly Clash: Why Its Future Is Not Up to White Women." *Salon*, September 24.

Cowan, T. L., and Jasmine Rault. 2014. "The Labour of Being Studied in a Free Love Economy." *Ephemera: Theory & Politics in Organization* 14 (3): 471–88.

Cross, Katherine. 2014. "The Chapel Perilous: On the Quiet Narratives in the Shadows." *Nuclear Unicorn*, February 6. http://quinnae.com/2014/02/06/the-chapel-perilous-on-the-quiet -narratives-in-the-shadows/.

Daniels, Jessie. 2014. "Trouble with White Women and White Feminism." *Racismreview.com*, January 28. http://www.racismreview.com/blog/2014/01/28/trouble-white-women-white -feminism/.

Giroux, Henry A. 2000. "Public Pedagogy as Cultural Politics." *Cultural Studies* 14 (2): 341–60.

———. 2003. "Public Pedagogy and the Politics of Resistance: Notes on a Critical Theory of Educational Struggle." *Educational Philosophy and Theory* 35 (1): 5–16.

———. 2004. "Cultural Studies, Public Pedagogy, and the Responsibility of Intellectuals." *Communication and Critical/Cultural Studies* 1 (1): 59–79.

Goldberg, Michelle. 2014. "Feminism's Toxic Twitter Wars." *Nation*, January 29. http://www .thenation.com/article/178140/feminisms-toxic-twitter-wars.

Gregg, Melissa. 2009. "Learning to (Love) Labour: Production Cultures and the Affective Turn." *Communication and Critical/Cultural Studies* 6 (2): 209–14.

hooks, bell. 1994. *Teaching to Transgress*. Abingdon: Routledge.

John, Arit, and Allie Jones. 2014. "The Incomplete Guide to Feminist Infighting." *Wire*, January 29. http://www.thewire.com/politics/2014/01/incomplete-guide-feminist-infighting /357509/.

Juhasz, Alexandra, and Anne Balsamo. 2012. "An Idea Whose Time Is Here: FemTechNet—A Distributed Online Collaborative Course (DOCC)." *ADA: A Journal of Gender, New Media, and Technology*, November 11. http://adanewmedia.org/2012/11/issue1-juhasz/.

Kaba, Miriame, and Andrea Smith. 2014. "Interlopers on Social Media: Feminism, Women of Color and Oppression." *Truthout*, February 1. http://www.truth-out.org/opinion/item/21593 -interlopers-on-social-media-feminism-women-of-color-and-oppression.

Khan, Aminah. 2014. "Toxicity: The True Story of Mainstream Feminism's Violent Gatekeepers." *Black Girl Dangerous*, February 25. http://www.blackgirldangerous.org/2014/02/toxicity-true -story-mainstream-feminisms-violent-gatekeepers/.

Lorde, Audre. 1997. "The Uses of Anger." *Women's Studies Quarterly* 25 (1/2): 278–85.

Loza, Susana. 2014. "Hashtag Feminism, #SolidarityIsForWhiteWomen, and the Other #Fem-Future." *ADA: A Journal of Gender, New Media, and Technology*, July 7. http://adanewmedia .org/2014/07/issue5-loza/.

Nakamura, Lisa. 2015. "The Unwanted Labour of Social Media: Women of Colour Call Out Culture as Venture Community Management." *New Formations: A Journal of Culture, Theory, Politics* 86:106–12.

Nyong'o, Tavia. 2014. "Civility Disobedience." *Bullybloggers*, August 18. https://bullybloggers .wordpress.com/2014/08/18/civility-disobedience/.

Rhodes, Deborah. 1995. "Media Images, Feminist Issues." *Signs* 20 (3): 685–710.

Sandlin, Jennifer A., Brian D. Schultz, and Jake Burdick, eds. 2010. *Handbook of Public Pedagogy: Education and Learning beyond Schooling*. New York: Routledge.

Sedgwick, Eve Kosofsky. 2003. *Touching Feeling: Affect, Pedagogy, Performativity*. Durham: Duke University Press Books.

Spender, Dale. 1995. *Nattering on the Net: Women, Power, and Cyberspace*. North Melbourne: Spinifex Press.

Tokumitsu, Miya. 2014. "In the Name of Love." *Jacobin*. January 13. https://www.jacobinmag.com/2014/01/in-the-name-of-love/.

11

Open Education as Resistance: MOOCs and Critical Digital Pedagogy

SEAN MICHAEL MORRIS AND JESSE STOMMEL

> There is no such thing as a *neutral* educational process.
> —RICHARD SHAULL (foreword to Paulo Freire, *Pedagogy of the Oppressed*)

Introduction

Massive open online courses (MOOCs) and critical pedagogy are not obvious bedfellows. The hype around MOOCs has centered mostly on a brand of *sage-on-the-stage* courseware at direct odds with critical pedagogy's emphasis on learner agency. Despite this—or, more to the point, because of this—we remain, like Paulo Freire, hopeful critical pedagogues. In *Pedagogy of Hope*, Freire writes, "I am hopeful, not out of mere stubbornness, but out of an existential, concrete imperative" (Freire 1994, 8). The simple truth is that we *must* be hopeful for in hope lies possibility. But, also like Freire, we recognize that hope must be balanced with action and struggle. There is no use in mere hopefulness. Critical pedagogy requires an engagement with reality that is persistent and demanding, and that engagement must result in real action, even if that action is exemplary and minute.

This chapter advocates for open education as a platform for engaging students and teachers as full agents of their own learning. Specifically we examine MOOCs (and our own work in MOOCs) through the lens of critical pedagogy and offer a series of theses that reimagine MOOCs, and open edu-

---

This chapter is revised from a three-part series previously published on *Hybrid Pedagogy*: Sean Michael Morris and Jesse Stommel, "Critical Digital Pedagogy: A Definition," "A Misapplication of MOOCs: Critical Pedagogy Writ Massive," and "If Freire Made a MOOC: Open Education as Resistance," *Hybrid Pedagogy*, http://www.hybridpedagogy.com/tag/OpenEd/.

cation more broadly, as potential sites of liberation. Freire writes in *Pedagogy of the Oppressed*, "A revolutionary leadership must accordingly practice co-intentional education" (Freire 1970, 69). Teachers must be learners, students must be empowered to be teachers, and classrooms must become collaborative sites of intrinsic motivation, networked learning, and critical practice. A critical digital pedagogy demands that open educational environments must not be repositories of content; therefore, a MOOC cannot be merely a delivery device but should be aimed first and foremost at building empowered communities.

In our own work with MOOCs this has been always at the forefront: make a space for open dialogue, and change can occur. MOOC MOOC, a seven-day meta-MOOC *about* MOOCs, ran in three iterations across 2012 and 2013. The course took the approach of a wildly open pedagogy, playfully investigating the form of the MOOC with an eye toward adapting its pedagogies for other learning environments.

MOOC MOOC: Dark Underbelly (MMDU) was a fourth iteration that diverged from the format of the other three with topics for discussion that were emergent and participant driven.[1] Where MOOC MOOC sought to understand the MOOC and its place within education, dissecting it with an almost laser focus, MMDU was designed as a catalyst to unearth deeper (and sometimes darker) issues implicated in the past, present, and future of education. The goal of our work has not been to make better MOOCs but to examine MOOCs and our experiences in them to put open education more deeply into conversation with critical pedagogy.

PART I: Critical Digital Pedagogy

Pedagogy is not ideologically neutral. This line has been for us almost a mantra over the last several years. We've written it as the first line on the "About Us" page for *Hybrid Pedagogy* (http://www.digitalpedagogylab.com /hybridped/about-us/), which is a digital journal of learning, teaching, and technology that we codirect. We've circled around this phrase, because we feel increasingly certain that the word "pedagogy" has been misread—that the project of education has been misdirected—that educators and students alike have found themselves increasingly flummoxed by a system that values assessment over engagement, learning management over discovery, content

1. These discussions were coordinated to intersect with Cathy N. Davidson's Coursera MOOC The History and Future of (Mostly) Higher Education. Each discussion responded directly to issues arising within Davidson's course.

over community, and outcomes over epiphanies. Education has misrepresented itself as objective, quantifiable, and apolitical.

Higher-education teaching is particularly uncritical and undertheorized. Most college educators (at both traditional and nontraditional institutions) do little direct pedagogical work to prepare themselves as teachers. A commitment to teaching often goes unrewarded, and pedagogical writing (in most fields) is not counted as "research."

The entire enterprise of education is too often engaged in teaching that is not pedagogical. There are a whole host of other words we'd use to describe this work: instruction, classroom management, training, outcomes driven, standards based, or content delivery. Pedagogy, on the other hand, starts with learning as its center, not students or teachers, and the work of pedagogues is necessarily political, subjective, and humane.

WHAT IS CRITICAL PEDAGOGY?

Critical pedagogy is an approach to teaching and learning predicated on fostering agency and empowering learners (implicitly and explicitly critiquing oppressive power structures). "Critical pedagogy" as a philosophical perspective was first outlined by Paulo Freire, then expanded by Henry Giroux, bell hooks, and others. The word "critical" in critical pedagogy functions in several registers:

- Critical, as in mission critical, essential.
- Critical, as in literary criticism and critique, providing definitions and interpretation.
- Critical, as in reflective and nuanced thinking about a subject.
- Critical, as in criticizing institutional, corporate, or societal impediments to learning.
- Critical pedagogy, as a theoretical field or disciplinary approach, which inflects (and is inflected by) each of these other meanings.

Each of these registers distinguishes critical pedagogy from pedagogy, but the current educational climate has made the terms, for us, increasingly coterminous (i.e., an ethical pedagogy *must be* a critical one). Pedagogy is praxis, insistently perched at the intersection between the philosophy and the practice of teaching. When teachers talk about teaching, we are not necessarily doing pedagogical work, and not every teaching method constitutes a pedagogy. Rather, pedagogy necessarily involves recursive, second-order, metalevel work. Teachers teach, but pedagogues teach *while also* actively investigating teaching and learning. Critical pedagogy suggests a specific kind of anticapitalist, liberatory praxis. This is deeply personal and political work, through which pedagogues cannot and do not remain objective. Rather, pedagogy, and particularly critical pedagogy, is work to which we must bring our full selves and work to which every learner must come with full agency.

In *Pedagogy of the Oppressed*, Paulo Freire argues against the *banking model of education*, in which education "becomes an act of depositing, in which the students are the depositories and the teacher is the depositor" (Freire 1970, 73). This model emphasizes a one-sided transactional relationship, in which teachers are seen as content experts and students are positioned as subhuman receptacles. The use here of "subhuman" is intentional and not exaggeration; for in the tenets set out in Freire's work (and the work of other critical pedagogues, including bell hooks and Henry Giroux), the banking model of education is part and parcel with efforts most clearly summed up in the term *dehumanization*. The banking model of education is efficient in that it maintains order and is bureaucratically neat and tidy. But efficiency, when it comes to teaching and learning, is not worth valorizing. Schools are not factories, nor are learning or learners products of the mill.

We are made deeply skeptical when we hear the word "content" in discussions about education, particularly when it is accompanied by the word "packaged." It is not that education is without content altogether, but that its content is coconstructed *as part of* and *not in advance of* the learning.

Critical pedagogy is concerned less with knowing and more with a voracious not knowing. It is an ongoing and recursive process of discovery. For Freire, "Knowledge emerges only through invention and re-invention, through the restless, impatient, continuing, hopeful inquiry human beings pursue in the world, with the world, and with each other" (Freire 1970, 74). Here, the language echoes the sort of learning Freire describes. With a flurry of adjectives and clauses separated by commas, his sentence circles around its subject, wandering, pushing restlessly at the edges of how words make meaning—not directly through literal translation into concepts, but in the way words rub curiously against one another, making meaning through a kind of friction. Knowledge emerges in the interplay between multiple people in conversation—brushing against one another in a mutual and charged exchange or *dialogue*. Freire writes, "Authentic education is not carried on by 'A' *for* 'B' or by 'A' *about* 'B,' but rather by 'A' *with* 'B'" (93). It is through this impatient dialogue, and the implicit collaboration within it, that critical pedagogy finds its impetus toward change.

In place of the banking model of education, Freire advocates for "problem-posing education" (84) in which a classroom or learning environment becomes a space for asking questions—a space of cognition not information. Vertical (or hierarchical) relationships give way to more playful ones, in which students and teachers coauthor together the parameters for their individual and collective learning. Problem-posing education offers a space of mutual creation not consumption. In *Teaching to Transgress*, bell hooks writes, "As a classroom community, our capacity to generate excitement is deeply affected by our interest in one another, in hearing one another's voices, in recognizing one another's presence" (hooks 1994, 8). This is a lively and intimate space of creativity and inquiry—a space of listening as much as of speaking.

WHAT IS CRITICAL DIGITAL PEDAGOGY?

Our work has wondered at the extent to which critical pedagogy translates into digital space. Can the necessary reflective dialogue flourish within web-based tools, social media platforms, learning management systems, or MOOCs? What is digital agency? To what extent can social media function as a space of democratic participation? How can we build platforms that support learning across age, race, gender, culture, ability, and geography? What are the specific affordances and limitations of technology toward these ends? If, indeed, *all learning is necessarily hybrid*, as we've argued,[2] to what extent are critical pedagogy and digital pedagogy becoming also coterminous?

Writers and educators like Howard Rheingold, Cathy N. Davidson, Seymour Papert, and the Feminist Technology Network (FemTechNet) community have considered this intersection explicitly and implicitly. The wondering at these questions is, in fact, not particularly new. In his forward to Freire's *Pedagogy of the Oppressed*, Richard Shaull writes, "Our advanced technological society is rapidly making objects of most of us and subtly programming us into conformity to the logic of its system [. . .] The paradox is that the same technology that does this to us also creates a new sensitivity to what is happening" (Shaull 1970, 33). And John Dewey writes in *Schools of To-morrow*, published decades earlier, "Unless the mass of workers are to be blind cogs and pinions in the apparatus they employ, they must have some understanding of the physical and social facts behind and ahead of the material and

2. In "Hybridity Part 2: What is Hybrid Pedagogy?," Jesse Stommel (2012a) writes, "My hypothesis is that all learning is necessarily hybrid. In classroom-based pedagogy, it is important to engage the digital selves of our students. And, in online pedagogy, it is equally important to engage their physical selves. With digital pedagogy and online education, our challenge is not to merely replace (or offer substitutes for) face-to-face instruction, but to find new and innovative ways to engage students in the practice of learning."

appliances with which they are dealing" (Dewey 1915, 246). If we are to keep every educative endeavor from becoming millwork—from becoming only a reflection of oppressive labor practices and uneven power relationships—we must engage deeply with its reality.

Increasingly, the web is a space of politics, a social space, a professional space, and a space of community. And, for better or worse, more of our learning is happening there. For many of us, distinguishing between our *real* selves and our *virtual* selves is increasingly difficult, and in fact, these distinctions are being altogether unsettled. In "The New Learning is Ancient," Kathi Inman Berens writes, "It doesn't matter to me if my classroom is a little rectangle in a building or a little rectangle above my keyboard. Doors are rectangles; rectangles are portals. We walk through" (Berens 2012). When we learn online, our feet are usually still quite literally *on the ground*. When we interact with a group of students via streaming video, the interaction is nevertheless *face-to-face*. The web is asking us to reconsider how we think about space and how and where we engage, as well as on which platforms the bulk of our learning happens.

In *Small Pieces Loosely Joined: A Unified Theory of the Web*, David Weinberger writes, "We are the true 'small pieces' of the Web, and we are loosely joining ourselves in ways that we're still inventing" (Weinberger 2002, xii). Ten years ago, following the publication of Weinberger's book, we wouldn't have imagined the learning networks we've now built with colleagues working together (sometimes simultaneously in real time) in places as seemingly remote as Portland, Madison, Manchester, Prince Edward Island, Sydney, Cairo, and Hong Kong.

This is not to say, however, that there aren't challenges to this sort of work. In *On Critical Pedagogy*, Henry Giroux argues,

> Intellectuals have a responsibility to analyze how language, information, and meaning work to organize, legitimate, and circulate values, structure reality, and offer up particular notions of agency and identity. For public intellectuals, the latter challenge demands a new kind of literacy and critical understanding with respect to the emergence of the new media and electronic technologies, and the new and powerful role they play as instruments of public pedagogy. (Giroux 2011, 175)

Most digital technology, like social media or collaborative writing platforms or MOOCs, does not have its values coded into it in advance. These are tools merely, good only insofar as they are used. And platforms that do dictate too strongly how we might use them, or ones that remove our agency by too covertly reducing us and our work to commodified data, should be rooted out by a critical digital pedagogy. Far too much work in educational technology starts with tools, when what we need to start with is humans.

We are better users of technology when we are thinking critically about the nature and effects of that technology. What we must do is work to encourage students and ourselves to think critically about new tools (and, more importantly, the tools we already use). And when we're looking for solutions, what we most need to change is our thinking and not our tools.

In short, critical digital pedagogy

- centers its practice on community and collaboration;
- must remain open to diverse, international voices, and thus requires invention to reimagine the ways that communication and collaboration happen across cultural and political boundaries;
- will not, cannot, be defined by a single voice but must gather together a cacophony of voices; and
- must have use and application outside traditional institutions of education.

A critical digital pedagogy demands that open and networked educational environments not be merely repositories of content but, rather, create dialogues in which both students and teachers participate as full agents.

Pete Rorabaugh writes in "Occupy the Digital: Critical Pedagogy and New Media":

> Critical Pedagogy, no matter how we define it, has a central place in the discussion of how learning is changing in the 21st century because Critical Pedagogy is primarily concerned with an equitable distribution of power. If students live in a culture that digitizes and educates them through a screen, they require an education that empowers them in that sphere, teaches them that language, and offers new opportunities of human connectivity. (Rorabaugh 2012)

Critical pedagogy is as much a political approach as it is an educative one, a social justice movement first, and an education movement second.

So, critical digital pedagogy must also be a method of resistance and humanization. It is not simply work done in the mind, on paper, or on screen. It is work that must be done on the ground. It is not ashamed of its rallying cry or its soapbox. Critical digital pedagogy eats aphorisms—like this one right here—for breakfast. But it is not afraid to incite, to post its manifestos, or to light its torches.

PART II: A Misapplication of MOOCs

If 2012 was the year of the MOOC (Pappano 2012), then 2013 was the year the MOOC died.[3] The public imagination around the MOOC has faded and become niche, now becoming the playground of political and social theorists, a dedicated (and mostly academic) audience, and learning hobbyists. The conversation has gone to its corners, and the biggest impact that MOOCs have had on education is to catapult edupreneurs like Sal Khan and Daphne Koller into a national spotlight that includes appearances on NPR and CNN. Lackadaisically, other universities are joining the MOOC movement, perhaps hoping for some windfall of either a larger student body or just some good local press, or perhaps simply as a great "why not?" But the MOOC moment has passed.

The shame of that, if it is true, is that the MOOC remains largely unconsidered. In July 2012 when we launched MOOC MOOC, *Hybrid Pedagogy*'s meta-MOOC inspection of MOOCs, we did not want to investigate the practical applications of connectivism or an iteration of the use of learning management systems; we entered the fray because MOOCs excited (molecularly) education. There was value in even the desperate attempts, the banal efforts, and the comical forays because of the conversations they initiated. Increasingly, that conversation has dulled to a murmur.

We have said variously that a MOOC is not a thing, a course, or a classroom. The MOOC is seen as a mere extension of a distance-learning experiment that's been going on for over a century; or, as a neoliberal, capitalist enterprise to co-opt traditional education and make learning into a for-profit, corporate product. In certain ways, and in examples that continue to proliferate across the educational landscape, the MOOC has become an engine for poorly considered pedagogy (in the same way that most online learning is that engine). Companies like Coursera quickly scrambled, shortly after their initial production of massive courses, to drum up a financial yield from their otherwise free offerings. And Udacity, an unabashedly Silicon Valley–based endeavor, within a year of launching its first MOOCs admitted what to many academics looked like defeat and changed its curriculum into one of massive open online training. In cases such as these, learning became a product, and

---

3. In "What is MOOCification?," the opening prompt for the third iteration of MOOC MOOC (http://www.moocmooc.com/articles_files/What_Is_MOOCification.html), Sean Michael Morris writes, "The MOOC is dead. It is a death that was predicted, inevitable, and one that will linger for some time, the odor of its putrefaction filling our hallowed halls. What is more interesting about the MOOC's death than its inevitability."

the humanitarian ideals of the university seemed to fall on fallow ground. But it was not the MOOC that caused this capitalization of education and its dialogues, nor the disillusionment and disappointment that followed.

The MOOC was an empty space—a potential site of resistance—on which we might have writ different expectations, as neither a product nor a thing.

When we say that the MOOC is not a thing, then, what do we mean? If it is not a course one enters and exits, if it is not the content bound up within its learning management system, or if it is not a product of which we can dispute the value, intentions, and results—activities that have been the centrifuge of the MOOC debate—what is it?

The MOOC is a strategy. In "March of the MOOCs: Monstrous Open Online Courses," the article that first announced MOOC MOOC, Jesse Stommel writes, "A MOOC isn't a thing at all, just a methodological approach, with no inherent value except insofar as it's used" (Stommel 2012b). As with all methodological approaches, the MOOC begins as a blank slate. Much like a screwdriver in a toolbox, a chalkboard in the classroom, or a phone in the pocket, the MOOC isn't this or that, positive or negative, good or bad, or well-intentioned or malicious, *until it is put into play.* Many people will argue with this position, and we're quick to admit that it's politically fraught, but it is this neutral, imaginative, and generative space that we must hold to understand what it is that we missed about MOOCs, and which we must not miss again. Also, for this exegesis to work, we must refuse to see "MOOC" as a mere acronym and must instead interrogate it alongside words like "approach," "lens," "pedagogy," and "praxis."

"Massive" and "open" suggest the typical limitations of the classroom have been lifted, including the strictures of social norms and power structures of the traditional (often dysfunctional) teacher-student relationship. Most efforts to realize the MOOC in any practical sense (e.g., Coursera, Udacity, and others) first begin by divesting themselves of true openness, instead inventing a partial openness, or a strategically reframed idea of "open" that can still include enough of the banking model of education to keep instructors, institutions, and students anchored. The reduction of "open" to mean "access" or "free," for example, is the result of a fundamental misunderstanding of what openness in education entails. "Free" suggests a product or transaction and "access" requires gatekeepers and permissions, whereas "open" suggests community. The openness the MOOC presages is one where agency trumps position, where a student can become a teacher or a teacher a student, and the whole endeavor of education becomes a collaboration. It is not openness like a door is open, it is open the way a mind is open.

If, as bell hooks writes in *Teaching to Transgress,* "The classroom remains the most radical space of possibility in the academy" (hooks 1994, 12), then the MOOC is the most radical of such spaces outside the academy. This is important: the MOOC represents a departure from the university-centric model of learning; not just a departure from the oppressive banking model of education but a relocation of education into previously unacknowledged learning spaces. To understand how we are seeing the MOOC as a site of resistance, we must be ready to embrace its inherent value, *even in its misapplication.*

The MOOCs of Coursera, Udacity, and edX—the MOOCs that still rest on the limestone of the banking model of education—while underutilizing the potential of the MOOC, nonetheless tinker with elements of true openness. Early Udacity MOOCs, for example, included high school students in courses that college seniors might take and encouraged on-ground meetups. Coursera, too, encourages on-ground collaboration and support for its students. The motivation, though, is to provide student "TAs" rather than student-teachers. This is an innovation—a dipping of the toes into a new pedagogical pool—but it is also fastidiously aligned with the banking model that limits the agency of those students. Still central to the learning experience is the teacher of the MOOC, the "content expert," who, in a strangely deft bait-and-switch by most MOOC providers, is less involved in the actual learning process.[4]

But even in these misapplications of the MOOC, a germ of radical possibility exists. In "What is a MOOC?" Dave Cormier says, "A MOOC is a course, it's open, it's participatory, it's distributed, and it supports life-long networked learning" (Cormier 2010). When learning is established online, it automatically enters a new space, one where distribution, collaboration, participation, and networked learning become possible; even if they remain ghosts in the room, they are natural parts of the environment. Where online learning has failed, by mimicking an off-the-Internet classroom, the MOOC offers the potential for greater integration with the vast creative and educative possibilities of the web. The connectivist MOOCs (as in "cMOOCs"), as opposed to the more corporate hierarchical "xMOOCs" of the Ivy League universities and Silicon Valley, seek to bring into alignment the learning environment with the web, making an Internet-as-learning space.[5]

---

4. In most cases, MOOCs are "led" by previously videotaped instructors delivering lectures—a phenomenon Audrey Watters (2013) addresses in her article "The Early Days of Videotaped Lectures," when she says: "Part of this is a failure of instructional design. Part of this is a failure of pedagogy. Part of it is a failure of community—a failure of both certain online education start-ups in fostering community and a failure on my part in joining it."

5. In "What Is the Theory That Underpins Our MOOCs?," George Siemens (2012) writes about the connectivist MOOC model: "At the core of the MOOCs that I've been involved with is a power question: what can learners do for themselves with digital tools and networks?"

Within the connectivist MOOC model, student agency is not only more possible but also entirely necessary, because the environment of the MOOC is literally built by students as they carve spaces and make connections across the web. If there has been one complaint about the connectivist MOOC approach, it is that it leaves too much unstructured; so much so, that the learner cannot know where to begin her learning process.[6] Radical possibility and liberation do not any more arrive from an anarchic learning environment than they do from the banking model. In *Pedagogy of the Oppressed*, Paulo Freire writes that "the oppressed must confront reality critically, simultaneously objectifying and acting upon that reality" (Freire 1970, 34). A do-as-you-will learning approach does little to motivate critical engagement with reality; even if an instructor, mentor, guide, or content expert sets the stage, the freedom to do or to not do can actually wrest critical engagement from the learner's hands. Mere freedom to roam the Internet can result in a drowning sensation, which can be just as debilitating to agency as oppressive leadership. Omission of leadership can result as much in oppression as can the misuse of power.

The teacher never disappears for Freire. Instead she must become repositioned, abdicating her authority and joining the students in the learning process, about which critical pedagogy is quite clear. The oppressor cannot free the oppressed without relinquishing his place as oppressor—as well as the mind, inclinations, and prejudices that go along with it—and joining the oppressed in their struggle for liberation. The teacher cannot preach against oppression from behind the podium but must leave the podium behind, removing it from the environment and mind of the classroom. In this way, the movement toward a liberating education does not become leaderless but rather leader saturated. Whether realized or not, this is the inherent promise, the ideology, of the MOOC.

Our work (here and in the various iterations of MOOC MOOC) is an intervention. We have come with our colleagues to sit the institution of education down and discuss its addiction and its dependency on poor pedagogy. The university balances on a precipice of irrelevance and refutability, bordering on becoming but a credentialing corporation; the knowledge aristocracy of the academy finds itself awash in an information age where authority based on reading, publishing, and experience is a negligible authority. What is hap-

6. Keith Brennan (2013) writes in his "Guide to Understanding the MOOC Novice," "One of the most important aspects of the learning experience is motivation. And one of the most important aspects of motivation is our sense of our own capability, and our sense that the environment we are learning in will allow us to achieve."

pening, and why critical pedagogy and the MOOC are so *mission critical*, is not that the edifice of education has lost its value; rather, unless learners are given agency within those walls, they will *take* agency elsewhere. They will leave and are leaving because they can find agency and information elsewhere.

Like any tool in the wrong hands, MOOCs can become agents of continued oppression—of the learner or the teacher, in a pedagogical or political-economic sense. We are peeking through a pinhole when we look at MOOCs. But what we continue to see through the pinhole is possibility, radical and social as much as educational. In "Massiveness + Openness = New Literacies of Participation?" Bonnie Stewart writes,

> [The] variety of responses to MOOCs is indicative of the fault lines becoming increasingly visible in the terrain of contemporary higher education. . . . Even if few of the largest MOOCs are currently designed to resemble Trojan horses for participatory culture, they nonetheless have the potential to expose large sectors of society to new literacies and meta-level processing around the idea of learning as a communicative practice. (Stewart 2013)

This is not mere idealism, and we should be clear that the potential does not lie within the MOOC itself—that *thing*—but within the zeitgeist that made the MOOC necessary and inevitable. Just as Twitter fueled the Arab Spring, or just as Luddites organized against the misuse of industrial technologies, so may MOOCs point out the much-needed shift in its fundamental pedagogical practices that the academy must attend to, and signal new, critical conceptions of education, learning, and learners.

PART III: If Freire Made a MOOC

In a recent event focused on building community in MOOCs, Al Filreis (2013) offered a keynote, "The Non-Automated Humanities MOOC," in which he remarked, "Don't talk about MOOCs as courses. That's a slippery slope to creating a thing that doesn't hybridize but colonizes." To see the MOOC as a course that reinforces ossified hierarchical relationships in learning environments is to carry forward a banking model of pedagogy that does nothing to empower students or teachers. The pedagogical value in openness is that it can create dialogue and can deconstruct the teacher-student binary by increasing access and bringing together disparate learning spaces. Openness can function as a form of resistance both within and outside the walls of institutions. But open education is no panacea. Hierarchies must be dismantled—and that dismantling honored as an ethic—if its potentials are to be realized.

We offer here six theses that work to reimagine what the MOOC is and what it can be. These theses are tentative, meant to invite conversation, in the nature of Freire's notion of dialogue.

THESIS #1: A COURSE IS A CONVERSATION AND NOT A STATIC RESERVOIR OR RECEPTACLE FOR CONTENT

Audrey Watters writes in "5 Things I've Learned from MOOCs about How I Learn," "When the C in MOOC feels like 'community,' I'm far happier than when the C feels like 'course'" (Watters 2012). And so, the body of the course must have as its limbs no less than the number of participants. Twenty-five, fifty, or two hundred thousand—each must be allowed the agency to be a co-author. In "Rhizomatic Education: Community as Curriculum," Dave Cormier argues that "curriculum is not driven by predefined inputs from experts; it is constructed and negotiated in real time by the contributions of those engaged in the learning process" (Cormier 2008). A course is a starting point, a space where learners can experiment with their agency, discover the complexity of their oppression, and begin to work toward more liberated action.

In *Pedagogy of the Oppressed*, Paulo Freire writes, "It would be a contradiction in terms if the oppressors not only defended but actually implemented a liberating education" (Freire 1970, 36). This work cannot originate from teachers alone. Participation is key and must be presented always not as an injunction (for participation that is forced is mandatory, not emancipatory), but as a call toward invention, self-invention, and humanization.

In most MOOCs, content replaces the teacher, making the interchangeability of the teacher's and students' roles impossible. Content is static and governed from the podium. It is written before students are available to read it, consult on it, or change it. Content cannot relinquish its authority. The teacher is not approachable, if indeed active in the MOOC at all, but is seen and read—and thus becomes irrefutable. Even if students are asked to refute, question, or append the teacher, the *teacher-as-content* is always at the center of the operation of education.

In MOOC MOOC, we provided content that spurred invention and conversation each day of the seven-day MOOC; but that content was self-undermining. The course invited learners in the MOOC to question and fill obvious gaps in the content. MMDU went one step further—there was no content at all besides that which participants brought to the fore. Topics and subject matter were announced on the *Hybrid Pedagogy* site, which served more as background music rather than as a strict framework. Our pedagogical imperative is to let a course unfold according to the whim and determination of the group—to replace *teacher-as-content* with *learning-community-as-content-maker*.

THESIS #2: EDUCATION CANNOT BE COMPULSORY, AND THE WORK OF LEARNING STARTS WITH AGENCY

To protect academic freedom in education, we must start in the classroom by fostering agency and inviting dissent. The first step in advocating for students and learners is to be one. We cannot demand that *this* is when students will learn *that*; instead we must approach learning as collaboration. This is at the heart of what Freire calls "co-intentional education," in which "teachers and students (leadership and people), co-intent on reality, are both Subjects, not only in the task of unveiling that reality, and thereby coming to know it critically, but in the task of re-creating that knowledge" (Freire 1970, 69). The collective knowledge of a group of students will almost always exceed the expertise of one instructor.

While connectivist MOOCs have made great strides in reimagining learning experiences as co-intentional, the majority of MOOCs do not ask questions about student agency. In general, they do nothing to innovate online pedagogies; but worse, almost as a response to the massive nature of the courses, MOOC designers have removed even further the opportunity for students to take control of their own learning by disconnecting them utterly from the power of the teacher. *Teacher-as-content* is unavailable for negotiation, inflexible not in the sense that a live instructor might be strict, but in the way of a museum display under glass: within most MOOCs, few options exist for students to make changes, meddle, or get their fingers dirty.

MOOC MOOC, which was essentially an experiment in learning about learning (and talking about talking about learning about learning), started from the assumption that teachers can't talk about learning adequately (or fully) without students in the room and without recognizing the ways that we are all students. We didn't merely work to deconstruct teacher-student binaries; instead we started from a place where students were automatically teachers and teachers automatically students, and all learning was a collaboration.

In chapter 3 of *Net Smart*, "Participation Power," Howard Rheingold writes, "In the world of digitally networked publics, online participation—if you know how to do it—can translate into real power. Participation, however, is a kind of power that only works if you share it with others" (Rheingold 2012, 112). In the classroom, and in what we can now call the traditional MOOC, the role of the teacher is imbued with authority in advance. Critical pedagogy demands the act of teaching be focused on abdicating and not guarding that

authority. Critical digital pedagogy demands a consideration of how we abdicate authority within digital environments. Given the degree to which the
learning management system (LMS) can assert its own authority ("management" is, after all, one letter of the acronym), participant pedagogy demands
that the teacher both abdicate authority *and also* actively invite students to
subvert the control of the platform within which they're working.

In "Best Practices: Thoughts on a Flash Mob Mentality," Janine DeBaise
writes, "Too often, faculty design pedagogy around the worst-case scenario
and then apply that pedagogy to every student" (DeBaise 2014). The critical
digital pedagogue sees imminent danger in any sort of "best practices." Best
practices, as they're conventionally understood, are not about meeting and
working mindfully and collectively with students, but about *keeping us from
needing to.* Freire writes, "In a humanizing pedagogy the method ceases to
be an instrument by which the teacher (in this instance, the revolutionary
leadership) can manipulate students (in this instance, the oppressed), because
it expresses the consciousness of the students themselves" (Freire 1970, 69).
The *best* best practices are those that are, as DeBaise (2014) also writes, "'Practices Worth Considering' or 'Things You Could Try' or 'Stuff That Just Might
Work.'"

The MOOC, perhaps in part because of its massive nature (and the ti-
midity of its innovators), relies far too heavily on the crude persistence and
adequacy of the "best practice." As a designer constructs the course, she will
endeavor to create an environment where the majority of students may succeed; she creates quizzes, content, and discussion fora meant to encourage
engagement and learning. She does this *before* she knows who will join the
course; a necessary evil, some would say, because the course, once launched,
will be without anyone at the helm. Best practices in MOOCs buttress the
content and allow a designer to sleep at night, knowing that the course will
turn a deaf ear to any riots fomented by the participants.

We argue that a MOOC should have no buttresses. The *best* best practice
is to imperil best practices. For example, having a video of the instructor(s)
at the head of each unit is often declared a best practice for online learning.
However, we have decidedly avoided using talking-head lecture videos in any
of our MOOCs, choosing instead to include videos of participants at the head
of each day's activities, allowing the voices of authority to proliferate rather
than congeal. Our goal is not to avoid showing up for the course but to make
ourselves part and parcel, sometimes a catalyst for the conversation that un-

folds but never its center. Courses can be built in advance certainly, but we argue that they're better when they *quite literally* build themselves.

The work of critical pedagogy is emergent, which means the notion of outcomes needs to be reimagined. Outcomes are bureaucratic devices employed to keep learning organized, predictable, and efficient; but bureaucracy, according to Freire, is the enemy of liberation. For Freire, "The moment the new regime hardens into a dominating 'bureaucracy' the humanist dimension of struggle is lost and it is no longer possible to speak of liberation" (Freire 1970, 57). Outcomes tell learners what is important in advance, making the act of learning neat and tidy, while deterring the unexpected and unruly epiphanies that arise organically from within a learning environment. Invention arises from self-governance. Henry Giroux says in *On Critical Pedagogy*:

> I have stressed that these new sites of education, which I call the realm of public pedagogy, are crucial to any notion of politics because they are the sites in which people often learn, unlearn, or simply do not get the knowledge and skills that prepare them to become critical agents, capable not merely of understanding the society and world in which they live but also of being able to assume the mantle of governance. (Giroux 2011, 175)

While outcomes theoretically prepare students to meet the requirements of an industrialized world—where deadlines and measurable productivity are the backbone of labor—they do not empower students to question labor practices, to demand change, or to genuinely innovate. Outcomes prepare students to be dull, listless participants in labor-for-labor's-sake.

Outcomes are programmed into the code of a MOOC, within the LMS itself. As flexible as a given LMS may be, the code behind the design assumes that outcomes, assessments, and grades will each be an integral part of the instruction. A course is taught in predetermined segments or modules, each building in some way from the previous segment and each relying on students meeting the outcomes of the previous modules. In some cases, new information is hidden behind an outcome firewall, so that content remains invisible until an outcome is met.

In our MOOCs, and in all our courses, we avoid predetermined outcomes. We assume, with the participants, that we will generate more questions than answers, and that we will do something together that none of us could have anticipated (and that none of us could have done on our own). We do not say,

"At the end of this unit, you will know / be able to / understand . . ." Instead we offer trajectories and then ask students what they've learned, what has surprised them, what questions remain unanswered, and what participants want to do with their epiphanies. Freire writes, "The pedagogy of the oppressed, which is the pedagogy of people engaged in the fight for their own liberation, has its roots here. And those who recognize, or begin to recognize, themselves as oppressed must be among the developers of this pedagogy" (Freire 1970, 35–36). It cannot be the LMS designers, the administration, or the teachers—masters of outcomes, all—who make pedagogical determinations; it is the learner who must participate actively in that pedagogy. We begin to make this possible when we rethink outcomes—and the technology that supports them.

THESIS #5: LEARNING SHOULD NOT BE STRUCTURED TO CONFORM TO ASSESSMENT MECHANISMS

Structuring learning toward assessment is another bureaucratic choice, one designed to create streamlined instruction, not to encourage learner empowerment and agency. In truth, learning is not a process that can be structured in advance without first hobbling it, like fitting a body into a box by chopping off its limbs. Much goes missing when we remove learning from learners' hands and manicure it for ease of instruction. When we ask students to conform their learning to the mechanisms by which we measure it, we are not permitting students to learn; we are asking them to pull the *right* lever at the *right* time to the *right* effect—like automatons.

Assessment is too often the enemy of innovation. Our inability to quantitatively assess something is often in direct proportion to its pedagogical value. The best work confounds us. Because of the rampant culture of assessment that devalues students and their work, we've internalized grading as compulsory in education; however, grading is done in many more situations than it is actually demanded. In "Ranking, Evaluating, and Liking: Sorting Out Three Forms of Judgment," Peter Elbow writes, "assessment tends so much to drive and control teaching. Much of what we do in the classroom is determined by the assessment structures we work under" (Elbow 1993, 187). We find ways to grade, even inside learning environments, like MOOCs, where grading isn't required.

Assessment and standards are elephants in almost every room where discussions of education are underway. Cathy N. Davidson (2009) offered a risky and still novel post titled "How to Crowdsource Grading," in which she described forgoing external summative assessment in favor of peer feedback and her own "feedback to the feedback." Assessment mechanisms should be formative, designed to create new opportunities for learning; but most importantly, our assessment practices should arise organically from within our learning communities and not from the technologies and methodologies that support them.

Assessment has political implications for MOOCs—and online learning more generally. Without measurable successes, alternative instructional delivery methods cannot prove themselves viable. Administrations and those who hold the purse strings of funding for education (or educational technology) want quantified results. But a MOOC whose participants score well on quizzes is not necessarily *teaching* well. John Warner, a blogger for *Inside Higher Ed*, asks in "The Costs of Big Data,"

> What if one of our goals for students is the development of agency, the ability to negotiate and exert control over their own lives? What if we believe this is an important goal because it is significantly correlated not only with success, but happiness and well-being? What if we believe that a student's education should extend beyond "tips, tricks, and hints," for getting better grades? (Warner 2014)

These are questions that standardized assessments can't answer and that their design doesn't acknowledge. In truth, assessment should not really be a *mechanism* at all. Assessment should be about curiosity and critical inquiry, a reflective and recursive process that emerges from within a learning community rather than structuring that community in advance.

THESIS #6: IN EDUCATION, WE RISE AND FALL TOGETHER

Critical digital pedagogy demands that we rethink labor conditions within education. A system that mistreats teachers is a system that mistreats students. There is a justified anxiety that MOOCs will further damage the tenuous role of teachers in higher education. To be clear, we do not believe technology like the Internet or platforms like MOOCs can replace teachers. Thinking critically about our technologies, though, can help assure that technology *will never* replace teachers.

In *Pedagogy of the Oppressed*, Freire writes, "Any situation in which some individuals prevent others from engaging in the process of inquiry is one of violence. The means used are not important; to alienate human beings from their own decision-making is to change them into objects" (Freire 1970, 85). Freire does not use the term "violence" lightly here, nor does he use it really as metaphor. Educational institutions are, increasingly, sites of real oppression, suffering, anguish, and uprising. The academy is full of discontent masses, and while dissenters often take themselves to a minimum safe distance before openly voicing their objections on blogs and social media, one cannot ignore the contingent labor crisis, students overburdened with debt, radical reduction of tenured positions, increasing corporatization, and deep, wounding cuts to funding given over to the actual work of educating at these institutions. The university, like 75 percent of its faculty (Weissmann 2013), is in a precarious position; that which consists primarily of adjuncts may yet become adjunct itself.

Freire also writes, "Education as the practice of freedom—as opposed to education as the practice of domination—denies that man is abstract, isolated, independent, and unattached to the world; it also denies that the world exists as a reality apart from people" (Freire 1970, 81). Open education as a practice, then, must also be protest. Openness is not an empty rhetorical strategy, but incendiary, bringing into conversation matters of learning, pedagogy, and power that classrooms with closed doors omit.

Few MOOCs have reflected on their own political economies. In the MOOCs we've run, like MOOC MOOC, and through our editorial practices on *Hybrid Pedagogy*, we have proceeded under the supposition that there are accidental pedagogues everywhere, teachers without classrooms who left the academy but kept their ears and eyes open for discussions of a new future for higher education. These are the optimists and introverts, the radicals, and the truly deeply irrevocably fringe. And they are most often lurkers in our MOOCs, precarious voices in our Twitter chats and lingerers in rooms at conferences. And their minds are full of ideas. As Freire has said, "The oppressed must be their own example in the struggle for their redemption" (Freire 1970, 36). We have tried to build spaces where voices that were unheard could find audience; and we did this not simply out of a practice of critical digital pedagogy, but because *none of the problems of higher education will be solved without the help of those it has made adjunct.*

Conclusion

We will be required to cede our authority many times over. Critical pedagogy is, according to Freire, "made and remade" (Freire 1970, 48). And, "critical reflection is also action" (Freire 1970, 128). This means that educators and students will need to return again and again to their fundamental assumptions about education—about open education, about MOOCs, about assessment, about outcomes, and about what it means to be part of a community of educators and students.

The field of critical digital pedagogy is yet nascent. We find ourselves, appropriately, with more questions than answers about how this work might continue to take shape. How can critical pedagogy help to examine, dismantle, or rebuild the structures, hierarchies, institutions, and technologies of education? What systems of privilege must we first dismantle? When we muster our pedagogy as a form of advocacy, how do we decide what counts as talk and what counts as action? How shall the scholarship of pedagogy—words like these ones right here—words that gape at world changing—give way to the voices of learners, gathered together in a networked community of radical generosity?

References

Berens, Kathi Inman. 2012. "The New Learning Is Ancient." *Kathi Inman Berens*, December 3. http://kathiiberens.com/2012/12/03/ancient/.

Brennan, Keith. 2013. "In Connectivism, No One Can Hear You Scream: a Guide to Understanding the MOOC Novice." *Hybrid Pedagogy*, July 24. http://www.hybridpedagogy.com /journal/in-connectivism-no-one-can-hear-you-scream-a-guide-to-understanding-the -mooc-novice/.

Cormier, Dave, 2008. "Rhizomatic Education: Community as Curriculum." *Dave's Educational Blog*, June 3. http://davecormier.com/edblog/2008/06/03/rhizomatic-education-community -as-curriculum/.

———. 2010. "What is a MOOC?" YouTube video, 4:26. Posted December 8. https://www.you tube.com/watch?v=eW3gMGqcZQc.

Davidson, Cathy N. 2009. "How to Crowdsource Grading." *HASTAC*, July 26. https://www .hastac.org/blogs/cathy-davidson/2009/07/26/how-crowdsource-grading.

DeBaise, Janine. 2014. "Best Practices: Thoughts on a Flash Mob Mentality." *Hybrid Pedagogy*, April 22. http://www.digitalpedagogylab.com/hybridped/best-practices-thoughts-flash-mob -mentality.

Dewey, John. 1915. *Schools of To-morrow*. New York: E. P. Dutton & Company.

Elbow, Peter. 1993. "Ranking, Evaluating, and Liking: Sorting Out Three Forms of Judgment." *College English* 55 (2): 187–206.

Filreis, Al. 2013. "The Non-Automated Humanities MOOC." Keynote address at Wisconsin Institutes for Discovery, Madison, November 14.

Freire, Paulo, 1970. *Pedagogy of the Oppressed*. New York: Penguin Books.

———. 1994. *Pedagogy of Hope*. New York: Bloomsbury Academic.

Giroux, Henry. 2011. *On Critical Pedagogy*. New York: Bloomsbury Publishing.

hooks, bell. 1994. *Teaching to Transgress*. Abingdon: Routledge.

Pappano, Laura. 2012. "The Year of the MOOC." *New York Times*, November 2. http://www .nytimes.com/2012/11/04/education/edlife/massive-open-online-courses-are-multiplying -at-a-rapid-pace.html.

Rheingold, Howard. 2012. *Net Smart*. Cambridge: MIT Press.

Rorabaugh, Pete. 2012. "Occupy the Digital: Critical Pedagogy and New Media." *Hybrid Pedagogy*, August 6. http://www.hybridpedagogy.com/journal/occupy-the-digital-critical -pedagogy-and-new-media/.

Shaull, Richard. 1970. "Foreword." In Paulo Freire, *Pedagogy of the Oppressed*. New York: Penguin Books.

Siemens, George. 2012. "What Is the Theory that Underpins *Our* MOOCs?" *Elearnspace*, June 3. http://www.elearnspace.org/blog/2012/06/03/what-is-the-theory-that-underpins-our-moocs/.

Stewart, Bonnie. 2013. "Massiveness + Openness = New Literacies of Participation?" *MERLOT Journal of Online Learning and Teaching* 9 (2). http://jolt.merlot.org/vol9no2/stewart_bonnie_0613.htm.

Stommel, Jesse. 2012a. "Hybridity Part 2: What is Hybrid Pedagogy?" *Hybrid Pedagogy*, March 12. http://www.hybridpedagogy.com/journal/hybridity-pt-2-what-is-hybrid-pedagogy/.

———. 2012b. "March of the MOOCs: Monstrous Open Online Courses." *Hybrid Pedagogy*, July 23. http://www.hybridpedagogy.com/journal/the-march-of-the-moocs-monstrous-open-online-courses/.

Warner, John. 2014. "The Costs of Big Data." *Inside Higher Ed*, July 6. http://www.insidehighered.com/blogs/just-visiting/costs-big-data#sthash.v7usTXuu.dpbs.

Watters, Audrey. 2012. "5 Things I've Learned from MOOCs about How I Learn." *HackEducation*, May 9. http://hackeducation.com/2012/05/09/5-things-ive-learned-from-moocs-about-how-i-learn.

———. 2013. "The Early Days of Videotaped Lectures." *Hybrid Pedagogy*, April 11. http://www.hybridpedagogy.com/journal/the-early-days-of-videotaped-lectures/.

Weinberger, David. 2002. *Small Pieces Loosely Joined: A Unified Theory of the Web*. Cambridge: Perseus.

Weissmann, Jordan. 2013. "The Ever-Shrinking Role of Tenured College Professors (in 1 Chart)." *Atlantic*, April 10. http://www.theatlantic.com/business/archive/2013/04/the-ever-shrinking-role-of-tenured-college-professors-in-1-chart/274849/.

Opening Education, Linking to Communities: The #InQ13 Collective's Participatory Open Online Course (POOC) in East Harlem

JESSIE DANIELS, POLLY THISTLETHWAITE, AND SHAWN(TA) SMITH-CRUZ

Introduction

Our institution, like many across the United States, is awash in discussion about the promise and perils of open education made possible through an array of digital technologies. Given the particular history of the City University of New York (CUNY), the public university system of New York City, whose mission is to "educate the children of the whole people" and whose history includes a fairly recent past of free tuition for students, we were particularly intrigued by the potential for creating a truly open, online course. With twenty-four institutions across New York City and about 270,000 degree-credit students and 273,000 continuing and professional education students, CUNY is the third largest university system in the United States and the nation's largest public urban university. The Graduate Center is CUNY's principal doctorate-granting institution offering more than thirty doctoral degrees in the humanities, sciences, and social sciences, with significant research on global and progressive policy issues.

A collective of approximately twenty members of the Graduate Center, funded by the Ford Foundation as part of the JustPublics@365 project, created a participatory open online course, or "POOC," titled Reassessing Inequality and Re-Imagining the 21st-Century: East Harlem Focus. The course hashtag #InQ13 (inequality, 2013) became the name for the collective working to produce the course. The course was offered for credit as a graduate seminar through the Graduate Center and featured training in community-based

The #InQ13 POOC was part of the JustPublics@365 project, which was supported in part by a grant from the Ford Foundation. The #InQ13 Collective involved a large number of people, including CUNY faculty, guest faculty and activists, Graduate Center students, JustPublics@365 fellows, librarians, and tech consultants.

participatory research methods. CUNY students who sought credit for the course enrolled in the usual way by registering for the course. The course was also open to the nonacademic community for participation. About half the in-person sessions were held at a CUNY campus in East Harlem, which were open to the community. Anyone could watch videos of the course sessions online and could access the readings assigned for the course online. None of these modes of participation required registration, but those who registered and participated online experienced a greater level of engagement than those who did not enroll. In addition, we held a series of smaller meetings with community leaders about the course that increased awareness about the POOC and about CUNY's interest in East Harlem and potential for future collaboration.

Launching a POOC against the MOOC Moment

The historical moment in which the 2013 POOC emerged influenced its structure and character. The *New York Times* proclaimed 2012 "the year of the MOOC"—Massive Open Online Courses (Pappano 2012). There was no shortage of hyperbole about MOOCs during that time. In perhaps the most egregious example of this hype, *New York Times* columnist Thomas Friedman extoled the revolutionary possibilities of MOOCs, suggesting that "[n]othing has more potential to enable us to reimagine higher education than the massive open online course, or MOOC" (Friedman 2013). Such claims are similar to those made about educational television in the middle of the twentieth century (Picciano 2014). The term "MOOC" was coined by educational technologists Dave Cormier and George Siemens in 2008 (Cormier and Siemens 2010). In fall 2011, Stanford University opened some of its computer science courses to the world through an online platform and found hundreds of thousands of students enrolling. As a result, MOOCs moved quickly from niche discussions among educational technologists to the forefront of conversation about higher education as sustained by the *New York Times* (Pappano 2012; Lewin 2013). These idealistic forecasts, however, were predicated on the condition that MOOCs can extend higher education, without payment or condition, to the people who might apply it to transform lives and society.

Premised on extending the experience of traditional university courses to massive audiences, MOOCs have provoked an array of responses. Commentators who believe that higher education is in need of reform argue that traditional educational practices have finally been subverted by a productively disruptive force (Shirky 2015). According to such arguments, the educational experiences offered at elite institutions can now be made available to students across the world, for free, thus making higher education possible for students who would not otherwise be able to afford it. Critics of MOOCs often view them in the context of a higher-education system that is being defunded and worry that higher-education administrators see, in MOOCs, possibilities for revenue generation through increased enrollments and cost-cutting through reduced full-time faculty hires.

Connectivist MOOCs, or cMOOCs, are designed to foster community, connection, and peer-to-peer learning. cMOOCs are generally produced using locally designed, often open-source platforms. The open online course we created is more aligned with cMOOCs. The much-hyped and well-financed corporate xMOOCs on platforms by Udacity, Coursera, and edX can extend lecture videos (and sometimes reading materials) to those who register and view (Wiener 2013), but courses that restrict their course materials to enrolled, sometimes paying customers are not open (Otte 2012), except by significant redefinition of the word "open."

Application of licensed content of any kind is arguably incongruent with the aim and purpose of a MOOC. Licensed access, even if freely available to course attendees, requires some form of registration. Such content is not "open and online." Clay Shirky asserts that the real revolutionary benefit of new cultural and education technologies is openness (cited in Parry 2012), yet current xMOOC models that keep course materials behind registration walls, building potential for revenue generation, compromise this benefit. The recent partnerships between Elsevier and edX (Elsevier 2013) and between Coursera and Chegg, consolidating textbooks by Cengage Learning, Macmillan Higher Education, Oxford University Press, SAGE, and Wiley (Doyle 2013), point to educational enclosure rather than openness (Watters 2013). xMOOC models currently amount to a shaded variation on current higher-education models providing licensed academic content to a defined and regulated student audience.

Three major xMOOC service providers have entered the market: Udacity, Coursera, and edX. Udacity and Coursera are for-profit enterprises assembling "open" course content in commercial software. edX is a not-for-profit platform developed by Harvard and MIT with an initial investment of $30 million and then offered to university partners to share the revenue they generate (Kolowich 2013). All these platforms are designed to extend the reach of higher education by delivering courses online to great numbers of students, including those in untapped, often far-flung markets, at lower, "affordable" costs. xMOOCs, subsidized by universities and their software providers, are intended to lower costs to student consumers, yet still return profits for universities and their xMOOC providers using traditional revenue-generating models.

MOOCs have been criticized for their paltry imagining of the educational experience. To date, most MOOCs have consisted of video lectures, sometimes accompanied by discussion forums or automated tests. Students are expected to absorb videos in ways consonant with what Paulo Freire described as the banking model of education, in which students are imagined as empty vessels into which the instructor deposits knowledge (Freire 1993). Within the mostly one-way communication structure of the truly massive MOOCs, the interaction between faculty members and students is necessarily constrained because of scale. While some MOOCs try to foster interaction between the professor and his (or her)[1] students, this has not met with much success (Bruff et al. 2013). There is little in the corporate MOOC model to recommend it as a vehicle for a graduate seminar, in which intimacy and sustained focused discussion, rather than massiveness and openness, are most prized.

Organizers of the POOC wanted to design the course to engage with New York City. We were also concerned with providing a focus for the breadth of disciplinary approaches featured in the course. Several faculty engaged in early discussions about the course suggested we create an educational experiment that resisted the "placelessness" of MOOCs by situating this course in a specific neighborhood.

East Harlem is a neighborhood that has simultaneously fostered a vibrant, multiethnic tradition of citizen activism and borne the brunt of urban policies that generate inequality. Several of the people in the #InQ13 collective had ties to East Harlem as residents, researchers, community activists, and workers, so the possibility of locating the course there was immediately tangible. In addition, CUNY recently located the new Silberman campus supporting public health and social work in this neighborhood. These factors taken together— the unique, vibrant history and present of East Harlem, the connection to the neighborhood from those in the #InQ13 collective, and the new CUNY East Harlem campus—provided a compelling case for situating the POOC there. So, the original questions that framed the course were joined by another set of questions. Could a course such as this one "open" the new CUNY campus to the East Harlem community in innovative ways? Given the troubled relationship of university campuses to urban neighborhoods, could we forge a healthy set of relationships? And, were there ways that the digital technologies used

1. Most high-profile MOOCs have featured men as instructors; the POOC was co-led by two women. For more on the gender imbalance in MOOCs, see Straumheim (2013).

in the course could offer a platform for community activists engaged in the struggle against the forces of inequality in East Harlem?

Community engagement with East Harlem began before the course started, and relationships took on more focused energy as course development began. Edwin Mayorga led these efforts as the official community liaison for the course, coordinating with eighteen community partners (Daniels and Gold 2014, par. 17). There were also meetings held outside of the course in East Harlem among the instructors, developers, and community partners during the semester.

Different parts of the CUNY Graduate Center also had to join forces in unprecedented ways. With POOC organizers aiming to afford every course participant unfettered access to course materials, a strong collaboration with librarians was required to create open-access reading lists. The course offered lectures and discussions that were both streamed live and video recorded, assigned readings, and scheduled a series of assignments. Many of the guest lecturers were also authors of the assigned readings. This confluence provided a unique opportunity to begin discussions with faculty about sharing their work openly on digital platforms with global, nonacademic audiences.

CUNY centrally licenses Blackboard software supporting password-protected course readings for enrolled CUNY students. (C)opyright@CUNY, a CUNY-wide library committee, posts guidelines and resources for CUNY instructors managing course-reserve readings. Several CUNY libraries additionally offer Sirsi Dynix ERes software and scanning services for local course support. Some CUNY Graduate Center faculty use Blackboard for reserve reading support; others use the CUNY Academic Commons and Open-CUNY platforms, both of which provide password protection for licensed course documents. Still other Graduate Center instructors employ commercial password-protected file-sharing sites (e.g., Dropbox and Google Drive) to post course readings. A few instructors continue the analog practice of distributing photocopies, while others provide only assigned reading lists to students who must find readings on their own.

The #InQ13 course could not apply these licensed course delivery platforms to serve students and lecturer-participants without CUNY affiliation. Our library-licensed academic works—journal articles, books, book chapters, and other media—could not be extended to audiences other than Graduate Center–affiliated students without violating license agreements. Assigning licensed readings for the #InQ13 course accessible only to those with Graduate Center credentials was antithetical to the goals of the course. Organizers refused to adopt a tiered-access scenario that would fail to provide full access to course readings to invited non-CUNY course participants. From the outset, there was little question that the readings assigned for the #InQ13 course had to be open access.

At the time the POOC was offered, CUNY did not yet support open-access publishing with an institutional repository. In November 2011, CUNY's University Faculty Senate passed a resolution calling for an open-access institutional repository. In response, the CUNY Office of Library Services with the University Faculty Senate convened a task force to develop a repository (Cirasella 2011). In October 2012 the task force forwarded specific recommendations to its conveners, outlining a plan for implementation of a CUNY-wide repository. In fall 2013, the CUNY Graduate Center licensed Digital Commons software to provide a platform for a Graduate Center repository called CUNY Academic Works, and in fall 2014 the CUNY-wide institutional repository was launched, built on Digital Commons software.

But CUNY librarians had to find a repository platform to support the POOC in spring 2013. Many of the #InQ13 authors unaffiliated with CUNY had posted works in their own university open-access repositories. And, we directed several CUNY and non-CUNY authors to deposit works in the Internet archive "Community Texts" section that we established for use with #InQ13.

Structure of the Course

Each session was both live-streamed for those who wanted to participate synchronously and then, several days later, a more polished video recording of the class session was released and posted to the #InQ13 course website for those who wanted to participate asynchronously. The assignments for the course were designed by the faculty and by educational technologists (Daniels and Gold 2014, par. 23 and 39). Students posted their completed assignments on the course blog at the #InQ13 website. To facilitate group work, students could use a "groups" feature on the site to collaborate around specific projects. These groups were intended to foster connection between online learners and CUNY-based learners, but the "group" feature was not heavily used. The faculty provided feedback and grades on assignments produced by CUNY-based learners, and the digital fellow provided feedback for online learners (Daniels and Gold 2014, par. 49) At the end of the semester, students were invited to present their projects at a community event at La Casa Azul Bookstore in East Harlem (this was in addition to the four regular sessions held in the neighborhood).

Libraries have traditionally offered faculty copyright guidance, supporting courses with reserve software and scanning services, shepherding extension of licensed-library content for exclusive use by a well-defined set of university-affiliated student users. Under current licensing models, this content cannot be extended to the massive, unaffiliated, undefined, and unregistered body of MOOC enrollees without tempting lawsuits. And, as we have seen in the Georgia State University case, publishers will sue universities providing traditionally enrolled students access to course-reserve readings, even if the published readings are password-protected and selected according to reasonable interpretations of fair use guidelines (Smith 2013). Though universities may open courses to anyone with an Internet connection and the will to participate, the vast majority of supporting course content—including academic books, book chapters, articles, and films—are not currently available to universities to redistribute openly. Course readings must either be published open access with copyright owner consent or licensed explicitly for open online course use (Fowler and Smith 2013).

Curtis Kendrick and Irene Gashurov discuss several potential models for MOOC enrollment and revenue generation that offer access to licensed textbooks and scholarly material. Licensed textbooks and journals inaccessible to nonpaying customers might be free or discounted for "premium"-paying MOOC customers, for example (Kendrick and Gashurov 2013; Courtney 2013). Coursera negotiated to license resources, just like libraries do, to expand access to textbooks and scholarly journals for their registered MOOC students. Access is supplied at a cost to the course provider, and it is limited to a pale fraction of scholarship available to university-affiliated students through traditional course-reserve systems and, increasingly, through open-access scholarship.[2] The Coursera and edX licensing models ask universities to subsidize registered MOOC students' access to some licensed body of scholarly work, under defined terms, for some determined time. University-supported Coursera and edX are poised to expand MOOC student access to academic content, but only within regulated, publisher-imposed limits.

The moment licensed scholarly material is on the MOOC syllabus, the MOOC compromises one of its Os ("openness"). A course may be massive and may be online, but its content is no longer open if students are required to register for access or encouraged to pay to gain enhanced access to course content. Restricted access is antithetical to the project of open access and eviscerates the transformative potential of MOOCs.

2. See *The Dramatic Growth of Open Access Series* in *The Imaginary Journal of Poetic Economics*, a blog by Heather Morrison: http://poeticeconomics.blogspot.ca/2006/08/dramatic-growth -of-open-access-series.html.

Open-access scholarship, in contrast to licensed content, is available to a broad variety of readers and to any student with an Internet connection, online or on campus, in any economy. Scholarship published in "gold" or completely open-access journals or scholarship posted "green" open-access on author websites or in institutional repositories is accessible by anyone and can be included, free of charge, in any course. Only open-access publishing will expand the quality and variety of academic works available to the web-browsing worldwide public. A critical mass of open-access scholarship, currently estimated at no more than 25 percent of scholarly output (Gargouri et al. 2012), must form the backbone of the project for MOOCs to realize their much-touted potential to transform higher education. Securing scholarship in open-access contexts must go hand-in-hand with MOOC building. They are two logical, inseparable parts of the same project to enhance global public access to higher education. To achieve revolutionary potential, MOOCs require a transformed system of scholarly communication.

At the March 2013 University of Pennsylvania conference *MOOCs and Libraries: Massive Opportunity or Overwhelming Challenge?*, Jennifer Dorner, Head of Doe/Moffitt Library Instruction and User Services at University of California, Berkeley, recognized MOOCs as "a real opportunity to educate faculty about the need for owning the rights to their content and making it accessible to other people" (Howard 2013). Librarian-faculty collaboration in MOOC building also involves conversation with authors about transforming scholarly communication. Activists, artists, and academic authors who participated in our POOC were called on to make their work open access.

MOOCs offer authors a unique opportunity to widen readership and to raise the profile of their work. Prompted by authors' potential to increase exposure to additional readers through MOOCs, book publishers proved to be willing, and even eager, to make traditionally published works open access, at least temporarily and in part, if they were assigned readings for our POOC. Several book publishers, when approached by librarians, with an author cc'd, made copyright-restricted books and book chapters openly available online, particularly when the author appeared in our open online presentation series.

Forging Open Access for Community Engagement

Making course readings open access required a great deal of work with divisions of labor and responsibility. These divisions of labor, fuzzy at first, became clearer as the course progressed and as librarians worked with instructors to review course readings. In a conventional course, one instructor

selects readings to teach a small group of students. In this unique participatory course, a twenty-member team was required to *produce* the course,
with two instructors, for thousands of potential students, both enrolled at
the Graduate Center and not enrolled, participating from geographically dis-
persed locations (Daniels and Gold 2014). While all embraced open access to
scholarly and artistic works as a worthy goal, none were experienced in the
mechanics of open-access discovery, identification, permissions seeking, and
posting.

Course instructors provided initial "wish list" sets of readings for course
modules selected for content only, without considering licensing restrictions
that amounted to 117 total requested articles, book chapters, websites, blogs,
films, and entire books. Daniels and her production team reviewed the syllabus, and in conjunction with instructors, found or forged open-access equiva-
lents for 47 titles, or about 40 percent of the traditionally licensed required
readings. Librarians then reviewed the team's remaining list to examine the
licensing status of the readings and to determine what steps the team might
take to obtain key readings in open-access formats. Librarians reviewed electronic journal articles for author self-archiving possibilities. Books and films
required publisher (or other rights holder) permissions and cooperation. A
more thorough report of our pursuits has been published elsewhere (Smith-
Cruz, Thistlethwaite, and Daniels 2014).

COMMUNITY MEMBERS AS COPYRIGHT OWNERS

Librarians contacted book publishers, cc'ing authors, lecturers, and course
organizers on all correspondence. This librarian-author collaboration proved
to be compelling to publishers. Many authors were honored to have their
work included and volunteered to contact publishers via personal correspondence. Three of the nineteen publishers contacted understood the nature of
our request and seized the opportunity to offer open, unlimited distribution
of materials for the duration of the course. Publishers provided free online access for a defined time with course traffic directed to and access governed by
their websites. Some publishers were unable to be contacted, whereas others
declined our invitation to participate.

Early in the term, #InQ13 course coordinators approached filmmaker Ed
Morales about his 2008 documentary film, *Whose Barrio?: The Gentrification
of East Harlem*, requesting that he post it free online for the course's second
module. Morales retains the copyright for his work, and he was also a guest
for the course. He readily complied, posting his film to be viewed free, open,

and online via the Internet Movie Database. Morales's eager participation was early inspiration to organizers who went forward to convince other authors and publishers to make their work openly available.

Another early instance produced a thornier result. One course lecturer believed she retained copyright of her forthcoming book. She assured course organizers that publisher's correspondence confirmed permission to post chapters on the course website. However, librarians' end-of-course review of the email correspondence revealed a misinterpretation of the publisher's correspondence. The publisher had in fact withheld permission to post the work. The posted chapters were removed from the temporary course repository when we discovered the error. A different book publisher responded with a course-pack license agreement requesting a fee to permit fifty-seven pages to be copied no more than twenty times. While Daniels's letter to the publisher had been clear about the nature of the "open, online" course and the author's appearance as a guest lecturer, the publisher either misunderstood the request or was at a loss about how to respond. Upon clarifying this issue, this publisher of left-leaning academic texts described the book as a bestseller. The publisher was willing to negotiate a license and fee to allow online distribution of two requested chapters, but only if distribution could be limited to a specified number of students. A subsequent attempt to clarify went unanswered.

Three academic publishers allowed temporary open online posting for the #InQ13 course: University of California (UC) Press, New York University (NYU) Press, and University of Minnesota (UMN) Press. UC posted the introduction and chapter 3 of Arlene Dávila's 2004 *Barrio Dreams: Puerto Ricans, Latinos, and the Neoliberal City*. Before our request, the press featured the book's introduction on its website, as a teaser. UC also posted two chapters of Laura Pulido, Laura Barraclough, and Wendy Cheng's 2012 *A People's Guide to Los Angeles* and chapter 5 of Ruth Wilson Gilmore's 2007 *Golden Gulag: Prisons, Surplus, Crisis, and Opposition in Globalizing California*. NYU Press provided Johana Londoño's chapter "Aesthetic Belonging: The Latinization and Renewal of Union City, New Jersey" from the 2012 anthology *Latino Urbanism: The Politics of Planning, Policy, and Redevelopment* edited by David Diaz and Rodolfo Torres. UMN offered the biggest win as measured by pagination, posting the entirety of Cindi Katz's 2004 *Growing Up Global: Economic Restructuring and Children's Everyday Lives* in downloadable PDF format, which was available through a link on the press's website. Publishers kept all links live from the time we reached agreement through the end of the semester-long course.

Choosing Articles Everyone Can Access

The Directory of Open Access Journals (DOAJ; doaj.org) and the SHERPA/RoMEO tool (www.sherpa.ac.uk/romeo) were essential for reviewing course readings. The DOAJ hosted by Lund University lists over ten thousand peer-reviewed scholarly journals that are entirely open access, or "gold" open access. The SHERPA/RoMEO database, hosted by the University of Nottingham, lists academic journals that are not "gold" open access, but that allow another sort of author self-archiving. SHERPA/RoMEO lists the so-called "green" open-access policies, covering over twenty-two thousand academic journals. Of the titles covered in 2011, 94 percent offered some form of author self-archiving after embargoes, ranging from zero to twenty-four months (Millington 2011). Publishers offer wildly varying terms for self-archiving. Some allow pre-peer-reviewed versions only; others allow self-archiving only in peer-reviewed versions, as long as the publishers final PDF is not used; and still others require any self-archiving to feature only the publisher's PDF. SHERPA/RoMEO also notes when publishers limit the type of repositories authors may employ for self-archiving. For example, some restrict postings to temporary repositories; others to author websites or institutional repositories; and others to nonprofit repositories.

Over thirty-two thousand scholarly periodicals are included in these two tools. Applying these tools to review the course lists we learned that scholarship is sometimes posted openly, without regard for publishers' restrictions. Posting policies are not at all immediately obvious to authors or to faculty forming syllabi. We also learned that, while author self-archiving is allowed by hundreds of traditional academic publishers, the opportunity to self-archive is not ubiquitously understood or enacted by authors. In conversation with librarians, though, the authors inevitably became at least aware of and in some cases, expert in, publisher's policies as it applied to their published work.

Evaluating the POOC

It is challenging to assess the impact of an experiment in education that took as its chief goal to be "participatory." When the goal is for a course to be "massive," the primary metric of evaluation is how many people registered for the course. We did not measure the massiveness of the POOC because participants were not required to register at the course website. Instead we opened the course to as many varieties of learners as possible. We measured a broader spectrum of factors meant to gauge the participatory quality of the course.

The #InQ13 POOC was an alternative to MOOCs, emphasizing openness and participatory action above massiveness of scale. While our model sometimes resulted in messy struggles with the complex social, political, and economic issues related to inequality, not the least of which is the inequality between academics and community partners, the POOC was nevertheless a bold reimagination of what it is to take seriously the idea of opening higher education. Graduate education can and should engage learners outside the traditional academy, but it must do so through thoughtful models, conceptualized with wide participation and equitable practice in mind. We offer the #InQ13 model in particular, and the idea of the POOC more generally, as one possible path for others considering future experiments in open graduate education.

Traditional measures of learning assessment are valuable, yet they often overlook the variety of learners and the wide range of their goals in engaging with such a course. One of the most relevant metrics is the number of people who attended the open events in East Harlem, participating in person, which was nearly five hundred. And, as further testimony to the global potential of online learning, we found that people from twenty-six countries visited the course website or watched the videos.

Conclusion: Opening Education, Linking to Communities

We began the POOC with an emphasis on participatory pedagogy, on concrete interactions between a student community and a geographically specific urban community, which necessitated a model far removed from the sage-on-a-stage, broadcast teaching environments employed in most MOOCs. While MOOCs have spurred discussions about online courses extending the reach of higher-education institutions (and, in the process, proffering new, more profitable business models for them), our experiences with the #InQ13 POOC suggest that online courses that emphasize interaction among faculty, students, and broader communities are accompanied by significant institutional and economic costs. On the #InQ13 course website, our credits page lists nineteen different individuals who played a role in creating the course experience. If MOOCs are sometimes imagined by administrators and businesses as a labor-saving, cost-cutting device for higher education, then the POOC model offers another model; it was, in fact, a job-creation program. It modeled higher education with the potential to enliven academic-community partnerships in interesting ways. It required a significant investment of time, money, and labor to succeed, and heavily relied on libraries and librarians to navigate the often daunting terrain of open access.

One of the key lessons learned from our POOC is that engaging with communities means making scholarly materials available to people who do not hold academic credentials. While MOOCs claim openness, what they offer is restricted or tiered access to licensed scholarship, and thus little potential to transform higher education. A successful opening of higher education to communities requires a robust academic infrastructure of open-access scholarship. Libraries become the bridge between scholars and communities for this more open future.

References

Bruff, Derek O., Fisher, Douglas H., McEwen, Kathryn E. and Smith, Blaine E. 2013. "Wrapping a MOOC: Student Perceptions of An Experiment in Blended Learning." *Journal of Online Learning and Teaching* 9 (2): 187.

Cirasella, Jill. 2011. "CUNY Institutional Repository: Coming Soon-ish?" *Open Access @ CUNY*, November 23. http://openaccess.commons.gc.cuny.edu/2011/11/23/cuny-institutional -repository-coming-soon-ish/.

Cormier, Dave, and George Siemens. 2010. "Through the Open Door: Open Courses as Research, Learning, and Engagement." *Educausereview* 45 (4): 30–39. http://er.educause.edu/articles /2010/8/through-the-open-door-open-courses-as-research-learning-and-engagement.

Courtney, Kyle K. 2013. "The MOOC Syllabus Blues: Strategies for MOOCs and Syllabus Materials." *College and Research Libraries News* 74 (10): 514–17.

Daniels, Jessie, and Matt Gold. 2014. "The InQ13 POOC: A Participatory Experiment in Open, Collaborative Teaching, and Learning." *Journal of Interactive Technology and Pedagogy* 5. http://jitp.commons.gc.cuny.edu/the-inq13-pooc/.

Dávila, Arlene. 2004. *Barrio Dreams: Puerto Ricans, Latinos, and the Neoliberal City.* Berkeley: University of California Press.

Diaz, David R., and Rodolfo D. Torres. 2012. *Latino Urbanism: The Politics of Planning, Policy, and Redevelopment.* New York: New York University Press.

Doyle, Caity. 2013. "Coursera and Chegg Partner Up to Provide Free Textbooks for Online Courses." *Technapex*, May 8. http://www.technapex.com/2013/05/coursera-and-chegg -partner-up-to-provide-free-textbooks-for-online-courses/.

Elsevier. 2013. "Elsevier to Provide Textbooks for Five New edX MOOCs." October 23. http:// www.elsevier.com/about/press-releases/science-and-technology/elsevier-to-provide -textbooks-for-five-new-edx-moocs.

Fowler, Lauren, and Kevin Smith. 2013. "Drawing the Blueprint as We Build: Setting Up a Library-Based Copyright and Permissions Service for MOOCs." *D-Lib Magazine* 19 (7/8). doi: 10.1045/july2013-fowler.

Freire, Paolo 1993. *Pedagogy of the Oppressed.* New York: Continuum.

Friedman, Thomas L. 2013. "Revolution Hits the Universities." *New York Times*, January 26. http://www.nytimes.com/2013/01/27/opinion/sunday/friedman-revolution-hits-the -universities.html.

Gargouri, Yassine, Vincent Lariviere, Yves Gingras, Tim Brody, Les Carr, and Stevan Harnad.

2012. "Testing the Finch Hypothesis on Green OA Mandate Ineffectiveness." Open Access Week 2012, October 26. http://eprints.soton.ac.uk/344687/.

Gilmore, R. W. 2007. *Golden Gulag: Prisons, Surplus, Crisis, and Opposition in Globalizing California*. Berkeley: University of California Press.

Howard, Jennifer. 2013. "For Libraries, MOOCs Bring Uncertainty and Opportunity." *Chronicle of Higher Education*, March 25. http://chronicle.com/blogs/wiredcampus/for-libraries-moocs-bring-uncertainty-and-opportunity/43111.

Katz, Cindi. 2004. *Growing Up Global: Economic Restructuring and Children's Everyday Lives*. Minneapolis: University of Minnesota Press.

Kendrick, Curtis, and Irene Gashurov. 2013. "Libraries in the Time of MOOCs." *Educausereview* 48 (6). http://www.educause.edu/ero/article/libraries-time-moocs.

Kolowich, Steve. 2013. "How EdX Plans to Earn, and Share, Revenue From Its Free Online Courses." *Chronicle of Higher Education*, February 21. http://chronicle.com/article/How-EdX-Plans-to-Earn-and/137433/.

Lewin, Tamar. 2013. "Massive Open Online Courses Prove Popular, If Not Lucrative Yet." *New York Times*, January 6. http://www.nytimes.com/2013/01/07/education/massive-open-online-courses-prove-popular-if-not-lucrative-yet.html.

Morales, Ed, and Laura Rivera. 2009. *Whose Barrio? The Gentrification of East Harlem*. New York: Ed Morales.

Millington, Peter. 2011. "60% of Journals Allow Immediate Archiving of Peer-Reviewed Articles—But It Gets Much Much Better. . . ." *SHERPA Services Blog*, November 24. http://romeo.jiscinvolve.org/wp/2011/11/24/.

OCLC Research. 2013. "MOOCs and Libraries Event Videos Now Available." *OCLC Research*, April 9. http://www.oclc.org/research/news/2013/04-09.html.

Otte, George. 2012. "Degrees of Openness?" *Tributaries: Occasional Affluents to the Confluence*, November 12. http://purelyreactive.commons.gc.cuny.edu/?s=degrees+of+openness.

Pappano, Laura. 2012. "The Year of the MOOC." *New York Times*, November 4. http://www.nytimes.com/2012/11/04/education/edlife/massive-open-online-courses-are-multiplying-at-a-rapid-pace.html.

Parry, Marc. 2012. "The Real Revolution Is Openness, Clay Shirky Tells Tech Leaders." *Chronicle of Higher Education*, November 7. http://chronicle.com/blogs/wiredcampus/the-real-revolution-is-openness-clay-shirky-tells-tech-leaders.

Picciano, Anthony. 2014. "MOOCs: The Hype the Backlash, and the Future!" *University Outlook* 1 (4). http://anthonypicciano.com/pdfs/Hype-Backlash-Future.pdf.

Pulido, Laura, Laura R. Barraclough, and Wendy Cheng. 2012. *A People's Guide to Los Angeles*. Berkeley: University of California Press.

Shirky, Clay. 2015. "The Digital Revolution in Higher Education Has Already Happened. No One Noticed." *Medium*, November 6. https://medium.com@cshirky/the-digital-revolution-in-highter-education-has-already-happened-no-one-noticed-78ec0fec16c7.

Smith, Kevin. 2013. "A Discouraging Day in Court." *Scholarly Communications @ Duke*, November 20.

Smith-Cruz, Shawnta, Polly Thistlethwaite, and Jessie Daniels. 2014. "Open Scholarship for Open Education: Building the JustPublics@365 POOC." *Journal of Library Innovation* 5 (2): 15–28.

Straumheim, Carl. 2013. "Masculine Open Online Courses: More Female Professors Experiment with MOOCs, but Men Still Dominate." *Inside Higher Ed*, September 3. https://www

.insidehighered.com/news/2013/09/03/more-female-professors-experiment-moocs-men
-still-dominate.

Watters, Audrey. 2013. "Coursera, Chegg, and the Education Enclosure Movement." *Hack Education*, May 8. http://hackeducation.com/2013/05/08/coursera-chegg.

Wiener, Jon. 2013. "Inside the Coursera Hype Machine." *Nation*, September 4. http://www
.thenation.com/article/176036/inside-coursera-hype-machine.

PART FOUR

The Pathos of the MOOC Moment

13

Digital Universalism and MOOC Affects

ELIZABETH LOSH

In responding to Coursera cofounder Daphne Koller from the stage of the 2012 Tanner Lectures on Human Values, which were delivered at Stanford University during a barrage of news coverage focusing on massive open online courses (MOOCs), economist and former university president William Bowen (2015) described Koller as a "true believer" and lauded her "missionary spirit" (157). Bowen was not alone in identifying secular evangelism as a key feature of the oratory of the MOOC moment. As de Vise (2012) pointed out in a *Washington Post* editorial, "EdX and Coursera allow top schools to expand their global brand and share their intellectual capital with the world in the manner of academic missionaries." Popular TED Talks featuring MOOC founders and CEOs cite the existence of desperately needy people from Johannesburg (Koller 2012) to Kolkata (Khan 2011) as an imperative to support the growth of MOOCs as an alternative to traditional education. This essay asks how the digital universalism and MOOC affects associated with charity and philanthropy can be read as part of a longer rhetorical tradition in open education. It also explores how intensely negative feelings might be generated by the substitution and deferred gratification at the heart of MOOCs, including the shame and contempt that founders claimed such courses were designed to avoid.

The emotional appeals to pathos from stories of trampled mothers and destitute street kids as potential beneficiaries are obvious. Certainly tropes about the developing world, the inner city, and the sick ward deployed in the speeches of MOOC founders are rhetorically powerful, but the call to action does not necessarily follow from the tales of woe. Furthermore, this missionary MOOC rhetoric smacks of what Cole (2012) has called "the white-savior industrial complex," which he claims is typified by the Kony 2012 viral video campaign that was targeted to white American youth and urged them somehow to facilitate the capture of Ugandan guerilla leader Joseph Kony. Such rhetoric relies on stereotypes about the global South and confidence that those with problems do not need to be consulted about their choices among possible solutions (Cole 2012).

As an example of how Cole's "white-savior industrial complex" may be manifested in MOOC rhetoric, promotional materials for the Khan Academy's KA Lite initiative and the Kolibri application ("the offline app for universal education"; https://learningequality.org/kolibri/) clearly emphasize charity for the dispossessed in foreign countries with videos featuring schoolchildren from Africa and the Indian subcontinent. In other essays in this collection, the problems of adopting the pose of the MOOC missionary are explored from a global perspective. Siva Vaidhyanathan sees the trope of the "white man's burden" in the rhetoric of MOOCs, and Nishant Shah argues that education is particularly likely to be identified with postcolonial agendas of development, progress, affluence, and reform in which MOOCs are seen as a form of crisis response.

In contrast, Shah's own experiences as a facilitator of an experiment in MOOC education at Leuphana University in Germany depended on other kinds of affective investments and was premised on attitudes of friendly collegiality rather than heroic intervention in tragedy. The course Managing the Arts: Marketing for Cultural Organizations (https://www.mooc-list.com /course/managing-arts-marketing-cultural-organizations-leuphana) began with the assumption that cultural managers in Lagos and Bangkok are as competent and capable as their counterparts in Budapest and Berlin. This transnational MOOC sponsored by the Goethe-Institut also drew attention to the affective labor both of cultural managers and of participants in the course and emphasized how the subject matter required people to be mediators, moderators, and diplomats.

In courses from Coursera, edX, Udacity, and the Khan Academy, MOOCs attempt to have global reach, but they often reflect particular and distinctively American premises about US exceptionalism, technosolutionism, and entrepreneurialism, as well as the virtues of direct democracy unencumbered by parliamentary processes. Of course, in the longer American oratorical history, open education has often presented a powerful and popular theme. Such cultural narratives defined the US nation-state in relationship to its opportunities for access to pedagogical resources. At the beginning of the last century, skilled public speakers like Booker T. Washington and Jane Addams drew audiences by emphasizing removing barriers to learning. The character development revealed in their own autobiographical writings (which highlighted origins in abjection and privilege, respectively) demonstrated their deep investments in the rhetoric of educational reinvention. The moving pitches of Washington, Addams, and many others for facilitating pedagogical salvation also frequently included fundraising appeals for schooling and training facilities for specific at-risk populations and infrastructural investments necessary for long-term growth. For example, Tuskegee's Movable Schools to provide instruction in modern agricultural methods and home economics required highly specialized vehicles to reach rural students in their pioneering early distance education plan (Mayberry 1991). Mobile units were sometimes referred to by the name of the philanthropist who had financed them, as in the case of the "Jesup Wagon" that was stocked with demonstration materials including farm machinery, livestock, and elaborate educational exhibits. In contrast, the TED Talks of contemporary MOOC advocates tend to avoid discussions of specific revenue models and infrastructural requirements, just as they may skirt around US exceptionalism with regard to the topoi of opportunity. In other words, Koller may describe herself as an Israeli-American child of privilege, and Khan may refer to his family's own Bengali immigrant success story, but specific corporate leadership and organizational communication challenges seem to be excised from their personal stories—in ways that they never were in the stories of Addams and Washington—just as anxiety about the sustainability of the institutions that they have founded seems to be less important than celebrating the buzz of a Silicon Valley start-up.

The rhetoric of top MOOC evangelists is also characterized by an appeal to universalism in the nineteenth-century sense of the term, as the categorical denial of the existence of damnation and the absolute affirmation of universal salvation. In the secular context, liberation from predestined fate or irreversible error means that no one will be denied an education regardless of how disadvantaged or ill prepared. The brand identity of Coursera makes its universalism especially explicit: its mission statement has been revised from "We envision a future in which everyone has access to a world-class education that has so far been available to a select few" (http://www.sscnasscom.com /ssc-article/development-initiatives/education-training/development-moocs /coursera/) to "We provide universal access to the world's best education" (https://www.coursera.org/about/) With this revision in language, the digital universalism of Coursera is of the present rather than of the future and exists without reference to any class of the elect.

Charismatic nineteenth-century universalists such as Olympia Brown and Hosea Ballou were once important figures in nineteenth-century oratorical culture. They made powerful affective appeals to an American cult of happiness that was emerging in US popular culture. Their public speaking performances also inspired a deluge of pamphlets weighing both the pros and cons among those participating in print discourse. It is noteworthy that these earlier universalists embraced other universalisms beyond religious ones. For example, universal suffrage and universal education were also explicit goals of the nineteenth-century universalists.

Digital universalism—or the belief that anyone can be rescued by computational media technologies—could also be said to be a feature of the rhetoric of many technology companies and of the Silicon Valley culture from which many MOOCs developed. Elsewhere Vaidhyanathan (2011) has argued that universalism is central to the ideology of Google, although it conflicts with the particularism of personalization, customization, and targeted advertising that assumes that algorithms can locate individual data bodies and markers of difference. In her work on Peruvian hackerspaces, Anita Say Chan (2013) has warned that this type of digital universalism has many consequences for local media ecologies and communities of practice, because it has a tendency to impose one-size-fits-all solutions in imagining how digital learning and literacy is constituted.

Moreover, digital universalism should not be confused with universal design, despite the fact that the Bill and Melinda Gates Foundation has provided funding for both the MOOC Research Initiative and the promulgation of Universal Design for Learning (UDL) principles through the Center for Applied Special Technology (CAST). UDL builds on the universal design movement for disabled people that contributed to curb cuts, close captioning, and many other improvements to transportation and communication infrastructures. Unfortunately, MOOC course content often seems to give little consideration even to students who are nonnative speakers of English, despite the fact that designing curricular features for nonnative speakers might improve learning for everyone, as Paul Kei Matsuda (2014) has asserted. Because MOOC lectures are pitched to a very low level of expertise, they are assumed to be assessable, but most assignments are designed to have few alternatives, and the curricula lack flexibility to support different learning styles by UDL standards.

Lauren Berlant (2011) has argued that the false inclusivity of neoliberal structures dependent on the entrepreneurship of the self only encourage forms of "cruel optimism" that demand affective responses to opportunities for participation from those habituated to the conditions of permanent precarity. Such cruel optimism enforces using "technologies of patience" while the subject whose satisfaction is perpetually deferred becomes worn out. The promise of safety from educational perdition can make powerful affective appeals, as can the possibility of proxies for traditional educators. As Berlant notes, the figure of the "substitute teacher" is a key character in affective investments, even if this character is often subject to ridicule and abuse: "often students are cruel to substitutes, out of excitement at the unpredictable and out of not having fear or transference to make them docile or even desiring of a recognition that has no time to be built" (46).

If the conventional substitute teacher is "a placeholder, a space of abeyance, an aleatory event" (46), according to Berlant, it would seem that the MOOC format delivers the ultimate substitute teacher, a video deliverable serving as a remote proxy for live teaching at scale. In my book *The War on Learning: Gaining Ground at the Digital University* (2014), I describe the powerfully negative affective responses associated with this particular digital form of substitute teaching, from "flipped classroom hate Tweets" on social media to diatribes on peer forums in designated online-course space. Facing a hostile audience once open to possibilities, the substitute teacher can easily become a figure of loathing, ridicule, contempt, and disgust.

In their analysis of how contemporary affect theory emerged from the era of cybernetics, Eve Kosofsky Sedgwick and Adam Frank (1995) have focused on the writings of early affect theorist Silvan Tomkins and the ways that shame and contempt (or disgust) presuppose positive affect and produce "bodily knowledges" in response. According to Sedgwick and Frank, "Without positive affect, there can be no shame: only a scene that offers you enjoyment or engages your interest can make you blush. Similarly, only something you thought might delight or satisfy can disgust" (22). Following Sedgwick and Frank, I might assert that it is the initial investment of positive affect in these "free" video courses and their promises to spread the gospel of digital universalism that can turn so violently toward negative expressions of contempt. Although MOOCs are generally associated with superficial affective engagements, the small percentage of students who complete assigned work may be comparatively deeply invested, as may be the faculty who choose to engage their institutional reputations.

The closer that the potential learner might assume the role of the teacher, the more likely that student-participants may manifest collusion and generate an atmosphere of generally negative affect. When Fatimah Wirth taught the ill-fated Coursera course Fundamentals of Online Education: Planning and Application to her fellow educators in winter 2013, news accounts dramatized "forums full of venom" and "scathing declarations" on Twitter (Strauss 2013). After UC Irvine emeritus economics professor Richard McKenzie dropped out of his own Coursera course a few weeks later, his subsequent lawsuit alleged that he should be compensated for "significant emotional injuries in the form of shame, mortification, and hurt feelings" (Kolowich 2016).

Yet promoters of MOOC experiences promise liberation from the negative affect of the traditional classroom, particularly in regard to the mortification of shame. In his memoir *The One World Schoolhouse*, Salman Khan (2013) tells how video lessons enable "no shame or stigma in progressing slowly" (9) and "no embarrassment or shame" when content must be "explained again" (23), as well as conditions in which failure is a "an opportunity for learning rather than a mark of shame" (250). The conditions of mutual recognition in the traditional classroom in which teacher and student may be understood as similarly vulnerable to the shame of being an object of contempt or disgust are obliterated by technology that separates the participating parties in time and space. Learners are spared the postlapsarian shame associated with their previous academic records and come to the MOOC with a perpetually clean slate free of educational sin. Most professors at companies like Coursera and edX also are first-timers to online teaching and may hope to begin with clean slates.

In her essay "Desiring Recognition, Accumulating Affect," Megan Watkins (2010) worries that online learning saps educational experiences of critical desires and contagions. She points out that the separation of learning from teaching predates current trends for digital self-directed learning and online delivery and can be traced to the antiauthoritarianism of theorists of critical pedagogy, such as Henry Giroux and Peter McLaren. For Watkins, technology exacerbates this bifurcation of knowledge acquisition and instruction. As she observes, although "recognition" is often associated with "a positive process with the elicitation of positive affects," it "can also function in a negative way, carrying the resultant force of negative affects" (273). If one is interacting with a neutral technology rather than other human beings, it is impossible to be "singled out" in Watkins's terms "for poor academic performance or behavior" (273). Unfortunately, according to Watkins, minimizing contact has many hidden costs not only for the affective state of the learner but also for the affective state of the teacher.

At the most basic level, relative anonymity fosters conditions of avoidance, which may explain the staggeringly high attrition rates in MOOC enrollments. Many online courses offer "certificates of accomplishment," but it is often adequacy that students pursue rather than excellence. Those pursuing recognition for outstanding performance risk being ignored by their digitally detached professors or peers. It is these students who crave attention who often most vociferously digitally express their negative affect either inside or outside the confines of the course platform. As a protective strategy, the bulk of students follow the cues of the learning management system to have the affectless demeanor of those on a vocational track, much like the working-class peers described by educational theorist Mike Rose (1989) who "just wanna be average" rather than stand out as eggheads or nerds. In Rose's classic work of autobiographical narrative in the pedagogical literature of college composition about working-class students content with marginally passing grades, he credits a beatnik English teacher at his Catholic high school who took a personal interest in his college plans with motivating him to seek recognition and risk. Without these personalized affective investments, MOOC participants who do not "just wanna be average" risk disappointment and disillusionment. As more MOOC companies move toward an employee certification model in which the MOOC primarily serves as corporate-required training, "going through the motions" without any affective investments might become increasingly the norm.

Yet by focusing on "affective computing," Rosalind Picard (1997) insists that computer science rationalists should not continue to dismiss the existence of emotional investments from the scene of computation. Logicians may desire neutral calculations rather than embarrassing displays of affect, but Picard questions their biases. For her, "too little emotion" can impair decision-making activities (10), since emotions serve as "a powerful motivator, influencing perception, cognition, coping, and creativity in important ways" (1), and digital activities involve limbic system functions at a profound level. She ends with a "manifesto" in its closing pages that credits Donald Norman for his leadership in cognitive science. Norman—in addition to calling for more research on the role of affect in regulatory systems and acknowledgment of the subservience of the cognitive component—was the author of the volume *Emotional Design*, which is famous for asserting that "attractive things work better" (2004, 17).[1] Norman and Picard argue that affects—both positive and negative—are inseparable from the scene of technological engagement.

In popular talks delivered to the TED conference devoted to "technology," "entertainment," and "design" and subsequently posted on the TED website, the gospel of learner analytics that many MOOC evangelists espouse accentuates the "data-driven mode" (Koller 2012) or "data-centric reality" (Khan 2011) that will supposedly allow learners to recognize themselves and to be recognized in the data without the subjective clouding and randomization dictated by affect. Thus MOOC students can be interpellated or hailed by their own numbers and serve simultaneously as researcher-subjects seeking meaning and research-subjects being mined for information.

1. It is worth noting that Picard and Norman use the terms "affect" and "emotion" interchangeably, although many self-identified affect theorists observe that "affect" functions as a more impersonal force or nonhuman actant, while "emotion" presupposes a liberal subject or Cartesian cogito for whom the body can be mastered by the mind (Gregg and Seigworth 2010, 1–2; Massumi 1987, xvi; Hemmings 2005, 551–52).

However, data might actually give us a variety of affective attachments and repulsions to respond to rather than exclusively offering us access to objective facts. MOOCs as instantiations of the larger "quantified self movement" may be characterized by magical thinking, strong feelings around wish fulfillment, and obsessions and compulsions traditionally associated with religiosity. "Tracking data isn't simply about the data," Jill Walker Rettberg writes (2014). "Once we have personal, quantified data about ourselves, we look at it and we interpret it. We use the data to adjust the stories we already tell ourselves about our lives, and we use our stories about our lives to adjust, excuse or understand our data" (71). Rettberg argues that these "affective ties" to data can be profound for self-trackers and represent a long history of "seeing ourselves through technology."

Yet MOOC advocates contend that data encourage objectivity and spur cutting sentimental ties. For example, at one point in his *One World Schoolhouse* (2013), Salman Khan uses an extended analogy to the temporality of particular dietary schedules as a way to understand the rigidity of ritual practices in education, such as assessment. He questions why breakfast, lunch, and dinner are served in a specific order in the day in a standard three-meal regimen when one meal might suffice and fasting might be preferable for good health. Khan maintains that this mealtime sequence is totally arbitrary and contends that it is a relic of path dependencies reinforced by workplace economics and social conventions. (Ironically the same structure of consuming specific kinds of food at specific times in the day was praised by Booker T. Washington in *Up From Slavery* (1901) as part of the civilizing mission of education that would separate human beings from chattel.) Khan dismisses the three-meal schedule as an antiquated habit we "cling to" nostalgically (2013, 62). "As with our eating habits, so with our teaching habits" (63), Khan declares.

We can examine Khan's language closely for cues and clues that give us insight about his own negative affects when he expresses contempt or disgust with phenomena that frustrate him or irritate him. For example, while Washington enshrined labor as virtuous, for Khan the word "labor" is associated with "manual labor," "menial labor," and "low-cost labor." Following this logic, the MOOC format of online video serves as a labor-saving device that is far more efficient than conventional classroom learning, which currently appears to occupy a disproportionate amount of the time and energy of both teachers and students. According to Khan, the labor of participating in the conventional educational system drains them of the positive affect that they should be experiencing.

Bureaucracy is another major villain in Khan's narrative, which is allowed to be the focus of much of the negative affect that he represses elsewhere in his optimistic account of win-win learning. In *One World Schoolhouse* Khan bemoans the "resistance of administrators and bureaucrats" (2013, 41) and the obstacles created because "[b]ureaucrats and organizations" have a "built-in aversion to new ideas and approaches" (42). He pines for the resources that would be freed if "bureaucracy" were to get its "fat" "trimmed" (120). His alternative online paradigm to the strictures of traditional bricks-and-mortar education, which is supported by an online library of educational video, is supposedly "nonbureaucratic, open-minded, and located in the very heart of Silicon Valley" (164), which are all assumed to be positive descriptors.

But what if we follow the advice of David Graeber in *The Utopia of Rules* (2015) and instead embrace bureaucracy as our own happy object with its own "secret joys" for our affective engagement? Instead of accepting the account of MOOC missionaries and their urgings to revile bureaucracy as the enemy, we can disobey their dictates about what deserves our affection in higher education. After all, Graeber praises bureaucracies for having a number of admirable qualities. Although antiauthoritarian "fantasy worlds" may be imbued with more "charisma" (184), the indifference, regularity, predictability, and transparency of rule-bound and mechanically operating institutions should inspire more open love and fidelity rather than furtive romance.

Extrapolating from Graeber, I will confess my own infatuation with the delights of PDFs, org charts, committee structures, and parliamentary procedures, in speaking as a serial employee of several state-run public research universities. As Clark Kerr (1963) once remarked, the "university" really is a "multiversity" of many stakeholders, so disputes need to be resolved fairly and consistently. What's inside the black box of Coursera's proprietary software and legalistic end-user license agreements is often more mysterious, and even open-source efforts like those of edX can vary widely in ways that make predicting outcomes by participants difficult.

Just as critics of MOOCs might allow themselves to acknowledge the positive affects that are potentially attached to bureaucracies of higher education, MOOC skeptics should also acknowledge their own delights at the downfall of disruptive alternatives to the conventional campus. It is understandable for traditionalists to experience a certain amount of schadenfreude in the passing of the "MOOC moment," particularly when MOOCs have struggled to gain new adherents, and campus public relations offices have turned to promoting newer forms of splashy instructional innovation and outreach. It may even be predictable for institutional academics to experience joy in the misery of hubristic MOOC-creator Sebastian Thrun, who found himself saddled with the shortcomings of his company Udacity, which at the end of 2013 the *New*

York Times called a "flop" in failing to provide measurable improvement in the academic success of San José State University students (Lewin 2013). Thrun himself confessed to delivering "a lousy product" and wore his digital hair shirt of failure before the online public. If social media initially spread positive MOOC affects as students signed up for courses, social media has also delivered negative MOOC affects in the scathing criticism of blog postings, YouTube commentary, Twitter status updates, and snarky posts on platforms for the ephemeral voicing of mean spirits and bad moods.

It is worth reminding readers that, as a rhetorician, I don't think "rhetoric" is a dirty word. To speak of the "rhetoric of MOOCs" is not intended as disparagement per se, because rhetoric shouldn't be equated with deception or empty promises. The issue for scholars studying discourses around instructional technology is how MOOC rhetoric may assume certain universals about technology and education that are problematic and how MOOC rhetoric attempts to redirect affects it dismisses as improper. For doubters who were concerned about how MOOCs may have celebrated the branding of the Ivy League, white male privilege, the "great man" theory of history, and solo inventor myths, perhaps they can also relish how they might have acted as killjoys during the euphoria at the height of the MOOC moment.

At the same time, many technophobic purists and fundamentalists in the university may feel that turnabout is fair play for the negations and slights that they feel they may have experienced at the height of the MOOC moment. As I noted in *The War on Learning*, at its worst the MOOC moment encouraged procedures for faculty governance to be suspended, sticklers for rules to be silenced, and critics to be shamed, and these humiliations affected Luddite conservatives and progressive technological experimenters alike.

In her book *The Promise of Happiness*, Sara Ahmed (2010) argues that the killjoy should not be treated as a villain, because taking the unenviable killjoy position often occupied by feminists, queer people, precarious workers, and others unable to form attachment to proscribed "happy objects" is "to open a life, to make room for life, to make room for possibility, for chance, for alternative ways of living" (20). By resisting the happy objects of MOOCs and locating pedagogical pleasures elsewhere, perhaps readers of this book are opening up possibilities other than digital universalism for future learners.

There is a long history of affective ebb and flow around the rhetoric of open education efforts. It is worth remembering that the Chautauqua circuit had lectures and demonstrations by noted nineteenth-century experts and intellectual celebrities that may have been comparable in many ways to the material delivered digitally today by esteemed scholars representing elite university brands. Yet most of the Chautauqua speeches were pedagogically very superficial and followed the tried-and-true scripts of reform sermons and inspirational talks. Chautauqua also had comical everymen, zither players, yodelers, and bell ringers (Antczak and Siemers 1993, 213) and a general atmosphere of spectacle and heightened enthusiasm. When expectations about information, entertainment, and technology changed among its core audience (Canning 2005), Chautauqua went into decline. Now that MOOCs seem to be similarly falling out of favor, perhaps we should remember and commemorate the euphoria and derision they once inspired.

References

Addams, Jane. 2013. *20 Years at Hull-House*. Philadelphia: Addams Publications.

Ahmed, Sara. 2010. *The Promise of Happiness*. Durham: Duke University Press.

Antczak, Frederick J., and Edith Siemers. 1993. "The Divergence of Purpose and Practice on the Chautauqua Keith Vawter's Self-Defense." In *Oratorical Culture in Nineteenth-Century America: Transformations in the Theory and Practice of Rhetoric*, edited by Gregory Clark and S. Michael Halloran, 208–25. Carbondale: Southern Illinois University Press.

Berlant, Lauren Gail. 2011. *Cruel Optimism*. Durham: Duke University Press.

Bowen, William G., Kelly A. Lack, and Kevin M. Guthrie. 2015. *Higher Education in the Digital Age*. Princeton: Princeton University Press.

Brown, Olympia. 1983. *Suffrage and Religious Principle: Speeches and Writings of Olympia Brown*. Metuchen: Scarecrow Press,

Canning, Charlotte M. 2005. *The Most American Thing in America: Circuit Chautauqua as Performance*. Iowa City: University Of Iowa Press.

Chan, Anita Say. 2013. *Networking Peripheries: Technological Futures and the Myth of Digital Universalism*. Cambridge: MIT Press.

Cole, Teju. 2012. "The White-Savior Industrial Complex." *Atlantic*, March 21. http://www.theatlantic.com/international/archive/2012/03/the-white-savior-industrial-complex/254843/.

Graeber, David. 2015. *The Utopia of Rules: On Technology, Stupidity, and the Secret Joys of Bureaucracy*. New York: Melville House.

Gregg, Melissa, and Gregory J. Seigworth. 2010. *The Affect Theory Reader*. Durham: Duke University Press.

Gross, Daniel M., and Jonathan Alexander. 2016. "Frameworks for Failure." *Pedagogy* 16 (2): 273–95.

"'Hate This Flipped Class'—A Collection of Tweets Collated 8 September 2013 by @attackcomplex." https://irvingtonparentsforum.files.wordpress.com/2014/01/flipped-classroom-tweets.pdf.

Hemmings, Clare. 2005. "Invoking Affect: Cultural Theory and the Ontological Turn." *Cultural Studies* 19 (5): 548–67.

James, Felix. 1971. "The Tuskegee Institute Movable School, 1906–1923." *Agricultural History* 45 (3): 201–9.

Jaschik, Scott. 2013. "Coursera Forced to Call off a MOOC amid Complaints about the Course." *Inside Higher Ed*, February 4. https://www.insidehighered.com/news/2013/02/04/coursera-forced-call-mooc-amid-complaints-about-course.

Kerr, Clark. 1963. *The Uses of the University.* Cambridge: Harvard University Press.

Khan, Salman. 2011. "Let's Use Video to Reinvent Education." TED Talk Subtitles and Transcript. https://www.ted.com/talks/salman_khan_let_s_use_video_to_reinvent_education/transcript.

———. 2013. *The One World Schoolhouse: Education Reimagined.* New York: Twelve.

Koller, Daphne. 2012. "What We're Learning from Online Education." TED Talk Subtitles and Transcript. Posted August. https://www.ted.com/talks/daphne_koller_what_we_re_learning_from_online_education/transcript.

Kolowich, Steve. 2016. "After the Gold Rush." *Chronicle of Higher Education,* June 5. http://chronicle.com/article/MOOCs-Moneythe-Untold/236708.

Lamott, Anne. 1995. *Bird by Bird: Some Instructions on Writing and Life.* New York: Anchor.

Lewin, Tamar. 2013. "After Setbacks, Online Courses Are Rethought." *New York Times,* December 10. http://www.nytimes.com/2013/12/11/us/after-setbacks-online-courses-are-rethought.html.

Massumi, Brian. 1987. "Notes on the Translation and Acknowledgments." In Gilles Deleuze and Felix Guattari, *A Thousand Plateaus,* xvi–xix. Minneapolis: University of Minnesota Press.

Matsuda, Paul Kei. 2014. "Local Is Global: Teaching Writing to a Global Student Population." Presented at the UC Writing Conference, UC San Diego, October 10.

Mayberry, B. D. 1991. "The Tuskegee Movable School: A Unique Contribution to National and International Agriculture and Rural Development." *Agricultural History* 65 (2): 85–104.

Noble, David F. 2001. *Digital Diploma Mills: The Automation of Higher Education.* New York: Monthly Review Press.

Norman, Donald A. 2004. *Emotional Design: Why We Love (or Hate) Everyday Things.* New York: Basic Books.

Ogrizek, Irene. 2013. "Daphne Koller and the Problem with Coursera." *Irene Ogrizek,* May 18. http://ireneogrizek.ca/2013/05/18/8932/.

Picard, Rosalind W. 1997. *Affective Computing.* Cambridge: MIT Press.

Rettberg, Jill Walker. 2014. *Seeing Ourselves through Technology: How We Use Selfies, Blogs and Wearable Devices to See and Shape Ourselves.* Basingstoke: Palgrave Macmillan

Rose, Mike. 1989. *Lives on the Boundary: The Struggles and Achievements of America's Underprepared.* New York: Free Press; London: Collier Macmillan.

Sedgwick, Eve Kosofsky, and Adam Frank. 1995. "Shame in the Cybernetic Fold: Reading Silvan Tomkins." *Critical Inquiry* 21 (2): 496–522.

Strauss, Valerie. 2013. "How Online Class about Online Learning Failed Miserably." *Washington Post,* February 5. https://www.washingtonpost.com/news/answer-sheet/wp/2013/02/05/how-online-class-about-online-learning-failed-miserably/.

Vaidhyanathan, Siva. 2011. *The Googlization of Everything (And Why We Should Worry).* Berkeley: University of California Press.

Vise, Daniel de. 2012. "U-Va. Takes Major Step in Online Education." *Washington Post,* July 16. https://www.washingtonpost.com/local/education/u-va-takes-major-step-in-online-education/2012/07/16/gJQAF3YOqW_story.html.

Washington, Booker T. 1901 [1995]. *Up from Slavery.* Reprint. New York: Dover Publications.

Watkins, Megan. 2010. "Desiring Recognition, Accumulating Affect." In *The Affect Theory Reader,* edited by Melissa Gregg and Gregory J Seigworth, 269–87. Durham: Duke University Press.

14

The Prospects and Regrets
of an EdTech Gold Rush

ALEX REID

Over a period of less than three years, the massive open online course (MOOC) has traveled the familiar path of hyped technologies. As proclamations of the failure of MOOCs ring as loudly now as the prior proclamations of the MOOC revolution not long ago, online higher education rolls onward. The challenge that MOOCs promised to meet, of bringing postsecondary education to a new population of underserved students, remains unmet, and the potential of the Internet to serve as a platform for formal education remains largely unrealized. Even though a growing number of college students take at least one online course each year, the vast majority of coursework continues to take place on campus, which might give one the sense that little has changed in higher education. On the surface this is accurate. Students follow much the same curriculum, that is, sit in the same classrooms and complete similar assignments to students a decade ago. However, the information-media environment of the face-to-face course has shifted significantly in the last decade through technological developments from course-management systems and digital libraries to social media and mobile devices. Higher education happens online today, regardless of how the courses are catalogued. The very public rise and fall of a particular kind of MOOC experience demonstrates, if nothing else, that we still struggle to understand and discuss online pedagogy, whether it is happening among thousands of MOOC students or a dozen in an otherwise traditional seminar. Either way, the online world continues to confront higher education as an opportunity (to fail) to grasp and in this respect is part of a cycle that is far more ancient than the familiar story of techno-hype. It is a story of kairos and metanoia. One might say that kairos is the watchword, the patron demigod, of higher education and information technology today. Kairos, the Greek god of opportunity, both

.eds and haunts the academy as our disciplines and institutions alternately leap to grasp at a new technology or hold back, averse to the risks involved. In Greek myth, Kairos was depicted as young and swift; he could only be caught by grasping the hair hanging over his face. Once he passed you by, it was too late. Even in ancient Greece, opportunity was fleeting. Found in the passing shadow of Kairos was Metanoia, the personification of regret, of missed opportunity. In Christian theology, kairos becomes the time in which God acts, and metanoia becomes a central principle of Christian practice, that is, repentance. The words take on slightly different meanings in classical rhetoric where kairos becomes the skill of matching a rhetorical act with its appropriate time, and metanoia becomes a strategy for correcting or modifying a statement, for demonstrating a change in thinking. Across each of these evolving uses runs a familiar dualism of opportunity and regret.

Regardless of the viewpoint one brings toward the opportunities presented by digital media, the valuation of emerging technologies is measured in relation to a fairly static view of who students are and how learning happens. That is, the traditional humanist and the technolibertarian posit new technologies either as a potential threat or as a boon to an already existing human with independent and self-contained capacities for thought, agency, and expression. A more contemporary postmodern view may be less certain about human agency but continues to view technology as distinct from human thought or action. However, an alternate *posthuman* view suggests that human thought and action is interwoven with technology in such a manner that judgments of threat or benefit, good or bad, become very complicated. Posthumanism refers to a broad movement in the humanities that integrates recent research in cognitive science, cybernetics, and related fields with cultural theories to understand the sociocultural and ecological effects of emerging technologies.[1] In taking up concepts such as Edwin Hutchins's (1995) distributed cognition and Andy Clark's (2010) extended mind, posthumanism implies a different view of what learning might be and what role technologies might play in it. In some respects, our contemporary concerns about the effects of emerging technologies on learning, if not thinking in general, have a long history. Plato famously wrote of the threat of writing to human memory in the *Phaedrus*, though obviously today it would be difficult to imagine human intelligence and knowledge without writing and reading, to say nothing of the educational practices that have been built on literacy. If our views of how

---

1. Posthumanism is thoroughly explored in texts such as Katherine Hayles's (1999) *How We Became Posthuman: Virtual Bodies in Cybernetics, Literature, and Informatics*, and Cary Wolfe's (2010) *What is Posthumanism?*

thinking and learning work are tied to technological and historical conditions, then it is not surprising that a different technological context creates challenges.

Expecting those new conditions to produce the same thinking and learning experiences as we have encountered in the past is unrealistic. It is the inverse of the cliché about repeating the same acts and hoping for a different result. Here we take up a new set of processes and hope to get the same outcome. That is, we define the success and failure of digital pedagogies on their ability to replicate the brick-and-mortar campus. The opportunities and, by extension, the regrets we associate with MOOCs begin with this expectation that we already know what learning should be. Furthermore, based on that expectation, we also express faith in a particular future where we believe that educational technologies should take us. However, if we instead imagine that thinking and learning will shift with the technologies that we employ, then our ideas about what is best and where the future might lead must also shift. This is not a form of technological determinism. It is not an argument that our ability to learn is determined by the technologies we use, but it is an argument that learning relies on, and is shaped by, technologies. As much as we may recognize that college students can encounter a wide range of learning experiences and pedagogies, it is also clear that they widely experience large lecture halls, textbooks, and exams. Though a variety of online, college learning experiences are likewise to be had, students widely experience the online version of those lecture halls, and this is the image MOOCs tend to raise. However, as I will discuss, once one gets beyond the faculty video lecture and the provided course materials, MOOCs open students to a vast network of participants and media. The twentieth-century lecture hall operated at a time when information and expertise were relatively inaccessible. Lectures, textbooks, and the other familiar mechanisms of the college curriculum developed in those contexts. Participants in a MOOC, much like most of us online, face very different conditions: a deluge of information and many expert voices (or at least claims to expertise). Twentieth-century students on a brick-and-mortar campus had many ways to meet and collaborate face-to-face that are unavailable to online students, but those online students have their own opportunities for communication and collaboration on a scale unthinkable a few decades ago. However, those opportunities come with their own challenges. In short, rather than being deterministic, emerging technologies like MOOCs open significant questions about what the future of learning might be. That future is open and dynamic, and as such, we need to consider the opportunities presented by MOOCs and other educational technologies in that light.

Bruno Latour's Prospects

Bruno Latour is a sociologist best known for his work in science studies and his role in the development of actor-network theory. Fundamentally, Latour argues that we must rethink the divide we have established between nature and culture and recognize the role that nonhuman actors, including technologies, play in our lives. Coincidentally, he has offered a MOOC course of his own, Scientific Humanities, through the France Université Numérique, which, at least, indicates some implicit interest in MOOCs, as does his digital humanities project surrounding his most recent book, *An Inquiry into Modes of Existence*, which reimagines the shape of academic collaboration through an extensive, collaborative website (http://www.modesofexistence .org/). Indeed, his work indicates the importance of recognizing that research and teaching practices are interwoven; it is difficult to imagine revolutionizing teaching practices, as MOOCs promised to do, without some similar shift in research paradigms, particularly in terms of the dissemination and discussion of research. Instead one might view learning, whether one is referring to what is learned through research or scholarship or what is learned in a classroom, as an experience that emerges from a network of human and nonhuman actors rather than as some intrinsic human characteristic that is either enhanced or disrupted by technologies. I am particularly interested here in Latour's assessment of the modern conception of futurity, that is, the way we imagine where educational technologies might take us. Any conception of kairos, of opportunity, is built on our imagination of the future, as is metanoia, our sense of regret or desire to rethink past choices.

In his essay "An Attempt at a 'Compositionist Manifesto,'" Latour (2010) approaches futurity from a broad historical perspective. He takes up Walter Benjamin's angel of history as an emblem for modernist futurity and suggests that, "contrary to Benjamin's interpretation, the Modern who, like the angel, is flying backward is actually not seeing the destruction; He is generating it in his flight since it occurs behind His back! It is only recently, by a sudden conversion, a *metanoia* of sorts, that He has suddenly realized how much catastrophe His development has left behind him" (485–86). We might see academia in a similar position relative to MOOCs. Our future, too, has been built more on fleeing the past than facing the future. While in some respects, particularly in the humanities, we romanticize a prior age of higher education when there were more tenured faculty (and more majors in our departments), we have also arrived at the present moment by fleeing a less egalitarian, less open, and less diverse institutional past. As Latour continues, "just at the time when people are despairing at realizing that they might, in the end, have 'no future,' we suddenly have many prospects. Yet they are so utterly different from what we imagined while fleeing ahead looking backwards that we might cast them only as so many fragile illusions. Or find them even more terrifying than what we were trying to escape from" (486). Although Latour's compositionist manifesto is not about higher education, a historical view of progress and prospects can illuminate our own task, which is not only to build or participate in a particular vision of the future for higher education but also to understand futurity itself, especially as that concept is composed in relation to technological innovation. In my Latourian-inspired perspective, the prospective view of the future is neither technologies solving our problems or a messianic moment of justice but rather the composition of a new set of conditions: not ones that attempt to leave the past behind as we see with modernity but ones that understand the past very differently. That is, conventionally we say that "necessity is the mother of invention," which implies, among other things, that technologies develop to solve existing problems. Clearly solving contemporary problems is a motivation for some innovations, but the eventual effects of emerging technologies are less predictable, especially when their cultural impact is on the scale of the Internet. As rhetorician and media scholar Gregory Ulmer (2002) observes, it is likely that "the ethical dilemma of self/other will not be solved in an electronic apparatus, but simply that it will become irrelevant, just as 'appeasing' the gods, which was the problem addressed by ritual, became irrelevant in literacy" (114). Perhaps we stopped appeasing the gods, but not because we no longer required a good crop. Instead we came to see our relationship to crops differently. Similarly, we will likely not solve the technolibertarian/humanist dilemma of developing technologies that empower rather than dominate their human users. Instead we will come to see our relationship with technology differently. In this way, the problem mutates and becomes productive of a new set of prospects, a new future.

Like Benjamin's angel, the criticism of MOOCs sees technological progress as driving us toward destruction and the end of higher education. And that criticism is not totally wrong; it clearly identifies problems that need to be addressed. However, as Latour addresses elsewhere, criticism is not enough.

> What would critique do if it could be associated with more, not with less, with multiplication, not subtraction. . . . That is, generating more ideas than we have received, inheriting from a prestigious critical tradition but not letting it die away, or "dropping into quiescence" like a piano no longer struck. This would require that all entities, including computers, cease to be objects defined simply by their inputs and outputs and become again things. (Latour 2004, 248)

In shifting from objects to things, Latour is suggesting that we must treat nonhumans as active participants in the networks we share with them rather than as mute servants of human will or some amorphous and spectral ideology. In doing so, he offers a means to associate critique with multiplication. When nonhumans become actors in our networks, those actors multiply the prospects for activity rather than reducing the situation to a bipolar future of liberation or domination. Unfortunately, it is bipolarity that always seems to emerge from such conversations. We are either the hapless angel, pushed forward by the storm of progress, or clever technicians carving a future from the natural world. Latour has been accused of being on both ends, perhaps because he rejects this bipolar ontology. In his hybridized world, humans are neither automatons nor demigods. We are, in Latour's words, made to do. We are made to eat, drink, sleep, breathe, walk, talk, think, and so on. We do these things in relation to food, water, beds, air, the ground, language, and so on. Agency is not inside but in relation. This perspective offers a different way to understand our relations with technology where the question is not whether a device enhances, obstructs, or dominates some innate agency but rather how the networks in which we participate produce agency. As such, one might investigate what we are made to do as participants in a MOOC and consider how these activities relate to learning.

Of course, when we discuss "learning," we are discussing a rather general human experience. Every sensation offers an opportunity for learning about our environment. Formal, institutional learning capitalizes on that general human capacity, and the particular ways in which higher education operates can be historically traced through a vast network of actors. The practices of credit hours, semesters, seminars, lectures, majors, and general education requirements all emerge from this history, as do our expectations of what college learning should be. Although we are all very well aware of these institutional elements and continually press up against them as administrators, faculty, and students, we also tend to obscure their role in defining learning. That is, we view learning as what Latour (2005) terms a "matter of fact": an empirically observable reality. In place of matters of fact, Latour offers us "matters of concern," where we "learn how to feed off uncertainties, instead of deciding in advance what the furniture of the world should look like" (115). In the case of MOOCs, this means not deciding in advance what formal learning should look like and instead recognizing the wide range of human and nonhuman actors who gather together in the production and experience of a MOOC. Of course, this also means not deciding in advance that MOOCs are the future either. Instead MOOCs offer a site of experimentation for investigating how learning might happen in a massive online environment.

Although a MOOC may not reproduce the learning experience or out-comes of a conventional classroom, it also opens capacities that would not otherwise be possible. Some of these are fairly obvious, such as being free to the students. Others are subtler. For example, my discipline, rhetoric and composition, has had mixed success (at best) with delivering MOOC versions of first-year composition courses, especially if one sets as an outcome deliver-ing a course that might substitute for an existing conventional composition course. Writing courses seem unlikely candidates for "MOOCification," since they have always relied heavily on the ability of the instructor to respond to each student's writing. This tutorial model of instruction produces outcomes that are impossible to replicate with a 10,000:1 student-faculty ratio, and the adoption of computerized "reading" of student work does not solve the prob-lem. Even if it did become possible to develop automated scoring software that reliably simulated human readers, providing formative assessment is well beyond our technological means. That said, there have been a few MOOC experiments in this direction. In the Coursera composition courses offered by Duke University and Georgia Tech, the faculty in both instances observed the low rate of completion among the students (Comer 2014; Head 2013). They recognized the impracticality of such courses serving the same objectives as traditional composition courses, although meeting a college composition re-quirement did not seem to be a significant motive for the participants either (Comer 2014, 132). Instead as Denise Comer, lead faculty member for the Duke composition MOOC, observes, "As the course draws to a close, we have over 80,000 people enrolled. That's 80,000 people who thought about writ-ing, or watched a video on writing, or contributed to the forum, or drafted a writing project, or gave feedback to another writer. . . . Forum posts suggest that even if someone participated in one segment of the course, they had the opportunity to think about themselves as writers" (147–48). So a MOOC may appear to be a failure in terms of its ability to deliver traditional college cur-ricula but seen from a different perspective, one that does not cling to that outcome, a different set of values emerge.

If one imagines that the outcomes we have for college students in relation to communication involve developing their ability to communicate and col-laborate in a digital, networked environment, then it is hard to say that tradi-tional classrooms can meet that outcome either. What a MOOC or other on-line environment can provide is a space where students can find communities that share their interests, audiences who will read their writing, and even real-world purposes that students might value and pursue through writing. While I do not have a specific solution to offer, predicating the educational goals for communication on what one can do with one-to-one, instructor-student mentoring is shortsighted and backward-looking. If, rather than insisting that we already know what the future of literacy will be (and thus fear a future of no literacy), we considered the many prospects of future literacies built from the things that are available and participating in our thinking and learning, then we might discover a rich array of possibilities. From this perspective one does not ignore the criticisms directed at MOOCs regarding their pedagogy, but one also does not stop at the point of criticism. Instead one opens a large field of inquiry and opportunity where our conceptions of literacy, learning, and teaching become intertwined with the network of technologies and tools that participate in these activities.

A larger matter of concern than pedagogical effectiveness, however, is at stake with MOOCs, one that examines their broader effect on the culture of higher education. For some, MOOCs, especially xMOOCs like Coursera, are a tool for disruption.[2] For others, particularly the brand name institutions that have partnered with xMOOCs, these technologies might be tools for marketing and student recruitment. Many universities hope that MOOCs will serve as a cost-cutting measure in the ongoing pursuit of student enrollment and the increasing demand for postsecondary education. For still others, MOOCs represent a cultural war on tenure and faculty, as well as on the underprivileged students whom universities aim to serve this way. In other words, MOOCs are a prototypical "matter of concern" in that they bring together many human and nonhuman participants with a wide range of epistemological, social, and political views that are often difficult to integrate. How does scholarly research into the educational effectiveness of MOOCs speak to the political pressures from state governments or boards of trustees to adopt MOOC platforms or the concerns of professional scholarly organizations and faculty unions? How might those conversations intersect with the interests of college students or prospective MOOC participants (two different groups of people) or the shifting capacities of emerging technologies or the interests of those investing in the development of these platforms? In addressing these political, institutional matters of concern, all the human and nonhuman actors must be represented as they come together not through shared values but through shared concerns. There are obviously no simple answers.

2. The conversation around MOOCs has generally divided them between cMOOCs and xMOOCs, terms coined by education technologist Stephen Downes (2012). "Connectivist MOOCs," or cMOOCs, emphasize shared learning among participants, tend to be more informal, and typically take place across a variety of social-media platforms. A good example of a cMOOC would be DS106 (ds106.us), which is a course on digital storytelling. xMOOCs are those offered by Coursera, Udacity, and related ventures, which tend to be more focused on the delivery of video and textbook content.

This is not solely a matter of establishing the facts. Instead it is a matter of composing new networks and associations that redefine the relations among these many humans and nonhumans, or, as Latour puts it, composing new prospects for the future.

Digital Prospecting

To follow through on Latour's recommendation of prospecting in imagining a future for online higher education (MOOC or otherwise), it might be useful to explore a more literal version of digital prospecting, *Minecraft*. For those unfamiliar with it, *Minecraft* is a popular video game that offers a variety of gameplay options, including a "creative mode" where users build custom virtual worlds, a survival mode where players must mine for resources and defend themselves against various monsters, and a multiplayer mode where players compete against one another in a variety of settings. As the game's title suggests, however, the core activity involves mining one's world for resources and then crafting useful items. Of course *Minecraft* is not the only game that works this way. Many massively multiplayer online role-playing games (MMORPGs) require players to gather resources and acquire items. Often this involves collaboration and trade. How might critique, teaching, and learning become like *Minecraft* where what gets taken apart becomes the basis for what gets put together? Much of the pedagogical exploration of *Minecraft* has focused on the creative mode, where one can build models of historical buildings or construct complex machines like graphing calculators, or on taking advantage of student interest and literacy in gameplay to build more conventional literacy skills.[3] While the example of *Minecraft* might immediately set one's mind toward the growing interest in using games for learning (or "gamification" as it is sometimes termed), I am not interested in that angle here.[4] Instead *Minecraft* offers a simplified world of actors that helps to exemplify the Latourian task of prospecting.

In *Minecraft* one must learn the relationships that pertain among the universe of objects that can be combined to make armor, weapons, tools, houses, and fortifications. In more complex gaming worlds, like *World of Warcraft*, an elaborate community of "theorycrafting" has developed to compute the tactical uses of different tools in combination with one another, but *Minecraft* is simpler than that. It is relatively easy to see how different actors can be com-

---

3. Daniel Short (2012) and Jeffrey Brand and Shelley Kinash (2013) investigate the pedagogical uses of *Minecraft*, which have gained some mainstream news attention as well (Ossola 2015).
4. Gamification has both its proponents (e.g., McGonigal 2011) and its critics (Bogost 2015).

bined for the simple purpose of survival. Survival, or perhaps more optimistically, thriving, is a key element here both for *Minecraft* players and for the actors in a MOOC or other online learning environment. While there might always be some abstract gesture toward the relationship between "getting an education" and thriving in the real world, such matters do not really inform pedagogy. This is not to suggest that courses need to aim their content more directly toward "real-world" application. That would be the general form of the argument made about *Minecraft* in most educational research: that playing the game aides in succeeding at something else. Prospecting suggests something very different. It suggests understanding how actors thrive and learn *within* the context of their environment. That is, as a *Minecraft* player, one prospects to uncover the available resources, strategically combines them, and collaborates with other players so as to continue surviving. The game does not come with a readymade future or a preset endpoint. One has to build one's future just as one must build one's armor. The activities of searching, composing, and sharing, both individually and in groups, which underlie *Minecraft*, are not just gaming activities, they are core practices of both web culture and constructivist pedagogy. It is not unusual for college students to be asked to engage in such activities, but it is harder to discover similar kinds of prospecting taking place at the level of faculty, pedagogy, and curriculum, which is where it will need to take place if we are to address the challenges of digital media.

To prospect in the space of online learning means neither fleeing the past nor importing some prebuilt outcome. Instead it requires an emergent approach linking together the capacities of human and nonhuman actors. The primary difference between the large-scale xMOOCs and the ethos of digital prospecting is that the former has been built primarily on a lecture-based pedagogy where learning is more about consuming or digesting knowledge than making it. It has imagined that, in the end, a massive open online course should produce similar learning experiences and outcomes to traditional courses. Read or watch a lecture. Discuss the lecture with other students and class facilitators (if not the professor herself). Take a test to verify that you have learned what you should. If a *Minecraft*-inspired view of digital prospecting might inspire metanoia, a changing of one's mind, about the missed opportunities of a digital academy, it would not begin with regrets about technological platforms but with recognizing the missed opportunities to rethink learning itself. It would begin with mining existing resources and using those parts to craft something different. As the corporate interests of privately owned public spaces grasp at the kairotic moment of MOOCs, we might lament the missed opportunity of some alternate online learning or wax nostalgic for a brick-and-mortar education that will never be the same. It is easy to feel as though one is being blasted backward into the future. In this context, critique is, at best, a half-measure. When academics and journalists from the *Chronicle of Higher Education* to the *New York Times* observe that, for whatever good a MOOC may serve, it can never replace the value of face-to-face learning, one wonders if their memory of sitting in a lecture hall with several hundred peers has been colored by nostalgia.[5]

Metanoia might be better than nostalgia as a way of rethinking the regrets of missed opportunities of online education. As Anil Dash (2012) observes, the web is shifting from pages to streams, from the static webpages of early HTML or even blogs and wikis to the continuous updates of social media. This tension is quite visible in a MOOC where one moves from the static content of recorded lectures to the deluge of participant discussion forums to say nothing of ancillary channels in Twitter, Google+, and elsewhere. Pages and streams suggest two different kinds of prospecting: mining pages and panning streams. And both are quite different from the literacy practices of the print era. In the print-era lecture hall, the one we still try to emulate online, there was a lot of information to cover, but as faculty one could create a manageable body of knowledge, instructing students to read specific books and listen to specific lectures. There was always more information out there on any given subject, but it was far harder to access. Practices of reading, listening, note taking, memorizing, and testing all operated on that scale.

In the digital classroom, we are deluged with information. We don't need to go in search of it; we must actively ignore it. Traditional courses begin to resemble games, filled with unnecessary, artificial obstacles where we ask students to take tests and pretend that they can't find the answers to the questions in a few seconds on their smartphones. From banning books to banning laptops in classrooms, institutions have often responded to changes in information flow with censorship. Here censorship is perhaps just a form of nostalgia. Looking back at the print era, rather than defining those classroom activities as the be-all and end-all of learning, as what it means to acquire knowledge, we might instead see students learning how to participate in technology-specific information systems. When we ask students to participate in the same basic activities but in the very different information systems of an online environment, then it is hardly surprising when the two do not mix.

What would online education look like if it resembled digital prospecting? Perhaps it would bear some resemblance to the affinity spaces James Paul

5. For examples of op-ed pieces in this genre, see Doug Guthrie (2012), David Youngberg (2012), and Steve Lohr (2013).

Gee describes that emerge around video games and other objects of cultural interest. As Gee and Elisabeth Hayes (2011) write, "Passionate affinity-based learning occurs when people organize themselves in the real world and/or via the Internet (or a virtual world) to learn something connected to a shared endeavor, interest, or passion" (69). However, it is difficult to build a sustained, professionalizing curriculum based on affinity spaces. Certainly the motivations of students vary and may not rise to the level of passion; furthermore, the roles of grades and credits significantly shift the relationship among the participants. A professor can never simply be the more learned peer. The unanswered question then is what else might there be besides the informal passion-based learning of affinity spaces, which cannot sustain the formal curriculum needed to credential college graduates, and the status-quo online education environments, which too often seem a byproduct of the worst elements of online and face-to-face interaction. Put differently, we know that twentieth-century methods can reliably produce twentieth-century graduates. The question we appear to be asking now is which twenty-first-century methods can produce twentieth-century graduates: a question with obvious built-in contradictions. That, of course, raises the question of what twenty-first-century graduates should look like, with the tautological answer being that they should look like the reliable product of twenty-first-century methods, whatever those are. It is within the conversation between outcomes and methods that digital prospecting needs to occur.

While higher education remains primarily beguiled by the bells and whistles of technological innovation, the more significant shift in the move toward digital literacy is gaining a different abstract view of pedagogy and curriculum. Our historical expectations for graduates from English to engineering developed in concert with the network of material and discursive structures that built the modern university: lecture halls, labs, libraries, semesters, credits, general education, textbooks, and so on. They also reflected our scholarly practices, which developed in a similar network, so we have asked students to do work that mirrored our own, albeit at a less expert level. The outcomes of a course given in a lecture hall emerge from a discovery of what it is possible to teach and learn in that space over a semester. The same can be said of a seminar room or laboratory. In the end, the expectation of a graduate from an English department is the amalgamation of a series of lecture hall and seminar room experiences with their final exams and final essays and, of course, the many books read along the way. It is also the particular social experience of working with peers and faculty over that time. Without these physical structures, without institutional practices and regulations, without professorial essays and monographs, and without the print literacy culture of the mid-twentieth century, the English major, or any major, appears an arbitrary collection of outcomes and practices with a strangely affected set of social interactions. The late-twentieth-century English classroom or scholarly essay bore only the vaguest resemblance to the book club or newspaper book review, and also little resemblance to the English classes of the nineteenth century. Similarly we might expect that twentieth-first-century digital courses and scholarship will have only a little in common with contemporary social media or with the curriculum of the last century.

If the point, as I have been suggesting, is to begin by investigating the relation between the affordances of digital technological structures and the outcomes we determine for online education, then the most salient point might be the recognition that digital learning places a far greater premium on collective, collaborative learning. In these smart, always-connected spaces in which we learn and work, it is perhaps less important (though not unimportant) what we know and can accomplish individually. In my own field of English, individual accomplishment is valued above all, a fact best exemplified by the single-author monograph necessary for tenure. However, in my experience, such accomplishments rarely translate to expertise with online collaborative environments. Rather than asking students to compose individual essays or take exams, courses would need to develop and assess a different set of activities that demonstrate an ability to understand disciplinary content, practice disciplinary methods, and communicate in disciplinary genres, as well as perhaps professional and public ones. Admittedly, that suggestion is vague. However, the essay and the test only gain their solidity through their connection to an institutional network of agents that make these products into viable tools for measuring student knowledge. Addressing the matters of concern surrounding the future of higher education, represented in the synecdoche of MOOCs, will require rebuilding those networks and agents to foster new understandings and ultimately new measures of student learning. These are the opportunities—the kairotic moments—that might be sought and fostered through the development of new educational technologies and pedagogies.

References

Bogost, Ian. 2015. "Gamificiation Is Bullshit." In *The Gameful World: Approaches, Issues, Applications*, edited by Steffen P. Walz and Sebastian Deterding, 65–80. Cambridge: MIT Press.

Brand, Jeffrey, and Shelley Kinash. 2013. "Crafting Minds in Minecraft." *Education Technology Solutions* 55:56–58.

Clark, Andy. 2010. *Supersizing the Mind: Embodiment, Action, and Cognitive Extension*. Oxford: Oxford University Press.

Comer, Denise. 2014. "Learning How to Teach . . . Differently: Extracts from a MOOC Instructor's Journal." In *Invasion of the MOOCS: the Promises and Perils of Massive Open Online Courses*, edited by Steven D. Krause and Charles Lowe, 130–49. Greenville: Parlor Press.

Dash, Anil. 2012. "Stop Publishing Web Pages." *Anil Dash*, August 14. http://dashes.com/anil/2012/08/stop-publishing-web-pages.html.

Downes, Stephen. 2012. "Massively Open Online Courses Are 'Here to Stay.'" *Stephen Downes*, July 20. http://www.downes.ca/post/58676.

Gee, James Paul, and Elisabeth Hayes. 2011. *Language and Learning in the Digital Age*. Abingdon: Routledge.

Guthrie, Doug. 2012. "Jump Off the Coursera Bandwagon." *Chronicle of Higher Education*, December 17. http://chronicle.com/article/Jump-Off-the-Coursera/136307/.

Hayles, Katherine. 1999. *How We Became Posthuman: Virtual Bodies in Cybernetics, Literature, and Informatics*. Chicago: University of Chicago Press.

Head, Karen. 2013. "Lessons Learned from a Freshman-Composition MOOC." *Chronicle of Higher Education*, September 6. http://chronicle.com/blogs/wiredcampus/lessons-learned-from-a-freshman-composition-mooc/46337.

Hutchins, Edwin. 1995. *Cognition in the Wild*. Cambridge: MIT Press.

Latour, Bruno. 2004. "Why Has Critique Run Out of Steam? From Matters of Fact to Matters of Concern." *Critical Inquiry* 30 (2): 225–48. doi:10.1086/421123.

———. 2005. *Reassembling the Social: An Introduction to Actor-Network-Theory*. Oxford: Oxford University Press.

———. 2010. "An Attempt at a 'Compositionist Manifesto.'" *New Literary History* 41:471–90.

———. 2013. *An Inquiry into Modes of Existence: An Anthropology of the Moderns*. Cambridge: Harvard University Press.

Lohr, Steve. 2013. "Beware of the High Cost of 'Free' Online Courses." *Bits Beware of the High Cost of Free Online Courses Comments*, March 25. http://bits.blogs.nytimes.com/2013/03/25/beware-of-the-high-cost-of-free-online-courses/?_r=0.

McGonigal, Jane. 2011. *Reality Is Broken: Why Games Make Us Better and How They Can Change the World*. New York: Penguin Press.

Ossola, Alexandra. 2015. "Teaching in the Age of Minecraft." *Atlantic*, February 6. http://www.theatlantic.com/education/archive/2015/02/teaching-in-the-age-of-minecraft/385231/.

Short, Daniel. 2012. "Teaching Scientific Concepts Using a Virtual World—Minecraft." *Teaching Science* 58 (3): 55–57.

Ulmer, Gregory. 2002. "Reality Tables: Virtual Furniture." In *Prefiguring Cyberculture: An Intellectual History*, edited by Darren Tofts, Annemarie Jonson, and Alessio Cavallaro, 110–29. Cambridge: MIT Press.

Wolfe, Cary. 2010. *What Is Posthumanism?* Minneapolis: University of Minnesota Press.

Youngberg, David. 2012. "Why Online Education Won't Replace College." *Chronicle of Higher Education*, August 13. http://chronicle.com/article/Why-Online-Education-Wont/133531/.

15

Always Alone and Together: Three of M
Student Discussion and Participation Exp....

STEVEN D. KRAUSE

Alone in a Crowd: Listening to World Music

My first extensive experience as a student in a MOOC came in the late summer/early fall of 2012 in Listening to World Music. MOOCs were at their zenith then—at least in the eyes of the mainstream and educational media. Coursera was growing in leaps and bounds, with major universities rushing to sign on as "partners." In a March 2012 interview in *Wired* magazine, Udacity founder Sebastian Thrun predicted, "In 50 years . . . there will be only 10 institutions in the world delivering higher education and Udacity has a shot at being one of them" (Leckart 2012). The *New York Times* declared 2012 "The Year of The MOOC" (Pappano 2012). And among my faculty colleagues around the country, there really was a palpable fear that we might all very well be out of a job in the next few years.

Despite the rapidness of the rise of MOOCs and the grand predictions of their future, nothing I was reading seemed based on actual experience from participants. Both MOOC proponents and critics seemed extraordinarily comfortable making claims based on absolutely *zero* experiences or observations of actual MOOCs. So in late July 2012, I enrolled in the Coursera course Listening to World Music, which was taught by Carol Muller, a professor of music specializing in ethnomusicology at the University of Pennsylvania. I was interested in the course in part because the description reminded me of a general education "music appreciation" sort of class I took as an elective near the end of my undergraduate career: that course was a lot of fun, and maybe this one would be fun, too.

Ultimately, I blogged extensively about the experience in summer and fall 2012, and I also published an essay as part of a two-article "symposium" on MOOCs in *College Composition and Communication (CCCs)*, which focused ımarily on the peer review process for writing assignments (Krause 2013). (Jeff Rice [2013] wrote the other article in the series; interestingly enough, he, too, wrote about his experience with the Listening to World Music course.)

Early on, I was surprised how much the course had the apparatus of a traditional and credit-bearing college course. It struck me as a kind of "remediation" of the college experience in the sense that Jay David Bolter and Richard Grusin (2000) discussed it in their book *Remediation: Understanding New Media*. In a nutshell, Bolter and Grusin don't mean "remedial" as in something like "remedial education"; rather, they mean the "remaking" or "remediating" of something when represented in a new medium. Remediation has happened throughout history, though Bolter and Grusin argue that "remediation is a defining characteristic of the new digital media" (45), and much of their book traces this in media such as computer games, digital photography, and, of course, the World Wide Web. After all, "web page" is a "remediation" of print, and the first web pages very much looked like newspapers and magazines of the time.

All the apparatus of a "real class" were in place. There was a syllabus outlining the course objectives and requirements, a calendar for the upcoming lectures, and even an "honor code" agreement. There was also a "Monday through Friday" schedule to the course very much akin to the kind of schedules that your typical University of Pennsylvania student probably kept with their courses—though early in the course, this schedule was adjusted to reflect the fact that most of the twenty thousand students from all over the world did not have the schedule of an early-twenty-something student attending an elite university in Philadelphia. In effect, the designers of this course "poured" the familiar face-to-face into this website.

Muller's teaching method was lecture/sage on the stage, her "standing and delivering" with her simple slides projected on a green screen set up behind her. I have no doubt that Professor Muller is a talented teacher and lecturer *in person*, but this frankly did not translate well in the MOOC. She appeared to be recording these lectures without any rehearsal or previous work in front of the camera. Further, the videos were shot with all the production values of a midwestern public access television station, and a rather poorly funded one at that. As I wrote in the *CCCs* symposium article:

> The lectures were broken up into ten to fifteen minute segments and were interrupted with pauses and links to YouTube clip examples of the music she was discussing. Most videos also ended with a short quiz covering the highlights of these lectures. It became clear early on that the lectures were all recorded well in advance; Muller occasionally commented in the discussion forums for the class (her graduate assistants were much more present), but for the most

part, she was not actually "there"; she was more of a show host than a professor. (Krause 2013, 689–90)

Each unit of Listening to World Music also included videos called "Graduate Student Discussion." These six- to ten-minute videos were discussions by
a group of graduate students (some of whom introduced themselves as "TAs"
[teaching assistants] for the class), which were about some key issues raised in
Muller's lectures about the music of that unit. Like Muller's videos, these re-
cordings had poor production values and were impromptu and unrehearsed;
for the most part, the graduate students spoke from notes and "discussed"
those notes and lectures with each other. The goal seemed to be to imitate the
kind of small group discussion section typically taught by graduate assistants
as supplements to the larger lecture. Of course, these videos didn't actually
feature students from the class; rather, they were of graduate students talking
to other graduate students, and, as is often the case when graduate students
talk with each other about a topic that they're studying, it was way over the
heads of casual students like me. So instead of being anything close to being
like a "give and take" exchange between students about Mueller's lectures
through the mediation and explanation of her TAs, these were instead oddly
stilted and staged discussions among the TAs themselves.

    And then of course there were interactions with other students in the class.
In Listening to World Music, student-to-student interaction happened indirectly in the peer review process of the short writing assignments and directly
in the discussion forums, which I described and critiqued in some detail
(Krause 2013). But in brief, each of the short writing assignments were peer
evaluated based on a rubric with a simplistic scoring process on a scale of zero
to two. Simultaneously, the rubric was also oddly complex, asking students,
for example, to distinguish a paper's "strength of argument" based on a "one-
point" score for a paper that was "Convincing, but pedestrian" from a "two-
point" score for a paper that was "Convincing and nuanced." While many
students in the discussion forums expressed liking the peer review process,
I didn't see any discussion about the grading rubrics themselves. Of course,
it was difficult to know how seriously anyone actually took this grading process since we weren't accountable for the quality of the reviews we did for our
peers, which for me meant reading and commenting on my peers' writing as
quickly as possible and not paying a lot of attention to their comments on my
writing. Further, this peer review process wasn't directly interactive at all: that
is, students read and submitted their assignments anonymously, meaning my
peers had no idea who I was when they were reading my writing and I had no
idea who was commenting on my essay. We read and commented on literally

disembodied student writing projects, and there was no mechanism to connect and ask other questions about the grades and comments.

Structurally, the discussion forums were well organized. Each week of the
course was organized around "subforums" about that week's music and lectures. For example, week two's topic was Paul Simon's album *Graceland*, and
subforums included "'The Boy in the Bubble' discussion" and "'Homeless'
discussion," along with discussions on other topics connected to the lectures.
Students started new threads under each subforum topic—there were thirty-
six such threads in the "'The Boy in the Bubble' discussion," for example—
and the discussions could be sorted by "top threads," "last updated," and "last
created."

This is not to say that these discussions were always on topic or that the
students' responses were equally orderly and organized. The busiest (as far as
I could tell) thread in this subforum was titled "We create and build on what
we know," which included 55 posts from about 30 different writers, and the
Coursera software indicated that it had 709 "views" (though I assume that
was only when the class was actually active). I don't think it would be right
for me to quote directly from the discussion since I don't have the permission
of the other students, but I think a brief summary illustrates my point about
the give-and-take of the discussion. This specific thread kicked off with a post
about a Peter Gabriel cover of the song "Boy in the Bubble," one that has a decidedly somber tone compared to Simon's original. This led to a comparison
to the song "Sound of Silence" from Simon's days with Art Garfunkel, along
with a discussion on the "African" (and then jazz) nature of Simon's original
version of "Boy in the Bubble." A number of readers made connections to the
video of "Boy in the Bubble" that appeared in the early days of MTV, which
in turn lead to some discussion on the value (or lack thereof) of music videos
generally. Along the way, there were many interpretations of the lyrics of the
song, including the politics of South Africa and the mixed role of technology
as expressed through the line "lasers in the jungle." And of course, this was
but one of over thirty other threads discussing only this song.

On the one hand, what takes place here is clearly analogous to the sort of
free-form exchange that would take place in any small-group seminar digging
into an interpretation of "Boy in the Bubble." On the other hand, it was far
from a "small-group" discussion because of the numerous contributions, and
without an instructor acting as a discussion leader, it lacked the coherence of
an intellectual exchange, a dialogue. There were many interesting points and
observations, but in my mind, this conversation and interaction didn't result
in a coherent "thread."

At the end of the Listening to World Music, I received an email from the

"Listening to World Music Course Staff," which included some basic information on some of the "key stats" for the course. For the discussion forums, the course staff reported:

Total threads: 8,045
Total posts: 17,339
Total comments: 5,419
Total views: 243,711

For me, these numbers tell two contradictory stories. First, given that the class started with over thirty-six thousand students (though it finished with fewer than four thousand based on the statistic "active users last week"), that's actually not a lot of posts and comments per student over a seven-week period, especially given that there were some students who posted well over one hundred times. As a point of comparison: during the semester when I was finishing up time as a student in the Listening to World Music MOOC, I was also teaching an online version of a graduate course titled Rhetoric of Science and Technology. One of the major components of that course was the discussion forums, and most students posted sixty or more comments during the course of the semester. That to me points to the difference between the discussion forums for Listening to World Music, where interaction between students was an afterthought rather than an integral part of the course.

Conversely, these statistics also point to the inherent problem of connecting and interacting with other students in these discussion forums, the drinking from a firehose phenomenon. Even though only a small percentage of students participated, the number of participants and posts was still far too much for anyone to reasonably follow. There was "togetherness" with my peers in the same sense that we connect to an audience watching a television show—though I don't mean watching a popular television show like *The Walking Dead* or what have you with family and friends in the same room; I mean watching the show alone in the privacy of your own room and knowing that out there, completely disconnected from me, there were thousands of others passively experiencing the same thing.

Still in a Crowd, but At Least Together: E-Learning and Digital Cultures

If Listening to World Music was an attempt to remediate the content and conventions of a typical face-to-face general education college class into a MOOC, my next major MOOC experience, E-Learning and Digital Cultures (EDC MOOC) was an effort to ignore the conventions of both traditional and online educational delivery. EDC MOOC was organized and taught by a group of faculty at the University of Edinburgh's Digital Education program: Siane Bayne, Jeremy Knox, Hamish Macleod, Jen Ross, and Christine Sinclair. I first learned about the program at Edinburgh and their MOOC via their "Manifesto for Teaching Online" (2011; http://www.swop.education .ed.ac.uk/edinburgh_manifesto_onlineteaching.pdf). I was intrigued by the manifesto's many provocative claims; for example:

- Online courses are prone to cultures of surveillance: our visibility to each other is a pedagogical and ethical issue.
- Online spaces can be permeable and flexible, letting networks and flows replace boundaries.
- Online teaching should not be downgraded into "facilitation."
- Community and contact drive good online learning.

So, with little more to go on than the manifesto and EDC MOOC course description, I decided to assign EDC MOOC as part of my own teaching in winter 2013, in a course called Computers and Writing, Theory and Practice. This is a graduate course I have taught regularly since the late 1990s, and it is a somewhat misnamed course because, besides being about issues regarding technology and writing that go beyond merely "computers," this course also has a specific writing pedagogy emphasis. I wrote about this experience in some detail on my blog and also in the essay "MOOC Assigned" (Krause 2014).

Another wrinkle with things during that term was that I taught this specific section of Computers and Writing online. This meant "we were simultaneously experiencing, studying, and discussing MOOC pedagogy while we were ourselves within a MOOC—we were the rats in the maze and simultaneously we were the scientists watching how that rat negotiated the turns" (Krause 2014, 123). In other words, we were reading emerging scholarship and articles about the MOOC phenomenon while simultaneously participating and studying a "live" MOOC *and* we were also doing all this online. Of course, my graduate course was only eight students, all of whom I also interacted with in person and on campus, obviously a different student experience of the EDC MOOC with tens of thousands of students from all over the world.

I originally assigned the EDC MOOC for two reasons, both of which turned out to be interestingly inaccurate. First, the description for EDC MOOC in 2011 (https://onlineteachingmanifesto.wordpress.com/the-pdf/) implied at least some pedagogical focus since it said it was going to explore digital cultures and their implications for learning online, and also because of this statement: "The course is not about how to 'do' e-learning; rather, it is an invitation to view online educational practices through a particular lens—

that of popular and digital culture" (Krause 2014, 124). In reality, there was no attention to pedagogy; rather, the course was broken up into two broad "blocks" or units—the first concerning utopias and dystopias, and the second on "being human" (which included materials about humanism and post/anti-humanism). This wasn't a complete disconnect with the course I was teaching, but this focus wasn't quite what I was expecting.

Second, I wanted to give my graduate students an experience of what I had assumed would be a "typical" MOOC driven by a lecture hall–styled peda-gogy with a lecturing professor and some teaching assistant–led discussions. But the apparatus and teaching approach in EDC MOOC were radically dif-ferent from any other MOOC I had visited, heard about, or dropped out of—not to mention the first MOOC Listening to World Music that I experienced in great detail. There were no lectures from the professors, "talking head" or otherwise; in fact, the professors who put the course together were only occasionally visible as coparticipants in the discussion forums and in a few Google Hangout discussions. In hindsight, this is hardly surprising given the manifesto that had attracted me to this course in the first place. Clearly, the EDC MOOC faculty were trying to problematize the conventions of instruc-tion that courses like the Listening to World Music MOOC were trying to embody in an online format. But even the most deconstructed course still needs a teacher.

As I wrote on my blog while in the course, one of the better discussions about halfway through the course was a thread titled "Where are the profes-sors?" To paraphrase the anonymous student/poster who started the thread, the course was a collection of videos and readings we were being asked to in-terpret without guidance from any professor. Does that mean it was a "course" at all? Both Sinclair and Bayne responded to the thread, and they made it very clear that their goal was to avoid the "guru professor" mode. Fair enough. But the problem is the *complete* lack of a center with no professor (or professors) as the leader meant this wasn't so much a course as it was more like a collec-tion of potentially interesting texts.

My students and I were together in EDC MOOC through our own class, though otherwise alone within it. We discussed this alienation and "alone-ness" within the larger MOOC in some detail because, while the delivery and role of faculty in EDC MOOC was purposefully at odds with other MOOCs, the results in the discussion forums were exactly like other MOOCs I've en-countered: chaotic and lonely. In *Invasion of the MOOCs* (Krause and Lowe 2014), we included two essays from my graduate students in that class, and both of them articulate this student loneliness in some detail. In her essay "More Questions Than Answers," Jackie Kazua (2014) pointed out that, even in face-to-face lecture hall classes, you have a sense of the other "bodies" around you and of the professor doing the lecturing, and she also discusses in some detail the problems of peer review feedback that is a "one-shot deal, a one-time, one-sided 'conversation'" (110). And let me quote at a bit more length part of Melissa Syapin's essay, "Those Moot MOOCs," mainly because I think she's expressing the point I'm trying to express here:

> This might seem like a strange statement given that MOOCs offer thousands of students the ability to make sense of these resources with their classmates, but I found myself feeling like it was just me in the class. I would seek out comments or discussions on the videos or readings I chose to read in order to find connections, but I rarely felt I was connected to another student. . . . I felt as if everyone was individually learning the content as opposed to a classroom learning the content together. (Syapin 2014, 116)

Interestingly enough, in the third iteration of the course that ran in late fall 2014, the EDC MOOC organizers added a series of short video lectures each week that serve as introductions to that week's readings, videos, and discussions. But these aren't simply videos of professors giving lectures. Rather, each of these five videos (one for each week of the course, and each one featuring one of the five EDC MOOC faculty leading the course) are shot at different locations—at an old anatomy lecture theater; near sculptures of Eduardo Paolozzi; in the midst of Edinburgh's old town and next to a statue of David Hume; in the digital location of a *Second Life* virtual world; and on a walk through a reflective walking labyrinth in a garden in campus at the University of Edinburgh. The videos have the look of a nationally syndicated public television show, professionally produced with multiple scene changes while the well-rehearsed and focused voiceovers from the professors continue. These videos were short—the longest one just over five minutes—and they end with questions designed to help lead students through that week's discussion. I haven't visited the discussion forums in this version of the course and I have no real way to measure the effectiveness of these videos, but it is easy for me to imagine how they might have helped me and my students me feel more of a connection to the EDC MOOC professors and, by extension, the other students.

Still Alone, but Together in Other Ways: Dropping in and out of Internet History, Technology, and Security

The "MOOC Mania" has calmed, both in the media and in my own life. In November 2013, almost exactly a year after the *New York Times* infamously labeled 2012 the "year of the MOOC," Sebastian Thrun (who about eighteen months earlier had so provocatively predicted that his MOOC company would be one of the great remaining universities in fifty years) described Udacity as a "lousy product" (Chafkin 2013). In the terminology of the frequently cited Gartner Hype Cycle (http://www.gartner.com/technology /research/methodologies/hype-cycle.jsp), MOOCs had descended from the lofty "peak of inflated expectations" to the lowly depths of the "trough of disillusionment." My own MOOC studies had slowed considerably as well. I've started a few and dropped out of them all.

What happened? Arguably, the inflated expectations were so outrageously high that the rapid sink into disillusionment was preordained. How could *any* educational phenomenon possibly live up to this early hype? But to be more specific, I think two broader problems emerged from the first wave of MOOCs.

First, MOOCs have had a fundamental audience problem: instead of attracting would-be college students around the world who cannot afford or who otherwise lack access to higher education, the vast majority of MOOC students already have college degrees, are professionally employed, and residing in developed world countries. Gayle Christensen and Brandon Alcorn (2014) summarized their large study of MOOC students. According to their survey of four hundred thousand active MOOC students conducted in 2014 by the University of Pennsylvania (one of Coursera's MOOC partners and the host institution for Listening to World Music), two-thirds of MOOC participants come from the developed world. Further, "83 per cent of MOOC students already have a two or four-year diploma or degree, even in regions of the world where less than 10 per cent of the adult population has a degree. Meanwhile, 69 per cent of them are employed" (Christensen and Alcorn 2014). The survey also found that the majority of MOOC students are male and "the gap between male and female participation if far greater for these courses than in traditional education" (Christensen and Alcorn 2014).

Second, the performance of students in MOOCs versus students in more traditional college classes is quite poor. This became clear most notoriously in a partnership between Udacity and San José State University. As Tamar Lewin (2013) reported, "Despite access to the Udacity mentors, the online students last spring—including many from a charter high school in Oakland— did worse than those who took the classes on campus. In the algebra class, fewer than a quarter of the students—and only 12 percent of the high school students—earned a passing grade."

This is not to say that MOOCs haven't continued and haven't stopped evolving. From what I have seen from my own scattered experiences, MOOCs in mid- to late-2014 are a remediation of themselves from just a couple years ago: still recognizable as a remediation of a college course, but revised and remade from their previous versions. The same but different.

In summer 2014, I dropped into (and ultimately out of) Internet History, Technology, and Security, which was taught by University of Michigan's Charles Severance, a clinical associate professor in computer science. This was far from Severance's first foray into online teaching and social media. Severance served as the executive director and the chief architect of the Sakai Project (an open-source learning management system), he's written a number of books on various aspects of programming, and he has an active social media presence as "Dr. Chuck." In the 1990s, he hosted a couple of different television shows devoted to the then-emerging Internet, and his past experience in front of the camera shows. While his lectures were in the genre of the "talking head" professor with PowerPoint slides (he appears to have recorded about half his talks in his university office and the other half in what looks to be a home office or den), he is comfortable and experienced in the art of giving a lecture with no actual audience present. Further, Severance fleshes out the history part of the course with a series of videos with some of the early pioneers of computing generally and the Internet specifically, interviews that mostly date back to his days as a television host.

Once again, the discussion forums for the class were a nearly useless stream of white noise, but Severance made different efforts for students to connect to him and each other. Severance's class was the most "open" in the sense of trying to get out of the Coursera course shell/walled garden that I've experienced to date. Granted, there was a Facebook group about Listening to World Music, though it was a group never acknowledged officially by the course, and the EDC MOOC leaders used Twitter. But Severance's efforts to connect beyond the class were different both in quantity and quality. The Coursera course shell for Internet History, Technology, and Security had *direct* connections to the class Facebook page, Severance's homepage, and his "@drchuck" Twitter feed.

Then there were Severance's "office hours" videos, which are available via his YouTube channel. These were two-or-so-minute videos Severance shot with a cell phone at different public gathering spots—Starbucks and similar coffee shops appeared to be popular—all over the world. During my summer with Internet History, Technology, and Security, Severance recorded these videos in Barcelona; Washington, DC; Seoul; Las Vegas; Maribour, Slovenia; and Puebla City, Mexico (Severance 2014). It's not that the content of these videos was all that interesting; it was mostly Severance doing a shaky job operating his camera phone while meeting with a handful of Coursera students who briefly introduced themselves. Severance wasn't the first Coursera professor to attempt face-to-face contact with her or his students; for example, Elizabeth Losh (2014) recounts an early Coursera meet-up picnic in Northern California, a gathering where hundreds of Coursera students from all over the world came to interact with their fellow MOOC students and with professors. But here, Severance is the one going to the students, setting up small group opportunities for them where they are.

Was it enough? Of course not. For the few dozen students who got the opportunity to make those connections with each other and with Severance, I am certain it was important and valuable. And for the thousands of us looking in via YouTube at these meetings, it was probably useful in that we got the chance to look in at a group of fellow MOOC students and likely recognize in that group someone like us. So even though these short videos and the social media around the course helped create another place where we could at least imagine being together, we were all still alone together, still alone in front of our own screens looking in on these gatherings.

I'll close with an uncertain prediction about the future of MOOCs. I suspect I will find myself enrolling in MOOCs again out of curiosity and a desire to learn something new, and I am also sure I'll assign MOOCs again to my students both as a space to experience and as a highly interactive "textbook" of sorts. I doubt I'll ever try to use MOOCs as a place to make connections with other students in the course or to have meaningful discussions and exchanges.

Perhaps that's the ultimate role of MOOCs in higher education, at least into the near future. We can't evaluate the usefulness of MOOCs with the same tools and benchmarks we use to evaluate conventional higher education, but that doesn't mean MOOCs have no value. As Jeffrey Selingo (2014) ponders it, MOOCs are a sort of "just in time education. . . . Students can register, with no financial risk, for as many courses as they want. Some might want to sample a particular lecture, or prepare a business plan for investors, or take a lesson for a presentation the next day." In that sense, it doesn't really matter if MOOCs can sustain interaction between students and teachers or if students complete the course at all.

The question remains though whether this is enough for for-profit enterprises like Coursera to make money or to allow the many not-for-profit MOOC providers to justify the expense. As Selingo (2014) writes, "The companies that rode to fame on the MOOC wave had visions (and still do) of offering unfettered elite education to the masses and driving down college

tuition. But the sweet spot for MOOCs is far less inspirational and compelling."

References

Bolter, Jay David, and Richard Grusin. 2000. *Remediation: Understanding New Media.* Cambridge: MIT Press.

Chafkin, Max. 2013. "Udacity's Sebastian Thrun, Godfather of Free Online Education, Changes
Course." *Fast Company,* November 14. http://www.fastcompany.com/3021473/udacity
-sebastian-thrun-uphill-climb.

Christensen, Gayle, and Brandon Alcorn. 2014. "Online University Courses Can't Change the
World Alone." *New Scientist,* March 10. http://www.newscientist.com/article/mg22129590
.200-online-university-courses-cant-change-the-world-alone.html#.VO9W31PF86k.

Kazua, Jackie. 2014. "More Questions Than Answers." In Krause and Lowe, *Invasion of the
MOOCs,* 105–13.

Krause, Steven D. 2013. "Symposium on Massive Open Online Courses: MOOC Response about
Listening to World Music." *College Composition and Communication* (64) 4: 689–695.

———. 2014. "MOOCs Assigned." In Krause and Lowe, *Invasion of the MOOCs,* 122–29.

Krause, Steven D., and Charles Lowe, eds. 2013. *Invasion of the MOOCs: The Promises and Perils
of Massive Open Online Courses.* Anderson: Parlor Press.

Leckart, Steven. 2012 "The Stanford Education Experiment Could Change Higher Learning Forever." *WIRED,* March 21. http://www.wired.com/2012/03/ff_aiclass/all/.

Lewin, Tamar. 2013. "After Setbacks, Online Courses Are Rethought." *New York Times,* December 10. http://www.nytimes.com/2013/12/11/us/after-setbacks-online-courses-are-rethought
.html.

Losh, Elizabeth. 2014. *The War on Learning: Gaining Ground in the Digital University.* Cambridge: MIT Press.

Pappano, Laura. 2012. "The Year of the MOOC." *New York Times,* November 2. http://www
.nytimes.com/2012/11/04/education/edlife/massive-open-online-courses-are-multiplying
-at-a-rapid-pace.html.

Rice, Jeff. 2013. "What I Learned in MOOC." *College Composition and Communication* 64 (4):
695-703

Selingo, Jeffrey J. 2014. "Demystifying the MOOC." *New York Times,* October 29. http://www
.nytimes.com/2014/11/02/education/edlife/demystifying-the-mooc.html.

Severance, Charles. "Coursera IHTS/PR4E Office Hours." *Chuck Severance.* YouTube Channel.
https://www.youtube.com/user/csev.

Syapin, Melissa. 2014. "Those Moot MOOCs." In Krause and Lowe, *Invasion of the MOOCs,*
113–21.

PART FIVE

MOOC Critiques

16

The Open Letter to Michael Sandel and Some Thoughts about Outsourced Online Teaching

THE SAN JOSÉ STATE PHILOSOPHY DEPARTMENT

During summer and fall 2013 and well into 2014, the San José State University (SJSU) Philosophy Department's open letter to Michael Sandel became an icon of academics' disapproval of massive open online courses (MOOCs) and privatized online teaching in higher education.

In press conferences with Governor Jerry Brown and Lieutenant Governor Gavin Newsom, our president, Mohammad Qayoumi, had predicted that online courses, especially MOOCs, would solve the major problems of higher education in California. Our president referred to three, very real, areas of concern: (1) high school students in California come to the California State University (CSU) system inadequately prepared for college work and need extensive remedial teaching; (2) the number of qualified students seeking admittance to state universities well exceeds the current supply of brick-and-mortar classrooms; and (3) students in the CSU system take a discouragingly long seven to eight years, on average, to graduate.

In his 2012 white paper, coauthored with Kim Polese, a Silicon Valley entrepreneur with no apparent credentials in higher education, our president stated that these problems could be solved by the introduction of MOOCs and SPOCs (Qayoumi and Polese 2012). You've heard of MOOCs? But what are SPOCs? They are small private online courses. Qayoumi's plan was to teach 25–40 percent of all lower-division classes using MOOCs and SPOCs. He proposed that the MOOCification (and SPOCification) of first- and second-year courses would be instituted not only at SJSU but also throughout the CSU system: all community colleges, all CSUs, and all universities within the University of California system (UCs) (Qayoumi and Polese 2012, 12). That was the first step. The next step, as he wrote, "will be redesigning upper-division programs. . . . Each institution, or group of institutions, can build degree programs using a number of possible sources, such as materials already available in open-source courseware, learning modules developed by corporations, national labs, public broadcasting services, libraries" (Qayoumi and Polese 2012, 12). We, in the Philosophy Department, along with educators across the land, knew that such a proposal might appear to be a magic bullet to taxpayers and a lucrative source of income to private vendors eager to expand into higher education.

As part of our president's plan to revamp the entire CSU system, the Philosophy Department was asked to "pilot" a version of Michael Sandel's edX Justice course. We respectfully declined but were subject to continuous pressure and not terribly subtle threats for noncompliance. We decided that we would continue to refuse, but we wanted to document our refusal. We first wrote a letter to our dean stating our refusal and our reasons. But we still feared retaliation for our refusal. Moreover, we were well aware that the threat was not only to our department but also to the students and faculty at our sister campuses around the country. Thus, we decided to address our concerns to a national audience.

The open letter to Michael Sandel first appeared in the *Chronicle of Higher Education* on May 2, 2013 (http://www.chronicle.com/article/the-document -an-open-letter/138937). The *New York Times* noted our stand on the same day (Lewin 2013). The letter was cited and discussed subsequently by numerous national and international newspapers and journals.[1] More than one critic described us as Luddites, but, happily, most either cheered us on or at least presented our side of the story fairly. It has been made into Exhibit 1 in a Harvard Law Case Study, "MOOCs and Consequences for the Future of Education" (Young and Nesson 2014). The editors of the *Chronicle of Higher Education* in their December 9, 2013, issue included in their 2013 Influence List the SJSU Philosophy Department.

In this chapter, we elaborate on the concerns we expressed in our letter.

Part I: Our Objections to Sandel's edX Justice Course

A. BAD SCHOLARSHIP AND INFERIOR PEDAGOGY

There are two basic and essential components to a good university education: the quality of the professoriate and the pedagogical approach. MOOCs and

---

1. To mention some of the most circulated: *Los Angeles Times, Wall Street Journal*, the weekly national magazine, *Nation*, and then several times again by the *New York Times*.

blended courses remove the expertise from the classroom and transfer it to one remote videotaped lecturer. MOOCs offer no teacher-student interaction, and in blended classes the expert is not the one who is interacting with the students.

A good university is an institution where knowledge is being generated as well as taught, and good teaching involves demonstrating how students can and should integrate themselves into a current discussion and further contribute to a field of learning. Thus, a good-quality college course not only has to be up-to-date but also must be relevant and tailored to the specific needs and interests of specific groups of students in specific institutional contexts. In other words, a prepackaged, one-size-fits-all, cookie-cutter course will inevitably not match the particular student body to which it is sold.

To date, MOOCs have been pedagogical failures. Good universities strive for two fundamental educational goals: literacy and intellectual skill and virtue. By literacy we mean acquiring an understanding of and competence in a subject. We ask students to demonstrate command of the material; for example, to know what Plato, Confucius, Mary Wollstonecraft, and so on have argued. Intellectual skill and virtue involves learning how to think, learning how to analyze and interpret, learning how to learn, developing epistemic virtues such as open-mindedness and attention to evidence, and acquiring tools to continue learning. Intellectual skill and virtue is more important than, and a necessary condition for, literacy.

There are three essential pedagogical methods to achieve the goal of making our students more skillful and virtuous learners:

1   *Dialogue.* We want students to learn how to articulate and defend their positions, and for that to happen a dialogue is required. We need to be able to ask a question, hear the answer, and challenge it. We need to encourage them and show them where an idea can go. We need to make students think about something they didn't think about before, which can be achieved only through conversation or class discussion. Online classes can achieve this objective as long as they involve substantive interaction between and among students and their professors of the sort described above.

2   *Active Engagement.* Learning how to think requires active engagement. Active engagement involves more than clicking through various segments in MOOCs or taking an online quiz, but participating in the learning process. Students become a part of the learning process when they are asked questions and they come up with answers themselves or help another student work out an idea. A MOOC on the other hand is a one-way road of transmission of information that hardly differs from the mail-order

courses of old: students read the textbook on their own and take a quiz at
the end.

3   *Evoking Affect.* Memory and understanding partly depend on affect and
students best retain knowledge when they care, are moved, and are inspired. Successful professors get their students to care about the material
being taught (as opposed to caring only about their grade). Getting students to care about a subject requires interacting with them.[2]

What underlies the three pedagogical methods we noted is the most
significant aspect of education that MOOCs omit: feedback. A MOOC is a
course without feedback (MOOCs usually rely on automated or peer grading). We hold that feedback is the mechanism whereby the most essential
components of learning take place. Thus we argue that MOOCs can provide
information but not education. Therefore, they can only offer literacy and
not intellectual skill and virtue. Without feedback, expertise, and current
and relevant material, MOOCs and blended courses are not real university
courses with real university professors and thus inherently not up to par with
the level that is required for a university education.

Our critics will object that these concerns relate to MOOCs and that Sandel's edX course is not a MOOC but a "blended course." We now turn to our
concerns about edX's blended version of Sandel's Justice course.

What would our students learn about justice through a purchased blended
course from a private vendor? This is part of a broader question of what students at a university like SJSU would learn in any class from such a course.
What, first, is a "blended course" and how do such courses look when they
are provided by private vendors? Our open letter was a response to a specific
request that we teach a course constructed by edX and based on a series of
videos by Professor Sandel. We had no specific problem with the content of
Sandel's class. Some of us have even enjoyed viewing Sandel's lectures, which
were readily available for free through the PBS website. The problem is with
the very concept of "blended class." There have been many definitions of
"blended course," but perhaps most useful for our purpose is a definition provided in an article cowritten with three others by the president and provost of
our own university (Ghadiri et al. 2013). The "blended model of online learning" is defined there as "combining the online MOOC content with highly
structured, student team-based, in-class learning. . . . This form of a flipped

2. An alternative model can be found in the UK's Open University where curriculum, pedagogy, and technology are in the hands of faculty who have successfully developed distance learning since the 1970s.

classroom was employed [in a course they discuss] to replace the traditional face-to-face (F2F) lecture classroom instruction." So, according to their definition, blended learning involves (1) MOOC content, (2) student team-based in-class learning, and (3) a flipped classroom. In our case, the MOOC content would have been structured within a platform provided by edX. It would be a "flipped classroom" in that the SJSU instructor would no longer provide the content of the class in lecture and discussion of class readings but would have the students gain that content from Professor Sandel outside of class while sitting in front of a computer. The things students would have done traditionally at home (i.e., homework) would be flipped into the classroom. The most expensive part of instruction, the faculty person teaching the class, could be dispensed with, thus saving money for the university and ultimately the taxpayers, students, and parents.

There is some confusion surrounding the term "flipped classroom" especially in the case of philosophy. Many advocates of the flipped classroom have raved about the possibility of opening up discussion in the classroom since the lectures would now be viewed at home. This assumes that there is no valuable discussion in the classroom already, or that classroom activity now is mainly a matter of a professor delivering a lecture. In our discipline (and related ones, such as English and history) discussion has long been an essential aspect of classroom activity. Plato used it in the Academy he founded around 300 BCE. Traditionally, Asian philosophy is dialectical as well, as are Arabic and Jewish philosophy. Another aspect of the "flipped classroom" concept, which itself is essential to the "blended class" concept, requires that the work done at home consist mainly of viewing videos of lectures (videos which, in the case of the edX Justice class, include videotaped discussion with Harvard students), as well as taking some multiple-choice quizzes based on this content. This assumes that students in the "traditional class" are basically passive watchers of lectures and takers of quizzes. So the "flipping" is getting this passive activity out of the schoolroom and into the home. But this is a totally inaccurate description of what does go on in the typical liberal arts classroom. This is not the only problem with the flipped classroom.

Let us now look at the other thing that is flipped. What traditionally do we expect students to do at home? Homework is of course expected, including the writing of papers, which generally requires the kind of quiet that one can seldom find in a noisy classroom especially one which mainly consists of group activities. Another thing traditionally expected is that the students do their assigned reading, for example, reading Plato's *Phaedo* or Harriet Taylor Mill on women's rights or Nāgārjuna on emptiness. Yet, in the blended and flipped classroom, there is no room for close reading and reflective, careful writing. The *time* previously allotted to those activities is assigned now to watching canned videos and taking multiple-choice quizzes. In essence, the blended/flipped classroom replaces close reading and reflective writing both at home and in the classroom. The educational result couldn't be worse.

Again, our critics might concede that some upper-division liberal arts cannot be taught in MOOCs or blended courses, but insist that MOOCs or blended classes are ideal for undergraduate basic-skills courses. Let us consider the folly of this response by examining the problems with using these formats to teach critical thinking, which is initially taught as a basic skill. We begin with an account of what constitutes a critical-thinking education at the undergraduate college level and then discuss using MOOCs to teach critical thinking.

Critical-thinking education involves learning the following: (1) concepts of good argumentation, such as validity, soundness, cogency, and adequate inferential support; (2) techniques for identifying and avoiding errors of reasoning in argument construction, such as fallacies; (3) techniques for analyzing arguments, such as argument mapping and diagramming; (4) formal techniques for testing validity, such as truth tables, natural deduction, and semantic trees; (5) techniques for critically engaging issues of social justice; and (6) concepts of social epistemology, such as fact versus opinion, appropriate sources, problems surrounding joint deliberation, and basic philosophy of science that facilitates how to demarcate between genuine science and pseudoscience. In addition, critical thinking education involves (7) teaching the epistemic virtues, such as epistemic courage, humility, nonnegligence, persistence, diligence, autonomy, compassion, self-scrutiny, awareness of implicit and cognitive bias, awareness of emotions while reasoning, and regulation of emotion in response to reason. It also involves providing students with a trajectory toward the formation of a *critical identity*—a way of thinking about the world that involves both an evaluative matrix for engaging social issues and personal issues of the self, as well as a metaunderstanding of how to move through disagreement with others in an effective and respectful way. Finally, a good education in critical thinking should provide one with the ability to perform all of what goes into critical thinking in the relevant context in which it is to be performed: engagement with others in both an online context and in a face-to-face context, such as in town hall deliberation or a corporate boardroom.

Let us now turn to one of the arguments in favor of using MOOCs to teach critical thinking: that MOOCs, by comparison to traditional critical-thinking courses, provide a lower cost, are comparably reliable, and are equal to quality critical-thinking education.

Cost: Are MOOCs cheaper than teachers who teach critical thinking in actual classrooms? The advertised position is something like the following: One MOOC can teach more students than twenty teachers because the Internet facilitates greater access while delivering the same or better quality education than an actual teacher in a classroom teaching, for example, forty students. But the cost savings advertised is not the true cost. What is not presented are the hidden background costs which include: (1) research and development cost involved in creating a good critical-thinking program, (2) customer support cost, and (3) licensing cost. Furthermore, the companies that make MOOCs might initially offer them at a low cost to get adoptions, but eventually, because they need to make a profit, will increase the cost.

There are also costs borne by the students. They will need reliable access to high-speed Internet, as well as a computer. This raises an obvious question: *How can a MOOC teach someone critical thinking if they don't have a computer or a digital device or access to high-speed Internet?* These are the people we should really want to reach and provide access to higher education, especially to foster critical thinking. However, in the case of this population, we can't supply an education via a MOOC, unless we provide, for *free*, computers, digital devices, and high-speed Internet. If we want to provide critical-thinking education globally, we probably also need to throw in running water, a safe place to study, and a community that supports learning for women.

The key question is: what is the true cost of providing a critical-thinking education to those who need it most? The people in this group typically don't come from families with strong educational backgrounds, don't have sufficient means for basic necessities, and generally fall on the wrong side of the digital divide. Can MOOCs do anything for this group? We think not. To deprive them of education in critical thinking, a fundamental set of skills and virtues that are crucial to personal and professional success and political engagement is simply unjust in a democracy.

Reliability: Are MOOCs more reliable that what a good teacher can do in a classroom? They appear to be more reliable on the surface, since they don't get sick, there is always customer support, and the day-to-day performance does not vary. But, *the Internet does break down.* Customer support has a wait time. Students get impatient when they can't get their instructor's attention to help with a problem, so they walk away from their computer. Learning styles differ. Finally, the rhetoric of reliability has to be weighed against what the reliability is about—quality critical-thinking education. If a MOOC is reliable for providing a lower quality critical-thinking education, then that reliability won't be relevant, but if they are not reliable for fostering crucial components of critical thinking, such as epistemic virtues, then they are not reliable.

Quality: Do MOOCs provide a quality critical-thinking education across all components of critical thinking? We believe that people learn epistemic virtues best when they have the appropriate relationship to a person displaying the epistemic virtue in the relevant context and when they are attentively observing the person with the intention to acquire the virtue. There are three components to this. The first is that observation of a person performing the epistemic virtue is key to the acquisition of it. The second is that observing someone perform it in the relevant context provides one with inspiration and guidance on how to execute the performance when in the appropriate context. The third is because they have the appropriate relationship to the person displaying the virtue the positive feedback and reinforcement that they gain from that person when they display the epistemic virtue will support the development and sustainability of the virtue. A MOOC surely can provide a video of a TED talk where someone argues for a position and performs an epistemic virtue. And through watching the video, a student can see the relevant epistemic virtue in action. However the other three components of teaching epistemic virtues cannot be done in a MOOC.

What we should want are critical thinkers who can display the epistemic virtues in the engaged context of joint deliberation. This is a context that can be found everywhere in the world from corporate boardrooms to small town discussion halls, as well as on the Internet. We do not want critical thinkers who *only* feel comfortable engaging in critical thinking when their identity is shielded through the anonymity of Internet communication. What good would it be to have a generation of critical thinkers that suffer from the *medium-dependence problem*—their critical thinking is tied to a medium, the Internet, which does not reflect one of the most important actual contexts in which we need critical thinking to be displayed.

Finally, we note that critical thinking is the foundation of success in all learning. This provides an additional reason to object to MOOCs and other blended courses in upper-division courses, such as justice. If these courses rely on critical thinking and critical thinking cannot be taught in these formats, then these other courses cannot be responsibly taught in these formats. But this is not our only concern about teaching a course on justice using an off-the-shelf course provided by an outside vendor.

B. SUBSTITUTING EDX'S VERSION OF SANDEL
FOR OUR LOCAL COURSES IS UNJUST

There are additional problems with the edX "blended model" of teaching a course on justice offered by a professor at a privileged institution like Harvard. Those who advocate this model of teaching envision thousands of students watching these videos and taking these quizzes, thus producing the educational equivalent of a monoculture in which only a few voices will ever be heard. Since students will not be encouraged to engage in reflective reading or writing (there is no time for that, remember, if they are to get through their videos and quizzes), they will simply massively reproduce whatever Sandel and his Harvard students, for example, think about justice. This will become the norm throughout the country and much of the world. If Sandel believes that there are two kinds of utilitarianism, for example, and this appears on the quiz, then there will always, and everywhere, be only one authoritative position on this, who says that there are only two kinds of utilitarianism. Moreover, possibility for dynamic intellectual interaction between professors from all over the United States and students from different classes and ethnicities is significantly reduced. Now, only a few star professors are part of the conversation.

Further, both Professor Sandel and his students represent a certain strata of society. Although there are students from many ethnic groups in the audience when he gives his lectures, they all are experiencing enculturation as part of an educational elite. These students will have their own perspective on justice based at least in part on their social position and the model of justice they learn as part of an educational elite. Many of them will not know what it is like to face the issues of justice that are faced by typical students at colleges that serve students from other social contexts. Views of justice that question the establishment will not be heard or will not be heard with any vigor. Moreover, students in the flipped classrooms will see privileged college students interacting with the "real" teacher, Professor Sandel, whereas they only get to interact with other students and their "lesser" teacher at SJSU, a teacher whose own views on justice are now seen as having no importance because he or she is no longer a "content provider." Professor Sandel will not answer *their* questions. They will not interact with him: only "his" students will do that. Imagine how disempowered that will make our students feel.

It may well be that in the world of blended/flipped classes the superstar college professors like Sandel who provide the actual content of the course will try to be open-minded, but the categories of thinking risk being set by them and by their for-profit content packagers. The end result of this is sadly ironic. For justice, on one model, involves creating a society that is more egalitarian and/or democratic, where the goods of society, including higher education, are distributed in a fair manner. Yet a course on justice based on predominance of the ideological content of teachers in privileged universities cannot avoid being designed to sustain the upper class in a country where class divisions are becoming more striking every day and where the members of the upper class (the well-named 1 percent) increasingly dominate through the influence of their mounting wealth. With the blended model and flipped classroom, we begin with something that seems like an innocuous experiment yet end by promoting the rise of plutocracy and class division in America by promoting two kinds of universities: the one with real teachers and real students on the one hand (Harvard) and the one with MOOCs and teaching assistants on the other (SJSU of the future).

Many who critically responded to our open letter argued that our main concern is to save our jobs and that our bias in this makes our arguments illegitimate. It is true that, with the advance of blended classes, flipped classes, and MOOCs (if this happens), the need for as many PhDs and MAs, or even for philosophy departments, will not exist. The whole thing can be taken over by employees of edX with little academic qualification, incredibly low wages, and no interest or ability to participate in unions. It is not only the loss of jobs but also the loss of all the values that public higher education ever stood for which is at risk. Intellectual integrity, for example, goes out the door. But the important point is that, in the end, our students are harmed the most. They only get a pseudodegree in pseudo–higher education. They will learn how to take quizzes well, how to parrot whatever Sandel, for example, preaches. They will learn how to satisfy the "facilitator" in their seldom-visited classroom. They will even learn how to "game the system" through cheating and highly selective studying, which will become incredibly easy under this new system, since standardization will lead to standard answers. They will get basically what they currently get from some of the worst for-profit online universities—that is, virtually nothing and for a lot of money. To put it bluntly, if we taught Michael Sandel's edX Justice course, we would be casting our students in an upstairs-downstairs scenario and make no mistake about it, our students would be in the servants' quarters.

Part II: Lessons Learned

A. WHOM DO YOU TRUST?

On February 13, 2013, a Little Hoover Public Hearing on California Higher Education (Little Hoover Hearing 2013) took place, which included remarks from SJSU administrators (Junn and Cheal 2013). The hearing focused on financing and student aid, online education, and the role of the faculty. The following items were addressed in the hearing:

1   The financial shape and history of the UCs, CSUs and community colleges;
2   Corporate plans for higher education;
3   The state of UC and CSU online; and
4   How the UC and CSU teachers think the MOOCs will affect the people.

Two distinct and countervailing philosophies and attitudes about higher education are evident in these hearings. The public employees who spoke at the hearing used words like "institution," "tradition," and "good" when describing the university. They called themselves "stewards" and "servants" serving students. This reflects the old idea that universities serve the common good by educating the young so they can wisely run the world as adults. In contrast, the language of the Silicon Valley corporate leaders embodies technocratic-business values. Coursera refers to "communities" instead of "classes" and "students" become "participants." Udacity's Sebastian Thrun says he is creating a "marketplace for instructors." With tech start-up zeal, Dean Florez wants to "disrupt" universities like a "lightning bolt" from the sky. Given these attitudes, why should California give these people control of our public institutions?

Will it make a difference whether higher education is public or private? Public institutions are open to public scrutiny, control, and accountability. Private institutions are not. California public institutions have to follow the Brown Act of 1953, which makes holding private meetings to make public decisions a criminal offense. An agenda must be publicized three days in advance. Anyone can attend these meetings, download the documents, and complain to the public officials and the public record. Public institutions cannot use taxpayer money to advocate for or against any public policy. Private companies, by contrast, make all their decisions behind closed doors. Except for their annual report and the tax filing, they are required to say little else. Since *Citizen's United v. FEC* 558 U.S. 310 (2010), they can also use unlimited funds to affect political results. Currently, there are no laws forcing private companies to hold public meetings. We the people would never know if a corporation uses taxpayer money to enrich itself and act against the public interest.

B. FOR-PROFIT EDUCATION AND DISRUPTIVE TECHNOLOGIES

The open letter to Michael Sandel represents in microscopic form a business relation between private for-profit online companies and academics. Private for-profit universities in affiliation with academics who made their reputation on excellent academic contributions might seem to have the best of two worlds—the efficiency of a profit-based company and the proven expertise of a renowned scholar. Yet, our experience would suggest there is much to be wary of in such an arrangement. There are several circumstances that raise a red flag about the relation between a private for-profit online company and its claims for gainful education. In particular, three caveats are outstanding.

Caveat #1: The online course provider relies on an affiliation with a privileged institution rather than a clear account of the faculty member's credentials and history of teaching evaluations. For example, edX trades on the imprimatur of Harvard, MIT, Stanford, and a few other prestigious universities. This is a practice marketing specialists know as branding. But in Harvard's edX Course, *Introduction to Computer Science*, no permanent Harvard faculty member teaches the course. The current Harvard edX course, Introduction to Computer Science, is taught by a senior lecturer, David J. Malan, and two undergraduates, Ron Bowden and Zamlya Chan.

Data supplied by a Harvard law professor, Terry Fisher, suggest that a professor from a university with a less-hallowed name, whose evaluations are available to students, would be as good or a better choice for instruction in this subject if the class were conducted face-to-face rather than online (Walters 2014). On February 2, 2014, we had a statement from Stanford president John Hennessey in which he specifies data that indicate the failure of Stanford-sponsored MOOCs and, at this point more relevantly, data he offers regarding an exemplary SPOC. About MOOCs, Hennessey states: "The range of student capability within the course simply becomes so large that you've got 10 students that are way ahead of the class—or 1,000 students that are way ahead—you've got 5,000 that are lost and you have some in the middle—and it just doesn't work. . . . [When] you give an exam, that exam is going to be a cakewalk for some students and it's going to be a disaster for others—and you could see that in some of the early experiments we've done with the really massive activities" (Walters 2014)

As for SPOCs, Hennessey cites the results of Professor Terry Fisher, who offered his course in copyright law, not to a massive amount of students but to five hundred students broken into individual sections of twenty-five students each, "chosen after extensive applications," each section with its own teaching assistant, some with live discussions and some with asynchronous discussions. Of the 500 people who signed up for the course, 307 completed it, although 60 did not take the final exam and 52 who did failed. The dropout and fail rates in this SPOC, although better than MOOCs on average, unquestionably are worse than students' success rates in face-to-face teaching (Walters 2014). Thus if quality is the goal, colleges and universities should begin by looking within the existing faculty and teach the courses on their own campuses.

Caveat #2: The online course provider is more interested in the cosmetic aspects of the online spokespeople and the eye-catching quality of visuals rather than clear, organized, and substance-filled presentations. Consider some remarks made by edX's CEO, Anant Agarwal, about the hiring of movie or television celebrities in place of teachers with records of excellent teaching:

> "From what I hear, really good actors can actually teach really well," said Anant Agarwal, CEO of edX, who was until recently a computer-science professor at MIT. "So just imagine, maybe we get Matt Damon to teach Thévenin's theorem," he added, referring to a concept that Agarwal covers in a MOOC he teaches on circuits and electronics. "I think students would enjoy that more than taking it from Agarwal." (Sumagaysay 2013)

Coursera, edX, and Udacity minimize the screen presence of instructors without good looks. "Udacity, another MOOC provider . . . apparently already uses "camera-friendly" staffers to appear in videos with professors," as reported by Sumagaysay (2013) from her interviews with Coursera, edX, and Udacity personnel. Obviously the for-profits assume students can be lured by the good looks or the movie-star fame of an online spokesperson. If the for-profits are right, neither the instructor's credentials nor her record of successful teaching is relevant. As long as a course is branded by the right university, the for-profits have an incentive to prioritize good looks over good credentials and good teaching.

A final concern is that once students are used to getting information from good-looking people they might then become cognitively biased to only paying attention to good-looking people. But most people are not exceptionally good-looking. Do we want to reduce our students' ability to cognitively and emotionally engage with people by priming them on the acquisition of information only from "good-looking" people? And what if that group is not sufficiently diverse, such as only including attractive white people?

Caveat #3: The ratio that for-profit online universities spend on public relations and advertising compared with faculty expenditures widely exceeds the ratio between the same as spent by both private nonprofit or public colleges and universities. Here we may summon the practice of the leader in the field of online teaching.

Apollo Education Group, Inc., is an S&P 500 corporation that owns several postsecondary learning institutions. By far the greatest revenue, approximately 90 percent, accrues from the University of Phoenix, which Apollo has described as "the nation's largest regionally accredited private university" (Apollo Annual Report 2004, 2).

In 2011, Apollo Education Group, including the University of Phoenix, spent $655 million on marketing. It spent $415 million on what it labeled as "admissions advisory." Since the University of Phoenix accepts anyone who fills out its forms and pays its tuition up front, it is highly unlikely that the $415 million went to pay admissions staff who were pouring over applicants' entry documents. In fact, Apollo is very active in lobbying at federal and state governmental levels, especially concerning its possible loss of accreditation status.[3] In 2011 the net revenue of Apollo was $4.7 billion (Apollo Group form 10-K 2013). In other words, about 23 percent of Apollo's revenue was spent on marketing and "admissions advisory." Compare that to the CSU system, which spends about 1 percent of the budget on marketing.[4] In other words, Apollo Education Group, for whom the University of Phoenix provides 90 percent of its revenue, spent a ratio of over seventy-five times greater of its revenue on marketing and admissions advisory than that of the CSU system.

But there are more telling criteria for comparing the worthiness of educational institutions whether for-profit, nonprofit, private, or nonprofit public. The US Department of Education recently adopted a very hard-nosed cri-

---

3. For a further discussion, see "University of Phoenix Maxing Out on Defaults" (http://banktalk.org/2012/06/26/university-of-phoenix-maxing-out-on-defaults), *Bank Talk*, June 26, 2012. See also Bob Johnson, "Bob Johnson's Blog on Higher Education Marketing—Bob Johnson's Blog on Higher Education Marketing," *Bobjohnsonblog.com*, January 11, 2013.

4. The overall expense of the twenty-three-campus CSU system in 2012–13 was $4.77 billion, of which $93.2 million was spent on public relations (about 0.2 percent of the budget) and $55.4 million was spent on admissions advisory.

terion to determine whether a higher-education program succeeds or fails. Here is its rule: If a higher-education institution graduates students who cannot make enough money to pay back their student loans, regardless of how penurious and careful their spending might be, then the program from which they received a degree or certification may be considered to have failed. If the program nears this criterion, it may be considered in a "warning" zone (http://www2.ed.gov/policy/highered/reg/hearulemaking/2012/gainfulemployment .html). As published in the *New York Times*, for-profit private institutions of higher learning have a very high failing rate, much higher than private non-profits and public colleges and universities (Carey 2014). There is no reason to think that MOOCs are immune from this trend.

Conclusion

We have argued that MOOCs and flipped courses are educationally deficient. But we are not Luddites. We understand and use technology when we think it appropriate. Our faculty teach online courses—which we have developed—and we blog and tweet. We do these things when we think they will help our students and with an understanding of how to best educate our students. The SJSU student population is diverse and with a variety of particular challenges that contribute to our values and how we serve our students. Students who are the first in their family to attend college, commuter students, students of all ages, and traditional students help make up the campus student population. SJSU students are smart and tech-savvy; however, many of them are also working not only to pay for their own education but also to help their families. We believe that our students do better when engaged with faculty who understand the issues they face, and we are committed to giving them the education they deserve.

Finally, one of our primary objections to President Qayoumi's MOOC project is that it is an effort to transfer control of curriculum and pedagogy from faculty to outside vendors. This is a usurpation of one of the faculty's primary responsibilities. Further, a prime responsibility of the administration of a public university is to act as a conservator of a public trust, rather than as an agent in the transfer of a public good to private interests.

References

"The Document: An Open Letter from San José State U.'s Philosophy Department." 2013. *The Chronicle of Higher Education*. May 2. http://www.chronicle.com/article/the-document -an-open-letter/138937/.Carey, Kevin. 2014. "Corinthian Colleges Is Closing. Its Students

May Be Better Off as a Result." *New York Times*, July 2. http://www.nytimes.com/2014/07 /03/upshot/corinthian-colleges-is-closing-its-students-may-be-better-off-as-a-result.html ?_r=0.

Apollo Group, Inc., 2004 Annual Report, http://www.annualreports.com/HostedData/Annual ReportArchive/a/NASDAQ_APOL_2004.pdf.

Ghadiri, Khosro, Mohammad H. Qayoumi, Ellen Junn, Ping Hsu, and Sutee Sujitparapitaya. 2013. "The Transformative Potential of Blended Learning Using MIT edX's 6.002x Online MOOC Content Combined with Student Team-Based Learning in Class." https://www.edx .org/sites/default/files/upload/ed-tech-paper.pdf.

Junn, Ellen, and Cathy Cheal. 2013. "Little Hoover Commission Public Hearing Written Testi- mony: San José State University Responses," February 26. http://www.lhc.ca.gov/studies /activestudies/highereducation/San%20Jose%20State%20testimony.pdf.

Lewin, Tamar. 2013. "San José State Philosophy Dept. Criticizes Online Courses." *New York Times*, May 2. http://www.nytimes.com/2013/05/03/education/san-jose-state-philosophy -dept-criticizes-online-courses.html.

Little Hoover Commission Hearing on CA Higher Education Financing, Online Classes and Faculty. 2013. YouTube video, 4:55:00. Posted February 26. https://www.youtube.com/watch ?v=ByWlWwRRTiY.

Qayoumi, Mohammad H., and Kim Polese. 2012. "Reinventing Public Higher Education: A Call to Action." http://www.sjsu.edu/president/docs/reinventinghighered_full.pdf.

Sumagaysay, Levi. 2013. "Movie Stars As Teachers? Plus Other Celebrity And Tech News." *SiliconBeat*, November 6. http://www.siliconbeat.com/2013/11/06/movie-stars-as-teachers -plus-other-celebrity-and-tech-news/.

Walters, Richard. 2014. "MOOCs in Transition: Not So Open, Open or Even Online." *Financial Times Web Blog*, February 2. http://blogs.ft.com/tech-blog/2014/02/moocs-in-transition-not -so-massive-open-or-even-online/.

Williams, Keith R. 2013. "Responses to Questions Posed by the Little Hoover Commission." http://www.lhc.ca.gov/studies/218/February%202013%20Hearing/Williams%20testimony .pdf.

Young, Jeffrey R., and Charles Nesson. 2014. "MOOCs and Consequences for the Future of Edu- cation." *Harvard Law School Cases*, February.

17

The Secret Lives of MOOCs

IAN BOGOST

Massive open online courses (MOOCs) are usually discussed as an educational technology, as a new way of teaching. This is true to some extent, even if these courses look far less "disruptive" when understood in relation to the long tradition of online and distance learning. For example, the *Slate* columnist Will Oremus (2012) has offered a convincing (and deflationary) account of MOOCs' potential as course material, suggesting that they are best understood as a replacement for traditional textbooks.

Even if MOOCs do sometimes function as courses (or as textbooks), a minority of their effects arises from their status as educational experiences. Other, less obvious aspects of MOOCs exert far more influence on contemporary life. This article discusses some—but certainly not all—of the different but important ways of understanding what MOOCs are and how they function in the contemporary educational, economic, and media ecosystem.

MOOCs as Marketing

MOOCs allow academic institutions to signal that they are with-it and progressive, in tune with the contemporary technological climate. They make an institution's administration appear to be doing novel work on "the future of higher education" and offer professors an opportunity to reach a large number of students who might also spread their ideas, buy their books, or otherwise publicize their professional practice. Less cynically, MOOCs can help deliver a taste of on-campus offerings to future students, parents, or the general public—although this latter function is hardly novel; for example, iTunes U has distributed free lectures for years.

In 2012, twelve higher-education institutions, including Georgia Tech where I work, announced their partnership with the MOOC provider Coursera to offer online courses (Kolowich 2012). Reactions to the announcement were dramatic, an outcome both Coursera and its new partner institutions surely hoped for. At the *Atlantic*, Jordan Weissmann (2012) penned a panegyric to the partnership, entitled "The Single Most Important Experiment in Higher Education." A key excerpt: "The fundamental challenge for U.S. universities as they struggle to contain their costs is figuring out how to teach more students using fewer resources."

This is the biggest and most insidious misconception of the format, the one that pervades every conversation about online education. The fundamental problem isn't one of cost containment but one of funding—of understanding why the cost-containment solution appeared in the first place (Mitchell, Palacios, and Leachman 2014). We collectively "decided" not to fund education in America. Now we're living with the consequences. Lost on those who mount such defenses is the fact that running these online courses costs *more* rather than less money in the short term; most Coursera faculty take on the task in addition to their normal work, and institutions bear the costs of creating and managing this new form of learning.

The more we buy into the efficiency argument, the more we cede ground to the technolibertarians who believe that a fusion of business and technology will solve all ills. But then again, perhaps that's what some MOOC proponents want. The issue isn't online education per se but the logics and rationales that come along with certain implementations of it.

Georgia Tech and the other dozen institutions that began the Coursera partnership probably weren't doing so out of some sort of carefully reasoned strategic implementation plan. Indeed, an all-campus email sent from the Georgia Tech Provost's office (Guzdial 2012) suggests that wasn't the case:

> Many members of our community express a desire to "try out" new techniques, to reach new Georgia Tech students and stakeholders, and to provide more flexible approaches to classroom instruction and course design. Coursera is just the first step in a strategy that will give us the freedom to investigate these new approaches and rapidly adopt the ones that have a positive impact on the Institute.

Institutions of higher learning are afraid of the present and the future yet drunk on the dream of being "elite" and willing to do anything to be seen in the right crowd making the hip choices. The provost's email also notes, "It also is significant that Georgia Tech is a founding member of this group." Group membership is a key obsession of university administration, and it's why they take systems like the *US News & World Report* rankings so seriously. Of course, all such structures are partly fictions we invent to structure our lives and society. The Ivy League isn't a natural law or a God-given lineage.

In this respect, Coursera got the upper hand among institutions that fancy themselves elite: once they were able to secure a critical mass of respected institutions, others didn't want to appear left behind. Given the drama surrounding University of Virginia (UVA) President Teresa Sullivan, who was pushed out of her post in 2012 partly for failing to adopt online learning strategies quickly enough, only to be rehired after a PR nightmare that played out weeks before UVA announced their participation in Coursera anyway, you can see how presidents and provosts across the land might be ready to sign on for defensive reasons alone (Jaschik 2012).

Claiming that MOOCs and their ilk signal "the beginning of the end" for higher education makes good headlines (Adams 2012). But that's mostly blustery rhetoric. As Siva Vaidhyanathan (2012) retorts, "I wish pundits would stop declaring that MOOC's are revolutionary when they are merely interesting (not that there is anything wrong with that)." But the revolutionary language serves a purpose, and that purpose is to market the idea of MOOCs as a possible future for institutions, and especially for the administrators who lead them. Buying into Coursera or its ilk associates an institution with a vague signal of futurism and reinvention, associates a purportedly "elite" institution with its elite brethren, and buys some time while the whole thing shakes out. Facebook page? Check. Twitter account? Check. Coursera courses? Check.

MOOCs as Financial Policy

But can MOOCs be *more* than marketing? Researchers and teachers at dozens of institutions have been pondering such questions for years, for decades. Of course, like all good research, progress comes slowly, in fits and starts, with as many failures as successes. Nobody wants to hear this though, because the age of Silicon Valley technolibertarianism sees real value as the most rapidly produced and untamed value. If it's immediate attention we're after, then there's another way to get it, by doing something that's not just new and me-too but also thoughtful and different and right. It's much harder to do that work within the academy, because few have any time to think about it seriously (even at the level of provosts' offices and the like) because of the austerity measures producing the illusion of the need for efficiency in the first place. And so, we reap what we sow.

In this respect, MOOCs exemplify what Naomi Klein (2008, 6) has called "disaster capitalism": policy guilefully initiated in the wake of upheaval. The need to teach more students with fewer resources is a complex situation. It's partly caused by hubris, especially the blind search for higher institutional status through research programs, and it's exacerbated by the tax-base crises of the ongoing and seemingly permanent Great Recession. MOOCs offer the next logical step in this process of "cost containment." But those who would call current funding models "unviable" and offer MOOCs as a convenient alternative fail to admit that the very need for an alternative presumes that we want to abandon public education in favor of a corporate-owned infrastructure in the first place.

Such problems infect all uses of MOOCs whether or not we want to admit that they do, even when trustworthy agents try to repurpose them for more egalitarian ends. Consider the scholar and educational futurist Cathy Davidson's case for an exceptional use of MOOCs, as exemplified by her own somewhat metadiscursive online course, The History and Future of (Mostly) Higher Education, offered via Coursera in 2013. The "experiment," as she calls it, was partly inspired by Davidson's ongoing (and much needed) critique of contemporary schooling as a system that has long outgrown the original contexts for its invention during industrialization (Bogost et al. 2013)

Of course, concomitant with the decline of industrialization, we have also seen the decline of affordable higher education, particularly in the last thirty years (US Government Accountability Office 2014). Davidson criticizes the lack of affordable access to education, admitting that "MOOCs aren't the answer" to these problems (Bogost et al. 2013). Yet Davidson doesn't address the evidence suggesting that MOOCs may actually *exacerbate* such problems. For example, they seem to reproduce rather than reform the lecture-based model Davidson also laments; they are primarily pursued by students who have already completed the higher education to which Davidson wants to increase access (Duke University 2013). They are overwhelmingly populated by white, male students, whose privilege already helps them evade the downsides of low-contact learning situations (Balch 2013).

Given these incompatibilities, Davidson still hopes her History and Future of (Mostly) Higher Education course might unearth better approaches to future learning for those students excluded from higher education. And efforts like hers will probably produce interesting observations. But I can't help but wonder if the excluded students Davidson hopes to help wouldn't rather have access to affordable (even if "Taylorist" in its orientation toward efficiency and scientific management, to invoke one of Davidson's favorite slurs) state education instead of the opportunity to phone into an extravagant "storyboarding" session hosted by Duke, an immensely wealthy private university, some of whose faculty have told me that they "didn't even register" the post-2008 financial apocalypse that forged the final nail in the coffin of educational access in the United States in particular.

MOOCs' ability to rectify access and affordability in higher education might exemplify *the politician's syllogism*, which goes like this:

1   We must do something.
2   This is something.
3   Therefore, we must do this.

The Silicon Valley solutionist version of the politician's syllogism assumes that the "something" of premise one is a problem addressable by technological change, and that the "something" of premise two is a technological solution. Such is one of the ways MOOCs are often presented.

When one refuses to accept this position at face value, it's common to endure a response that rejects the validity of all concern: *well, what's your solution, then?* No critique is deemed valid without a complete alternative program. Davidson is sensitive to this criticism, and her approach emphasizes her interest in defining such an alternative. But a valid response to a solutionist proposal may also involve rejecting the desirability of a particular solution wholesale, or observing that the problem it hopes to solve isn't actually a problem in the first place. If MOOCs are necessarily bound up with an endorsement of increased austerity, privatization, and elitist exclusivity, then those features cannot simply be short-circuited by the isolated acts of well-intentioned agents.

Perhaps it is irrelevant whether MOOCs are "good" or "bad" educational apparatuses, or whether individual "positive" examples of the uses of MOOCs can be found to disprove wholesale rejections for the form. Instead a more important question might ask what MOOCs as a form do to the educational, technological, cultural, social, and economic landscape: in how they function at large. Individual examples of MOOCs illuminate a part of that picture, but not the whole of it. That whole picture is complex; MOOCs may function on many registers all at once, with interdependencies in between. But, overall, MOOCs seem to function *first* and *most powerfully* as new instruments of fiscal and labor policy, rather than as educational technologies. Their value as instruments of learning is less important than the choices they are making on our behalf while we argue about their educational potential.

MOOCs as Standardization Practices

In 2013 President Obama announced a White House plan to make college more affordable. MOOCs enjoyed a positive mention in the plan, along with a related concept that might be less familiar, the "flipped classroom":

> A rising tide of innovation has the potential to shake up the higher education landscape. Promising approaches include three-year accelerated degrees, Massive Open Online Courses (MOOCs), and "flipped" or "hybrid" classrooms where students watch lectures at home and online and faculty challenge them to solve problems and deepen their knowledge in class. Some of these approaches are still being developed, and too few students are seeing their benefits. (White House 2013)

Even among those who have become accustomed to hearing about MOOCs in the media, the "flipped classroom" might have been a new concept. The idea is that a typical or "traditional" classroom involves listening to lectures in class and doing homework outside of class, while a flipped or "inverted" classroom asks students to listen to or watch MOOC-style video lectures before class and to perform exercises or other learning activities in class.

Educators seem to have warmed to the idea of the flipped classroom far more than that of the MOOC, even though the two are intimately connected. MOOC start-ups like Coursera have advocated for flipped classrooms, since those organizations have much to gain from their endorsement by universities. MOOCs rely on the short, video lecture as the backbone of a new educational beast, after all, so any incremental adoption of those materials benefits MOOC providers. Whether in the context of an all-online or a "hybrid" course, a flipped classroom takes the video lecture as a new standard for knowledge delivery and transfers that experience from the lecture hall to the laptop.

And the idea of a "flipped classroom" does sound good on first blush. After all, modern classrooms are hardly the pride of the educational experience, for students or for teachers. Flipping them might be for the best.

I already mentioned Cathy Davidson's dissatisfaction with the industrialist lecture as a learning format. No matter the learning content deployed in a classroom, its form embraces a disciplinary practice purpose-built for the factory or corporation who might later hire its compliant graduates. Given the collapse of industrialism and the rise of the knowledge economy, Davidson advocates for a more process-oriented, distributed, and exploratory method of learning more suited to today's postindustrial age.

But that dissatisfaction with the structure of classrooms is hardly a new enterprise. Fifty years ago, Marshall McLuhan ([1964] 2003, xvii, 444) cited the lecture hall as an example of a "hot" medium, one that exercises a single sense and therefore obviates the need for students to fill in the details. By contrast, for McLuhan the seminar exemplifies "cool" media, those that require more conscious effort from their participants. In *The Gutenberg Galaxy*, McLuhan (1962, 125) had made the same observation about the print book, arguing that its single-origin, single-sense method of knowledge recording and delivery set the stage for industrialization.

Perhaps surprisingly, a flipped classroom doesn't fundamentally alter the nature of the experience in the way that McLuhan and Davidson propose. Both MOOCs and flipped classrooms still rely on the lecture as their principal building block. In a typical classroom, students listen to lectures. In a flipped classroom, students still listen to lectures—they just do so as homework, edited down into pleasurably digestible chunks. The lecture is alive and well, it's just been turned into a sitcom.

Of course, a flipped classroom is not meant *just* to deliver prerecorded lectures. It hopes to allow the reclamation of class meetings for other sorts of "learning activities." Given the luxury of a small, McLuhan-cool seminar-style class, one can easily imagine that such an arrangement would prove beneficial. Indeed, the original concept of the "inverted classroom," which can be traced back to 2000, suggests that such a classroom "requires lower student enrollment" and has as a strength "the opportunity for faculty-student interaction" (Lage, Platt, and Treglia 2000, 37).

But flipped classrooms and MOOCs are not meant to enable a larger number of smaller, more personalized classes. Or, when they do, such success is purely accidental and secondary. These new courses are first-efficiency measures that hope to aggregate fewer higher-level (and higher-cost) educational encounters and standardize them for regularized future delivery. In practice, flipped classroom meetings usually involve additional assessments and exercises, most of which are nonsynthetic and automated (e.g., clicker responses, low- or unmoderated online discussions, quizzes, and so forth). The abstract, open-ended engagement with ideas (what makes the seminar "cool") is subordinated to efficient, measurable productive acts.

An astute observer might start to wonder . . . what's so flipped about the flipped classroom? Looking at the two side-by-side reveals one major difference that will help us reformulate this concept without the bluster of its trendiness.

A traditional classroom has readings before class, lectures during class, and assignments after class. A flipped classroom has lectures before class, assignments during class, and assessments after class. Flipped classroom

supporters like to argue that traditional classrooms only provide first exposure to materials via lecture, but that claim assumes that nothing whatso-
ever happens before such classes, that students enter class blind (see, e.g.,
the "Flipped Classroom Field Guide"; https://docs.google.com/document
/d/1arP1QAkSyVcxKYXgTJWCrJf02NdephTVGQltsw-S1fQ/pub#id.suag
qb7wve21). In reality, digging deeper than hearsay is a hallmark of university
education. Classes in all disciplines ask students to engage with primary and
secondary materials beforehand—and to experience analyzing, synthesizing,
and putting those materials to use with their own minds and hands.

The flipped classroom abstracts these materials, overloading them into
the lecture, which itself is usually shortened and condensed, typically into
modules less than twenty minutes in length. This condensed primary material then becomes fodder not for discourse or practice—as in the case of the
seminar—but for evaluation.

And furthermore, the new "primary" materials in question are reduced
in number and diversity—thus the idea of "star" professors serving as the
celebrities of global MOOC lectureships. Such a direction corresponds well
with other efforts to standardize education at the primary, secondary, and
postsecondary levels. A cynic might say that the flipped classroom ushers
in the CliffsNotesfication of university courses. A moderate might rehearse
Oremus's (2012) suggestion, that MOOCs replace textbooks and other reading materials students traditionally encounter in university, spinning that take
into a certain benefit.

But "replacement" is an imprecise characterization, particularly for courses
in which a singular, canonical textbook doesn't (or shouldn't) exist (hint: most
of them). More specifically, video lectures compress both primary materials
(readings) and their clarification (lectures) into a single format, one shorter
and necessarily less detailed than would be possible with a combination of
preclass readings and in-class lectures or discussions.

In essence, the flipped classroom is really a *condensed*, an *abstracted*, and
a *standardized* classroom, one in which primary and secondary materials are
refactored into prebuilt lectures for the sake of value propositions other than
the student's direct encounter with the currency of ideas. A flipped classroom
is a compromise.

Even so, such a classroom isn't *necessarily* a bad thing. A guide published
by Vanderbilt University suggests that flipped classrooms offer better opportunity and incentive for students to gain exposure to material before class
(Brame 2013). For example, it's possible that nonmajor students taking introductory courses might find more gratification in a short, summary lecture than they would reading esoteric textbook chapters or difficult primary

material. In this case, condensation means encapsulation, compression: making materials more condensed so as to render them more easily and broadly digestible.

But then again, one could easily argue just the opposite: that a condensed classroom is a false copy, one that exchanges detail for facility—a particular concern especially in introductory courses whose students *won't* later enjoy deeper contact with primary materials. Thumbnailing or abridging a subject might be fine in a magazine article or a TED talk, but isn't higher education supposed to provide genuine mastery, not just glib adequacy? Aren't college courses meant to place students in direct contact with the history of knowledge, not just to offer another channel of short-form entertainment students can collect and assemble into a credential?

No matter its benefits or faults, it is inaccurate to call this flipped classroom "flipped," when really it is condensed, abstracted. But you can see why it's an effective rhetorical term. "Flipping" implies an ambitious and visionary overturning of the sort Davidson advocates, rather than a simple refactoring of resources that might allow classes to better prepare students for assessment—one of the other principal benefits cited in the Vanderbilt findings. Worse yet, many instructors who are legitimately interested in increasing the "cool" and reducing the "heat" of their lecture classes may be inadvertently tricked into thinking they are "flipping" their classrooms, thus lending credibility to a project with incompatible aims.

MOOCs as Speculative, Silicon Valley–Style Financial Leverage

Today's business practices privilege the accrual of value in the hands of a small number of network operators. Anything unable to be maximally leveraged isn't worth doing. MOOCs subscribe to leverage as a primary value proposition ("massiveness"), implicitly rejecting the premise that some things benefit from "inefficiency." MOOCs also evangelize the Silicon Valley ideology of technological salvation that Evgeny Morozov (2013, 6) has called "solutionism" and David Golumbia (2009, 7) has called "computationalism." For example, MOOC researchers-turned-entrepreneurs Daphne Koller and Sebastian Thrun assume that computational methods for instructional automation can "solve" the problems of education—just as a service like Uber is seen to "solve" taxi-hailing among entrepreneurs, venture capitalists, and other technology boosters.

Citing enormous enrollment numbers against very small numbers of instructors and instructional support personnel is a common way to justify the promise of MOOCs ("Massive Online Open Courses [MOOCs] with

100,000+ students" is the line in the Snowbird session description; Spector, Khan, and Norvig 2012). Yet, we also know that these courses also exhibit very high attrition rates, from 90 percent to as high as 97 percent (Black 2012; Rivard 2013).

Some proponents argue that attrition doesn't really matter, that even a student who enrolls in such a course and simply learns something about the area is benefitting in some way. This is probably true, but such a feat can be accomplished in any number of ways, from blogs to books to lectures to "ordinary" web videos. There's something "massive" going on, perhaps, but let's be clear about what it is. If it's publicity for more traditional courses of study, even in the very long-term, so be it. If it's the size of the potential audience for such longitudinal messages, all right then.

Likewise, to call the participants "students" suggests that something akin to learning is going on for all of them. But that doesn't seem to be the case—at least not yet. They're more like potential students, or would-be students, or interested bystanders, or, at worst, just the people who filled out a sign-up form. In ordinary web-service businesses, they're called "users," and it's interesting to note that MOOC proponents have so carefully avoided that sort of dehumanizing, instrumentalist language. In any case, to call the participants who were involved "massive" numbers of "students" is misleading. Would you call an interstitial web ad for a new car a "massive online open road?" Probably not.

As edtech learning practices become commonplace, we would do well to remember that technology does not improve some underlying, pure nature of their subject. Rather, it *changes* those things, transforming them into something new, something different. The telephone doesn't improve communication; it alters it. Facebook doesn't improve socialization; it alters it. When it comes to the process of condensation, blanket statements slip through our fingers. Condensed milk isn't necessarily worse or better than fresh milk. Winnie the Pooh likes it. It can be spread on toast or dolloped atop New Orleans snowballs. But it is not an improvement over fresh milk. It's something else entirely. Likewise, phenomena like the MOOC-derived condensed classroom ought not to be thought of as an evolution. Instead we should see them just for what they are: one approach to learning whose merits are hardly sufficiently justified by its correspondence with current trends in Internet culture.

Indeed, flipped classrooms may not even offer the benefits of efficiency touted by edtech start-ups and parroted by the White House. Contrary to the common wisdom about MOOCs and their ilk, condensed classes actually seem to require *more* work rather than less. Not only because they require the creation of elaborate video lectures, but also because in-class activities have to be designed, monitored, and evaluated. Like the unseen labor of all technology solutions—the moderators who delete offensive posts from Facebook, or the drivers who pilot Google cars to collect street-view images—these efforts will likely be hidden away behind the scenes, transformed into menial labor activities (cf., Chen 2014). The likely endgame of MOOCs and flipped classrooms isn't a proliferation of high-contact, expert-run seminars, but the condensation of fewer, more readily distributable "online textbooks" with armies of low-paid instructional personnel cleaning up after them.

Stripped from its current context of cost-cutting and oversight amplification, the more abstract idea of flipping the classroom harkens back to Marshall McLuhan's hot and cool learning environments. If anything, a truly flipped classroom would just look more like a seminar, not more like a series of TED Talks with associated assessments. The error of flipped classroom advocacy is not a distaste for the big lecture classroom, but that its reversal entails online lectures and in-class assessments instead.

Of course, it's theoretically possible to turn every classroom into a small-scale, discussion-heavy period of reflection and exercise. But such a feat requires investment, and both Obama's plan and the MOOC advocates make the false assumption that today's educational austerity is both incontrovertible and acceptable. Now we can get on to the privatization of education via Udacity, Coursera, and their kindred, or the administrative bureaucratization of it via ObamaEd, which has been called the higher-education version of the No Child Left Behind Act (Fichtenbaum 2013). Parents and students who have worried about increasing size and decreasing attention in K–12 classrooms should note that flipped classrooms are an extension rather than an interruption of this practice, one tightly aligned with long-term financial deprivation in education (despite also costing more in the short-term).

The proliferation of such signals help us imagine what a truly "flipped" classroom might look like, one that really did reverse the worst aspects of education for the sake of improving it as a long-term social practice rather than converting it into a short-term appraisal contraption. It would be one in which administration and commercialization take a backseat to high-touch teaching and learning, one in which educators have the resources required to conduct what we've long known is better for students, and perhaps most of all, one in which compromises and short-cuts aren't palmed off as innovation.

As a consequence of the financial policy just described, MOOCs are amplifying the precarity long experienced by adjuncts and graduate-student assistants, and helping to extend that precarity to the professoriate. There are many academic labor implications of MOOCs. They encourage an ad hoc "freelancing" work regime among tenured faculty, many of whom will find the financial incentives for MOOC creation and deployment difficult to resist—particularly among public institution faculty who have gone years without raises after the 2008 financial collapse. Some institutions have offered considerable remuneration—amounting to tens of thousands of dollars, potentially, when doled out as months of summer salary, for example—for MOOC development and teaching. And, in some cases, MOOCs offer direct access to student tuition and direct competition among faculty for those new resources, extending the "entrepreneurial" institutional politics of professional schools (and corporate life more generally) to all disciplines.

The purpose of an educational institution is to educate, but the purpose of a start-up is to convert itself into a financial instrument. The two major MOOC providers, Udacity and Coursera, are venture capital–funded start-ups and thus are beholden to high leverage, rapid growth with an interest in a fast flip to a larger technology company or the financial market. The concepts of "disruption" and "innovation," so commonly applied to MOOCs, come from the world of business. As for edX, the MOOC consortium started by Harvard and MIT, it's a nonprofit operating under the logic of speculation rather than as a public service. If anything, it will help the for-profits succeed even more by evangelizing their vision as compatible with elite nonprofit educational ideals.

"The three leading MOOC providers, Udacity, Coursera and edX, have grown at a remarkable rate, adding hundreds of courses with dozens of college and university partners," according to Tamar Lewin (2013) in the *New York Times*' coverage of an online master's degree in computer science offered at Georgia Tech. But the statement is true only for certain definitions of "growth." Really, the MOOC providers have grown exclusively on the usual Silicon Valley premise of speculative, short-term bets that have little concern about long-term prospects. Certainly their revenues haven't grown much; only their reach, as they manage to convince universities to give away the "content" of courses and teaching to produce a beneficial network effect for these private technology services.

The growth of private MOOC companies is driven almost entirely from financial speculation, speculation with an interest in private, short-term gain via industrialized scale. It's worth imagining what other kinds of growth might be possible if we had the stomach for a different kind of speculation meant to benefit long-term social institutions like schools instead of the market. There's an alternate universe in which the *New York Times* published a story about how strong public investment in educational programs reduced costs and increased quality without selling the farm to bankers, one in which the key measure of "growth" is related to educational practice rather than industrialization. But that's not our universe, at least for now.

Conclusion: MOOCs as Entertainment

We are living in an age of para-educationalism: TED Talks, "big idea" books, and the professional lecture circuit have reconfigured the place of ideas (of a certain kind) in the media mainstream. Flattery, attention, appeal of celebrity, aspiration to become a member of a certain community, and other triumphs of personality have become the currency of thinking, even as anti-intellectualism remains ascendant. MOOCs buttress this situation, one in which the professor is meant to become an entertainer more than an educator or a researcher. The fact that MOOC proponents have even toyed with the idea of hiring actors to present video lectures only underscores the degree to which MOOCs aspire to reinvent education as entertainment.

But not just education as entertainment: MOOCs also offer destruction as entertainment. Perhaps this is the ultimate purpose of the MOOC, which is to give us something to gawk at. And like the summer blockbuster action film, the entertainment experience MOOCs are most capable of producing offers the catharsis of destruction. When the Silicon Valley news rag *TechCrunch* (Ferenstein 2013) reports that a Udacity partnership with a state university "will end college as we know it," they offer the ultimate action entertainment promise: the pleasure of watching something burn.

Except, action films fictionalize destruction, offering the cathartic harmony of watching a foe destroy before being destroyed in turn. But today, technology carries out massive transformations, which we feel no qualms about calling by names like destruction, disruption, or tsunami. The latter is the word David Brooks (2012) used to describe the rising tides, as it were, of MOOCs. Even the form of Brooks's article adopts the three-act structure common to screenwriting: the setup of an old, stodgy institution, education, contrast to a lithe, amorphous, powerful foe: the Internet ("What happened to the newspaper and magazine business is about to happen to higher education"). A conflict erupts between the two, full of anxiety and doubt. Great uncertainty prevails as world old and new compete, stone versus silicon ("If a few star professors can lecture to millions, what happens to the rest of the faculty?"). But as it turns out, "there are more reasons to feel optimistic"—competition turns to collaboration, as the agents of educational authority and the technological upstarts who would unseat them figure out how to work together, to "blend online information with face-to-face discussion."

More than anything else, MOOCs are one giant reality show about all of us who have a stake in higher education—which is, hopefully, all of us who live in a society that educates people. Even the book you hold in your hands participates in this process, creating angst and dread and hope and fancy. MOOCs are many things, but one of them is an activity performed for its own sake, outside the purview of disruption or corporatization or access. For now, anyway. Eventually—inevitably—we will all move on from them, whether through abandonment, victory, failure, or simple loss of novelty.

Perhaps this is the most important lesson of MOOCs: university management and labor has always been subjected to trends from outside, but we have not embraced them with such open arms and not as rapidly. MOOCs may or may not be the future of education. But following, adopting, and fending off the rise and fall of trends and hype for university operations are sure to become a part of our future work and perhaps a large part. Administrators, faculty, parents, and students will continue to debate about the benefits and detriments of this new normal. But normal it has become. The future of MOOCs, it would seem, already looks beyond them, to the next thing, or the next-next one, an arms race of speculative futures.

References

Adams, Susan. 2012. "Is Coursera the Beginning of the End for Traditional Higher Education?" *Forbes*, July 17. http://www.forbes.com/sites/susanadams/2012/07/17/is-coursera-the-beginning-of-the-end-for-traditional-higher-education/.

Balch, Tucker. 2013. "MOOC Student Demographics (Spring 2013)." *Augmented Trader*, January 27. http://augmentedtrader.com/2013/01/27/mooc-student-demographics/.

Black, Chad Thomas. 2012. "Attrition and the Year of the MOOC." *Parezco y Digo*, June 3. http://parezcoydigo.wordpress.com/2012/06/03/attrition-and-the-year-of-the-mooc/.

Bogost, Ian, Ray Schroeder, Cathy N. Davidson, and Al Filreis. 2013. "MOOCs and the Future of the Humanities: A Roundtable (Part 2)." *Los Angeles Review of Books*, June 15. https://lareviewofbooks.org/article/moocs-and-the-future-of-the-humanities-a-roundtable-part-2/.

Brame, Cynthia J. 2013. "Flipping the Classroom." Vanderbilt University Center for Teaching. http://cft.vanderbilt.edu/guides-sub-pages/flipping-the-classroom/.

Brooks, David. 2012. "The Campus Tsunami." *New York Times*, May 3. http://www.nytimes.com/2012/05/04/opinion/brooks-the-campus-tsunami.html.

Chen, Adrian. 2014. "The Laborers Who Keep Dick Pics and Beheadings Out of Your Facebook Feed." *Wired*, October 23. http://www.wired.com/2014/10/content-moderation/.

Davidson, Cathy. 2011. *Now You See It: How the Brain Science of Attention Will Transform the Way We Live, Work, and Learn*. New York: Viking.

Duke University. 2013. "Bioelectricity: A Quantitative Approach (Duke University's First MOOC)." February 5. http://dukespace.lib.duke.edu/dspace/bitstream/handle/10161/6216/Duke_Bioelectricity_MOOC_Fall2012.pdf.

Ferenstein, Gregory. 2013. "How California's Online Education Pilot Will End College as We Know It." *TechCrunch*, January 15. http://techcrunch.com/2013/01/15/how-californias-new -online-education-pilot-will-end-college-as-we-know-it/.

Fichtenbaum, Rudy. 2013. "Statement on the President's Proposal for Performance Based Funding." *AAUP*, August 24. http://www.aaup.org/news/statement-president's-proposal -performance-based-funding.

Golumbia, David. 2009. *The Cultural Logic of Computation*. Cambridge: Harvard University Press.

Guzdial, Mark. 2012. "Georgia Tech Will Partner with Coursera." *Computing Education Blog*, July 17. http://computinged.wordpress.com/2012/07/17/georgia-tech-will-partner-with -coursera/.

Jaschik, Scott. 2012. "The E-Mail Trail at UVa." *Inside Higher Education*, June 20. https://www .insidehighered.com/news/2012/06/20/e-mails-show-uva-board-wanted-big-online-push.

Klein, Naomi. 2008. *The Shock Doctrine: The Rise of Disaster Capitalism*. New York: Picador.

Kolowich, Steve. 2012. "Into the Fray." *Inside Higher Ed*, July 17. https://www.insidehighered.com /news/2012/07/17/uva-and-11-others-become-latest-plan-moocs.

Lage, Maureen J., Glenn J. Platt, and Michael Treglia. 2000. "Inverting the Classroom: A Gateway to Creating an Inclusive Learning Environment." *Journal of Economic Education* 31 (1): 30–43.

Lewin, Tamar. 2013. "Master's Degree Is New Frontier of Study Online." *New York Times*, August 17. http://www.nytimes.com/2013/08/18/education/masters-degree-is-new-frontier-of -study-online.html.

McLuhan, Marshall. 1962. *The Gutenberg Galaxy: The Making of Typographic Man*. Toronto: University of Toronto Press.

———. (1964) 2003. *Understanding Media: The Extensions of Man*. Reprint, New York: Gingko Press.

Mitchell, Michael, Vincent Palacios, and Michael Leachman. 2014. "States Are Still Funding Higher Education Below Pre-Recession Levels." *Center on Budget and Policy Priorities*, May. http://www.cbpp.org/cms/?fa=view&id=4135.

Morozov, Evgeny. 2013. *To Save Everything Click Here: The Folly of Technological Solutionism*. New York: PublicAffairs.

Oremus, Will. 2012. "The New Public Ivies." *Slate*, July 18. http://www.slate.com/articles /technology/future_tense/2012/07/coursera_udacity_edx_will_free_online_ivy_league _courses_end_the_era_of_expensive_higher_ed_.html.

Pinhoster, Ginger. 2013. "Massive Open Online Courses Help Make STEM Education More Accessible, But Do They Work for All Students?" *AAAS*, May 22. http://www.aaas.org/news /releases/2013/0522_moocs.shtml.

Rivard, Ry. 2013. "Measuring the MOOC Dropout Rate." *Inside Higher Ed*, March 3. https://www .insidehighered.com/news/2013/03/08/researchers-explore-who-taking-moocs-and-why-so -many-drop-out.

Spector, Alfred, Salman Khan, and Peter Norvig. 2012. "Reflections on Teaching Massive Online Open Courses," Computing Research Association Conference at Snowbird, July 22–24. http://archive2.cra.org/events/snowbird-2012.

US Government Accountability Office. 2014. "Higher Education: State Funding Trends and Policies on Affordability." December. http://www.gao.gov/assets/670/667557.pdf.

Vaidhyanathan, Siva. 2012. "Going Public the UVa Way." *Chronicle of Higher Education*, July 18. http://chronicle.com/blogs/innovations/going-public-the-uva-way/33623.

Weissmann, Jordan. 2012. "The Single Most Important Experiment in Higher Education." *Atlantic*, July 18. http://www.theatlantic.com/business/archive/2012/07/the-single-most-important-experiment-in-higher-education/259953/.

White House. 2013. "FACT SHEET on the President's Plan to Make College More Affordable: A Better Bargain for the Middle Class." August 22. http://www.whitehouse.gov/the-press-office/2013/08/22/fact-sheet-president-s-plan-make-college-more-affordable-better-bargain-.

18

MOOCs, *Second Life*, and
the White Man's Burden

SIVA VAIDHYANATHAN

Imagine an online digital platform that stirs such excitement that pundits predict it will radically change the ways humans teach, learn, and relate to each other. It's bound to be "disruptive," we are told. Imagine if tens of thousands of people rushed to enroll with this platform.

Imagine that soon after the platform's launch hundreds of colleges and universities around the world began online ventures on the platform, hoping to be seen as "cutting edge" and—most of all—frightened to be left behind as the world turns toward the Next Big Thing.

This actually happened. Back in 2006 *Second Life* was all the rage. We were advised (or warned) by *Business Week* that "your next cubicle could well be inside a virtual world" (Hof 2006). In the *Chronicle of Higher Education*, Andrea Foster (2005) described the rush that many researchers and teachers were making to *Second Life*, assuming that, as one professor said at the time, "students are going to play around in virtual worlds anyway."

As it turned out, *Second Life* did not revolutionize higher education. It did not revolutionize the office. It did not revolutionize much of anything. The media mania over *Second Life* was in a large part self-fulfilling because the more people wrote about it the more people signed up to try it out and the more people eventually forgot about it, leaving their avatars to wander the desert of the unreal.

That's not to say that *Second Life* was—or is—a failure. It is a commercial venture from a corporation, Linden Labs. It has had as many as thirteen million registered users in 2008, and the number of "concurrent users" logged on to *Second Life* reached a peak of 88,200 in 2009. The buzz has long since worn off. And Linden Labs has gone through many changes. But thousands still animate their avatars and exchange virtual goods and services with regularity.

Academic teachers and researchers continue to experiment with *Second Life* and, increasingly, other virtual worlds (Peachy et. al. 2010). While many remain active on *Second Life*, other professors and universities became annoyed at the predictable problems (e.g., trolls, pranksters, changing corporate policies, poor interface design, etc.), so they have been experimenting with other commercial and open-source platforms for virtual engagement and research.

So the lessons to be learned from the *Second Life* mania is that virtual education is interesting, even encouraging. And it's clear that research into how markets, norms, and laws succeed and fail in virtual worlds remains fascinating (Lastowka and Hunter 2003).

Second Life and virtual education are now useful additions to the toolkit of higher education. We can learn something from such experiments. But we should have known better than to rush in and declare this platform revolutionary based on nothing more than a naive faith in the allegedly transformative power of digital technology.

Flash forward to late 2012. The *New York Times* Education Life supplement declared 2012 "The Year of the MOOC," or massive open online course (Pappano 2012). Why? Because many other buzz-inducing publications, including the *Chronicle of Higher Education*, *Wired*, and even *Technology Review* had also run long, in-depth pieces and packages on this phenomenon.

New York Times columnist and innovation-enthusiast Thomas Friedman wrote two op-ed pieces in early 2013 celebrating the MOOC "revolution." In his usual style,

> Imagine how this might change U.S. foreign aid. For relatively little money, the U.S. could rent space in an Egyptian village, install two dozen computers and high-speed satellite Internet access, hire a local teacher as a facilitator, and invite in any Egyptian who wanted to take online courses with the best professors in the world, subtitled in Arabic. (Friedman 2013)

MOOCs hit all the buzz targets and terms: Silicon Valley launched; Stanford graduates and disaffected professors involved; free (as in free beer); open (as in open-source, even when they are not); potentially "disruptive" (based on nothing but faith-based speculation); and "revolutionary" or "transformative." Whenever one reads words such as these, along with "unsustainable" and "the new normal," one should quickly assume that the author has put very little actual thought into the subject. If I teach my students anything useful, it's to beware of all-too conventional wisdom clad in unconventional clothing.

Does all this mean we should dismiss MOOCs as a mere fad? Or worse, are MOOCs a waste of precious university time and money? Certainly not. MOOCs are something worthwhile and potentially something good. MOOCs should be promoted or demoted based on their merits. But their merits will take years to assess.

Academia should be the last place in society in which principals rush toward the bright, shiny objects without thought, evidence, data, or deliberation. As Elvis sang, "Fools rush in." Alas, that is what's happening.

The University of Virginia, my employer, rolled out a handful of Coursera "courses" in 2012. It has offered a few more during each of the past four years. No one has ordered professors to make such a move. Only those highly motivated by curiosity are doing the hard work of refashioning appropriate content for worldwide distribution. The university is committed to intensive study of student behavior and achievement through these efforts. The goal is to improve education at UVA, not to revolutionize or transform anything. And we shall do so carefully and deliberately, with trial and error, and guided by data and experience.

The UVA deal with Coursera was in the works for some time before the leader of the university's governing board, Helen Dragas, informed President Teresa Sullivan that she had the votes on the board to fire Sullivan in June 2012. Sullivan resigned, but she was effectively fired by that threat. Dragas gave no specific reason publicly to justify this move, which student, alumni, faculty, and community protests managed to reverse just six weeks later. But when the student newspaper, the *Cavalier Daily*, acquired the emails among board members concerning the firing, it discovered that several of the emails among the small group of instigators mentioned that UVA had not been listed in the national press coverage of MOOC development along with Stanford and Harvard (Jaschik 2012). To Dragas, this meant that UVA was complacent and comfortable, so she blamed Sullivan, who was widely acclaimed as a first-rank scholar and a longtime university administrator. This small element of the story—the role of MOOCs (or their absence) became blown up into seeming like the major reason behind the firing. This was not the case. MOOCs, to Dragas, were an example of one thing that UVA could and should be doing, but Dragas's problem with Sullivan was that the president was not "dynamic" enough. Dragas wanted the university to reinvent itself, along the lines that Harvard Business School professor Clayton Christensen outlined in his work on "disruptive innovation" (Rice 2012).

In the public mind the larger ideological clash over the overall future and role of higher education became reduced to a "MOOC or no MOOC" debate that fit well into the technocratic moment. If the putsch had happened in 2010 or 2015 it might have garnered a richer analysis nationwide. Alas, be-

cause 2012 was "the year of the MOOC," we at UVA had little to respond with
beyond the truth that we actually were happy and ready to produce these
expensive luxury services that would generate no revenue for the university.
Before Dragas pushed Sullivan out, she had failed to ask anyone whether we
were planning to produce MOOCs. And, as anyone well versed in technological experimentation in labs and classrooms would know, UVA has long been
a leader in the field (Vaidhyanathan 2012). Dragas could have known that
had she cared to investigate. Instead UVA was mischaracterized as slow and
resistant to change.

As I write, Coursera has more than one hundred university partners
around the world. edX is a partnership among MIT, Harvard, UC Berkeley,
and University of Texas. And Udacity is a for-profit venture launched by a
Stanford professor and unaffiliated with any particular university. Hundreds
of thousands of students across the world have registered for MOOC services
through these and other platforms. A slight fraction of those who register
ever finish the course. Few institutions have figured out how to grant credit
for work done in a MOOC. And none have figured out how to recoup the
substantial cost of producing a MOOC.

Let's be clear. MOOCs offer some shallow advantages to elite institutions
of higher education. And those few universities would be foolish to miss out
on them, regardless of the empty rhetoric surrounding the MOOC madness.
MOOCs offer opportunities for established colleges and universities to market themselves in clever new ways. Instead of showing off videos or images
of lovely campuses filled with happy young students, universities can invite
prospective students into a lecture (hopefully a good one) with a famous—
and usually male—professor.

The great pretension of MOOCS is that they offer even better opportunities for great populations of humanity who do not have access to high-quality
education courses. If even one young person in a corner of the world without
universities gets excited and motivated by physics or poetry, then the whole
MOOC endeavor has paid off. But by 2015 we know better than to ride on that
promise. MOOCs seem to offer little to those not already highly educated,
fluent in English, and connected to high-speed data services. In other words,
like so much else, MOOCs are making the rich richer.

As of 2016, MOOCs are a public service that America's wealthiest universities have engaged in at great expense with no measurable return. Designing and running a MOOC is expensive, just like almost everything else in
higher education. But these universities see a duty in sharing knowledge and
expertise beyond their walls. This is not a new ethic among universities. But
it's easier to do than ever before. But let's be clear: MOOCs are mostly about

marketing. A successful MOOC can raise the profile of star faculty around the globe. And since MOOCs generally appeal to those already educated and thus likely wealthy and likely to produce children who might pursue higher education in an elite and expensive setting, MOOCs do exactly what they are meant to do, which is to help the educated identify with the university and professor who produced the MOOC.

MOOCs also potentially render more pricey for-profit ventures such as the Learning Company and for-profit colleges increasingly irrelevant. The Learning Company hurts no one. But for-profit colleges have played a dispro-portionate role in the growing student debt problem of late (Vara 2015). They often offer their expensive courses online to cater to working people and par-ents. If MOOCs can serve some of the skill-building demand that drives these ventures, then for-profit colleges might feel real market pressure to reform.

Just as importantly, MOOCs can shake major universities of their long-held fantasy of using online courses to generate money. Back in 2003 Co-lumbia University shuttered its early venture in online "boutique learning," called Fathom.com (Tomsho 2003). Columbia leaders pushed their fantasy of revenue generation until it became clear that few people would pay real money for the experience of reading text on a screen—something many pub-lications have discovered the hard way as well. And more recently, the Uni-versity of California system has found that enthusiasm has declined for its efforts to generate revenue from UC Online (Asimov 2013). Private funding sources have dried up as MOOC mania has spread (Hechinger Report 2015). So perhaps one positive externality of MOOCs is that universities will be less optimistic about the ability to sell online course materials and will refocus their efforts on their core missions.

There are many misperceptions and misunderstandings about MOOCs, but chief among them is the widespread conflation of MOOCs on online edu-cation in general. Universities have been offering online courses and degrees for almost fifteen years. Many of these have been remarkably successful. And some have not. We have learned much from these efforts. And it's a rare uni-versity course that lacks some online component. The rise of powerful online course-management platforms allow any professor to post videos, link to web content, foster wiki or blog discussion, host a chat room, or require video projects as part of the graded assignments for the course. MOOCs could benefit from the toolkits that online educators have been developing for years. And online (and mostly offline) educators should certainly be able to learn from the trials and errors of MOOCs as well.

The biggest problem with MOOCs as they currently operate is that they highlight the least attractive aspects of higher education: the packed lecture with limited student-faculty contact. Most MOOCs involve videos of professors lecturing with slides. Then they are supplemented with some assignments and collaborative discussion. This is hardly an ideal method of student interaction. And no one has yet figured out how to make a brilliant seminar "massive."

One could think of current MOOCs as simulating the experience of sitting in the last row of the largest lecture hall in the universe. Or you could think of MOOCs as multimedia textbooks, supplements to courses and not courses in themselves. The most advanced digital textbooks contain online modules, quizzes, and projects built into them. They even offer audio and video. And they are expensive. So perhaps the great value of MOOCs could be the undermining of expensive multimedia textbook production for those courses that use textbooks (largely lower-level introductory courses in the sciences).

To make MOOCs successful as actual courses, MOOC developers face some daunting challenges. First and foremost, cheating is rampant and identity certification difficult, especially with a global collection of "users" (Coursera calls them "users" instead of "students"). Second, quality control is hard to maintain in such courses. Where is the incentive to improvise or update course materials? Rerecording a lecture after a new court case or election will be costly and time consuming. So MOOCs are going to have to be designed to be more flexible and updatable than they have been so far.

To avoid the recapitulation of massive lectures, some of which can be very effective with the right lecturer, MOOC developers will have to share that goal and trade techniques that offer rich interactivity even with thousands of users. This is not as easy as it seems. This is one reason that online courses through standard university degree programs have been so successful. MOOCs might not end up as massive or open as their advocates hope them to be.

The biggest threats to MOOCs are the biggest threats to any online venture: bots and trolls. It's too easy to program a small batch of code that can disrupt a MOOC, pretend to be a "student," or scrape and publicize student work and data. And soon enough we should hear horror stories of disruptive pranksters or bigots entering MOOCs to mess with students and professors. There is not much we can do to limit such behavior as long as MOOCs remain massive and open. So, again, we might find that the best lessons of MOOCs are that the online experiments that universities have been pushing for years work best.

Privacy rarely comes up in public discussion of MOOCs. But if advocates ever hope that users earn transferable credit for work done through MOOCs, then universities are going to have to push for strong protections so that personal information, including grades, never leak beyond authorized education officials. This limits the potential for MOOC companies to exploit private information for marketing and customized services for which they might charge a premium. Users could be tricked or coerced into allowing full and broad sharing of data and records upon registration (Lane et al. 2014).

But universities have a moral obligation to resist such dangerous tactics. Universities should never fall to the level of Google or Facebook when it comes to respecting students or even "users." So far, I have not seen problems of this type. The Coursera user agreement promises that it will not sell data to third parties, for instance. Of course, Coursera could change this policy if financial winds change. So far, there is no regulation that stops a MOOC firm from treating its users very badly. For these companies, as long as users are "users" and not "students," then federal student privacy law does not protect users like it would actual students.

If universities wanted to take seriously the obligation of spreading knowledge around the world, they would publish MOOC material themselves in an open format, eschewing partnerships with commercial firms like Coursera. They would also choose to use Creative Commons or other similar licenses that would encourage people to remix and reuse the content.

No MOOC firm has figured out a way to make money. So it's silly to assume that MOOCs offer higher education a way either to save or to make money. These things cost a lot to make, launch, and maintain. It would be frustrating but not surprising if MOOCs never make money for their host companies and thus never make money for their partner institutions. But it would be far worse if they did make money for colleges and universities.

The only thing worse than failing to make money from MOOCs is succeeding to make money from MOOCs. If universities started making substantial money from MOOCs, they could corrupt the mission of universities. Lucrative MOOCs could create perverse incentives to pander to the largest possible audiences. They could push or force professors to avoid controversial topics for fear of alienating potential "customers." And they could create internal reward systems at universities that favored the mass production of credits and degrees over the careful cultivation of knowledge and wisdom. Universities already face too many pressures from state legislatures and board members to move in the direction of mass production of degrees. We should not invite more.

The biggest misperception about higher education and thus the biggest misperception about MOOCs is that education consists of injecting information into a person—or that education is even about information. Education is supposed to be about wisdom, experience, acculturation into the life of the mind, and guided experimentation in collaboration with experienced teachers and enthusiastic peers. Education fails when we assume it's about what students retain after the information injection.

In 1938 Orson Welles's broadcast of the radio drama of *War of the Worlds* caused massive panic among listeners. Early scholars of communication used this event to cement their belief in what was called the "hypodermic needle" theory of communication. According to this model, a speaker or producer injected content into a passive audience. That audience would receive the message and react in predictable ways. Audiences were susceptible to propaganda and misinformation, but also capable of benefitting from high-minded content delivered by reputable sources. While it did not take long after World War II for more sophisticated media and communication scholars to challenge and reject the hypodermic needle theory, it stubbornly reemerges in the worst popular media criticism today (Katz et al. 1955). You hear it in whines from the right about "liberal media bias." You see it when liberals blame Fox News for their inability to get more working-class Americans to vote for what liberals assume are their economic interests.

Sadly, the hypodermic needle theory also dominates the assumption about higher-education teaching and renders most recent discussions about MOOCs shallow and hyperbolic. We see it at work in an interesting and potentially persuasive essay by economist Alex Tabarrok published by the Cato Institute, in which Tabarrok conflates teaching with informing. Tabarrok (2012) writes, "The productivity of teaching, measured in, say, kilobytes transmitted from teacher to student per unit of time, hasn't increased much," but MOOCs offer just that opportunity to substantially increase the rate of transfer.

Ah, if only education were that simple—or anything like the injection or "transfer" of information from one person to another. I fear that his willingness to be uncritically dazzled by the efficient delivery of content has distracted Tabarrok from appreciating how academics experiment with a variety of teaching tactics, tools, and methods. The cartoon Tabarrok draws of higher education being a series of huge lectures taught by less-than-master professors does not accurately capture the diversity of higher education in the United States or the world. Beyond that, Tabarrok conflates being a student with being a consumer. He writes "In the online world, consumers need not each consume at the same time, and suppliers need not produce at the moment of consumption" (Tabarrok 2012).

Higher education is a complex process through which one is merely guided. It's a series of experiments that test one's capacities, assess one's talents, and focus one's interests, as well as enable the acculturation into the educated middle class. Along the way there are licensing procedures, awards, successes, failures, heartbreaks, and hangovers. There is, of course, a tangle of productions, consumptions, and commercial transactions embedded within higher education. But there is no single act of production or consumption that captures either the purpose or value of higher education.

Tabarrok acknowledges the value of the "college experience," but he makes a mistake of distinguishing it from what happens in a course. Courses don't end when the lecture is over and the book is closed. They are essential and embedded parts of a rich, humane project. Sometimes courses are the least important element of the process of education. Some people, like Bruce Springsteen, learn "more from the three-minute record baby than [they] ever learned in school" (*Born in the U.S.A.* 1984). But many of us would not have encountered that three-minute record without the social and intellectual petri dish we call the American university campus.

The classroom has rich value in itself. It's a safe, almost sacred space where students can try on ideas for size in real time, gently criticize others, challenge authority, and drive conversations in new directions. But that does not mean that classrooms can't or shouldn't be simulated. And for the economic reasons Tabarrok cites there are good reasons to simulate classrooms.

However, courses are not anything like plays—unless they are very bad courses. And online courses are not anything like movies—unless they are really boring movies. I have taught online for years with some success and some failure, as well as a lot of experimentation and learning. But online teaching and MOOCs are not the same thing. In many ways they are antithetical. Online teaching has been succeeding for almost twenty years now. When done well or poorly, online teaching overcomes the very costs Tabarrok cites—transportation, opportunity, etc. Yet when done well, online courses include rich, almost constant interactions among students and faculty, a constant forum for feedback and correction, and space and time for conversation beyond the contours of the course material.

MOOCs, on the other hand, are more like fancy textbooks. They are all about the mass market and not the rich connectivity that established online courses offer their limited collection of students. MOOCs condense and fracture course material and present it in the pithiest, shallowest form. They lack improvisation, serendipity, and familiarity. They pander to the broadest possible audience, because in the MOOC economy—such as it is—enrollment is currency and quality is measured by the number of people who have checked in without subtracting the number who have checked out.

That's not to say that MOOCs could not improve greatly, as I trust they will. But the unfounded hyperbole surrounding MOOCs ignores the real outstanding work professors in all fields have been doing in integrating digital and multimedia tools into their courses and the outstanding work being done with online courses that have reasonable controlled enrollments. Of course, you can't make headlines with an outstanding traditional online course on accounting. You can only make headlines by "enrolling" more than five hundred thousand "students" (most of whom disappear almost instantly) in a MOOC or—better yet—"branding" a MOOC as an extension of a celebrity academic.

That leads me to Tabarrok's and Friedman's claim that MOOCs offer a way for the most students to encounter the best teachers. How do we know that the best teachers are the ones doing the MOOCs? How do we know that the most popular MOOCs are the best? Are we to assume that popularity is a proxy for quality? In short, we should not assume that.

Quality teaching is contextual. My sister teaches math in a community college. She has students of all ages, most with a limited foundation in math. Most have children and work several jobs. She draws them into the field, inspires them to push further, gives them frank feedback, and spends hours with them after class. I, on the other hand, stand in front of hundreds of the brightest, most privileged young Americans and tell them how copyright works and privacy doesn't. I have a global reputation as an author and scholar. My sister has a local reputation as a caring yet demanding teacher. Which Vaidhyanathan is the better teacher? Anyone who witnessed our courses would conclude that my sister is. But "the market" foolishly rewards me with prestige, a higher salary, more prepared and acculturated students, and global recognition. Which one of us would attract a bigger MOOC following? For this reason and others, you are not going to see either Vaidhyanathan performing for the MOOC audience any time soon.

MIT president Rafael Reif, in his inaugural address in September 2012, declared that MOOCs represent "a great step forward for humanity, a step that we should all celebrate. I am deeply proud that MIT and its edX partners, Harvard and UC Berkeley, are helping to lead this revolution, higher education's most profound technological transformation in more than 500 years" (Koch 2012). How could President Reif possibly know that MOOCs represent any significant change to American higher education, let alone its "most profound technological transformation in more than 500 years"?

As someone who has sat in many a classroom in Austin, Texas, I would nominate air conditioning for that honor. And as someone who researches the ways that technology affects society and vice versa, I would nominate the rise of the mainframe computer in the 1950s and 1960s before a simple web-based platform that hosts text and video.

This may or may not be the dawn of a new technological age for higher education. But it is certainly the dawn of a new era of unfounded hyperbole.

So let's focus on what we can learn and accomplish from the MOOC experiment and leave behind the unfounded hyperbole. And, let's take some time to examine the damage that MOOC madness has done to higher education.

When saying MOOC, the accent is on the "Massive." Everything exciting about MOOCs comes from their potential (if often fleeting) massive enrollments. And everything troubling and challenging about MOOCs reflects their massiveness as well.

MOOC "madvocates" continue to presume fame is some sort of proxy for teaching ability. They also presume that the part-time status of the great majority of America's college teachers indicates that the quality of their courses is necessarily below those of star professors at the constellation of elite research universities, without realizing that most courses in America are taught by struggling adjuncts for absurdly low remuneration is a problem that can be solved by increasing their status, pay, and benefits. It's not a reason to double down on the star system and dream that MOOCs can render those hardworking adjuncts redundant. As someone who has hired, fired, and assessed dozens of adjunct and full-time instructors, I can attest that there is no correlation between one's status and one's teaching skills.

If we support the MOOC experiment it would be foolish to do so without confronting the serious incentive problems that MOOCs present to teachers, students, and institutions of higher education. These are not reasons to quit MOOCs. They are reasons to take them seriously and strive to maximize the rewards of MOOCs while curbing the perverse incentives. We should offer MOOCs that aim for many levels of expertise and in many languages. We should not reward universities or faculty based on initial, inflated enrollment. We should question the "O" as in "open" because the flood of trolls will show up in MOOC discussions, threatening to ruin everyone's best efforts. We should ask why universities are not hosting and launching their own homegrown MOOCs when the software is simple and the talent is all in-house. Why engage with private companies that have completely different missions and demands than that of universities?

The current incentives are all out of whack. And all this attention paid to MOOCs is counterproductive to their potential success. We should be encouraging and rewarding experimentation at all levels of enrollment, in the widest array of platforms, with a goal of enhancing quality teaching instead of merely crowing about quantity.

We should be investing in skill development across the teaching faculties and putting part-time teachers on full-time salaries. We should be championing the potential synergies between great research and great teaching. We should reverse the dangerous trend of federal disinvestment from scientific research, the sort of funding that paid for Sergey Brin's graduate work at Stanford and directly funded the development of PageRank, the core algorithm that has made Google ubiquitous and Brin rich and famous.

We should be justifiably proud of the remarkable and enviable triumphs of American higher education. Instead we find most recent conversations about higher education echoing around this one tiny (and so far trivial) aspect of the complex and diverse ecosystem of higher education. This focus on technological platforms at the expense of actual threats, challenges, and successes robs us of the ability to have sober, informed debates about the proper level and style of investment in higher education. So I suggest we let MOOCs grow and do their best work, learn from successes and mistakes, and stop assuming that they are the simple answer to anything meaningful and profound in the production and distribution of knowledge.

References

Asimov, Nanette. 2013. "UC Online Courses Fail to Lure Outsiders." *SFGATE*, February 22. http://www.sfgate.com/education/article/UC-online-courses-fail-to-lure-outsiders-4173639.php.

Foster, Andrea L. 2005. "The Avatars of Research." *Chronicle of Higher Education*, September 30. http://chronicle.com/article/The-Avatars-of-Research/13850.

Friedman, Thomas L. 2013. "Revolution Hits the Universities." *New York Times*, January 26. http://www.nytimes.com/2013/01/27/opinion/sunday/friedman-revolution-hits-the-universities.html.

Hechinger Report. 2015. "End of California's Digital Campus Is a Blow for MOOCs." *US News & World Report*, April 14. http://www.usnews.com/news/college-of-tomorrow/articles/2015/04/14/end-of-californias-digital-campus-is-a-blow-for-moocs.

Hof, Robert. 2006. "My Virtual Life." *BloombergView*, April 30. http://www.bloomberg.com/news/articles/2006-04-30/my-virtual-life.

Jaffe, Sarah. 2015. "'We Won't Pay': Students in Debt Take On For-Profit College Institution. *Guardian*, February 23. http://www.theguardian.com/education/2015/feb/23/student-debt-for-profit-colleges.

Jaschik, Scott. 2012. "E-Mails Show U.Va. Board Wanted a Big Online Push | InsideHigherEd." *Inside Higher Ed*, June 20. https://www.insidehighered.com/news/2012/06/20/e-mails-show-uva-board-wanted-big-online-push.

Katz, Elihu, Paul F. Lazarsfeld, Columbia University, and Bureau of Applied Social Research. 1955. *Personal Influence: The Part Played by People in the Flow of Mass Communications.* Glencoe: Free Press.

Koch, Katie. 2012. "A President Next Door." *Harvard Gazette*, September 12. http://news.harvard.edu/gazette/story/2012/09/a-president-next-door/.

Lane, Julia, Victoria Stodden, Stefan Bender, and Helen Nissenbaum. 2014. *Privacy, Big Data, and the Public Good: Frameworks for Engagement.* Cambridge: Cambridge University Press.

Lastowka, F. Gregory. 2010. *Virtual Justice: The New Laws of Online Worlds.* New Haven: Yale University Press.

Lastowka, Greg, and Dan Hunter. 2003. "The Laws of the Virtual Worlds." Social Science Research Network. Posted May 29. http://papers.ssrn.com/abstract=402860.

Losh, Elizabeth M. 2014. *The War on Learning: Gaining Ground in the Digital University.* Cambridge: MIT Press.

Moore, Janet C. 2004. *Elements of Quality Online Education: Into the Mainstream: Wisdom from the Sloan Consortium.* Needham: Sloan Consortium.

Pappano, Laura. 2012. "The Year of the MOOC." *New York Times*, November 2. http://www.nytimes.com/2012/11/04/education/edlife/massive-open-online-courses-are-multiplying-at-a-rapid-pace.html.

Peachey, Anna, Julia Gillen, Daniel Livingstone, and Sarah Smith-Robbins. 2010. *Researching Learning in Virtual Worlds.* London: Springer Science & Business Media.

Reif, L. Rafael. 2013. "MIT's President: Better, More Affordable Colleges Start Online." *Time*, September 26. http://nation.time.com/2013/09/26/online-learning-will-make-college-cheaper-it-will-also-make-it-better/.

Rice, Andrew. 2012. "What the Failed Removal of UVA President Teresa Sullivan Means for Higher Education." *New York Times*, September 11. http://www.nytimes.com/2012/09/16/magazine/teresa-sullivan-uva-ouster.html.

Tabarrok, Alex. 2012. "Why Online Education Works." *Cato Unbound*, November. http://www.cato-unbound.org/2012/11/12/alex-tabarrok/why-online-education-works.

Thackray, Liz, Judith Good, and Katherine Howland. 2010. "Learning and Teaching in Virtual Worlds: Boundaries, Challenges and Opportunities." In *Researching Learning in Virtual Worlds*, edited by Anna Peachey, Julia Gillen, Daniel Livingstone, and Sarah Smith-Robbins, 139–58. Human-Computer Interaction Series. London: Springer. http://link.springer.com/chapter/10.1007/978-1-84996-047-2_8.

Tomsho, Robert. 2003. "Columbia University to Close Fathom.com E-Learning Service." *Wall Street Journal*, January 6. http://www.wsj.com/articles/SB104188231770411424?mg=id-wsj.

Vaidhyanathan, Siva. 2012. "The Right Way to Lead Higher Education through the Digital Age." *Chronicle of Higher Education Blogs: Innovations*, June 25. http://chronicle.com/blogs/innovations/the-right-way-to-lead-higher-education-through-the-digital-age/33031.

Vara, Vauhini. 2015. "A Student-Debt Revolt Begins." *New Yorker*, February 23. http://www.newyorker.com/business/currency/student-debt-revolt-begins.

ng the "C" in MOOC: Of Crises, Critique, and Criticality in Higher Education

NISHANT SHAH

In 2013, a seventy-four-year old man in India, Shyam Singh, who runs a corner photocopying shop on the campus of the Delhi School of Economics in New Delhi, found himself fighting what might be one of the most crucial battles around online and connected learning. Singh, who has spent a large part of his life—three decades—working at the University of Delhi's Central Research Library and the Ratan Tata Library, operating unwieldy machines of reproduction, saved for thirty years to buy a couple of digital photocopying machines and start a small photocopying shop after retirement (Roshan 2012). His shop—the Rameshwari Photocopy Service—was actually authorized by the Delhi School of Economics, which offered him an official license to facilitate the photocopying needs of the students and faculty in the school who would come to get their course material photocopied out of books that they could almost never afford to buy and were not easily available in the university's public lending libraries. Singh compiled course packs—a collection of different texts prescribed in a course, anthologized and bound together—which allowed students to buy all the texts prescribed for their curricula at affordable rates.

It came as quite a surprise to Singh, when one day, he was sued by a consortium made of three of the largest academic publishers—Oxford University Press, Cambridge University Press, and the Taylor and Francis Group—in the High Court of New Delhi, claiming damages of six million Indian rupees for copyright infringement for commercial gains (Liang and Basheer 2013). Singh, who had grown up in a country that has always deployed the rhetoric of universal education as a fundamental right of its citizens,[1] had always

---

1. In the interview with Roshan (2012), Singh says, "They speak of *sarva shiksha* (universal education). Why don't they sell cheaper books? . . . There are IAS officers' children here, but

thought of his work as facilitating equal access to students who would otherwise have been unable to afford the education. Hence, he was taken aback when the high court issued an injunction restraining him from providing copies of chapters from textbooks published by the three international publishers. In effect, Rameshwari Photocopy Service was shut down. Singh's legal battle found some respite, as the high court, in September 2016, dismissed the copyright infringement petition initiated in August 2012, by the consortium of publishing houses (Liang 2016). Although Singh in his fight against the intellectual property conglomeration of publishers who made a "scapegoat" and an "example" of his small photocopying shop has found unexpected support from academic, student, university, and popular media, much of the conversations around this case has been ensconced in lawyer-speak about limits and exceptions to intellectual property and copyright regimes both in the global and the national arena (Bhatia 2013). The populist debates have drawn a David-versus-Goliath picture, where the underdog is being crushed under the mighty heels of evil publishing houses, where the focus is on economics, numbers, and revenues, as well as the absurdly disproportionate value of the claim made by the triumvirate of publishers.

As Liang points out, Singh's expensive and long-drawn legal battle has culminated in an exceptional judgment that proclaims that copyright is "a statutory right and not a natural right," and not a moral right either. This is going to have definitive and lasting impact on the intellectual property laws and copyright exceptions in India, which have been heavily lobbied by global trade and political forces for harsher enforcement and more conservative interpretations. The petitioners are ready to appeal this judgment, and there will be longer nuanced readings of the fair rights clause of the copyright act in India. And yet, this critical legal battle has had no space in conversations at the heart of education transformation and digital education infrastructure in India or, indeed, in the global discourse. The jury is still out on what massive open online courses (MOOCs), which includes digital, online, connected, and distributed learning mechanisms, and platforms are and what function they play in imagining the future of higher education.[2] But, to make the debates more concrete, I want to locate MOOCs at the pivotal

---

poorer kids also come here to study," clearly showing that the photocopying services were the mainstay of access to knowledge for students with socioeconomic disadvantages.

2. It might be possible to understand MOOCs as a "wicked problem"—problems that refuse to be understood and cannot be named or resolved because they are systemically a part of the larger complex and extricating them is impossible. For more on "wicked problems," see the project the Wicked Series at https://www.kl.nl/projecten/the-wicked-series/.

point of choosing between a university of the future and the future of the university.

The case of the Rameshwari Photocopy Service illustrates this tension wonderfully. On the one hand, it is about the infrastructure of education. And yet, it doesn't get recognized as legitimate infrastructure in the MOOC debates. Given the nature of funding and the power of those who are defining the infrastructure for this new learning environment, MOOC infrastructure has emerged as an extremely normative structure.[3] Even as it standardizes learning experiences into information-exchange protocols, it also invalidates other kinds of creative, remixed, reappropriated forms of infrastructure that have made access to knowledge possible in emerging parts of the world.

On the other hand, the case is not seen as critical to our construction of the university of the future. This university is gentrified, available only to those who are legitimate users[4] and clearly only for those who can afford to have access to these new resource bases. Hence, even when Singh received support from academics, it was more a personal endorsement rather than a professional examination of the ways in which universities are actively pursuing closing of access for those that are not deemed worthy (Lessig 2013).[5] In this essay, using broad strokes, I look at two key narratives that interlace the idea of a crisis and the concern of higher education that inform the practice, policy, development, and infrastructure building in contemporary global MOOC debates.

I shall show, in looking at the specificity of the location of Rameshwari Photocopy and the particular figure of Shyam Singh, how we need to question the persuasive construction of the higher-education crisis that emerges from a few knowledge centers but is perceived as a global concern. I shall argue that there are indeed fundamental crises that this battle around copyright and intellectual property generates for education and learning, but they are very different from the preoccupations that are engineered in MOOC conversations but are oblivious to historical privilege and patronage.

3. FemTechNet has questioned the normative MOOC structure by proposing and operating a distributed open collaborative course (DOCC) that embodies new and alternative forms of learning, pedagogy, and collaborative research. More about it can be found at http://femtechnet .org/docc/.

4. Gibson (1984) in his coinage of the word "cyberspace" had deliberately used the idea of a "legitimate user" on the web, indicating that the web had a prescriptive, normative, and legitimizing function that excludes those that are not eligible.

5. Lessig's (2013) moving eulogy to open-access activist Aaron Swartz, who died in 2013, following persecution by MIT and the US government, shows the complicity of universities in supporting the intellectual property rights of corporations at the cost of human lives.

Higher-Education Crises

It might be an easy, albeit facetious, argument to make that the increased focus on MOOCs is a response to a set of perceived and growing higher-education crises (Blumenstyk 2014; Sommer 1995). The digital turn seems to have introduced such an unprecedented transformation of social, cultural, political, and economic orders that the foundational values of liberal higher education seem to be obsolete or in need of a dramatic upgrade. The seismic rupture that the digital paradigm produces invokes two warring factions.

On the one side are people who are convinced that this is history in the making, where we can do away with the behemoth of walled-garden disciplines and academic silos to make way for new conditions of knowledge production and learning (Drucker 2009). This death knell of the traditional educational complex often finds its proponents who advocate for a radical restructuring of the role, the function, the relevance, the form, and format of education in contemporary global societies (Corneli and Mikroyannidis 2012). They believe that the "time-space distanciation" (Harvey 1990) and shrinking of our lives offers a new possibility for reimagining what the university of the future is going to look like (Kamenetz 2010). This opportunity of redesign and reengineering of education in networked information societies finds interest simultaneously from new information markets that are shaping information and attention economies, as well as from neoliberal development states that are depending increasingly on public-private partnerships to build physical and digital educational infrastructure.

On the other side are people who see this call for upgrading the university as a threat to the future of the university (Barnett 2012). They insist that the university, historically speaking, has been an evolving, changing, adapting, and mutating form, and that the future of the university is not in shutting down the education system as know it, but in examining the new possibilities that arise (Jeffrey and Manganiello 1998). Voices on this side argue that the focus on the university of the future, rather than the future of the university, erodes the values of autonomy, critique, intellectual freedom, and creative spirit of education and learning, reducing it to skill-based rote learning tailored toward market demands of labor and employment (Losh 2014). They have shown how an emphasis on evaluating humanities and social sciences through quantified matrices produced by technology developers and administrators who are constructing new universities as professional spaces focused more on gross enrollment ratios and deskilled adjunct labor rather than on intellectual rigor or creative experimentation (Rajadhyaksha 2011).

It is not my intention to argue for either side. I am more intrigued by the fact that, regardless of which side of the battle line people pitch their tents, there remains a complicit agreement that we are living in a time of higher-education crises. All efforts on both sides—or even for those who straddle that hyphenated in-betweenness—are invested in looking at how these crises will be resolved. There is no questioning of the nature, the validity, or the scope of the crises. It is imagined as universal, definitive, prescriptive, and normative, and already understood. This then gives two expected, prewired responses to the interlaced relationship between higher education and crises that I seek to unpack and resist from the location in new knowledge societies like India.

The Crisis of Higher Education

The first and the most prominent crisis narrative that remains central to the MOOC-based imagination of the world is that higher education is in a state of crisis. There are enough symptoms that are identified for such a crisis. There is declining state investment and a slowing down of public infrastructure for public education. There is an accounting of education that is not the same as the accountability of education, thus leading to a trend of counting and quantifying that constructs education systems in the service of the market, with universities losing their intellectual autonomy (Zajda 2007). There is an apparent decline in the quality of education since it seems irrelevant and incapable to deal with the accelerated transformation that we experience.[6] While all these narratives—largely emerging from the global North centers of knowledge and privilege—are indeed to be taken seriously because they mark the end of an academic system as it has been known, it is a problem to take them as global crises.

Many of these narratives are marked by an unacknowledged privilege and a sense of entitlement that most of academia in newly emerging information societies cannot take for granted. This crisis narrative is marked by a romantic imagination of education as outside the folds of logics and logistics of late capitalism. It proposes a prelapsarian past for the university, imagining it as a safe haven of cerebral celebrations and intellectual inquiry. In many ways, it mimics the same argument that education critics like Karl Jasper (1961) have been proposing since the 1960s—a self-generated condition of anxiety

---

6. This is the most clearly visible in the high number of opinion editorials in popular media that insist that educational quality has been deteriorating, especially with the arrival of the digital technologies; see, e.g., Gordon (2013) and *Economist* (2012).

that justifies the deliberate separation of the university from the "real world," especially in the humanities and social sciences, which mistake their critique of the powers of market and state as a sign of being outside the realms of politics and economics.

The first separation of the political can be experienced in a cloistered existence that has resulted in the "disciplinization" of education. Look at almost any young scholar's account of their own work, conference presentations, or, indeed, strategies for publication, and they all revolve entirely around questions of method, citation, references, and impact factors. This separation of education from the realms of politics and activism is both futile and sinister, and it pervades both sides of the MOOC discourse. For people worried about the future of the university, the political seems to rob them of the space for experimentation, rhetoric, reading, and aesthetics that they perceive as removed from the quotidian practices of living and survival. For those interested in creating new universities of the future, it becomes a hindrance that distracts the learners from the professional goals of relevant learning.

In both cases, the new metrics of measuring the relevance and defining the role of education in the future are confused. They work with utopia or dystopia as their models, and thus continue to cling to dreams of a knowledge that is either "pure" or "functional" without recognizing its role in political battlegrounds that universities embody. They ignore the basic lessons that feminists have shown us that knowledge and learning are political. They refuse to acknowledge the power that universities wield to disrupt and reengineer the world around us. They hence perceive the digital as either a threat to the separation from politics or an opportunity to escape the political possibility. In both the cases, the response is to guard academia from the realm of political activism and propagate the futile quest for an objective and pure knowledge. In fact, we play into the hands of administrative nightmares, where we concentrate all our efforts at quantifying tasks, time, resources, outputs, and committees, rather than focusing on impact, critique, resistance, and politics, which are the founding principles of education and learning.

The second separation is in how the university is imagined outside the logics and logistics of economic circulation and market demands. This is not a condition that is familiar for most postcolonial and developing societies. In countries like India, education has always clearly been associated with socioeconomic mobility and aspiration. Indeed, it is a key characteristic of most postcolonial societies that education, even when it is enshrined as a fundamental right, has been perceived as having a deep and inextricable connection with the idea of development, progress, affluence, and reform. Universities have not only been at the heart of knowledge industries but also are often seen as a state apparatus toward building the new social and economic order (Nair 2005).[7]

Similarly, the lament about declining infrastructure is hard to believe, when compared to the global standards of education in developing and underdeveloped countries. It seems to be located in a geographical bubble that seems to resist the reality that, as globalization circulates capital and bodies, it also circulates debt and precariousness. The loss of resources and authority that generates the anxiety that is attributed to the digital turn is a reluctance to realize that new knowledge and information centers are growing in other parts of the world. Hence, in India, for instance, educational infrastructure is not declining. In fact, we are not experiencing the same kind of crisis that dominates the "global" discourse. The last decade has seen not only a proliferation of new resources and campuses for public higher education but also a steady growth of learners, including first-generation learners, entering the university system. There are increased opportunities for research, education, and employment, as well as a renewed investment through public-private partnerships in creating centers of academic and research excellence. This has reversed the "brain drain" that had marked the outflow of students to Europe and North America in the last decades of the twentieth century. There is a quest by universities in these continents to open satellite campuses and new educational systems in these countries. State initiatives like the National Mission for Education through Information and Communication Technologies (NMEICT) are deploying networked education plans and models to connect the interiors of the nation on an information superhighway leading to both unprecedented infrastructure growth and employment for new educated workforces.[8]

This burgeoning information economy and the recognition of new futures of education in a country like India inspire cases like the publishing houses versus Rameshwari Photocopiers. This might seem low-tech, but they are about establishing power over the informational futures of education complexes. But the global crisis discourse is so wedded to infrastructure and in-

7. Nair (2005) looks at the history of Bangalore as the IT City and maps out how entire regimes of education and knowledge were established over many decades to produce a city like Bangalore (or indeed Gurgaon in Northern India), which brings together the impulses of education in close synergy with the demands of the state and the market.

8. Documentation around this state initiative, including the massive financial and economic infrastructure, but also the political and social vision of the role that education has to play in the massive transformation of India from being a developing country to becoming an information superpower, can be found at http://www.nmeict.ac.in/.

novation that it does not accommodate for these low-tech and fundamental battles around intellectual property, access, and the war that governments and markets from the erstwhile knowledge centers are waging against the global commons. The first proposition I have, then, is to question the global nature of this crisis that is naturalized in both the deployment of and the resistance to MOOCs—both sides imagine either that there is a global crisis that needs to be resolved by either implementing MOOC-based projects that make traditional education accountable and countable, or that there is a global crisis that is being constructed equally and evenly because education and resources are being digitized, virtualized, and technologized. Instead I am going to propose that indeed a crisis is emerging in higher education, but this crisis is not about building infrastructure and metrics of quantification. It is about access, possession, authorship, and authority of knowledge, which we are losing increasingly, and, with an inward focus on the university and its survival, we ignore our complicity and safeguarding of walled gardens of the traditional university system.

The Crisis in Higher Education

The second narrative around crisis and higher education is a shift from the global to the national, where, even when there is no crisis *of* higher education in India, there is an invocation of a crisis *in* higher education. Conversations of this crisis within higher education center on merit, quality, autonomy, rigor, and relevance. Thus, for the proponents of MOOCs there is a growing argument that the university is in ruins (Readings 1996). Classrooms are filled with students who are not interested or engaged in education because they find it irrelevant (Kim 2014). They argue that teachers in the classrooms are not competent enough because they are outdated, both in their research and in their technologies of teaching. The digital web has produced such a huge information surplus that the teacher is redundant in classrooms, and indeed, classrooms are redundant in the DIY, each-one-teach-one distributed networked space of information exchange and learning. MOOCs are a response to all these problems—MOOCs highlight only the competent teachers who can produce material of excellent pedagogical value and deliver it to students on platforms that are collaborative, mixed media, engaged, and more in tune with the immersed web environments already occupied by these millennials.

For the detractors of MOOCs, these same problems persist, but they believe that MOOCs will only amplify and augment these problems. Because MOOCs are imagined as extension or virtualization of the existing classrooms, they not only replicate all the problems of the traditional classroom

(Chesley 2013) but also add a new set of difficulties because of the distanced and distributed nature of pedagogy that they deploy (Littlefield 2014). Pointing to other failed efforts at distance and connected learning using print and telecommunications technologies, MOOC detractors argue that MOOCs are not the answer to this crisis (Lurrilard 2014). But they do acknowledge that the MOOC offers the possibility of connecting to students who might not have access to educational possibilities because of a number of disadvantages, such as location, affordability, gender, sexuality, or physical mobility. Hence the bigger question is whether the MOOC is a viable solution to the crisis in higher education. There is no questioning that the crisis is present, growing, and in need of being resolved immediately.

None of these sides would actually acknowledge the case against Shyam Singh as critical. They would see it as unfortunate or mark it as a sign of the greed of intellectual property regime owners, but not integral to the crisis in higher education. However, a quick look at the case gives us a different idea. Singh, in his corner photocopying shop made most of his living creating course packages. In a country like India, where a large majority of the students in a public university cannot afford to buy all their textbooks, and library resources are not adequate to store enough copies to cater to the students (Danish 2012), without the availability of photocopying services, students would be left with no access to their textbooks (Agre 2000).[9] This is why the fair use exception to copyright in India clearly allows for complete reproduction of books that are either scarcely available or too expensive for the students (Liang 2010). Even when the Union Grants Commission of India makes an effort to make the essential textbooks available at subsidized prices, the supplementary reading and other resource material is still prohibitively expensive, especially for a student community that does not get stipends and scholarships very easily.

The crisis, which is perceived or constructed in higher education in India, is a response to this growing student demography, which is more diverse than ever before. Educationalist and Dalit feminist Sharmila Rege[10] looks at the data of the last five decades and argues that years of affirmative action and systemic opening of universities to first-generation learners has finally started showing results in the diversity of students on campus. Students from castes

---

9. Agre's (2000) emphasis on how the most quotidian practices of learning and knowledge distribution in the academia are contingent on these low-cost processes that defy copyright regimes are particularly worth underlining in this argument.

10. In conversation with Sharmila Rege at the KrantiJyoti Savitribai Phule Women's Studies Centre at Pune University. More about Rege's work can be found at http://www.unipune.ac.in /snc/womens_studies_centre/.

marked as backward or underdeveloped, students from families with socioeconomic poverty, and students marked as female and queer are all slowly
becoming visible on the landscape of the university. In the last two decades,
India has seen two, massive upper-class, upper-caste, patriarchal student
protests that have sought to suspend the affirmative action that grants privileged access to education for students who are marked with sociopolitical-
economic disadvantage (Mathur 2004).[11] Rege suggests that the crisis in
higher education was generated, not because education was unable to keep
up with the rapid transformations of neoliberal development, but because
education is no longer the playground of the upper- and middle classes. It
is the appearance of the nonnormative bodies and the visible influx of these
identities that refuse to be assimilated or integrated into the facsimile of stu-
dentship created by those in power that leads to the engineering of this crisis.

The MOOC-based solution, then, is clearly a way of creating a new exclusive environment in a country with less than 20 percent broadband Internet
penetration (Walia 2012).[12] It is a solution that seeks to create new elite structures that are ostensibly open but without any supporting infrastructure that
would grant access to students on geographical or sociopolitical fringes. This
is exactly why the case against Singh is not thought of as important or crucial to the conversations on MOOCs—because they look at the students that
Singh caters to as the crisis, rather than their access to education as critical.
The argument about quality and excellence is bolstered by the new calls for
privatization of education, where the global standards of research and intellectual inquiry are to be preserved for those who can afford it, whereas the
public education system can now be disinvested from and left for the new
bodies that have gained entry into the old boys club that the university has
been. Whether or not MOOCs are an answer to the perceived crisis of quality
and relevance in higher education is a false question to ask. Instead we need
to examine what is at stake in the engineering of this crisis. It is necessary
to locate the anxiety that generates this crisis and calls for a resolution. The

11. Known as the protests against the Mandal Commission, which recommended continuing
affirmative action in the form of seat reservations and quotas for students from backward castes
in public education and employment, the agitations reached a wild frenzy when students tried
to self-immolate in protest against these "special favors." Mathur's (2004) work on the subject
is a good introduction for those seeking an inroad into these fairly large and complex historical
debates.

12. Fixed broadband penetration in India at the end of 2012 was a dismal 7 percent. However, as Walia (2013) points out, the smart mobile revolution gives a projected connectivity of
six hundred million users by 2015, of which a sizeable people will subscribe to data connections.
But broadband is still nascent.

proposition is to understand that the vocabulary of crisis management is actually about managing the unwanted bodies in the classrooms and separating them from those in power.

Critical Higher Education

When it comes to MOOCs, globally and in particular locations, there seems to be a whole lot of noise about whether MOOCs are good or bad, a cure or a problem, or an answer or the beginning of a new question. But all of them reiterate the idea that higher education is in crisis and that there is a crisis in higher education. The crisis narrative shuts down more nuanced questioning about who engineers this crisis, what is at stake in identifying this crisis, and how the idea of a crisis hides the shift in centers of power around knowledge, information, and learning. It is necessary to see the forced historical separation of the university and spaces of higher education from the realms of political action and economic logics to create better metrics for understanding the form, function, and role of the university in the future.

While examining the possibilities and perils of MOOC-based restructuring of universities is important, it is necessary to escape the either-or divide. And in doing that, it becomes important to understand that the perceptions of crisis in infrastructure of higher education and universities are not global. It is a crisis that gets constructed because erstwhile spaces of patronage and power are experiencing the global distribution and circulation of precariousness, even as new centers are emerging in the networked circuits of global knowledge production. It is a crisis that follows the same logic of economic slowdown and paranoia about jobs being stolen that followed the growth of the outsourcing industry as companies started looking for cheaper and more precarious labor in developing countries. It is important to remember that in the brouhaha that followed the outsourcing debates, the attention was paid only on the first world jobs being lost, and not on the precarious and perilous conditions within which the new service providers in developing countries were being hired by companies that turned a blind eye to their inhuman and subpar working conditions.[13]

Dealing with this "crisis" in the language used by those who generate the crisis adds another layer of problems. Identifying students as resources or

---

13. These questions were foregrounded, for instance, only when the Savar Mall collapsed in Bangladesh (Yardley 2013), killing workers employed in exploitative outsourcing markets, and when an investigation was made into the worker's suicides at Foxconn in China (Fair Labor Association 2012), which assembles Apple products.

investments and understanding them as "actors" and "active learners" instead of recognizing the costs of becoming actors, as well as the contexts that do not take active learning for granted, immediately create an elite group that would be equipped to deal with the solutions being offered. The intersections in MOOC discussions generally take into account the network infrastructure problems of access, usage, adoption, penetration, interfaces, interactivity, and collaboration. So embedded are we in this language of connected technologies that low-tech solutions or practices are not only disregarded but also considered superfluous and made invisible in the material practices of learning. These intersections are in the service of the infrastructure and operationalization of learning, with no interest in the learners and their situations. MOOC-driven debates need to focus more on the values and politics of learning rather than concentrating on the characteristics, manifestations, and appearances of these values. Openness, for instance, cannot be a self-explanatory word, and questions about who gets to be open, what needs to be opened, what infrastructure is required to attain openness, what are its limitations, and who can and cannot afford to participate in the open processes, need due attention.

Simultaneously, the crisis in higher education that suggests that universities are no longer relevant to the needs of our times also needs to be taken with a pinch of salt. It is important to figure out who perceives this crisis and who benefits from strengthening this narrative of crisis that allows for a disinvestment from public education and the building of MOOC-based education delivery platforms that emerge from public-private partnerships. Looking at questions of intellectual property regimes, copyright universes, modes and forms of access, the mechanisms of knowledge production, and systems of knowledge distribution becomes important. If MOOCs are to be taken seriously, they will have to address all these questions at the policy level, but these questions also need to be incorporated into substantial and academic debates about the university of the future that we stand for (Goldberg 2012).[14]

But this chapter is not to discount the crises that do surround higher-education debates. What it is asking to dismantle is the crisis narrative that almost demands a disaster management response, producing blueprints of short-term interventions and strategies of immediate relief. Instead it is proposing, that we replace crisis with critical. In systems engineering, a critical system is a system whose "failure" could threaten human life, the system's own

---

14. Goldberg (2012) argues that we need to think not only about the university of the future, but the university that we can actually stand for—making a call for repoliticizing our conversations around university infrastructure and engagement.

environment or the existence of the organization that operates the system. Failure, in this scenario, is not merely about failure to conform to a specification but refers to any potentially threatening system behavior. Thus, in thinking of higher education as a critical system, we have to debate not whether MOOCs are going to succeed or fail but what happens if our higher-education systems fail entirely. The focus has to shift from the MOOC, which is only one specification of connected learning, to the very idea of learning and teaching itself, reconfiguring it so that the spaces of higher education remain stable, functioning, and able to support MOOC-based projects, not as a threat to the system but as an integral and integrated function of the system.

Similarly, in software development for critical systems, there is a three-step process that is generally deployed. The first is process engineering and management. We thus need to think of the university not as a natural monolith but as an engineered artifact that has constantly and historically been in flux responding to and creating the realities of the contemporary. This allows us to stop thinking about the university as nonchanging or removed from the accelerated temporality of the digital. The second parameter is the selection of the appropriate tools and environments for the system. Only once we have the model of a future of the university and the university of the future can we start effectively testing the proposed system of higher education by emulation and observing its effectiveness. The third important parameter is to address the larger context of legal and regulatory requirements, thus opening our concerns about learning and education to the larger political battles of openness, sharing, copyleft, collaborative commons, and infrastructure of access. It is here that a standard can be established, which then becomes a norm that forces the designers of the critical system to stick to the requirements.

This shift from crisis management to critical systems construction is useful because it will question the crisis as a given and look at the impulses and agenda of those who design and engineer this crisis as a global phenomenon. It also opens a clear line of questioning the adequacy of MOOC-like systems to actually address the real problems at hand, foregrounding questions that actually threaten a system failure rather than questions that are only about the testing of different models. It entails intersectional politics where the fights around ownership and nature of the digital technologies—the kind of fights that Rameshwari Photocopy Service are fighting—have to be incorporated in our models of connected future learning to make it into a robust system. It makes people like Shyam Singh and his audience central to the debates around MOOCs, rather than invisible in the imagination of a hypothetical user who remains abstract and hence removed from the spheres of political and economic operations.

This chapter is a call to wed critique to the critical and see what emerges and what new flows and trajectories of future learning emerge. And this time the answers and solutions are not going to be in the structures of privilege that are suddenly experiencing precariousness or the erstwhile centers and communities of power who feel infiltrated by the opening of universities. Instead it is going to be examining the idea of the university, the form of education, the purpose of learning, and the mode of teaching, as well as treating each of them as a crucial function, whose collapse can threaten both the critical infrastructure of the university of the future and the critical faculty of the future of the university.

References

Agre, Philip. 2000. "Infrastructure and Institutional Change in the Networked University." *Information, Communication, and Society* 3 (4): 494–507.

Barnett, Ronald, ed. 2012. *The Future University: Ideas and Possibilities*. New York: Routledge.

Bhatia, Gautam. 2013. "Copyright and Free Speech—I: Constitutional Arguments against OUP et al in the Delhi University Photocopying Lawsuit." *Indian Constitutional Law and Philosophy*, October 7. https://indconlawphil.wordpress.com/2013/10/07/copyright-and-free-speech-i-constitutional-arguments-against-oup-et-al-in-the-delhi-university-photocopying-lawsuit/.

Blumenstyk, Goldie. 2014. *American Higher Education in Crisis?: What Everyone Needs to Know*. New York: Oxford University Press.

Chesley, Brent. 2013. "My Problem with MOOCs." *Inside Higher Ed*, August 6. https://www.insidehighered.com/views/2013/08/06/essay-mooc-debate-and-what-really-matters-about-teaching.

Corneli, Joseph, and Alexander Mikroyannidis. 2012. "Crowdsourcing Education on the Web: A Role-Based Analysis of Online Learning Communities." In *Collaborative Learning 2.0: Open Education Resources*, edited by Alexandra Lilavati Pereira Okada, Teresa Connolly, and Peter J. Scott, 272–86. Hershey: Information Science Reference.

Danish. 2012. "DU Students Photocopying Academic Books Is Legal." *FirstPost*, August 31. http://www.firstpost.com/india/du-students-photocopying-academic-books-is-legal-437852.html.

Drucker, Johanna. 2009. *Speclab: Digital Aesthetics and Projects in Speculative Computing*. Chicago: University of Chicago Press.

Economist. 2012. "Not What It Used To Be: American Universities Represent Declining Value for Money to their Students," December 1. http://www.economist.com/news/united-states/21567373-american-universities-represent-declining-value-money-their-students-not-what-it.

Fair Labor Association. 2012. "Foxconn Investigation Report," March 29. http://www.fairlabor.org/report/foxconn-investigation-report.

Gibson, William. 1984. *Neuromancer*. New York: Ace Books.

Goldberg, David Theo. 2012. "The University We Are For?" *Huffington Post*, January 21. http://www.huffingtonpost.com/david-theo-goldberg/university-california-protests_b_1106234.html.

Gordon, Robert J. 2013. "The Great Stagnation of American Education." *New York Times*, September 7. http://opinionator.blogs.nytimes.com/2013/09/07/the-great-stagnation-of -american-education/?mtrref=undefined&gwh=50C2E0979C7989D5C955DE1BE092457C &gwt=pay&assetType=opinion.

Harvey, David. 1990. *The Condition of Postmodernity: An Enquiry into the Origins of Cultural Change*. Cambridge: Blackwell.

Jasper, Karl. 1961. *The Idea of the University*. Translated by H. F. Vanderschmidt. London: Peter Owens.

Jeffrey, Lyle David, and Dominic Manganiello, eds. 1998. *Rethinking the Future of the University*. Ottawa: University of Ottawa.

Kamenetz, Anya. 2010. *DIY U*. Canada: Chelsea Green Publishing.

Kim, Paul, ed. 2014. *Massive Open Online Courses: The MOOC Revolution*. New York: Routledge.

Liang, Lawrence. 2010. "Exceptions and Limitations in Indian Copyright Law for Education: An assessment." *Law and Development* 3 (4): 197–240.

———. 2012. "Oxford and Cambridge University Publishers Versus Students of India." *Kafila*, August 27. http://kafila.org/2012/08/27/oxford-and-cambridge-university-publishers-v -students-of-india/.

———. 2013. "Why They Mattered: Aaron Swartz 1986–2013." *Politico*, December 22. http://www .politico.com/magazine/story/2013/12/aaron-swartz-obituary-101418.html.

———. 2016. "Historic Delhi High Court Judgement Dismisses Publishers' Copyright Infringe- ment Petition." *Kafila*, September 20. https://kafila.online/2016/09/20/historic-delhi-high -court-judgement-dismisses-publishers-copyright-infringement-petition/.

Liang, Lawrence, and Shamnad Basheer. 2013. "Of Gandhi and a Godfatherly Copyright Offer: Shamnad Basheer and Lawrence Liang." *Kafila*, May 27. http://kafila.org/2013/05/27/of -gandhi-and-a-godfatherly-copyright-offer-shamnad-basheer-lawrence-liang/.

Littlefield, Jamie. 2014. "The Dark Side of the MOOCs: Big Problems with Massively Open Online Courses." *About Education*, December 20. http://distancelearn.about.com/od/isit foryou/a/The-Dark-Side-Of-The-Moocs-Big-Problems-With-Massively-Open-Online -Courses.htm.

Losh, Elizabeth. 2014. *The War on Learning: Gaining Ground in the Digital University*. Cam- bridge: MIT Press.

Lurrilard, Diana. 2014. "Which Problems Would MOOCs Solve, and How?" *University World News*, July 11. http://distancelearn.about.com/od/isitforyou/a/The-Dark-Side-Of-The -Moocs-Big-Problems-With-Massively-Open-Online-Courses.htm.

Mathur, M. L. 2004. *Encyclopaedia of Backward Castes: Mandal, Media and Aftermath*. New Delhi: Kalpaz Publications.

Nair, Janaki. 2005. *The Promise of the Metropolis: Bangalore's Twentieth Century*. New Delhi: Oxford University Press.

Rajadhyaksha, Ashish. 2011. *The Last Cultural Mile: An Inquiry into Technology and Governance in India*. Bangalore: Centre for Internet & Society.

Readings, Bill. 1996. *The University in Ruins*. Cambridge: Harvard University Press.

Roshan, Manas. 2012. "The Copyright Fight." *Caravan Magazine*, October 2. http://caravan magazine.in/lede/copyright-fight.

Sommer, John W., ed. 1995. *The Academy in Crisis: The Political Economy of Higher Education*. Oakland: Independent Institute.

Vallianeth, Thomas. 2014. "The DU Photocopying Case Thus Far." *SpicyIP*, September 28. http://spicyip.com/2014/09/the-du-photocopying-case-thus-far.html.

Walia, Kunal. 2013. "The Changing Landscape of the Broadband Market in India: Supply-Side Challenges." *Analysis Mason*, April 11. http://www.analysysmason.com/About-Us/News/Newsletter/India-broadband-market-AMQ-Apr2013/.

Yardley, Jim. 2013. "Report on Bangladesh Building Collapse Finds Widespread Blame." *New York Times*, May 22. http://www.nytimes.com/2013/05/23/world/asia/report-on-bangladesh-building-collapse-finds-widespread-blame.html.

Zajda, Joseph. 2007. *Decentralisation and Privatisation in Education: The Role of the State*. Dordrecht: Springer Books.

Contributors

ELIZABETH LOSH is an associate professor of English and American studies at William and Mary.

DANIEL T. HICKEY is the program coordinator of the Learning Sciences Program and a professor at Indiana University Bloomington.

SURAJ L. UTTAMCHANDANI is a doctoral candidate in the Learning Sciences Program at Indiana University Bloomington.

ARMANDO FOX is a professor in the Electrical Engineering and Computer Sciences Department at UC Berkeley and a co-PI of the ASPIRE Lab.

OWEN R. YOUNGMAN is a professor and the Knight Chair in Digital Media Strategy at Northwestern University's Medill School of Journalism, Media, Integrated Marketing Communications.

CATHY N. DAVIDSON is a Distinguished Professor of English and the director of the Futures Initiative and HASTAC@CUNY at the Graduate Center, CUNY.

HOWARD RHEINGOLD is the author of several books about online communities and has taught at Stanford and UC Berkeley.

JONATHAN WORTH is a senior research associate at Open Lab at Newcastle University.

MIA ZAMORA is an associate professor of English at Kean University and the director of the Kean University Writing Project.

ADELINE KOH is an associate professor of literature and the director of the Center for the Digital Humanities (DH@Stockton).

RADHIKA GAJJALA is a professor of media and communication at Bowling Green State University.

ERIKA M. BEHRMANN completed her doctorate in media and communication at Bowling Green State University.

ANCA BIRZESCU completed her doctorate in media and communication at Bowling Green State University.

ANDREW CORBETT is a graduate student in American culture studies at Bowling Green State University.

KAYLEIGH FRANCES BONDOR is an undergraduate student at Bowling Green State University.

JASMINE RAULT is an assistant professor of culture and media studies in the Institute of Communication, Culture, Information and Technology and the Department of Sociology at University of Toronto Mississauga.

T. L. COWAN is an assistant professor of media studies in the Department of Arts, Culture and Media (UTSC) and the Faculty of Information (iSchool) at University of Toronto.

SEAN MICHAEL MORRIS is the director at the Digital Pedagogy Lab and an instructional designer at the Office of Digital Learning at Middlebury College.

JESSE STOMMEL is the executive director of the Division of Teaching and Learning Technologies at the University of Mary Washington and founding director of *Hybrid Pedagogy*.

JESSIE DANIELS is a professor of sociology at Hunter College and the Graduate Center, CUNY.

POLLY THISTLETHWAITE is a professor and chief librarian at the Graduate Center, CUNY.

SHAWN(TA) SMITH-CRUZ is an archivist at the Lesbian Herstory Archives and an assistant professor and the head of Reference at the Graduate Center, CUNY.

ALEX REID is an associate professor of English and the director of composition and teaching fellows at the University at Buffalo.

STEVEN D. KRAUSE is a professor of English at Eastern Michigan University.

THE SAN JOSÉ STATE PHILOSOPHY DEPARTMENT collectively authored their contribution to this volume.

IAN BOGOST is the Ivan Allen College Distinguished Chair in Media Studies and a professor of interactive computing at the Georgia Institute of Technology.

SIVA VAIDHYANATHAN is the Robertson Professor of the Department of Media Studies at the University of Virginia.

NISHANT SHAH is a professor of culture and aesthetics of new media at Leuphana University in Lüneburg, a knowledge partner with Hivos in the Netherlands, and a cofounder of the Center for Internet and Society in India.

Index